Katherine Byrne is Lecturer in English at Ulster University, UK, where she teaches nineteenth- and twentieth-century literature and women's writing. She has published articles and book chapters on Victorian fiction and medicine, and on adaptation and television, especially on the adaptation of Elizabeth Gaskell for the small screen. Her previous books include *Tuberculosis and the Victorian Literary Imagination* (2011) and a book on Neo-Edwardian period drama, called *Edwardians on Screen: From Downton Abbey to Parade's End* (2015).

James Leggott teaches film and television at Northumbria University, UK. He has published on various aspects of British film and television culture and is the co-editor of *Upstairs and Downstairs: British Costume Drama Television from* The Forsyte Saga *to* Downton Abbey (with Julie Anne Taddeo, 2014). He is the principal editor of the *Journal of Popular Television*.

Julie Anne Taddeo teaches British history at the University of Maryland, College Park, USA. She is the author of *Lytton Strachey and the Search for Modern Sexual Identity* (2002) and has edited and co-edited the following collections: *Upstairs and Downstairs: British Costume Drama Television from* The Forsyte Saga *to* Downton Abbey (with James Leggott, 2014); *Steaming into a Victorian Future: A Steampunk Anthology* (with Cynthia J. Miller, 2012); *Catherine Cookson Country: On the Borders of Legitimacy, Fiction and History* (2012) and *The Tube Has Spoken: Reality TV and History* (with Ken Dvorak, 2009).

'This volume makes a significant contribution to the literature on both masculinity and period dramas, and will be welcomed by scholars of both – as well as by the fan community.'

Cynthia J. Miller, Senior Affiliated Faculty,
Institute for Liberal Arts and Interdisciplinary Studies,
Emerson College

'This is a must-read for anyone interested in contemporary British period drama and/or televisual representations of masculinities. This comprehensive collection covers dramas from *Poldark* to *Downton Abbey* to *The Crown*, from *Pride and Prejudice* to *Peaky Blinders*. It observes the complexities of represented gender roles by connecting them to their historical period and the contemporary struggles of a revived patriarchy clashing with a re-energised feminist project. Byrne, Leggott and Taddeo have managed to bring together cutting-edge research that highlights that rarely before has British period drama been such a privileged site where the conflicts of the past and the present are consolidated in intriguing, sometimes traditionalist and sometimes subversive, period drama.'

Elke Weissmann, Reader in Film and Television,
Edge Hill University

'*Conflicting Masculinities* is a bold, fresh and important contribution to the ongoing debates around the ongoing so-called crisis of masculinity, as well as to broader works on TV period dramas and genre more generally. The various essays within the volume boast an impressive breadth across historical periods, spanning the sixteenth to the twentieth centuries, as well as a range of TV genres extending beyond the strictly "period" from classic heritage productions to edgy and even comic dramas with historical settings. Adopting a wide range of critical approaches, the editors have carefully amassed a series of thoughtful, insightful essays which force the reader to rethink the ways in which contemporary and historical masculinities are constructed, as well as the period drama's complicity in negotiating those conflicting and often fragile masculinities. The book is essential reading for scholars of gender and television studies alike.'

Andrew B.R. Elliott, Senior Lecturer,
School of Film & Media, University of Lincoln

Library of Gender and Popular Culture

From *Mad Men* to gaming culture, performance art to steam-punk fashion, the presentation and representation of gender continues to saturate popular media. This new series seeks to explore the intersection of gender and popular culture, engaging with a variety of texts – drawn primarily from Art, Fashion, TV, Cinema, Cultural Studies and Media Studies – as a way of considering various models for understanding the complementary relationship between 'gender identities' and 'popular culture'. By considering race, ethnicity, class, and sexual identities across a range of cultural forms, each book in the series will adopt a critical stance towards issues surrounding the development of gender identities and popular and mass cultural 'products'.

For further information or enquiries, please contact the library series editors:

Claire Nally: claire.nally@northumbria.ac.uk
Angela Smith: angela.smith@sunderland.ac.uk

Advisory Board:

Dr Kate Ames, Central Queensland University, Australia

Prof Leslie Heywood, Binghampton University, USA

Dr Michael Higgins, Strathclyde University, UK

Prof Åsa Kroon, Örebro University, Sweden

Dr Niall Richardson, Sussex University, UK

Dr Jacki Willson, Central St Martins, University of Arts London, UK

Published and forthcoming titles:

The Aesthetics of Camp: Post-Queer Gender and Popular Culture
By Anna Malinowska

Ageing Femininity on Screen: The Older Woman in Contemporary Cinema
By Niall Richardson

All-American TV Crime Drama: Feminism and Identity Politics in Law and Order: Special Victims Unit
By Sujata Moorti and Lisa Cuklanz

Bad Girls, Dirty Bodies: Sex, Performance and Safe Femininity
By Gemma Commane

Beyoncé: Celebrity Feminism in the Age of Social Media
By Kirsty Fairclough-Isaacs

Conflicting Masculinities: Men in Television Period Drama
By Katherine Byrne, Julie Anne Taddeo and James Leggott (Eds)

Fathers on Film: Paternity and Masculinity in 1990s Hollywood
By Katie Barnett

Film Bodies: Queer Feminist Encounters with Gender and Sexuality in Cinema
By Katharina Lindner

Gay Pornography: Representations of Sexuality and Masculinity
By John Mercer

Gender and Austerity in Popular Culture: Femininity, Masculinity and Recession in Film and Television
By Helen Davies and Claire O'Callaghan (Eds)

The Gendered Motorcycle: Representations in Society, Media and Popular Culture
By Esperanza Miyake

Gendering History on Screen: Women Filmmakers and Historical Films
By Julia Erhart

Girls Like This, Boys Like That: The Reproduction of Gender in Contemporary Youth Cultures
By Victoria Cann

The Gypsy Woman: Representations in Literature and Visual Culture
By Jodie Matthews

Love Wars: Television Romantic Comedy
By Mary Irwin

Masculinity in Contemporary Science Fiction Cinema: Cyborgs, Troopers and Other Men of the Future
By Marianne Kac-Vergne

Moving to the Mainstream: Women On and Off Screen in Television and Film
By Marianne Kac-Vergne and Julie Assouly (Eds)

Paradoxical Pleasures: Female Submission in Popular and Erotic Fiction
By Anna Watz

Positive Images: Gay Men and HIV/AIDS in the Culture of 'Post-Crisis'
By Dion Kagan

Queer Horror Film and Television: Sexuality and Masculinity at the Margins
By Darren Elliott-Smith

Queer Sexualities in Early Film: Cinema and Male-Male Intimacy
By Shane Brown

Steampunk: Gender and the Neo-Victorian
By Claire Nally

Television Comedy and Femininity: Queering Gender
By Rosie White

Television, Technology and Gender: New Platforms and New Audiences
By Sarah Arnold

Tweenhood: Femininity and Celebrity in Tween Popular Culture
By Melanie Kennedy

Women Who Kill: Gender and Sexuality in Post-Feminist Film and Television
By David Roche and Cristelle Maury (Eds)

Wonder Woman: Feminism, Culture and the Body
By Joan Ormrod

Young Women in Contemporary Cinema: Gender and Post-feminism in British Film
By Sarah Hill

CONFLICTING MASCULINITIES

Men in Television Period Drama

Edited by
KATHERINE BYRNE,
JAMES LEGGOTT and
JULIE ANNE TADDEO

BLOOMSBURY ACADEMIC
LONDON · NEW YORK · OXFORD · NEW DELHI · SYDNEY

BLOOMSBURY ACADEMIC
Bloomsbury Publishing Plc
50 Bedford Square, London, WC1B 3DP, UK
1385 Broadway, New York, NY 10018, USA

BLOOMSBURY, BLOOMSBURY ACADEMIC and the Diana logo
are trademarks of Bloomsbury Publishing Plc

First published 2018 by I.B. Tauris & Co. Ltd.
Paperback edition published by Bloomsbury Academic 2020

Copyright Editorial Selection © Katherine Byrne, James Leggott and Julie Anne Taddeo, 2018

Copyright Individual Chapters © Sarah Betts, Lucy Brown, Katherine Byrne, Sarah E. Fanning, Louise FitzGerald, Mark Fryers, Gemma Goodman, Stella Hockenhull, Caroline Langhorst, James Leggott, Rachel Moseley, Claire O'Callaghan, Jessica Saxon, Julie Anne Taddeo and James Ward

Katherine Byrne, James Leggott and Julie Anne Taddeo have asserted their rights under the Copyright, Designs and Patents Act, 1988, to be identified as Editors of this work.

For legal purposes the Acknowledgements on p. xx constitute
an extension of this copyright page.

All rights reserved. No part of this publication may be reproduced or transmitted in any form or by any means, electronic or mechanical, including photocopying, recording, or any information storage or retrieval system, without prior permission in writing from the publishers.

Bloomsbury Publishing Plc does not have any control over, or responsibility for, any third-party websites referred to or in this book. All internet addresses given in this book were correct at the time of going to press. The author and publisher regret any inconvenience caused if addresses have changed or sites have ceased to exist, but can accept no responsibility for any such changes.

A catalogue record for this book is available from the British Library.

A catalog record for this book is available from the Library of Congress.

ISBN: HB: 978-1-7883-1335-3
PB: 978-1-3501-4435-4
ePDF:978-1-8386-0817-0
eBook: 978-1-8386-0816-3

Series: Library of Gender and Popular Culture, volume 22

Typeset by OKS Prepress Services, Chennai, India

To find out more about our authors and books visit
www.bloomsbury.com and sign up for our newsletters.

To all the men we've loved ... even the complete bastards.

Contents

List of Figures	xiv
List of Contributors	xvi
Acknowledgements	xx
Series Editors' Foreword	xxi

Introduction 1
Katherine Byrne, James Leggott and Julie Anne Taddeo

Conflicted Men	4
Men at Work	5
Warfare	7
The Female Gaze	8

PART I   The Seventeenth and Eighteenth Centuries

1   The Masculine Economies of *Banished* 15
James Ward

Introduction	15
Masculine Economies	17
Violence and Sacrifice	22
Banished, Masculinity and Australian History	24
Conclusion	28

2   'I will not fight for my country ... for my ship ... my King ... or Captain': Redefining Imperial Masculinities in *To the Ends of the Earth* 35
Mark Fryers

Introduction	35
Empire, Masculinity and the Sea	36
This Ship of Fools is England	41
The Sea as a Philosophical and Nightmarish Space	42

	Masculinity, Sexuality and the Sea	45
	'I kill people without knowing it'	47
	Conclusion	49
3	**Television Costume Drama and the Eroticised, Regionalised Body: *Poldark* and *Outlander***	52
	Gemma Goodman and Rachel Moseley	
	Introduction	52
	Masculinities and Male Bodies	54
	Regional Identity and the Body	56
	Colonised Territory: Looking at the Naked Male Body	62
	Outlander: Body as Contested Territory	64
	Conclusion	67
4	**Power and Passion: Seventeenth-Century Masculinities Dramatised on the BBC in the Twenty-First Century**	71
	Sarah Betts	
	Seventeenth-Century Drama on the BBC	73
	Coming of Age	75
	Passion	79
	Interior and Exterior Masculinities	82
	Conclusion	85

PART II   Visions of the Nineteenth Century

5	**A Post-Feminist Hero: Sandy Welch's *North and South***	91
	Sarah E. Fanning	
	'The Darcy Model': Andrew Davies's *Pride and Prejudice*	92
	The Evolution of Post-Feminist Masculinities in the Televised Classic Novel	93
	Moving Beyond Darcymania: A Hero in His Own Right	96
	North and South (2004): Thornton's Re-inscription as a Post-Feminist Victorian Hero	98
	Men as Men: Male Community	100

Contents

	Wounded Masculinity: Male Emotion	101
	Homosocial Bonding: John Thornton and Nicholas Higgins	104
	Post-Feminism and the Father Figure	106
	Conclusion	107
6	'Because my daddy would protect them': *Ripper Street*'s Edmund Reid and the Competing Demands of Home and Public Lives *Jessica Saxon*	111
	Losing His Home: Series One and Two	114
	Regaining His Home: Series Three	115
	Reid and Neo-Victorian Representations of Masculinity	117
	Daddy/Detective	121
	Conclusion	124
7	'Pleasure and pain, again and again' – Between Monstrosity and Inner Turmoil: The Representation of Masculinity in *Penny Dreadful* *Caroline Langhorst*	127
	Introduction: 'Not a girl's heart. A man's heart'	127
	'When you transform a life, you're making it anew': *Penny Dreadful* and Victorian Gothic	129
	'For the monster is not in my face, but in my soul': The Portrayal of Conflicted Gothic Masculinity in *Penny Dreadful*	132
	'You're a very young man. I've long since learnt that the truth is mutable': Troubled Father and Son Relationships	139
	Conclusion	141
8	Pathological Masculinities: Syphilis and the Medical Profession in *The Frankenstein Chronicles* *Katherine Byrne*	146
	Monstrous Doctors and the Legacy of Mary Shelley's *Frankenstein*	147

Conflicting Masculinities

An Unlikely 'Hero': Marlott and Syphilis	150
Power and Education	153
Changing Masculinities: *Sharpe* for the New Millennium?	154
Conclusion	158

PART III Masculinities from World War I to the Cold War

9 'The war is done. Shut the door on it!': The Great War, Masculinity and Trauma in British Period Television — 165
Julie Anne Taddeo

Uniforms and Masculine Authority	167
Hysterical Men	171
The Manly Death, Shirkers and Disabled Bodies	174
The Veteran's Anger	177
Conclusion: Memorialising Male Sacrifice	181

10 Pride versus Prejudice: Wounded Men, Masculinity and Disability in *Downton Abbey* — 187
Claire O'Callaghan

The Dilemma of Disabled Masculinity	191
'Think of me as dead': Matthew Crawley's Disabled Masculinity	193
Disabled Masculinity: The Case of Mr Bates	196
Conclusion	201

11 A Minority of Men: The Conscientious Objector in Period Drama — 206
Lucy Brown

'His name is Coward. His name is Shirker': Realism and Melodrama in *The Village*	208
'Mixed with sour milk': *Downton Abbey*'s Idealistic CO	213

Contents

'You're not the man I thought you were':
Echoes of World War I in *Home Fires* and
Upstairs, Downstairs 216
Conclusion 218

12 **Cads, Cowards and Cowmen: Masculinity in
Crisis in World War II Television Drama** 221
Stella Hockenhull

Masculinity in British Cinema and Television Drama 222
Wounded Masculinity in Period Drama 229
The WI Saves the Day 233
Conclusion 234

13 **'Have you seen Walliams' Bottom?': Detecting
the 'Ordinary' Man in *Partners in Crime*** 239
Louise FitzGerald

Gender and Genre 240
Camp David, Camp Criticism and Otherness 241
The Two Tommys: *The Secret Adversary* and
Models of Male Identity 245
Of Bees and Men: Gender Dualism and the
Detective Figure 249
Conclusion 254

14 **'No Need to Matronise Me!': *The Crown*, the Male
Consort and Conflicted Masculinity** 259
James Leggott

The Feminised Monarchy and Melodrama 261
The Male Consort: Malcontent and Moderniser 264
The Crown and the Philip Problem 269
The Crown and the Twenty-First Century 271

Bibliography 278
Index 296

List of Figures

Figure 1.1 'Do it for our Rosses', © @naughtybanished, reproduced with their permission.   30

Figure 2.1 Talbot (Benedict Cumberbatch) is nauseous as Wheeler (Brian Pettifer) first directs him to his quarters in *To the Ends of the Earth*.   44

Figure 3.1 Ross in harmony with the landscape in *Poldark*.   60

Figure 3.2 Jamie and Claire in harmony with the landscape in *Outlander*.   61

Figure 3.3 Jamie's scarred back as object of the female gaze in *Outlander*.   66

Figure 4.1 Following the death of his wife, Philippe storms out of his brother's court in the company of his lover in *Versailles*.   83

Figure 5.1 Thornton is comforted by his mother after he is rejected by Margaret in *North and South*.   105

Figure 5.2 Thornton and Higgins sitting to dinner together in the mill outbuilding in *North and South*.   107

Figure 7.1 'All the broken and shunned creatures' – Victor Frankenstein, his Creature/John Clare and their ongoing painful struggle in *Penny Dreadful*.   136

Figure 7.2 Sir Malcolm and his boys: between male bonding, anger and despair in *Penny Dreadful*.   140

Figure 8.1 Marlott resurrected from the dead by Hervey in *The Frankenstein Chronicles*.   159

Figure 9.1 The white feather as symbol of cowardice in *Downton Abbey*.   170

List of Figures

Figure 9.2 'The war is done. Shut the door on it, like I did': Tommy to Arthur Shelby in *Peaky Blinders*. 179

Figure 10.1 'Mr Bates, a shadow of a man?' in *Downton Abbey*. 199

Figure 12.1 Injurious Men: the violent and cowardly Bob Simms in *Home Fires*. 232

Figure 13.1 Tommy as a gangster in *Partners in Crime*. 250

List of Contributors

Sarah Betts is a PhD candidate at the University of York, working on the cultural memory and representations of English Civil War Royalists and Royalisms. This research includes investigations into the presentation of the past, particularly the seventeenth century, in contemporary popular culture.

Lucy Brown recently completed her doctorate at the University of Sheffield on the subject of devotion in the sensational works of Edmund Yates and Wilkie Collins. Her research interests include Victorian fiction, devotion, queer studies and costume drama. She has published on the representation of gay men in *Downton Abbey* and *Upstairs, Downstairs* (in *Upstairs and Downstairs: British Costume Drama Television from* The Forsyte Saga *to* Downton Abbey, edited by Leggott and Taddeo, 2014), and, more recently, was published in *The Apollonian*'s 'Reading Queer' issue with her essay entitled, 'Mind the Road: Lesbian Tragedies in *Last Tango in Halifax* and *Call the Midwife*'.

Katherine Byrne is Lecturer in English at Ulster University, UK, where she teaches nineteenth- and twentieth-century literature and women's writing. She has published articles and book chapters on Victorian fiction and medicine, and on adaptation and television, especially on the adaptation of Elizabeth Gaskell for the small screen. Her previous books include *Tuberculosis and the Victorian Literary Imagination* (2011) and a book on neo-Edwardian period drama, called *Edwardians on Screen: From Downton Abbey to Parade's End* (2015).

Sarah E. Fanning is Lecturer at Mount Allison University in Canada. She received her PhD from the University of Exeter in 2013. The subject of her doctoral thesis, which is currently being revised into a book, was depictions of masculinity in film and television adaptations of *Jane Eyre* and *Wuthering Heights*. She has published in the Oxford journal *Adaptation*. An article based on a paper delivered at the Charlotte Brontë Bicentenary

List of Contributors

Conference (Manchester, 2016) will be published in *Brontë Studies* (2018). Her research interests include the Brontës, gender studies, the nineteenth-century novel, literary adaptation, period drama, the Gothic in film and literature, women's writing and afterlife study.

Louise FitzGerald is Senior Lecturer in Film and Screen Studies at the University of Brighton in Sussex where her teaching focuses on film and screen histories, women, girls and popular contemporary culture; authorship; race and representation; post-feminism; culinary culture; and screen comedy. Her research interests include heritage studies; identity politics; feminist film theory; maternalism; and British popular culture. She has published various articles and book chapters including a chapter on the feminist potential of *Call The Midwife* (in *Upstairs and Downstairs: British Costume Drama Television from* The Forsyte Saga *to* Downton Abbey, edited by Leggott and Taddeo, 2014) and has more recently collaborated with a television practitioner on a forthcoming book about TV and food, *Taste and the TV Chef: How TV Taught us to Eat*.

Mark Fryers was awarded his PhD in 2015 from the University of East Anglia, UK; his thesis is titled: 'Maritime Film and Television and British National Identity, 1960–2012'. He published a chapter on the series *The Onedin Line* in *Upstairs and Downstairs: British Costume Drama Television from* The Forsyte Saga *to* Downton Abbey (edited by Leggott and Taddeo, 2014); he has written for the *Journal of Popular Television* and the *International Journal of Film, Radio and Television* and has a chapter on the animated maritime film in *Beasts of the Deep: Sea Creatures and Popular Culture* (2018). His current research is particularly focused on the manner in which film and television constructs and disseminates notions of national and collective identity, particularly with regards to physical land and seascapes.

Gemma Goodman is Associate Fellow of the Department of English and Comparative Literary Studies at the University of Warwick. Her research focuses on Cornwall and its literary representation from the nineteenth century until the present day. She is co-editor of *Gender and Space in Rural Britain, 1840–1920* (with Charlotte Mathieson, 2014) and recent publications include a chapter on Daphne du Maurier and Cornwall in *Sea Narratives: Cultural Responses to the Sea, 1600–Present* (2016). She is currently working on her book, provisionally entitled *Writing Cornwall: Searching for Alternative Versions of Place* (forthcoming).

Stella Hockenhull is Reader in Film and Television Studies and Co-Director of the Research Centre for Film and Media at the University of Wolverhampton, UK. Her main interests are British cinema and television. She has published two books on British cinema and landscape entitled *Aesthetics and Neo-Romanticism in Film: Landscapes in Contemporary British Cinema* (2013) and *Neo-Romantic Landscapes: An Aesthetic Approach to the Films of Powell and Pressburger* (2008). She is the author of a number of journal articles and chapters in edited collections on film and television and is co-editor of a forthcoming collection of essays entitled *Spaces of the Cinematic Home: Behind the Screen Door*.

Caroline Langhorst holds a BA in Film Studies and British Studies and a MA in Film Studies (her master's thesis was on 'Multiple Boundary Crossings in the Films of Derek Jarman'). She is currently working on her PhD thesis on representations of sub- and countercultural tendencies in British culture (mainly 1960s to 1980s cinema and music) at the University of Mainz, Germany. Her main research interests include British and American cinema, literature and culture, gender (particularly constructions of masculinity) and Gothic studies, popular music, countercultural narratives as well as youth and subcultures.

James Leggott teaches film and television at Northumbria University, UK. He has published on various aspects of British film and television culture and is the co-editor of *Upstairs and Downstairs: British Costume Drama Television from* The Forsyte Saga *to* Downton Abbey (with Julie Anne Taddeo, 2014). He is the principal editor of the *Journal of Popular Television*.

Rachel Moseley is Associate Professor in Film and Television Studies at the University of Warwick. She has published widely on questions of gender and representation in television and film, and is writing a book on the place-image of Cornwall.

Claire O'Callaghan is Lecturer in English at Brunel University, London. Her research centres on gender and sexuality in Victorian and neo-Victorian literature and culture, gender and sexuality in the twenty-first

List of Contributors

century, and the writings of Sarah Waters. She has just published her book, *Sarah Waters: Gender and Sexual Politics* (2017). She is also the co-editor of *Gender and Austerity in Popular Culture: Femininity, Masculinity and Recession in Film and Television* (with Helen Davies, I.B.Tauris, 2017) in which her chapter on *Downton Abbey* considers the relationship with money and masculinity. Claire is an editorial board member of the *Journal of Gender Studies* and on the Executive Committee of the Contemporary Women's Writing Association (CWWA).

Jessica Saxon is a faculty member at a community college in New Bern, North Carolina, USA; she teaches British literature of the long nineteenth century, early American literature and composition. She is also a PhD candidate at Old Dominion University in Norfolk, Virginia, USA. Her dissertation explores paratextual and narratorial interventions in nineteenth-century 'illicit' British narratives. Her other recent projects include supplements to *An Insider's Guide to Academic Writing* and an article in *Nineteenth-Century Gender Studies* on the direct address of a female audience in Charles Devereaux's *Venus in India*.

Julie Anne Taddeo teaches British history at the University of Maryland, College Park, USA. She is the author of *Lytton Strachey and the Search for Modern Sexual Identity* (2002) and has edited and co-edited the following collections: *Upstairs and Downstairs: British Costume Drama Television from* The Forsyte Saga *to* Downton Abbey (with James Leggott, 2014); *Steaming into a Victorian Future: A Steampunk Anthology* (with Cynthia J. Miller, 2012); *Catherine Cookson Country: On the Borders of Legitimacy, Fiction and History* (2012) and *The Tube Has Spoken: Reality TV and History* (with Ken Dvorak, 2009).

James Ward lectures in eighteenth-century literature at Ulster University, UK. His current research focuses on representations of this period in contemporary fiction, film and television. Recent publications include book chapters on *The Draughtsman's Contract* and on the representation of the English Revolution in UK television and film. His book *Memory and Enlightenment: Cultural Afterlives of the Long Eighteenth Century* is forthcoming.

Acknowledgements

An edited collection is always the sum of its parts. With that in mind, we want to thank all of our contributors for making this book possible in the first place. Each of the editors wants to thank the other two for a collaboration that often felt more like play than work. We want to thank Angela Smith and Claire Nally, for including this collection in I.B.Tauris's *Library of Gender and Popular Culture* series and the entire production team at I.B.Tauris for their invaluable help in the editing process. Special thanks to Joe Shrubb and all at Mammoth Screen for their generosity in providing our cover image, and to Aidan Turner for allowing us to use it. Lastly, we are grateful to all the complex, brooding and troubled men who grace our small screens and who have made understanding their plight an academic labour of love.

Series Editors' Foreword

We have come some way from the famous Colin Firth wet shirt scene in the 1995 BBC TV adaptation of *Pride and Prejudice*. TV shows such as *The Crimson Petal and the White* (2011), *Penny Dreadful* (2014–16) or *Taboo* (2017) provide viewers with evidence of a shift in how masculinity is represented and constructed. Accompanied by the evolution of neo-Victorianism as a theoretical position, many critics have identified how period dramas navigate a masculinity that is anxious or compromised in some way. Such anxious masculinity manifests in myriad ways: violence, aggression, rape, criminality. As the chapters in this book show, whilst heterosexual masculinity is still a consistent frame of reference, these representations challenge conventional notions of hegemonic masculinity. Where the idea of the 'heroic' is more or less defined in such historical terms, in the twenty-first century this is more often associated with the exposed male body that has its origins in male porn, as shown in other books in this series. The 'female gaze' is thus shown to have been attended to in an increasingly graphic way, with the covered torso of Colin Firth in 1995 now seeming quite staid. The male leads in such shows are nonetheless striking because they are frequently unconventional or unlikely heroes. As with many other books in this series, readers are challenged to reconsider their expectations about gender and popular culture.

– Angela Smith and Claire Nally

Introduction

Katherine Byrne, James Leggott and Julie Anne Taddeo

In 2015 and 2016 the BBC's eighteenth-century-themed drama *Poldark* (BBC, 2015–) captured the top spot on the *Radio Times* readers' list of 'Biggest TV Moments'. Aidan Turner, in the role of Captain Ross Poldark, secured the adoration of fans with his now-infamous shirtless scything scene in the first series, followed by his top-rated 'tin bath scene' in the second.[1] But the number-four fan favourite on the 2016 *Radio Times* list is equally, perhaps more, interesting and certainly problematic: the controversial 'bedroom encounter' between Ross and Elizabeth, which some critics have called a rape, and others regard, at the very least, as an aggressive seduction and act of adultery on the part of the hero.[2] Turner's Poldark defies our expectations of a romantic male lead: in that tin bath he is positioned in much the same way we have come to expect our heroines – naked, bathed by his fully clothed spouse, vulnerable, and the object of desire. When he seeks forgiveness from his wronged wife – and perhaps from the disappointed fans watching – for his night with Elizabeth, he hopes 'for some understanding, knowing you as I do.' Such scenes and their popular reception say a great deal about the range of behaviours allowed our heroes (on screen and off); more and more the period drama is offering up complex male characters, often committing disturbing acts of violence, yet whose flaws and introspection make them palatable and relatable to twenty-first-century audiences.

Poldark, like many of the male TV characters discussed in this collection, is as much at war with himself as the larger social order. As a model of conflicted masculinity, he is in good company in contemporary

British historical TV drama, although not without precedent. Since the tortured and torturing anti-hero Soames made an impact upon the popular consciousness in the BBC's *The Forsyte Saga* (1967) in the 1960s, the portrayal and interrogation of masculinity has formed an important part of UK period drama on the small screen. Given that the audience for costume drama has been traditionally largely female, however, this has tended to be critically overlooked in favour of a focus on the central female characters that were so key to the decades that followed. As a result, even the male lead, by the 1990s, was deemed important largely as a focus of the female (or homoerotic) gaze. In recent years, however, as this book interrogates via case studies of twenty-first-century programmes and tendencies, new forms of historical fictions on television have begun to foreground and examine 'maleness' in nuanced and important ways.

The period dramas covered in this collection may seem very different from each other in style and tone, ranging from deliberately classic 'heritage' television like *Downton Abbey* (ITV, 2010 – 15) and literary adaptations such as *North and South* (BBC, 2004) to dark, edgy productions like *Peaky Blinders* (BBC, 2013 –), with everything from comic easy viewing (*Partners in Crime*, BBC, 2015), to post-modern Gothic (*Penny Dreadful*, Showtime/Sky, 2014 – 16) in between. Their production and industrial contexts are similarly variable from open-ended soap to mini-series, and from prominence on mainstream television to exhibition via non-broadcast or transnational arrangement – and many of our contributors demonstrate how complex interactions between genre, broadcast landscape and audience have a bearing on representational strategies and readings. Our case studies here also cover a wide historical timeframe, with the first section in the collection concerned with shows set in the seventeenth and eighteenth, the second section the nineteenth, and section three the twentieth century.

This division is indicative of the clustering of period drama around particular stretches of national history that continue to resonate politically, culturally or economically with the interests of contemporary audiences, writers and producers. The 'Seventeenth and Eighteenth Centuries' section – with new essays by James Ward, Mark Fryers, Gemma Goodman and Rachel Moseley, and Sarah Betts – has the broadest sweep, encompassing a period which has tended to be the backdrop for stories concerning piracy, royalty, colonialism and region. This entire collection is also bookended by an examination of the intersection of masculinity and monarchy from

Introduction

the seventeenth to the twentieth centuries: the excesses (especially sexual) of male monarchy on display in a series like *Versailles* (Canal+, 2015–) make for an interesting contrast to the neutered role of the royal male consort in *The Crown* (Netflix, 2016–). The second section – with chapters by Sarah E. Fanning, Jessica Saxon, Caroline Langhorst and Katherine Byrne – deals with representations of the nineteenth century, with an emphasis upon Victorian (or neo-Victorian) contexts and the relationship between masculinity, domesticity, science, crime and pathology. Lastly, the 'Masculinities from World War I to the Cold War' section considers the ways in which dramas have dealt with the political and psychic impacts of twentieth-century conflicts; proportionate to the notably high number of recent dramas set during the first half of the century, this longer section contains essays by Julie Anne Taddeo, Claire O'Callaghan, Lucy Brown, Stella Hockenhull, Louise FitzGerald and James Leggott.

This volume takes as its main thesis, and point of departure, that historical TV drama, with its multifaceted take on masculinity through time, has a capacity to disrupt conceptualisations of 'hegemonic masculinity', and thus demands a scholarly tactic that is comparably heterogeneous. Although this is the first academic book solely on the topic of British TV period drama and masculinity, it builds upon and furthers a budding subset of television studies that includes such pathfinding work as Rebecca Feasey's *Masculinity and Popular Television* (2008), Amanda Lotz's *Cable Guys: Television and Masculinities in the Twenty-first Century* (2014), Michael Albrecht's *Masculinity in Contemporary Quality Television* (2015) and Brian Baker's *Contemporary Masculinities in Fiction, Film and Television* (2015). However, as befitting the complex, hybrid form of period drama itself, the contributors to *Conflicting Masculinities* draw methodologies and influence from an expansive range of scholarly paradigms. Unsurprisingly, many of the case studies here invite and reward analysis via developments in the discipline of history, or specific subcategories such as maritime, military, economic, colonial, medical, disability and royal history; the literary origins or inspiration of many of the examples here similarly inspires authors to relate programmes to such concepts as the Gothic, (neo-)Victorianism and adaptation. But our authors also take interdisciplinary inspiration from currents in media, cultural, geographical, screen and (obviously) gender studies; from the politics of the audience 'gaze', to understandings of camp, monstrosity, trauma, regionality, and of gender as 'performance'.

Although our book concludes with scrutiny of programmes set during the 1950s, this is not at all to suggest that evocations of more recent times have irrelevancy to a project on historical representation of gender roles and identity; indeed, whilst they fall – for practical as much as conceptual reasons – beyond the scope of our analysis here, it is beyond dispute that series set in the 1970s and 1980s, such as *Red Riding* (Channel 4, 2009 – 10) and *This is England* (Channel 4, 2010 – 15), respectively, make important, timely statements about conflicted masculinity.

Conflicted Men

Despite the diversity of material discussed here, certain key preoccupations emerge across the chapters. Perhaps the most important is the question of masculinity in crisis. It has become commonplace to talk of the 'crisis of masculinity' since the rise of second-wave feminism in the 1970s and neo-liberalism since Thatcherism, and indeed one of the key questions asked by this book is to what extent that is still true in the twenty-first century, as represented on or by our television screens. The neo-liberal marketplace has irrevocably eroded traditional values, and undermined the old understandings of men as breadwinners, while placing new emphasis on 'self-making and self-management' under which successful masculinity becomes a project, a work in progress that must be undertaken by all.[3] In particular, there has been much discussion of late of how anxieties around gender norms and roles during the recent recessionary era – during which time the most economically vulnerable industries (such as manufacturing or construction) have tended to be male-dominated, whilst femininity, by contrast, has been 'presented often as adaptive and resourceful' – have resulted in definitions of masculinity, once again, as in crisis.[4] Certainly most of the chapters here discuss characters who, even when still in a position of patriarchal power, are defined by an ongoing struggle with their position in a rapidly changing world. Hardly any of the men under discussion are entirely content or confident with their identity, with the possible – and significant – exception of David Walliams's character in *Partners in Crime*, a figure which, as FitzGerald argues, is at ease with the multiplicity of modern gender meanings and performance. Most of the other male characters are 'troubled' by an ideal of masculinity – strong, virile and powerful – which they either cannot obtain, or once possessed can

Introduction

no longer maintain. These anxieties seem to be symbolised by the scars which adorn the faces or bodies of male leads so frequently that they've become a leitmotif throughout this volume.

Recent period drama is strongly aware of these inadequacies and frustrations, and frequently represents aggression and violence, especially sexual violence, as the inevitable response to male problems. Almost all the programmes examined here include rape or so-called 'seduction' plots, involving a central character, and accompanied with varying degrees of violence. Rape in period drama is not new, having been the source of controversy since the infamous attack on Irene Forsyte in the original *Forsyte Saga* in 1967. Then it reflected the struggles surrounding marriage in the years leading up to the feminist revolution; now, as with Ross's hotly debated coercing of Elizabeth in *Poldark*, it invites the viewer to engage with very contemporary debates about the politics of consent. Disturbingly, however, rape on the small screen is portrayed as a consequence of the perpetrator's identity crisis, and is more about that, and his lack of self-esteem (or, like Bates in *Downton Abbey*, that of the husband or lover he has wronged) than it is about the experience and suffering of the victim. Poldark bullies Elizabeth into sex out of frustration and despair with his life; 'Black Jack' Randall's rape of Jamie in *Outlander* (Starz, 2014–) is an attempt to undermine, possess and control the perceived 'superior' masculinity of the hero (as well as serve as blatant metaphor for England's 'rape' of Scotland). Furthermore, as Ward points out in his discussion of *Banished* (BBC, 2015), when the rapist is portrayed by an especially handsome actor, fans are more likely to interpret such moments as 'seduction' – suggesting that sexual violence has become dangerously whitewashed and normalised by the period drama. So rape has multiple meanings in popular culture, but either way seems an inescapable accompaniment to masculinity on screen. This can be regarded as a way of indicating the anti-heritage, anti-feminist nature of the past – an uncivilised, inhospitable place for women, as *Outlander*'s Claire finds out – or a reminder of the lack of progress of the still violent and unevolved present.

Men at Work

Rape reflects the dark side of masculinity in period drama, but there are other, more positive trends which all these shows share. One of the most interesting 'anti-heritage' developments in recent historical fictions is the large number of working-class characters who are increasingly their focus, in a way they would not have been ten or twenty years ago. There are important exceptions, of course, like the aristocratic families in *Downton Abbey* and *Versailles*, though both shows take pains to highlight the effort that privilege demands. Generally speaking, however, period drama today is increasingly interested in men who work hard for a living, from farmers in *The Village* (Channel 4, 2013–14) to hard-labour convicts in *Banished*. Perhaps now, in our post-recession, post-austerity society, industrious physicality is valued most in our male heroes. Ross Poldark may come from an old and privileged family, but he works up a sweat on his land and in his mine. Middle-class men also have an important presence on screen, but they usually have a strong work ethic, like the wealthy but self-made John Thornton in *North and South* (of course, this type of 'entrepreneurial masculinity' is another example of the effects of neo-liberalism on our gender politics).[5] And one profession is of particular interest to the creators of recent period drama: the detective. The 'heroes' of *Ripper Street* (BBC/Amazon, 2012–16) and the *Frankenstein Chronicles* (ITV, 2015–) are policemen, and *Penny Dreadful* and *Partners in Crime* feature more unofficial and unconventional investigators. That this is the employment of choice for so many period heroes may be pragmatic, a utilising of the popularity of crime dramas, one of the most watched genres on our television screens. It can also be regarded, however, as an acknowledgement of the way in which these programmes attempt to solve the mystery of the past, to impose modern moral values upon it, and bring order and stability to the chaos of history. Of course this is easier said than done: frequently these series show the hero tainted and contaminated by the same society he is struggling to police. And, indeed, in dramas like *Banished*, any hierarchies and instruments of state control and order are of themselves corrupt and abusive. This series, and others like *Peaky Blinders*, invite the audience to align with the rebels and criminals, suggesting that it is through resistance, not compliance, that 'true' masculinity is constructed.

It is not only men's work which is of interest in this collection, however. Most of these dramas have a very modern interest in the ways male characters cope with the often conflicting identities demanded by their working and family lives (which women are usually thought to have been

Introduction

juggling for several decades). Betts in Chapter 4 suggests the way in which fatherhood acts to construct masculinity and kingship in seventeenth-century period drama: that seems to be true in a number of the shows discussed here. To be a patriarch in one way or another is still represented as the pinnacle of masculinity for all but the most radical of shows. This is complicated, however, by an awareness of the problems, and at times the loss of status, which still marks this blurring of gender roles for men. Hence fatherhood in *Ripper Street* and *The Frankenstein Chronicles*, and even in *Downton*, is accompanied by loss, and in *Versailles* (with its illegitimacy plots) by distrust and disillusionment. Even Prince Philip in *The Crown*, as discussed by Leggott in Chapter 14, while portrayed as a loving father, must resist the inevitable emasculation associated with the position of royal consort. Once again, it is only David Walliams's detective, husband and father who seems contentedly reconciled to his domestic role.

Warfare

If work and fatherhood can be considered the most important markers or shapers of period masculinity, warfare and conflict is perhaps its greatest challenge. As Taddeo, citing historian Jessica Meyer, discusses in Chapter 9, no event has more affected our 'social and cultural understanding of what it was to be a man'[6] than World War I. Partly due to the recent centenary of 1914, there are a large number of dramas on television which deal with the war years, or, like *Peaky Blinders*, are set in the 1920s but represent the war as an important context. As with increasingly inclusive portrayals of men from different classes, recent historical fictions are sensitive and nuanced in their explorations of different perspectives and experiences of warfare, including plots about lower-ranked soldiers, conscientious objectors and so on. Most of these characters, however, are shaped and – once again – 'scarred', by the Trenches, or, as Brown in Chapter 11 illustrates, judged and emasculated by their determination to avoid its horrors. And these themes are picked up further by Hockenhull in her examination of the angry and disenfranchised men represented in *Home Fires* (ITV, 2015–16) and other World War II dramas in Chapter 12. Generally speaking, the narrative of men during and post-conflict is one of decline, as these dramas display the impossibilities of measuring up to the heroic ideal symbolised by the uniform, while simultaneously chartering the progress made by the feminist movement at these times. Warfare may be traditionally constructed as the true test of a man's mettle, but our contributors here suggest that is a test which most men failed. The two world wars thus had a profound effect on modern manliness, perhaps ushering in the 'crisis' of the later twentieth century – and these dramas try to validate the trauma experienced by men during war, and long after war ended.

The Female Gaze

If successful masculinity on screen is defined by hard work, it is unsurprising that perhaps the most iconic image of the genre is that of a man labouring on the land. This image, referenced earlier, is from *Poldark*, and it needs little introduction: the moment where Aidan Turner, perfectly muscled, sweaty and tastefully hairy, is stripped to the waist scything his crops, is one known to most period drama viewers around the world. Connected to the natural world, working alongside his employees, Ross Poldark represents a fantasy of dependable, trustworthy manliness and a rejection of modern metrosexuality. Turner's body can be regarded as largely responsible for the success of the series, and this scene and others like it are, of course, designed to appeal to the female or homoerotic gaze. Indeed, even in *The Crown*, newlywed Elizabeth frequently and adoringly films her husband Philip in his various states of undress. This is arguably the most crucial factor for success of any period drama today, given that the main audience will be female. As a result our collection is full of desirable men, often topless, frequently naked, offered up for the viewing pleasure of their audience. Prior to the last few years, classic period drama was restrained in its portrayal of sex and the naked body: the 1999 film *Wings of the Dove* was defined by Claire Monk as 'post-heritage' partly because it contained a sexual coupling.[7] Nowadays quite graphic sexuality and nudity have become an inevitable part of all but the cosiest Sunday night television. Colin Firth's wet but fully clothed emergence from his lake in the 1995 BBC television adaptation of *Pride and Prejudice* seems very tame compared to what we demand of today's male leads. All the dramas explored here either exploit male beauty – the *Poldark* formula for success – for audience gratification, or deliberately reject it by the

Introduction

revelation of less clean, less appealing bodies in an attempt to establish grittiness or realism. *The Frankenstein Chronicles*, as Byrne's chapter shows, significantly, does both, via the on-screen metamorphosis of its aging but still desirable star, Sean Bean. Indeed, the casting of the male leads operate in a similar way, as this collection discusses. For every *North and South*, famous for the brooding attractiveness of its John Thornton (Richard Armitage), there is a *Banished* or *Versailles* signalling its edgy subversiveness by featuring unconventional or unlikely leading men. Similarly, *Peaky Blinders* chooses, in Cillian Murphy, a famous Hollywood star, but one who is best known for playing villains. It is particularly striking that period television has become a home or return to desirability for the aging or fallen-from-grace heartthrob. *Penny Dreadful*, for example, is notable for the casting of former Bond Timothy Dalton and 1990s movie star Josh Hartnett who had both fallen somewhat from the public eye prior to being resurrected by the programme. Arguably the same could be said of another former Mr Darcy, Matthew Macfadyen, in *Ripper Street*. These dramas remind the audience that age is no barrier to male desirability and that, in fact, experience and damage shape the kind of rugged masculinity an austerity-scarred society values most (sadly, the same cannot be said of the female leads, still mostly young and beautiful even in the grittiest shows).

As this book goes to press, more and more stories of conflicted men are gracing our small screen – a trend we hope will generate further discussions about the intersections of gender and popular culture. The leather-clad, chest-baring pirates of *Black Sails* (Starz, 2014–17), for example, are haunted by past heterosexual and homosexual relationships as they assert their authority on the high seas; the young Prince Albert, royal consort in *Victoria* (ITV, 2016–), exudes hipster appeal for younger viewers, but like *The Crown*'s Prince Philip, must push back, sometimes quite peevishly, against his limited role within the royal household. Ridley Scott's *Taboo* (BBC, 2017–) recreates the hero as a problematic hybrid of 'Bill Sykes, Sherlock Holmes, and Hannibal Lecter' while engaging with the dark legacy of Britain's colonial past.[8] Even the clergy is getting a makeover, with the hunky, jazz-loving vicar-detective of *Grantchester* (ITV, 2014–). Viewers now expect much more than a hero who can rock a wet shirt and a tea cup like Colin Firth's Darcy: he can be haunted by demons of war, disabled by disease or injury, stifled by his class or aging body, but also willing to be nurtured and rescued by women. As these dramas suggest, it is not necessarily masculinity that is in crisis: perhaps it is our expectations about masculinity that have been challenged and subverted.

Finally, the development of this volume not only coincided with a rich period for the production of historical TV drama, but with political upheavals in Europe and the USA that are unfolding as we go to press. Many commentators have turned to debates around gender politics for explanation, with the concept of 'toxic masculinity' – whether as a means to define politicians, leaders or voters – gaining considerable traction.[9] Indeed, events like the British vote to leave the EU, and the divisive election of Donald Trump, have been attributed to the frustration and rage of the disillusioned and often disenfranchised white male voter.[10] Some of the male population seem to be currently responding to political movements that reject neo-liberalism and multi-culturalism, as though in a wish to recreate for the future the kind of fictional national past beloved of the more conventional period dramas discussed here. At the same time, the surprising outcome of the 2017 British election displays a galvanisation of the younger sections of society who are demanding different types of social change. Some of our own contributors acknowledge the cultural contexts that cause us to seek solace, lessons or parallel in historical stories, and we therefore wait with interest to see how key events of our time inspire future production and characterisation. We hope that Captain Poldark's aforementioned plea 'for some understanding', whatever we think of his actions, or of those of the complicated, fascinating characters discussed here, is at least partly met by this book.

Notes

1. 'Poldark's topless tin bath scene voted 2016's biggest TV moment', *Radio Times*, 30 December 2016. Available at http://www.radiotimes.com/news/2016-12-30/poldarks-topless-tin-bath-scene-voted-2016s-biggest-tv-moment (accessed 5 February 2017).
2. 'Poldark "rape" scene sparks controversy', *BBC News*, 24 October 2016. Available at http://www.bbc.com/news/entertainment-arts-37749637 (accessed 8 February 2017).
3. Andrea Cornwall, 'Introduction: Masculinities under Neoliberalism', in F. G. Karioris and N. Lindisfarne (eds), *Masculinities under Neoliberalism* (London, 2016), p. 10.

Introduction

4. Diane Negra and Yvonne Tasker, 'Neoliberal frames and genres of inequality: Recession-era chick flicks and male-centred corporate melodrama', *The Sociological Review*, 16/3 (2013), p. 347. See also Diane Negra and Yvonne Tasker, *Gendering the Recession: Media and Culture in an Age of Austerity* (Durham, NC, 2014).
5. Cornwall, 'Introduction', p. 10.
6. Jessica Meyer, *Men of War: Masculinity and the First World War in Britain* (Basingstoke, 2009), p. 2.
7. Claire Monk, 'The British Heritage Debate Revisited', in C. Monk and A. Sargent (eds), *British Historical Cinema* (London, 2002), p. 193.
8. Morgan Jeffery, 'Tom Hardy interview – on making *Taboo* the electrifying antidote to *Downton*: "People might not like this"', *Digital Spy*, 31 December 2016. Available at http://www.digitalspy.com/tv/interviews/a817930/tom-hardy-interview-taboo-bbc-one-fx-tv-series-2016-plot/ (accessed 16 February 2017).
9. See, for example, Jacqueline Rose, 'The twin curse of masculinity and male-dominated politics helped create Brexit', *Guardian*, 2 July 2016. Available at https://www.theguardian.com/commentisfree/2016/jul/02/twin-curse-masculinity-male-dominated-politics-brexit (accessed 7 February 2017).
10. See for example Anatole Kalestky, 'Trump's rise and Brexit vote are more an outcome of culture than economics', *Guardian*, 28 October 2016. Available at https://www.theguardian.com/business/2016/oct/28/trumps-rise-and-brexit-vote-are-more-an-outcome-of-culture-than-economics (accessed 21 July 2017). And for breakdown of the gender distribution of the Brexit vote, see https://www.statista.com/statistics/567922/distribution-of-eu-referendum-votes-by-age-and-gender-uk/ (accessed 3 July 2017).

PART I

The Seventeenth and Eighteenth Centuries

1

The Masculine Economies of *Banished*

James Ward

Introduction

Banished (BBC, 2015) is one of three series discussed in this book which dramatise masculinity against the backdrop of the eighteenth-century military and colonial state. It is set during the earliest days of the New South Wales penal colony, founded by transported convicts and marines after their first landing there in 1788. In Chapter 3 of the current volume, Rachel Moseley and Gemma Goodman discuss the strong and continuing appeal of *Outlander* (Starz, 2014–), based around the Jacobite rebellion of 1745, and *Poldark* (BBC, 2015–), which centres on a Cornish veteran of the American War of Independence. Unlike these two series, *Banished* was not recommissioned after its initial run. A number of factors contributed to its failure. An original historical fiction as opposed to an adaptation from a literary source, *Banished* lacked the established and dedicated, if fractious, fanbases of *Outlander* and *Poldark*.[1] Whereas each of these programmes sits 'comfortably within the genre of "heritage drama"', as Chapter 3 below notes, *Banished* offered darker themes and more graphic depictions of violence and punishment than the history and conventions of traditional costume drama might allow. Its author, Jimmy McGovern, has consistently framed violent and violated masculinities against failures of political authority and institutional justice, taking in notorious episodes in the recent history of the British state including Hillsborough and Bloody Sunday (in *Hillsborough* (ITV, 1996) and *Sunday* (Channel 4, 2002)). In depicting these events McGovern's work asserts the historical truth of state violence against working-class citizens prior to its belated recognition by enquiries into Hillsborough and Bloody Sunday respectively 27 and 38 years after the fact, thereby performing functions of testimony and protest strikingly at odds with the spectatorial pleasures traditionally associated with historical drama. Tracing the deep historical foundations of such state brutality, *Banished* presents an escalating crisis of masculine authority which, following the climax of the series, leaves behind an array of damaged, destroyed and destructive males.

Tommy Barrett (Julian Rhind-Tutt), the one male character who can be described, in his creator's words, as a 'noble, heroic individual',[2] is executed in the series' final episode. Even though viewers found an alternative in the anti-heroism of Major Robert Ross (Joseph Millson), the latter's appeal is complicated by his being a calculating sadist who advocates cannibalism. During the execution sequence, he orders the exemplary killing of convicts who refuse to face the scaffold at the moment of the hanging. Arthur Phillip (David Wenham), the governor of the colony, having ordered the execution against his better judgement, does not scruple on the scaffold to make political capital of it as soon as the act is accomplished. It is carried out by James Freeman (Russell Tovey), Barrett's fellow convict and sworn friend, who himself escaped execution on condition that he become the colony's hangman, a bargain which he has kept secret from fellow convicts. That Freeman will be his friend's killer only becomes apparent to Barrett and his wife Elizabeth Quinn (MyAnna Buring), whom he has promised to Freeman after his death, moments before the hanging is carried out. A further casualty is Corporal MacDonald (Ryan Corr). Ordered by Ross to carry out the exemplary killings, he has also seen the same commanding officer take up with the woman he loves, Katherine McVitie (Joanna Vanderham). The combined burden of guilt and depression renders MacDonald suicidal. The series therefore closes on repeated images of masculine abjection: Elizabeth Quinn pounds Freeman with her fists and spits in his face while MacDonald steps alone into the surf and puts his pistol to his own head.

The Masculine Economies of *Banished*

As its ending shows, *Banished* trades in complex, compromised and complicit masculinities. These are partly occasioned by the series' factual basis. Thomas Barrett was indeed the first convict to be hanged in the penal colony, James Freeman was its first hangman, and Robert Ross was by all accounts an obnoxious individual regarded even by fellow officers with 'inexpressible hatred.' Subsequent fictions also depict him as deeply unpleasant.[3] As well as historical realities, however, the series is driven by modes of crisis that are widespread in contemporary culture. Traditionally the preserve of the environmentalist and anti-capitalist left, crisis rhetoric has, since the global financial shock of 2008, become part of the political mainstream. Survival in the face of the ongoing emergency led governments to declare what recent commentary, citing Giorgio Agamben, calls a 'state of exception'.[4] The crisis means that foreign aid, hospitality to immigrants, assistance to refugees and support for sick and disabled people are dismissed as unaffordable largesse. In this worldview masculinity can be identified as one of several traditional norms and values long held to be in slow decline, which has been brought to the verge of sudden and catastrophic failure, and which therefore requires an emergency reset. While crisis limitation in the economic sphere takes the form of austerity, an implicitly gendered discourse of masculine discipline supported by a rhetoric of hard choices, tough measures and adaptation to survive,[5] its cultural counterpart has been a return to frontier masculinities through the self-conscious adoption of handicrafts, work clothing and facial hair. As men begin to look as if they have escaped from the set of a period drama, popular culture makes austerity fun by appropriating historical crises. The most pervasive manifestation of the crisis ethos and its gendered subtext has been what Owen Hatherley calls the 'completely and inescapably global' ubiquity of the slogan 'Keep Calm and Carry On.'[6] Adapted from an unused British propaganda poster designed in 1939 for circulation in the case of a Nazi invasion,[7] it counsels a masculine performance of routine and emotional restraint. These examples reflect some ways in which crisis rhetoric, across politics and culture, represents a new variant of masculine economy.

Masculine Economies

In the collocation popularised by Hélène Cixous, 'masculine economy' refers primarily to the distribution of psychic and libidinal energies rather than material resources. Proceeding from the observation that 'a mixture of difference and *inequality*' creates all desire, Cixous describes a self-replicating system in which the essentialising of difference creates and exacerbates inequality. Through a combination of 'stratagem and violence', masculine economy makes 'sexual difference hierarchical by valorizing one of the terms of the relationship.'[8] Masculine economy is a form of power that inheres in compulsions and aversions: as Olli Pyyhtinen observes, it 'cannot tolerate separation, detachment, expropriation and loss', and must 'recover [...] expenses, settle the scores and get even.'[9] Such remarks look, in present times, less like an explication of abstruse psychoanalytic terms and more like a straightforward, even obvious, description of the dominant tenets of post-crisis political economy in the West. Its themes of necessary reduction to basics in a system that cannot tolerate wastage, excess or generosity are also fundamental dramatic premises of *Banished*. The show, according to its creator, poses the question 'how far do you go to survive?'[10] Governor Phillip pins this survival to the livelihood of individual bodies: 'what you take in must equal what you put out. If it is more you go fat; if it is less you die.' *Banished*'s historical fiction of the body politic links crises of the present with those of the late eighteenth century. In circumstances which echo current contexts of apparent institutional overload, the landing in Australia by the ships of the First Fleet in 1788 was necessitated by a crisis of overcrowding in the British prison system, caused by the loss of the state's previously favoured destination for transported convicts, the American colonies. The series' plot reflects the historical reality of a colony settled by urban convicts and professional soldiers, with limited stores and no experience of food cultivation in an alien continent whose ecology they did not understand. The colony faced food shortages almost immediately and this subsistence crisis quickly merged with ones of discipline and morale. In historical accounts, as in the series, the crises of the early colony are often viewed through the prism of gender, specifically the fact that men in the colony outnumbered women by more than three to one.[11]

Banished telescopes these crises of scarcity, violence and sex into the story of its two central convict characters. James Freeman agrees to become the colony's hangman when, with the noose around his neck, Governor Phillip presents him with a choice between taking the position and being himself hanged. Freeman has been sentenced to death for the murder of the colony's blacksmith, Marston (Rory McCann). The killing was an act of self-preservation as Marston had been openly stealing Freeman's rations, turning on him for 'showing off' in his effort to defend a female convict, Anne Meredith (Orla Brady), who was Marston's initial target. Freeman reports his tormentor to Governor Phillip (itself a transgression, in the eyes of fellow convicts, punishable by death), but the complaint goes unheeded because Marston's skills are indispensable in the colony. Thomas Barrett helps Freeman to kill Marston and dispose of his body, the bond between the two men having been cemented through a previous crisis which saw Elizabeth Quinn flogged for fraternizing with a male convict and Barrett sentenced to death over the same issue, only to receive a last-minute reprieve from hanging. The Quinn-Freeman-Barrett erotic tringle is further consolidated when they cheat marine Private Buckley (Adam Nagaitis) at cards by offering Elizabeth as a stake in the game. Incensed at his loss, Buckley taunts Barrett with the revelation that he previously had sex with Quinn; in response Barrett beats him to pulp, an offence for which he is finally executed by his best friend.

The events of the series portray the workings of masculine economy in two different ways; as two economies, in fact, that operate in tension rather than in equilibrium. In the first instance, as its material circumstances worsen, the colony's disciplinary regime hardens to the point where Governor Phillip presents the convict population with a show of punitive retrenchment. It is difficult not to read this scene against austerity measures such as benefit sanctions, widely applied in Western economies at the time of the series' broadcast. After the hanging of Tommy Barrett, he addresses them from the scaffold and, referring to their show of defiance in turning their back on the hanging, says:

> Let this dispel the myth that I do not have it in me to hang a man. If I can hang a man like Thomas Barrett then I can hang any. This disobedience shows you have energy to burn [...] Accordingly I hereby reduce your rations by a further quarter. And for the first time in New South Wales, this cut applies to convicts only. And that is due entirely to your disobedience.

Phillip presents reduced rations as a discretionary punishment in response to the convicts' show of defiance. In fact, as previous scenes have made clear, the measure has become unavoidable in the face of spoilage and dwindling stores. Phillip ironically inverts contemporary austerity's presentation of ideologically driven economic retrenchment as unavoidable necessity, while underlining its punitive effects. Reframing a crisis of scarcity as one of discipline, and dwindling vitality as mutinous excess, he personifies a system of masculine economy that can neither tolerate misdirected energy nor countenance generosity in the form of mercy. He makes the latter clear when he rejects a plea for clemency that comes from the victim of the attack, Private Buckley. Refusing the request, Phillip offers the rationale based on the representational logic of sovereignty. 'Barrett is not being hanged for what he did to you', Phillip insists to Buckley: 'he is being hanged for what he did to the uniform. To the flag, to the King himself.' In addressing the convicts, Phillip also includes himself in this symbolic repertoire, saying: 'I represent the King. To turn your back on me is to turn your back on the King. And that will not be allowed to happen.'

Though he appeals to the abstractions embodied by trappings such as uniforms and flags, the Governor ultimately exerts sovereignty through a material economy which regulates individual bodies by monopolising sexuality, violence and nutrition: all of the deaths and punishments in *Banished* arise from prisoners or junior marines attempting to appropriate control of these resources. In this context, Phillip's use of starvation as political weapon recalls Agamben's discussion, in *Homo Sacer* (1998), of modernity as a threshold point at which political sovereignty extends to biological processes, where 'power penetrates subjects' very bodies and forms of life.'[12] Biopolitics, defined as the 'inclusion of bare life in the political realm', constitutes the original 'nucleus of sovereign power.'[13] Dramatising this moment of inclusion, the Governor's speech marks the consolidation of his personal rule in explicitly gendered terms. While Agamben discusses sovereign power without significant reference to gender, it clearly takes on such an inflection in the Governor's speech. This is shown in the way Phillip begins with an assertion of his own essential masculinity. Refuting the perception that the power of death was something he did not have in him to discharge, he goes on to define this power against a standard which represents both a threat and exemplar: 'a man like Thomas Barrett', whose masculinity Phillip describes in a later scene as 'brave, principled, heroic.' Thus while the hanging, the exemplary killings and the cuts to rations represent a masculine economy that the governor imposes, his framing of the execution as a vindication of his own

The Masculine Economies of *Banished*

inner essence indicates that there is a further economy, one in which he participates rather than directs. This is namely an economy where masculinity has the status of a commodity within the system rather than a principle which structures it.

Like other resources in the penal colony, it is a commodity marked by scarcity. Early scenes in the first episode establish this lack. When Marston steals Anne Meredith's ration and no one challenges him, she demands of the convicts: 'Is there not one man amongst you?' Her question involves a rhetorical figure of substitution which is characteristic of the series' representation of masculine power. To invoke the basis of his authority Governor Phillip uses a metonym whereby individual marines stand not for themselves but the uniform, the flag and ultimately 'the King himself.' Phillip in turn is a stand-in for the monarch and as such interprets the convicts' protest as a personal affront which warrants violent retribution. In a similar fashion, Meredith uses a synecdoche to define a 'man' by a limited number of chivalrous and heroic attributes, which are clearly absent from the colony because they represent forms of expenditure inimical to its subsistence economy. Given that neither of *Banished*'s male leads exactly conforms to marketable ideals of TV masculinity, her question is also directed extradiegetically to viewers of the series – a further problem of masculine economy that will be discussed at the end of the current chapter. Within the series, this dearth of true 'men' in a population ironically overabundant in males represents a crisis that the sacrificial execution of Barrett purports to resolve.

Up to this critical moment, masculinity presents as an unstable quantity subject to inflation and negation. Meredith's question forms part of a continual querying and undermining of its value and status, in the context of a larger assault on personhood which is undertaken by the convicts themselves as well as their guards. The denial not just of the lower orders' masculinity but their humanity is energetically pursued to extremes by Major Ross. He enforces the prohibition on contact between male and female prisoners with the decree that 'scum must not breed.' Later in the series he suggests to Governor Phillip, in the face of heightened shortages, that the bodies of sick convicts be fed to their healthy counterparts on the pretext that it is wallaby meat. Ross's figuring of his charges both as food and as untouchable, noxious matter can be understood with relation to Fintan Walsh's point that 'the process of constructing viable subjects is premised upon the existence of "abject beings".'[14] In *Banished*, naming and name-calling amount almost to ceremonial rites which confer and consolidate this abject status through rhetorical figures of substitution. When James Freeman tries to engage Anne Meredith in conversation, she says she is not interested and that she prefers 'real grown up men.' He perseveres, asking her name but she refuses and says, handing him his ration, 'one pancake.' Shortly afterwards Freeman confronts the blacksmith Marston telling him to give Meredith back her food. He replies: 'that is not a woman. She is scum.' Private Buckley, after his beating by Barrett, is described as a 'cabbage.' In addition to objects of consumption, the colonists debase themselves and each other with labels of bodily orifices and functions: Marston calls Freeman 'mouth', while, in the act of killing him, Freeman calls his tormentor 'you fuck.' These examples suggest that male and female convicts, along with junior officers, form not just an underclass deprived of political subjecthood but also an ontological substratum denied of meaningful subjectivity. This deprivation is realised linguistically through substitution of their integrity as persons by whatever is partial or adjunctive – formless organic matter, dismembered parts and agentless actions. These represent a ground on which the competitive acquisition of masculinity is played out.

Violence and Sacrifice

The idea that masculinity represents a commodity that can be quantified, acquired and traded, currently a staple of semi-ironic gender discourse in the popular realm,[15] is one that the men of *Banished* take seriously. A literal rendering of masculinity as value occurs when Major Ross effectively requisitions Katherine McVitie from her lover Private MacDonald. Promoted to Corporal in exchange for doing so, MacDonald is made to escort her to the Major's tent, where the sentry taunts MacDonald that Ross is 'ten times the man [...] and twenty times the soldier.' In a similar vein, Private Buckley asks Sergeant Timmins, after another of his many humiliations, to teach him to box in the hope that it will 'make me a better man.' This strategy fails when, having incensed Tommy Barrett, Buckley assumes his opponent will 'fight by the rules', and adopts a newly learned classical pugilist's pose to face up to him. Having been immediately flattened and badly injured by Barrett, Buckley then

The Masculine Economies of *Banished*

consults the colony's minister, Reverend Johnston (Ewen Bremner). He advises him that to forgive Barrett publicly and intercede on his behalf would enable Buckley to increase his personal stock of manly virtue, a strategy which, like his earlier effort to fight by the rules, fails. Buckley's effort to gain status by using the rules assumes a system that operates meritocratically and, by analogy with liberal models of market economy, as a network of instrumentality and reward peopled by rational actors. In fact, *Banished*'s economy of masculinity is grounded not in such principles but rather in modes of ritual violence and sacrifice.

Masculinity in *Banished*, I have suggested, is governed by figures of substitution, systems of exchange and assertions of power that can be grouped together as aspects of masculine economy. Violence is at the heart of this system and it is inflicted in ritualistic modes. A substantial body of critical work makes the now familiar argument that the apparently rational, secular practices of Western industrial societies can be difficult to distinguish, structurally as well as in their content and desired ends, from the beliefs and rituals of traditional or pre-modern societies.[16] This context is particularly applicable to *Banished*. The series dramatises the importation of a European society to a continent which, although it had by 1788 been continuously inhabited for 50,000 years, was nonetheless regarded in law as *terra nullius*, no one's land, because its occupants were not regarded by Europeans as having established a civilisation. While the series' failure to address this expropriation was a contentious issue, which the next section of this chapter will discuss, *Banished* does use troubled masculinities to suggest that colonial society represents not 'civilisation' but a regime founded on atavistic sacrificial violence.

Rhetorics of sacrifice are important to two contexts for *Banished* that this chapter has developed, namely the historical founding of the New South Wales penal colony and the crisis economics of the present. Historically, transportation to Australia was, with some irony, described as nationalistic sacrifice on the part of those transported: 'True patriots all, for be it understood,/We left our country, for our country's good.'[17] Sacrifice for the national good is also, as Brian Nail argues, a persistent theme in recent political justifications of economic austerity.[18] In contrast with these notions of sacrifice as discipline and self-denial, *Banished* brings ritual violence to the fore. 'If sacrifice resembles criminal violence', reasons René Girard in his influential theory of the sacrificial, 'there is, inversely, hardly any form of violence that cannot be described in terms of sacrifice.' Georges Bataille theorises sacrifice as an essentially economic form of 'unconditional consumption', a moment of licensed excess and therefore 'the antithesis of production, which is accomplished with a view to the future; it is consumption that is concerned only with the moment.'[19] *Banished*'s depiction of capital punishment reflects both Girard's description of sacrifice as a ubiquitous subtext in state-administered violence and its designation by Bataille as a heightened form of consumption. Tommy Barrett's first, aborted, execution is described in explicitly sacrificial terms. It is halted after Reverend Johnson cries 'this is a crucifixion!' In order to formalise his marriage to Elizabeth Quinn, prevented by his having a wife in England, Governor Phillip asks Barrett, still on the scaffold, to accept that 'that as far as England is concerned you are a dead man.' By accepting this condition he becomes what Agamben describes as a 'living dead man' who may be killed without retribution.[20] When, on the scaffold for a second time, the sacrifice is made good and Barrett is successfully executed, Phillip lays his interpretation of the act before the community of convicts. In the speech already quoted, he uses the spectacle to refute any notion that an inner core of masculine courage has been lacking in him. Read according to the logic of sacrifice, Phillip is not locating an essence within himself: rather he is attempting to appropriate from Barrett and internalise to himself a convincing masculine authority. Symbolically, it seems that Phillip has accepted Ross's recommendation of cannibalism: in a moment of sacrifice as consumption, Barrett's much-coveted masculine presence is something that Phillip now claims to have ingested through the sacrifice of execution. The series' climax is therefore impressive in terms of its rendering of masculinity as symbolic economy, but this counted for little in the commercial economy upon which *Banished* ultimately foundered.

Banished, Masculinity and Australian History

With its cancellation *Banished* fell victim to the regime of tough decisions, survival and adaptation which are the focus of its dramatic critique. Echoing some of the gendered terms highlighted at the beginning of this chapter, a statement explaining the decision on behalf of BBC executives said: 'the BBC2 drama budget only allows for a limited number of

The Masculine Economies of *Banished*

returning dramas a year which means we have to make hard choices.'[21] On learning of the show's cancellation, one of *Banished*'s male leads tweeted that 'The history of Australia will have to tell it's [sic] story without us.'[22] This comment from Russell Tovey, who played James Freeman in the series, reflects wider discourses around gender and historical fiction. The idea of television drama as informative, large-scale national storytelling invokes oppositions, which inevitably become gendered, between 'serious' fact-based historical drama on the one hand and, on the other, escapist fantasy and romance. These overtones of seriousness are underlined in the implication that the purpose of *Banished* was to help Australia 'tell its story.' This particular phrase resonates with functions of testimony performed by McGovern's work on Hillsborough and Bloody Sunday and highlighted in the introduction to this chapter. It implies the story in question had, before *Banished*, remained to some degree untold; that in recounting the early colonial history of Australia, the show followed McGovern's previous work in bearing witness to traumatic events that had largely been misrepresented or passed over. In Australian contexts, as opposed to British ones, this is not a credible idea.

Tovey's idea that Australia might need help to tell its story reveals an asymmetry between Australian and British popular awareness of the penal period. Even though *Banished* was a joint venture between companies operating in the UK and Australia, featured Australian actors and was broadcast in both territories, the reaction of many Australians, including the series' own crew, indicate that they did not see it as their story. For example Jeffrey Walker, who directed four of the seven episodes in the series, characterised it in his view as 'not the story of the forming of Australia' but rather 'a British story about British class and British society.' The Australian academic Gary Sturgess called the show a 'new British television series' whose main point of interest was its evidence that 'the Brits have found something else to bash themselves up about.'[23] His comment reflects the fact that early European settlement in Australia is, in the UK, a relatively unfamiliar object of public memory. Within Australia, by contrast, the penal era is a founding moment that has been intensely documented, debated and revised. Masculinity and its integrity to myths of Australian origin and identity have been central to these often bitter debates.

As Martin Staniforth writes, 'the figure of the convict [...] lies at the heart of the construction of Australia as an essentially masculine society.'[24]

Conflicting Masculinities

Given that the gender imbalance that began with the First Fleet continued past the end of the penal period in 1844, the society founded at Sydney Cove was by definition a hypermasculine one. 'Male bonding', as Jill Conway writes, 'was a necessity in convict society.'[25] Historical necessity gave rise to an ideal. The notion that the penal era represents a wellspring of rough but honest and authentic masculine values is shown, for example, in the branding of James Squire beer, named after a First Fleet convict.[26] In a reflection of the importance of homosociality to the Australian founding mythos, 'mateship' was identified as a fundamental Australian value in a preamble to the Constitution of Australia drafted in 1999.[27] Manly, where *Banished* was filmed, was named by Arthur Phillip in 1788 after the 'confidence and manly behaviour' of the Indigenous Australians he observed there.[28] While, as this last detail suggests, there has always been a more inclusive and complex story to be told, narratives of Australia's masculine foundations are more often associated with the convicts alone. John Rickard summarises the rise to prominence in public memory of the convict era:

> For several generations the convict inheritance was an embarrassment [...] Then [...] it dawned on many Australians that the primitive convict society of New South Wales was an extraordinary beginning for a nation, and more a cause for astonishment than shame.[29]

The re-evaluation described above is part of an ongoing reckoning with the past which became particularly charged by the clustering, around the turn of the century, of several landmark moments. These included the 1988 bicentennial of the First Fleet, the 1992 *Mabo* judgement of the Australian High Court (which rejected *terra nullius* and upheld for the first time an Aboriginal title to Australian land), the 2001 centenary of Australian federation and Prime Minister Kevin Rudd's 2008 apology to Australia's indigenous peoples. In these circumstances the initial, positive, re-evaluation of the penal era has increasingly given way to the recognition that the achievements and sufferings of the convicts cannot stand for the totality of Australia's history. By focusing almost exclusively on convict society, *Banished* repeats a problem widely identified in Australian historiography and historical fiction whereby the convicts effectively displace the other victims of what have been called the 'three great evils'

The Masculine Economies of *Banished*

brought by the British in 1788: 'the violence against the original inhabitants, the violence against the convicts, and the violence done to the land itself.'[30] *Banished* compounds this violence by making Indigenous Australians invisible. The series therefore replicates a paradox identified by Chris Healy where 'Aboriginal people and things appear in and disappear from public culture in strange but definite ways.'[31] The 'natives', as they are referred to throughout the series, are described but never seen. They are said to have contributed to food scarcity by slashing the colonists' fishing nets, and are offered as a reason why the convicts need the protection of the marines. When a marine is killed by a snake, the literate convict 'Letters' Molloy (Ned Dennehy), on the urging of Major Ross, provides a fictional account of the death in a letter to his relatives, stating that the soldier was killed in action bravely defending the colony against 'native' attack. When Ross orders the exemplary killings, Molloy's rendering of this service saves him from being shot. Allowing one convict to assert his value to the colony's survival economy, and therefore his right to stay alive, Indigenous Australians represent not just a disembodied threat but also a ground against which viable masculine subjectivities can be defined.

Interestingly, Jimmy McGovern turned to notions of economy to explain the omission of Aboriginal people from his script for *Banished*. He argued that because the events of the series took place over a space of just two weeks, there would not have been the time to do justice to the complexities of representing Indigenous Australians.[32] While it succumbs to convict narratives' historic tendency to efface Indigenous Australians, *Banished* is arguably more successful in challenging the celebration of foundational masculinities and mateship bonds. It does so through the catastrophic dénouement of Freeman and Barrett's friendship. On the scaffold, when he learns the identity of his executioner Barrett says to Freeman, 'I loved you too much to do this to you' and Freeman replies 'I loved you Tommy. But I loved life more.' At its termination, then, the relationship of the two men represents an accelerated evolution of the concept of male bonding from its origins in the convicts' honour-code, through freely chosen fraternity, to its failure in the face of a new economy of pragmatic individualism. In the character who most relentlessly and brutally embodies this facet of masculine economy, Major Robert Ross, some fans of the show found their champion. This phenomenon will provide some concluding reflections.

Conclusion

As suggested at the beginning of this chapter, *Banished* dramatises austerity's self-declared state of exception. The series uses the colony's geographical dislocation, its dilemmas of legal authority, and the gender imbalance in its population to stage a crisis of masculinity that manifests in an abundance of males but a lack of what Anne Meredith calls 'real, grown up men.' Although uttered in a fictive version of 1788, the comment has wider currency in a present characterised by intense anxiety about the alleged devaluing of normative masculinities, and what Jacqueline Rose has called 'nostalgia for sexual certainty.'[33] In such contexts, the casting of Julian Rhind-Tutt and Russell Tovey as Barrett and Freeman in these roles represents, I have suggested, an investment in complex masculinities rather than purely bankable ones. Both are well-known TV actors who tend not to be cast as romantic heroes or conventional leading males. Where they do take such roles, they tend to embody desirable masculinity in ironised or unconventional form. Rhind-Tutt has played heartthrob roles archly in comedies (*Green Wing* (Channel 4, 2004–7); *Black Books* (Channel 4, 2000–4)) and by his own admission is more often to be found portraying 'aristocratic people, politicians, advisors.'[34] Tovey is familiar from the comedy *Him and Her* (BBC, 2010–13) where his character repeatedly falls short in conventional rites of masculinity ranging from competition over penis size to the delivery of a best man's speech. Even so, in discussing their roles in *Banished*, both actors seemed to fall back on traditionalist and exclusionary masculinities. Rhind-Tutt welcomed the chance to play Barrett because he represented 'more of a manly man than any role I've had the chance to play recently' and complimented, referring to his preparation for the physical aspects of the role, the training he received 'from some real Australian men.'[35] In a press interview to promote *Banished*, Tovey credited being cast in a role that he 'never would have got before' to a newly gym-enhanced physique while also, with a remark that appeared to criticize other gay actors for effeminacy, igniting a row that resulted in accusations of 'internalised homophobia' and a subsequent apology.[36]

Reflecting anxious perceptions of masculinity as a hard-earned resource that must be protected and capitalised upon, the discourse around the show therefore participates in the gendered economy which the programme presents in dramatically heightened form. As glossed by Governor Phillip, Barrett's execution attempts to enforce a doctrine of sacrifice where, as in Girard's reading, 'elements of dissension scattered throughout the community are drawn to the person of the sacrificial victim and eliminated, at least temporarily.' In keeping with the series' persistent rhetoric of substitution, the execution of Barrett is promoted through such logic as an 'act of collective substitution performed at the expense of the victim and absorbing all the internal tensions, feuds, and rivalries pent up with in the community.'[37] Read from the perspective of Agamben's work on sovereign power, Phillip's gallows speech is also an assertion of control, extending dominion beyond the colony as a political abstraction and into the bodies of the colonists. Embodying Jean-Luc Nancy's observation that 'to be *banished* amounts not to coming under a provision of the law but rather to coming under the entirety of the law',[38] *Banished* names and frames masculine abjection within a regime of totalising political violence. For all its other shortcomings, this aspect of the series resonates deeply and disturbingly both with the contemporary political climate and within McGovern's sustained critique of the British state. Even in the face of its relentless, brutalising violence, however, some viewers of the series did respond affirmatively to Anne Meredith's question 'is there not one man amongst you?' by electing Major Robert Ross to this status.

In the wake of *Banished*'s cancellation, Joseph Millson's character began to earn honourable mentions alongside the BBC's more successful paragon of eighteenth-century masculinity, Ross Poldark. Before either series aired, stars of *Banished* and *Poldark* had already played off against each other. In *Being Human* (BBC, 2009–13), Aidan Turner's suave and sexually confident vampire played opposite Russell Tovey's diffident and self-loathing werewolf. This test run suggested that *Banished* might struggle to match the scopophilic appeal of the *Poldark* reboot – even with the visual pleasures and dramatic potential inherent in its depiction of hard labour, al fresco sex and ritual punishment under the Australian sun. But it was in such contexts that Joseph Millson's character came to be viewed as an object of straight female desire comparable to Ross Poldark. As Chapter 3 of this volume points out, one of the major spectatorial modes associated with costume drama is the inscription of a 'desiring, straight, female gaze [...] in paratextual spaces such as magazines, gifs and memes.' Major Robert Ross is an obvious, if problematic, object of this gaze. A graphic illustration is

Conflicting Masculinities

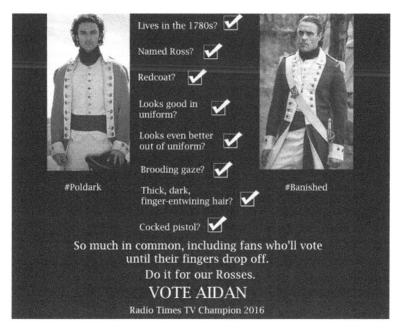

Figure 1.1 'Do it for our Rosses', © @naughtybanished, reproduced with their permission.

found in the checklist posted by the twitter user @naughtybanished and reproduced above. The punning association of military violence with phallic authority in the form of 'cocked pistols' is particularly striking because it seems indirectly to invoke the exemplary killings, suggesting that authoritarian violence is part of the character's appeal.

Links between sexuality and violence become particularly problematic in the context of Ross's 'seduction' of McVitie. Their initial encounter is a coercive, non-consensual exchange of sex for food. As well as echoing the contemporary reality of conditions endured during the refugee crisis of 2015, it can be connected to modern rape culture's reassertions through sexual violence of masculine power and authority in the face of its perceived devaluation.[39] In an apparent effort at mitigation, subsequent scenes attempt to contextualise Ross's character. He tells McVitie a story of his time at boarding school when he was singled out for humiliation after calling on a master to stop the beating of a fellow pupil. 'There have been many times since then that I have felt the urge to show compassion', Ross says; 'I have always managed to resist.' In a subsequent conversation with Corporal MacDonald, McVitie indicates that she accepts this interpretation, saying that Ross 'was kind once but he suffered for it so he is wary of ever being kind again.' This glimpse of repressed compassion becomes the basis for McVitie's acceptance of Ross, which culminates in apparently consensual sex. Presenting the engineering of apparent consent through coercion, these scenes replicate at an interpersonal level the imposition of consensus through political violence at Barrett's execution, further exemplifying Agamben's contention that modern political sovereignty extends into personal and corporeal spaces. Ross's anecdote does not so much expose a hidden vulnerability as present a lesson learnt in masculine economy, where compassion is revealed as a needless and shameful expense. His internalised, institutionally fostered violence raises the romantic stereotype of brooding, conflicted masculinity to a toxic extreme.

Mindful that his character embodies such qualities, *Banished* fan culture accepts the problems inherent in promoting Ross as an alternative romantic hero. As @naughtybanished explains, there is no question that his and McVitie's initial encounter is 'anything other than a rape'; indeed the reception of the scene anticipates the more widespread controversy surrounding a comparable one in *Poldark* and both are part of a renewed testing of boundaries around consent not just in period drama but more generally in popular culture.[40] In the face of such themes, memes use humour and fantasy to defuse the emotional impact of the series and to reverse the power dynamic it portrays: they are 'a relief and a release after the intensity of the actual drama' and are 'done half to glory in the masculinity, half to turn it on its head.'[41] Such imaginative responses bring paratextual closure to an issue that within the series itself remains troublingly unresolved. At the end of *Banished*, Ross is both the primary agent of its gendered violence and the most obvious object of the desiring gaze traditionally associated with costume drama. While it further explains the relatively limited popular success of *Banished*, this discomfiting combination also reflects larger shifts in the cultural expression of gender. Masculinities long subject to assertions of apparently never-ending crisis now adopt reactionary and retaliatory modes that both mimic and inform the violence of economic retrenchment. Perhaps even more than its depiction of judicial punishment, *Banished* dramatises this state of affairs through the violence of its own irreconcilable paradoxes.

Conflicting Masculinities

Notes

1. See, for example, http://outlanderaddiction.com and its comprehensive list of fan resources http://outlanderaddiction.com/outlandish_websites/; *Poldark* fandom is divided among devotees of Winston Graham's novels at The Winston Graham and *Poldark* Literary Society (http://poldark.activeboard.com), loyalists to the BBC's 1975–7 series (https://www.facebook.com/poldarkappreciationsociety/) and fans of the 2015 BBC adaptation (http://www.poldarked.com).
2. Jimmy McGovern, '*Banished*: A new drama for BBC set during the founding of the penal colony in Australia in 1788', *BBC Writers Room*, 4 March 2015. Available at http://www.bbc.co.uk/blogs/writersroom/entries/219f38a4-5c17-43ae-aee4-8fcdcf55d7a2 (accessed 19 August 2016).
3. The execution of the historical Thomas Barrett is discussed in Robert Hughes, *The Fatal Shore* (London, 2003), p. 91, and Tom Keneally, *The Commonwealth of Thieves* (London, 2007), pp. 160–2. On Robert Ross, see David S. Macmillan, 'Ross, Robert (1740–1794)', *Australian Dictionary of Biography*, National Centre of Biography, Australian National University. Available at http://adb.anu.edu.au/biography/ross-robert-2608/text3591, published first in hardcopy in 1967 (accessed 23 August 2016). The words quoted are those of Ross's fellow officer in the marines, David Collins. As a character in Thomas Keneally's novel *The Playmaker* (1987) and Timberlake Wertenbaker's theatrical adaptation *Our Country's Good* (1988), Ross is portrayed as cruel, authoritarian and sadistic.
4. Will Atkinson, Steve Roberts and Mike Savage (eds), *Class Inequality in Austerity Britain: Power, Difference and Suffering* (Basingstoke, 2013), p. 10, citing Giorgio Agamben, *State of Exception* (2005).
5. Diane Negra and Yvonne Tasker, 'Introduction: Gender and Recessionary Culture', in D. Negra and Y. Tasker (eds), *Gendering the Recession: Media and Culture in an Age of Austerity* (Durham, NC, 2014), pp. 1–30.
6. Owen Hatherley, *The Ministry of Nostalgia* (London, 2016), p. 14; Rebecca Bramall, *The Cultural Politics of Austerity: Past and Present in Austere Times* (Basingstoke, 2013), p. 4.
7. Ibid., p. 19.
8. Hélène Cixous, 'Sorties', in D. Tallack (ed.), *Critical Theory: A Reader* (Abingdon, 2013), p. 204 (emphasis in original) and p. 205.
9. Olli Pyyhtinen, *The Gift and its Paradoxes: Beyond Mauss* (Abingdon, 2016), p. 124.
10. *Banished* BBC Press Pack (2015), p. 3. Available at http://downloads.bbc.co.uk/mediacentre/banished.pdf (accessed 21 July 2017).
11. Many accounts present the arrival of female convicts as a transformational moment in the history of the colony. Hughes, *The Fatal Shore*, p. 89, discusses the disembarkation of the first female convicts on 6 February 1788 as inaugurating 'the sexual history of colonial Australia'. Grace Karskens critically

The Masculine Economies of *Banished*

dissects mythmaking around the arrival of further female convicts on the *Lady Juliana* in 1790 (Grace Karskens, *The Colony: A History of Early Sydney* (Crows Nest, NSW, 2009) p. 10).

12. Giorgio Agamben, *Homo Sacer: Sovereign Power and Bare Life*, trans. Daniel Heller-Roazen (Stanford, 1998), p. 5.
13. Ibid., p. 6.
14. Fintan Walsh, *Male Trouble: Masculinity and the Performance of Crisis* (Basingstoke, 2010), p. 24.
15. See, for example, Anon., *Man Points: The Definitive Guide to Measuring your Manliness* (London, 2015).
16. See, for example, Bruno Latour, *We Have Never Been Modern*, trans. C. Porter (Cambridge, MA, 1993).
17. George Barrington, *The History of New South Wales* (London, 1802), p. 152.
18. Brian Nail, 'Austerity and the Language of Sacrifice', *The Critical Religion Association*, 15 October 2013. Available at https://criticalreligion.org/2013/10/15/austerity-and-the-language-of-sacrifice/ (accessed 21 August 2016).
19. René Girard, *Violence and the Sacred* (Baltimore, 1977), p. 1; Georges Bataille, 'Sacrifice, the Festival and the Principles of the Sacred World', in F. Botting and S. Wilson (eds), *The Bataille Reader* (Oxford, 1997), p. 213.
20. Agamben, *Homo Sacer*, p. 131.
21. Paul Jones, 'Jimmy McGovern's *Banished* the victim of "limited" BBC2 drama budget as BBC confirms cancellation', *Radio Times*, 7 May 2015. Available at http://www.radiotimes.com/news/2015-05-07/jimmy-mcgoverns-banished-the-victim-of-limited-bbc2-drama-budget-as-bbc-confirms-cancellation (accessed 1 September 2016.).
22. @russelltovey, 5 May 2015. Available at https://twitter.com/russelltovey/status/595690814166151168 (accessed 31 July 2016).
23. *Banished* DVD material, 'Interview with Jeffrey Walker'; Gary Sturgess, 'Convicts and sex slaves: sorting the fact from the fiction in British TV series "Banished"', *Sydney Morning Herald*, 10 March 2015. Available at http://www.smh.com.au/comment/convicts-and-sex-slaves-sorting-the-fact-from-the-fiction-in-british-tv-series-banished-20150309-13yvc9.html (accessed 1 August 2016).
24. John Martin Staniforth, 'Re-Imagining the Convicts: History, Myth and Nation in Contemporary Australian Fictions of Early Convictism', unpublished PhD thesis, University of Leeds, 2015, p. 48. I am grateful to the author of the thesis for allowing me access to it in advance of its being made publicly available.
25. Jill Conway, 'Gender in Australia', *Daedalus*, 114/1 (1985), p. 350.
26. Carly O'Neill, Dick Houtman and Stef Aupers, 'Advertising real beer: Authenticity claims beyond truth and falsity', *European Journal of Cultural Studies*, 17/5 (2014), p. 590.
27. Staniforth, 'Re-Imagining the Convicts', p. 61; Mark McKenna, 'First Words: A Brief History of Public Debate on a New Preamble to the Australian

Constitution 1991–99', *Parliament of Australia* (n.d.). Available at http://www.aph.gov.au/About_Parliament/Parliamentary_Departments/Parliamentary_Library/pubs/rp/rp9900/2000RP16#Pre (accessed 31 August 2016). In the face of widespread objections, the word was removed from the preamble's second draft and the preamble as a whole was rejected when put to a referendum.

28. Hughes, *The Fatal Shore*, p. 15.
29. John Rickard, *Australia: A Cultural History* (London, 1988; 2nd edn 1996), p. 24.
30. Stuart MacIntyre and Anna Clark, *The History Wars* (Melbourne, 2003), p. 114.
31. Chris Healy, *Forgetting Aborigines* (Sydney, 2008), p. 10.
32. Anon., 'Boycott Banished, an All-White Drama about a Black Part of Our History', *New Matilda*, 10 March 2015. Available at https://newmatilda.com/2015/03/10/boycott-banished-all-white-drama-about-black-part-our-history/ (accessed 8 August 2016).
33. Jacqueline Rose, 'Donald Trump's victory is a disaster for modern masculinity', *Guardian*, 15 November 2016. Available at https://www.theguardian.com/commentisfree/2016/nov/15/trump-disaster-modern-masculinity-sexual-nostalgian-oppressive-men-women (accessed 17 November 2016).
34. *Banished* BBC Press Pack (2015), p. 11.
35. Ibid., p. 11 and p. 12.
36. Tom Lamont, 'Russell Tovey: "I was a scared, skinny little rat. Then I hit the gym …"', *Observer*, 1 March 2015. Available at https://www.theguardian.com/tv-and-radio/2015/mar/01/russell-tovey-looking-banished-interview (accessed 17 November 2016); Matthew Weaver, 'Russell Tovey says sorry for effeminate actor comments', *Guardian*, 3 March 2015. Available at https://www.theguardian.com/tv-and-radio/2015/mar/03/russell-tovey-sorry-effeminate-actor-drama-school (both accessed 17 November 2016).
37. Girard, *Violence and the Sacred*, p. 8 and p. 7.
38. Jean-Luc Nancy, *L'Imperatif Categorique* (Paris, 1983), p. 150; quoted in Agambem, *Homo Sacer*, p. 58.
39. Phoebe C. Linton, 'Modern Rape Culture and BBC's *Banished*', *The Public Medievalist*, 25 June 2015, Available at http://www.publicmedievalist.com/modern-rape-culture-and-bbcs-banished/ (accessed 5 August 2016).
40. 'Poldark "rape" scene sparks controversy', *BBC News*, 24 October 2016. Available at http://www.bbc.co.uk/news/entertainment-arts-37749637 (accessed 12 December 2016); Nickie D. Phillips, *Beyond Blurred Lines: Rape Culture in Popular Media* (Lanham, MD, 2016).
41. Email correspondence between author and @naughtybanished (16 November 2016). My thanks to @naughtybanished for permission to quote from this illuminating conversation and to reproduce the meme as an illustration to this chapter.

2

'I will not fight for my country ... for my ship ... my King ... or Captain': Redefining Imperial Masculinities in *To the Ends of the Earth*

Mark Fryers

Introduction

Rebecca Feasey states of the study of masculinity on television: 'masculinity and male sexuality continue to be understood as fixed, stable, unalterable and therefore, beyond enquiry'[1] despite increasing scrutiny of femininity in the same context. The three-part adaptation of William Golding's Booker Prize-winning literary trilogy, produced by the BBC in 2005 as *To the Ends of the Earth*, challenges and disrupts this notion of stability. It explores traditional modes of British imperial masculinity, only to suggest that this conception of a patriarchal, imperial masculine nexus of nineteenth-century 'success' was merely a downward hierarchy of violence, degradation and disenfranchisement. Primarily, the series addresses this through engagement with (and enquiry of) a number of established tropes of nineteenth-century British colonial power, especially the ship of state model, linear national progress and male maritime rites of passage symbolism. The series stands at odds with other naval narratives of the period, particularly the ITV series *Hornblower* (1998–2003) and the Hollywood film based on British writer Patrick O' Brian's seafaring novels, *Master and Commander: The Far Side of the World* (2003). Whereas these productions offer a gentleman, officer hero and a fairly straightforward dichotomy of heroes and villains (mainly the British versus the French/Spanish), *To the Ends of the Earth* offers no readily identifiable and uncomplicated nautical hero. This chapter will discuss how the series achieves this through its narrative and representational modes of address, in particular rendering in vivid detail 'the ways in which social power is both exercised and undermined.'[2]

Empire, Masculinity and the Sea

The British imperial 'project' was disseminated culturally as a certain set of overt British masculine values. For the officer class, it was judged by a display of gallant fortitude, whilst, for the others, it was typified by loyalty, hard labour and a robust sense of knowing one's place within the hierarchy. It is unsurprising therefore that the role of women was deliberately occluded. Culture, particularly literature and the printed press, were instrumental in constructing this vision. As Mangan asserts:

> From approximately 1850 imperial masculinity was methodically 'manufactured' by means of a cultural conveyor belt set up eventually throughout the empire with varying degrees of efficiency and with varying responses.[3]

This was particularly relevant within the armed forces, and especially so within the Royal Navy – the pride of these forces and the facilitator of much of Britain's success abroad. The ordinary British seaman – the 'Jack Tar' figure – was seen to champion the values of the nation at large[4] and the warship represented 'a [male] community comparable to a village or small town',[5] yet the greatest reverence was given to the officer classes of the navy or 'gentleman', as evidenced by the 'cult of Nelson.' Cynthia Behrman articulates this myth, describing how 'vital the British navy was to the national image, how deeply it was connected to the nation's history, and how easily its need for international superiority could be defended.'[6]

Redefining Imperial Masculinities

The sea was a space in which British masculinity, and the nation at large, could be explored, tested and celebrated. It was an appellation and extension of Empire but also a 'bourgeois space', in which, as Easthope suggested, 'the masculine ego can move as fast as thought, mastering nature as far as the eye can see.'[7] Again, literature provided the dramatic thrust in which to fuse this redolent ideology to tales of adventure and success, or what Green describes as the 'energising myths of empire.'[8] Novels such as Stevenson's *Treasure Island* (1883), Kipling's *Captains Courageous* (1897) or the nautical novels of Frederick Marryat gave fanciful narratives to the notion of male, imperial adventure. In these examples, the experience of being at sea and conquering the environment was central to the development of proper masculinity, providing a durable male 'rite of passage' scenario. Yet, in a revisionist sense, this can easily be interpreted as a fragile and performative sense of masculinity, suggesting its origins in Mangan's 'manufactured' evocation of colonial ideology. *To the Ends of the Earth* presents an opportunity to interrogate this performative display and its more insidious repercussions.

To the Ends of the Earth (2005)

The expensively produced (with a budget of ten million pounds)[9] three-part dramatisation of Golding's trilogy of books collectively known as *To the Ends of the Earth*, which comprised *Rites of Passage* (1980) and the sequels *Close Quarters* (1987) and *Fire Down Below* (1989), conflated the three books into one master narrative. It is set in and after 1812, seven years after Nelson's naval victory at Trafalgar, and three years prior to Wellington's victory at Waterloo. This particular historical moment is used as the basis for exploring established notions of nationalism and mythology. In the novel and the film, the period is used as a backdrop to interrogate the valour, heroism and mythology of the era and to vividly, viscerally and violently deconstruct them. Firstly, it places the sea journey from one side of the Empire to the other as its narrative trajectory, plotting a literal and metaphoric journey through the heart of Empire. The setting is a fighting British warship in the Napoleonic era, which also doubles as a passenger ship to Australia. This facilitates the inclusion of both women and non-naval personnel into the closed homosocial spaces of the Royal Navy. At a time when the myths of victory at Trafalgar were at their most vital, this ship, and its various inhabitants, presents both a microcosm of British society at sea,[10] placed under intense scrutiny, and its voyage offers an opportunity to interrogate the trope of the sea voyage as triumphant masculine rite of passage.

William Golding is perhaps best known for his novel *Lord of the Flies* (1954), which examines the moral choices facing humanity and the possibility of evil inherent in society. It explores these ideas through a group of shipwrecked schoolboys on a remote Pacific island who descend into factionalism and savagery in their enclosed and isolated surroundings. At the end of the story, a naval officer discovers the group, and having witnessed the evil manifested in the children, surveys his own warship anew. In the *To the Ends of the Earth* trilogy, Golding keeps the same theme of a small, isolated community far away from the mother country descending into partial depravity, but this time supplanting children with adults. Golding had a lifelong love of the sea, nurtured by his time as a Lieutenant in the Royal Navy during World War II, and this appreciation of the sea as a romantic space is fused with his themes of inhumanity and cruelty.[11]

The series was directed by Davis Atwood who had previously helmed the period drama *The Fortunes and Misfortunes of Moll Flanders* (ITV, 1996) (which is overtly referenced in the series' erotic episodes). Golding's novels were adapted by Tony Basgallup and Leigh Jackson, who were better known for work on contemporary soaps and dramas such as *Eastenders* (BBC, 1985-), *Casualty* (BBC, 1986-) and *Grange Hill* (BBC, 1978-2008). This perhaps explains why the finished product had much of the look and conventions of a period drama, but viewed the revered nineteenth century through a critical lens - dealing with decidedly social issues.[12]

In the adaptation, Benedict Cumberbatch portrays Edmund Talbot, a man of aristocratic bearing, travelling aboard a creaking warship, to take up a governor's position in Australia. His journey is also a personal journey of self-discovery. The ship is crewed by the Royal Navy under the watch of Captain Anderson (Jared Harris), and his Officers Lieutenant Summers (Jamie Sives) and Lieutenant Deverel (J.J. Feild). The ship is commissioned to engage with enemy ships if it encounters any on the long journey, but aside from that, the ship acts as a passenger vessel for Talbot and an assortment of other civilians heading for a new life in the colony.

Redefining Imperial Masculinities

These are comprised of the political radical Mr Prettiman (Sam Neill), the artist and his wife Mr and Mrs Brocklebank (Richard McCabe, Denise Black) and their companion Zenobia (Paula Jennings), Miss Granham, a governess (Victoria Hamilton), the craven Mr Pike (Jonathan Slinger) and his family as the principal leads. Tensions begin to arise in this small community almost immediately as Talbot incurs the wrath of Captain Anderson by walking on the quarterdeck, against his explicit instructions. Unable to discipline him due to Talbot's social position, Anderson instead humiliates the Parson Colley (Daniel Evans) by throwing him to the ground when he attempts the same. This sets off a chain of events, which lead to Colley being further humiliated by being forced to take part in the Neptune 'hazing' ceremony whereby crew are selected (often novice sailors) and are ritually abused and held underwater as the ship crosses the equator (see the BBC's 1978 series *The Voyage of Charles Darwin* for a much milder depiction).

Meanwhile, Prettiman falls gravely ill after a fall and he and Miss Granham decide to wed. There is an interlude in which another ship is spotted in the fog and both crew and civilians prepare themselves for battle. This sequence dramatically juxtaposes the rarely glimpsed working-class naval servicemen against the passengers of the upper decks, hastily and reluctantly pressed into service. However, the ship turns out to be a fellow British vessel, led by Sir Henry Somerset (Charles Dance) who brings news of the defeat of Napoleon at Waterloo. A lavish party takes place aboard Sir Henry's ship (the Jane Austen-style society ball is reproduced in these unusual circumstances, enforcing the notion of a stately home afloat) whereby Talbot falls in love with Henry's adopted daughter Marion Chumley (Joanna Page) and is distraught when they part. A swap takes place across the ships of Lieutenants as Deverel has fallen out of favour with Anderson, and likewise his replacement Lieutenant Benet (Niall McGregor) has fallen afoul of Sir Henry by having designs on his wife, Lady Somerset (Cheryl Campbell). Benet is a poet and a philanderer, who provides a contrast for the viewer between his and Talbot's own brand of aristocratic privilege. The two inevitably clash and their petty bickering over how best to assist Mr Prettiman in his incapacitated state leads to Talbot falling on him and exacerbating his swelling so badly that he almost dies, making Talbot almost responsible for two deaths.

Towards the end of the voyage, the creaking warship snaps its mast (an irresistible metaphor for fractured and emasculated masculinity) and Benet initially distinguishes himself by fixing the mast back into place despite causing both fires in the timbers below and the mistrust of Summers. Talbot is promoted to Midshipman and during one of his watches a mass of pack ice is spotted ahead, causing panic. The conflation here of primal elements (water, fire and ice), as well as Mr Prettiman's determination to shoot an albatross to debunk nautical superstition, invokes Coleridge's *The Rime of the Ancient Mariner* and the symbolism of a masculine fall from grace and attendant redemption. Talbot's trajectory throughout the narrative echoes the journey of sin and redemption the mariner undertakes. Even more significantly, it is his aristocratic arrogance that leads him through a journey of self-discovery. It is also pertinent to compare this evocation of a Napoleonic journey of nightmare and redemption, class and society, with Anne-Julia Zwierlein's[13] analysis of John Milton's *Paradise Lost* (1667), a text that also deals with a dramatic fall from grace. Zwierlein analyses the poem, particularly the section depicting Satan's sea voyage, in relation to the eighteenth-century seafaring trade, and changing attitudes to the sea and oceanic voyages. She suggests that the sea and ocean, considered as chaotic, dangerous and 'without dimension' in Renaissance times, begins to be viewed differently as it becomes the axis of trade and wealth for the burgeoning English, and later British, overseas Empire. The sea, particularly within a British context, is transformed by 'materialistic readings' in the 'secularised eighteenth century'[14] divesting oceanic metaphors of negative religious connotations and transposing them into commercialised spaces. The effect therefore, is of a leviathan tamed, a sea that can be conquered by military, but, more importantly, by commercial enterprise. *To the Ends of the Earth*, in its re-imagining of naval myth and secure institutional hierarchy, and its fidelity to literature like *The Rime of the Ancient Mariner*, returns the sea, voyage and ship metaphors, as well as the stable vision of social structure, to uncertainty and notions of humanity's hubris in the face of nature's awesome power (also evident in the continued Anglo-American cultural fascination with the tragedy of the RMS *Titanic*).

Eventually, Captain Anderson successfully steers the ship out of danger and it finally arrives safely. As a male naval Captain, Anderson is afforded the opportunity to redeem his earlier transgressions through nautical prowess, suggesting that it is the privileged, or those at the top of the hierarchy, who have a chance to atone for their sins. Talbot's final act also hints at his own redemptive conclusion. On arrival in Australia, he learns of the death of his benefactor, before spotting the ship burning in the distance (a legacy of Benet's repairs). Realising Summers is still on board, Talbot races to rescue him and is badly burned in the process, failing to retrieve him from the burning ship. The series ends with Talbot and Miss Chumley seemingly reunited on the jetty.

This Ship of Fools is England

By making the boat a ship-of-the-line, rather than a merchant vessel, both the novels and the series deliberately engage with British naval history and cultural tradition. This device also allows for the presence of women aboard a warship, a notable absence in so many nautical dramas. The navy itself is represented mainly by the officer class; Captain Anderson and Lieutenants Deverel, Benet and Summers, who all inhabit the social and professional spaces appropriate to their status. Anderson distinguishes himself after his brutal treatment of Colley, whilst Deverel as drunkard is heavily implicated in his degradation. Benet is a snob, whilst Summers, as the non-privileged officer, there on merit, is the man responsible for showing Talbot his position has responsibilities and consequences for everyone. It is clear that the navy is not glorified but shown to be human, fallible and capable of atrocity in its strictures and protocol, but also capable of social mobility and a possible arena in which a man can show himself to be great, like Admiral Nelson (therefore, not a total deconstruction of naval life and perhaps reflecting Golding's complicated attitudes towards it). This scrutiny of Britain's naval heritage elicits a conflicting and complicated set of associations not present in the likes of *Hornblower* or *Master and Commander: The Far Side of the World*, and offers a more diffuse projection of the founding myths of Britain. The conceit of *To the Ends of the Earth* invokes a number of long-established cultural and literal metaphors associated with the sea, ships, sailing and voyages. The voyage, or journey, metaphor is the most prevalent perhaps, as Golding originally used this device to de-stabilise the heroic, masculine rites-of-passage motif established in the aforementioned examples. In Golding's novel, as with the television adaptation, the sea journey as romance and adventure is transformed into a nightmare of death, disease and degradation.

As such, the series mixes elements of several generic customs, both stylistically and thematically and often in close proximity. The opening sees Talbot traversing the English countryside in a carriage, redolent of eighteenth-century costume dramas of the period. The carriage then alights at the docks, where Talbot first views them through his muddy carriage window (the first indication of grime). The bucolic countryside is juxtaposed against the romantic docks, accompanied by a jaunty theme that incorporates nautical motifs. As Talbot embarks upon the ship, there are several under-sail, under-mast, low-angle and panning shots, as is familiar from maritime filmic language, to emphasise the size and majesty, as well as the intimidating scale, of the three-masted frigate. The visual environment changes abruptly as Talbot enters the upper decks of the ship. The interiors are dark, grim and claustrophobic. The romantic image of the ship itself, so often revered within British culture, is revealed to be decrepit and befouled. The further down the ship Talbot ventures, the darker, more cramped and unpleasant it is: a literal metaphor for the social stratification of the era. Below decks, Talbot is greeted with sickness and drug-taking and he is mocked by the lower passengers, especially when he later attempts to man the cannons (an endeavour which leaves him concussed and humiliated). The lower depths are seen to be hellish and the inhabitants rarely glimpsed. They are given agency only when there is the prospect of warfare, suggesting something of the manner in which the subaltern were treated in eighteenth-century British society.

The Sea as a Philosophical and Nightmarish Space

In this series, the lead protagonist, Talbot, often governs the perception of space. As his perception is constantly altering and in flux, the visual and aural depiction of the ship and the sea are unstable, aligned to Talbot's own journey of self-discovery. This would explain the fluid handling of established nautical visual language in the programme. As such, the series has more in common with Milton's conception of seascapes:

> Milton's concept of space is not empirical, but hermeneutical: space is constructed through perception, and the uncharted ocean becomes a symbol of the instability of human knowledge.[15]

The instability of human knowledge is closely tied to Talbot as a character. As discussed, the individualised journey motif is established from the opening, as the dizzying grandeur of the ship is evoked from Talbot's nautical novice position, and the dreams and nightmares he has aboard sustain a consistent theme of subjectivity. Interstitial sailing scenes, usually a close-up of the prow of the boat, the wake from behind, aerial shots of the rigging or the ship in full sail from a long shot, are common tropes in nautical film and television to express and compress the passage of time, and/or to indicate forward motion. They usually have a positive connation and are often romanticised or fetishised evocations of sailing, matched by a romantic and sweeping soundtrack and visually aligned to sunlight or twilight. Their use here however is more complicated, and again, linked expressionistically to Talbot's shifts in mood. Talbot's first foray on deck is in poor weather, gloomy, wet and turbulent. He veers ungainly across deck, and is vomited on by the parson, again undermining the romantic notion of sailing. Talbot's entry into his journal concludes: 'added to the heat and humidity, a sea voyage, I am learning, can have an effect on a man's constitution.' As the narrative unfolds, this effect becomes more profound and is demonstrated visually and aurally for the viewer.

Unlike Talbot's partially redeemed aristocrat, it is Colley who suffers the most for traversing the lower depths after his rejection and humiliation on the upper decks. His situation is compounded as he is plied with alcohol and the narrative alludes to sex acts such as buggery and fellatio taking place between Colley and the crew. His possible homosexuality is also hinted at as he smiles longingly at a topless sailor shortly beforehand.[16] The punishment for his transgression is a painfully slow and agonising death as he lies indolent in his quarters for days until he expires: 'men can die of shame' as Talbot muses. Indeed, Colley's entire misfortune is at Talbot's hands. As Summers instructs Talbot, 'the captain humiliated the parson sir, because he could not humiliate you', blaming him for 'the arrogance of your class.' Talbot was also not present to put a stop to the ceremony as he was indulging in intercourse with Zenobia, a sequence intercut with the parson's humiliation for added resonance.

Virginia Heffernan's perceptive review in *The New York Times* observes that 'Golding writes, as usual, from the point of view of the bullies and this production shares that corrupted advantage.'[17] This is true as we see things almost entirely from Talbot's perspective. Not least is the

Conflicting Masculinities

Figure 2.1 Talbot (Benedict Cumberbatch) is nauseous as Wheeler (Brian Pettifer) first directs him to his quarters in *To the Ends of the Earth*.

peripheral treatment of women as well as the lower passengers and crew. Talbot has intercourse with Zenobia then refuses to acknowledge her, yet is smitten with Miss Chumley, the orphan raised by Sir and Lady Somerset. He upsets Miss Granham by assuming her status of governess yet eventually learns to respect her superior wisdom, despite Mr Prettiman claiming: 'Greek ... It's not for a woman's brain.' Indeed, much like the binary opposites of a Western, the women seem to be apportioned the archetypes of whore (Zenobia), homemaker (Miss Granham) and lady (Miss Chumley).

The series' pattern is established early on, as the romance of voyage and onward trajectory of novice sailor is undermined by the grungy reality of a nightmarish and dilapidated ship (certainly not a fit place for a lady, by the standards of the era). The heritage trope of country house and carriage, opulent interiors and wide open spaces is replaced by a foreboding and clustered interior more akin to Gothic horror. If the ship represents a microcosm of society at sea, a stratified stately home afloat, then it resembles the Gothic piles of Manderley (in Daphne du Maurier's *Rebecca*, (1938)) or the House of Usher (in Edgar Allen Poe's *The Fall of the House of Usher* (1839)) more so than Downton Abbey. The adaptation is clearly conversing with these tropes to undermine them and present a return of the repressed in 'polite' eighteenth-century British society.

We could therefore compare this iteration of Britain's 'Wild West' (the eighteenth-century Atlantic) to revisionist Hollywood Westerns. The series is punctuated with rotting and putrefying flesh, loveless fornication and fellatio, vomit, flatulence, sickness and fetid stench, demystifying the romance of the sailing ship, oceanic voyages, the Napoleonic era and British history in general. As such it has more in common with films like *McCabe and Mrs Miller* (1971) and *Unforgiven* (1992) or television programmes like *Deadwood* (HBO, 2004–6), which deliberately challenge the established myths of the American West, instead foregrounding the dirt and depravity. Similarly, contemporary costume dramas often foreground a gritty realism, such as *Ripper Street*'s (BBC/Amazon, 2012–16) grimy evocation of Victorian Whitechapel or *Peaky Blinders*' (BBC, 2013–) inter-war, gangland Birmingham, altogether offering an 'anti-heritage' representation of the British past.

Masculinity, Sexuality and the Sea

It is perhaps useful to consider the series in relation to the British films *HMS Defiant* and *Billy Budd*, which were both released in 1962. They both focus on the Nelsonian navy but specifically on the Spithead mutinies of 1797. As such they deal with the counter-myth of naval solidarity later subsumed by the glorious 'myth' of Trafalgar. As with *To the Ends of the Earth*, Hermann Melville's original novel *Billy Budd* (1924) used maritime existence as a metaphorical setting in which to explore the philosophy of man's (literal) condition and existence. Both films however follow a narrative of mutiny or alleged mutinous behaviour, a shocking injustice before 'order' is restored by a return to warfare. In both instances also, mutiny is engendered by the violence and bullying of a sadistic, rogue Master-at-Arms (Robert Ryan's Claggart in *Budd* and Dirk Bogarde's Scott Padget in *Defiant*). Unlike this series, these films position the middle-man as the villain and the Captain as paternal and just, forced to make hard decisions against his will (or 'benevolent despotism' as Reed finds in naval literature).[18] Similarly, the interruption of warfare to shift emphasis from internal scrutiny is not afforded here. The regenerative violence[19] that helps to fix myth and male solidarity is absent, and when the threat is raised, it prompts disconnection as women, radicals, narcissists and cowards populate the vessel. The distance from traditional, martial, masculine, imperial British values is perhaps best expressed by Mr Pike when he declares: 'I will not fight for my country ... my ship ... my king or my captain.'

Indeed, by deliberately keeping active warfare at bay, *To the Ends of the Earth* presents what has traditionally been represented as 'feminised' peacetime, which patriarchal society associated with 'unmanly' values as well as dangerous and radical thought. For Spicer, the dominant archetypes of masculinity in British film are characterised by an 'efficiently organised [...] close knit, disciplined group', whereby 'masculine comradeship is the dominant relationship, virtually excluding women altogether',[20] a situation readily created by naval ships crewed entirely by males. As Feasey observes:

> Society has long been accustomed to the gendering of the public and private spheres, and the hegemonic model of masculinity remains dependent on the demarcation of such gendered spaces.[21]

In other words, masculinity is defined as much by its supposed opposite of femininity or effeminacy. The discrete gendering of spaces in *To the Ends of the Earth* is denied by the presence of women and civilians within the maritime, masculine spaces, and indeed the public and private collide with devastating consequences for some. Therefore, hegemonic masculinity – its flaws, contradictions and iniquities – is on prominent and conspicuous display.

The male rite-of-passage paradigm is, however, still enacted partially through Talbot. It follows the convention in British cinema as discussed by Spicer:

> The masculine bonding at the heart of these films is shown primarily through the induction of the young new recruit, always middle class, into the fighting team, a process which becomes his passage into manhood.[22]

It is made clear that Talbot's arrogance in breaking protocol and standing on the quarterdeck uninvited sets off a chain of events that leads to the parson's humiliation and eventual death (quite the opposite of *Hornblower* as gentleman hero). His petty intellectual squabble with Benet also leads to Prettiman's misery, whilst he also initially treats Summers with disdain as he has been promoted to lieutenant from below decks rather than from commission. He patronisingly declares to him: 'A common sailor? Well then Mr Summers I must congratulate you [...] on imitating to perfection the manners and speech of a somewhat higher station in life.' The notion of the performance of class/masculinity underlines its artificiality, and the performative aspect is again emphasised by the scenes involving Talbot and Mr Pike as they prepare to play their (inept) part in the fighting, and are greeted as heroes despite doing nothing. Talbot swishes his sword and jumps up into the rigging like a child at play. He fails to impress those he seeks to, though, with Prettiman accusing him of being 'not exactly a boy ... but not exactly a man either.' There is a brief period where Summers invites Talbot to take part in the middle watch, to which Talbot claims to the other passengers: 'I am not just a civilian anymore, I am promoted to midshipman' (fittingly, the first position for both Horatio Nelson and the fictional Hornblower). The two enjoy a brief period of masculine bonding before the arrogance of Talbot's class interferes. When chastised by Summers for arriving late, he rebounds: 'I was discussing matters of a philosophical nature with Mr Prettiman, scarcely a discussion I could share with you.' As with Prettiman's comment regarding women and Greek, it seems education, or lack of it, was used to enforce artificial class and gender boundaries. The series therefore still discusses the unique virtues and celebrations of being an English *man*.

'I kill people without knowing it'

As stated, not only is the sense of space and perception linked to Talbot's perception, the production is also expressionistic in its evocation, particularly in dream sequences Talbot experiences, as he is plagued by fever, self-doubt and the consequences of his actions. In a surreal and deliberately ghostly sequence of events, Talbot's servant Wheeler (Brian Pettifer) vanishes overboard but later mysteriously turns up aboard Sir Henry's ship, only to then shoot himself in the head during heavy weather. Along with Colley and Prettiman, he is the third person that Talbot is accused of and accuses himself of being responsible for inadvertently killing (although Prettiman recovers). Talbot opines over voiceover, 'I kill people without knowing it', which could be read as the effect aristocratic or imperial masculinity has in general. Following this, Talbot dreams of seeing the deceased Wheeler and Colley, as dark and dirty water seeps down the walls and under the doors like an encroaching plague. Seawater as dirty and disgusting is a direct challenge to the 'ruler of the waves' motif of English mythology. This is compounded in the narrative, as the veneer of civilisation begins to break down, and the ship is initially without a doctor on board, and then without a parson, recognisable icons of eighteenth-century British society. It does have an artist, a philosopher and an aristocrat however. Indeed, the entire crew, in their decadence, peculiarities and bodily functions, resembles a satirical 'Hogarthian' sketch of English society. Yet, *To the Ends of the Earth* is a text about how society kicks downwards through its hierarchical structure and how uneven, unjust and jaundiced society is as a result of this practice. Talbot declares at the beginning 'my ambition is boundless', and due to his station in life, he has the opportunity to fulfil this.

There is a resonance and extratextual significance in the casting of the public school-educated Benedict Cumberbatch as the young aristocrat. Cumberbatch was raised in the exclusive London Borough of Kensington and Chelsea to a theatrical family with links to high society. This has become particularly relevant concerning comments about alleged discrimination against 'posh' actors made by Cumberbatch and others as part of a wider debate about social mobility in Britain between 2012–15. Cumberbatch claimed that he may decamp to 'classless America' as he had been 'castigated as a moaning, rich, public school bastard, complaining about only getting posh roles'[23] despite not being 'born into land or titles.'[24] However, Cumberbatch's comments identified himself with a self-pitying elite out of touch with the rest of society: a gap seemingly expanding at the time, supporting the structures of class society. He stated nostalgically of the Edwardian period:

> There was a social structure that had to be adhered to [...] Everyone was held in their place, but what was honourable about it was that there was a duty of care from the top down.[25]

This was exacerbated by his reference to black actors as 'coloured' in 2015,[26] yet complicated by his plea for increased representation of the former and his impassioned (and anti-government) plea for action on the refugee crisis in the same year.[27] Cumberbatch the actor compared with Talbot the out-of-touch colonial aristocrat therefore gives even more contemporary relevance to the interrogation of male, imperial and aristocratic privilege.

Conclusion

Recent television adaptations of *Treasure Island* (Sky, 2012) and *Jamaica Inn* (BBC, 2013) have gestured towards a revisionist history in the costume drama and adventure narrative by giving more prominent display to female and non-white characters whilst simultaneously highlighting the dirt and grime of nautical existence. Similarly, the nautical costume dramas *The Ebb Tide* (ITV, 1998), *Longitude* (Channel 4, 2000) and *Shackleton* (Channel 4, 2002) also question the myth of 'rule Britannia' by focusing on the seamier elements of nautical life and introducing science, technology and exploration to the 'great man' myth of maritime supremacy. These programmes offer different archetypes and conceptions of masculinity that probe the darker recesses of masculine maritime imperialism, more akin to historical verisimilitude. Likewise, *To the Ends of the Earth* represents the residual burnt ashes of imperial masculine identity and the gendered romance of nautical adventure. The series systematically undermines the ideological tenets of gallantry and presents, in often scatological detail, their effect upon the hierarchical formations of nineteenth-century Britain. It presents an obverse to Green's 'energising myths of Empire', showing instead how it is parasitic and not heroic; festering below the surface of heroic projections of imperial endeavour, it leeches off the disadvantaged whilst further nourishing the privileged. As with the revisionist Western, which questions the project of 'manifest destiny', *To the Ends of the Earth* is a revisionist colonial narrative and costume drama, which forensically dissects not just the notions of Empire and maritime/imperial masculinity, but also the very society assumed to be the beneficiary of these. It challenges the viewer to examine the disgrace as well as the grace of British history. The 'ship as England' metaphor which James Chapman identifies in *Master and Commander* (2003)[28] and which also certainly applies to programmes such as *Hornblower* is here de-stabilised, deconstructed and made to look 'hopelessly simplified.'[29] The ship is fragile and at breaking point; as Mr Talbot suggests, 'We are fragile, we are held together by ropes and cables', as indeed are some of the tropes that traditionally define masculinity.

Notes

1. Rebecca Feasey, *Masculinity and Popular Television* (Edinburgh, 2008), p. 2.
2. Marcia Landy, *British Genres: Cinema and Society, 1930–60* (Princeton, NJ, 1991), p. 55.
3. J. A. Mangan, *'Manufactured Masculinity': Making Imperial Manliness, Morality and Militarism* (Abingdon, 2012), p. 9.
4. John R. Reed, *The Army and Navy in Nineteenth-Century British Literature* (New York, 2011), p. 6.
5. Roy and Lesley Adkins, *Jack Tar: Life in Nelson's Navy* (London, 2008), p. xxvi.
6. Reed, *The Army and Navy in Nineteenth-Century British Literature*, p. 14.
7. Easthope quoted in David B. Clarke and Marcus A. Doel, 'From flatland to vernacular relativity: the genesis of early English screenscapes', in Martin Lefebvre (ed.), *Landscape and Film* (London, 2006), p. 216.
8. Martin Green, *Dreams of Adventure, Deeds of Empire* (New York, 1979), p. 3.
9. Ian Bell, 'It was all shipshape in a voyage packed with every known emotion', *The Herald* (Glasgow), 21 July 2005, p. 23.
10. Or as Gregor suggests: 'The ship becomes a theatre, and all its passengers the audience [...]' Ian Gregor, *William Golding: A Critical Study of the Novels* (London, 2012), p. 259.
11. Rachel Haugrud Reiff, *William Golding: Lord of the Flies* (New York, 2010), p. 58.
12. 'Big Brother afloat' as it has been described, in Jane Simon, 'We love telly', *The Mirror*, 6 July 2005, p. 39.
13. Anne Julia Zwierlein, 'Satan's Ocean Voyage and Eighteenth-Century Seafaring Trade', in B. Klein (ed.), *Fictions of the Sea: Critical Perspectives on the Ocean in British Literature and Culture* (Aldershot, 2002), pp. 49–76.
14. Ibid., p. 56.
15. Ibid., p. 61.
16. Wheeler Winston Dixon, *Straight: Constructions of Heterosexuality in the Cinema* (New York, 2003), p. 4.
17. Virginia Heffernan, 'Ah, Life at Sea: Sweaty, Sodden and Light on Nobility', *The New York Times*, 20 October 2006. Available at http://www.nytimes.com/2006/10/20/arts/television/20mast.html?_r=0 (accessed 15 August 2016).
18. Reed, *The Army and Navy*, p. 153.

19. Richard Slotkin, *The Fatal Environment: The Myth of the Frontier in the Age of Industrialisation, 1800–1890* (New York, 1985).
20. Andrew Spicer, *Typical Men: The Representation of Masculinity in Popular British Cinema* (London, 2001), pp. 33–5.
21. Feasey, *Masculinity and Popular Television*, p. 153. See also Alison Light, *Forever England: Femininity, Literature and Conservatism Between the Wars* (Abingdon, 1991).
22. Spicer, *Typical Men*, p. 35.
23. Hannah Furness, '"I'm definitely middle class", says actor Benedict Cumberbatch', *Telegraph*, 28 April 2013. Available at http://www.telegraph.co.uk/culture/tvandradio/10023710/Im-definitely-middle-class-says-actor-Benedict-Cumberbatch.html (accessed 15 August 2016).
24. Liz Thomas, '"I'm tempted to quit 'posh bashing' UK" says star of Sherlock Benedict Cumberbatch', *Daily Mail*, 14 August 2012. Available at http://www.dailymail.co.uk/tvshowbiz/article-2188010/Im-tempted-quit-posh-bashing-UK-says-star-Sherlock-Benedict-Cumberbatch.html (accessed 15 August 2016).
25. Anita Singh, 'Benedict Cumberbatch: "Downton Abbey is sentimental, clichéd and atrocious"', *Telegraph*, 16 August 2012. Available at http://www.telegraph.co.uk/culture/tvandradio/downton-abbey/9480067/Benedict-Cumberbatch-Downton-Abbey-is-sentimental-cliched-and-atrocious.html (accessed 15 August 2016).
26. Lanre Bakare, 'Benedict Cumberbatch apologises after calling black actors "coloured"', *Guardian*, 26 January 2015. Available at https://www.theguardian.com/culture/2015/jan/26/benedict-cumberbatch-apologises-after-calling-black-actors-coloured (acessed 15 August 2016).
27. Jessica Elgot, 'Benedict Cumberbatch stuns theatregoers with anti-government speech', *Guardian*, 30 October 2015. Available at https://www.theguardian.com/uk-news/2015/oct/30/benedict-cumberbatch-stuns-theatregoers-anti-government-speech-refugees (accessed 15 August 2016).
28. James Chapman, '"This ship is England": history, politics and national identity in Master and Commander: The Far Side of the World (2003)', in J. Chapman, M. Glancy and S. Harper (eds), *The New Film History: Sources, Methods, Approaches* (New York, 2007), pp. 55–68.
29. Peter Paterson, 'Sail of the century', *Daily Mail*, 21 July 2005, p. 59.

3

Television Costume Drama and the Eroticised, Regionalised Body: *Poldark* and *Outlander*

Gemma Goodman and Rachel Moseley

Introduction

Many shows in recent years, such as *Hinterland/Y Gwyll* (BBC, 2013–), *Shetland* (BBC, 2013–) and *Jamaica Inn* (BBC, 2014) have been set in the British Celtic peripheries, making use of locations at the geographical edges of Britain. *Outlander* (Starz, 2014–) and *Poldark* (BBC, 2015–), set in eighteenth-century Scotland and Cornwall respectively, have created the biggest buzz in the UK and America, with dedicated fan bases and media hype which increases with each series. Both are adapted from popular literary sagas: Diana Gabaldon is due to publish book nine of her *Outlander* novels in 2018 and Winston Graham wrote 12 *Poldark* novels. The programmes sit comfortably within the genre of 'heritage drama': stories set in the past and often adapted from literature. The genre has, conventionally, been seen as a conservative, nostalgic form in the 'quality' television tradition, in which the focus on visual splendour and historical detail can paper over the socio-political tensions present in the literary source texts.[1] At the same time, however, and especially in its cinematic incarnation, heritage drama has also been recognised as a space in which passion and desire can, in the best melodramatic tradition, be spoken in the mise-en-scène, for instance through costume.[2] More recently, dramas such as *Tipping the Velvet* (BBC, 2002), *Desperate Romantics* (BBC, 2009), *The Crimson Petal and the White* (BBC, 2011) and *Victoria* (ITV, 2016 –), have been much more direct in their representation of (particularly female) sexuality and desire. Both of the programmes explored here feature strong central female characters and handsome aristocratic leading men in their twenties – Jamie Fraser (Sam Heughan) in *Outlander* and the eponymous Ross Poldark (Aidan Turner) who are both constructed as objects of the female gaze.[3] While there are plenty of frock coats, frills and flowing locks, then, these shows are not so predictable, particularly in relation to masculinity, the male body and the female gaze.

Poldark was last adapted by the BBC in the mid-1970s, and returned in 2015, the year after Diana Gabaldon's novels were adapted for television. This was the year of the referendum on Scottish independence; the vote took place during the narrowcast of *Outlander* in the UK via Amazon video. The second series of both programmes appeared in 2016, the year in which the UK voted to leave the EU; there was further talk of Scotland's independence, and questions of territory, borders, power and devolution remain prominent socio-political issues on national and global scales. In such a context, the conjunction in these dramas of the display of both contested places and the male body suggests the on-going, if re-figured, significance of the relationship between body and landscape. In June 2015 we wrote a piece on *Outlander* and *Poldark* for *The Conversation* where we refocused discussion of the male body and desire onto questions of regionality and nationhood.[4] While typically the female body has been theorised in relation to nation and identity in both film and literary studies, we argued that 'atypically [...] it is the male bodies, and not the female, that bear the symbolic weight of representation in relation to landscape, region and nation' within these shows.[5] It is this premise that we wish to explore further here, in its complex relation to an active, desiring female gaze, more common in a 'post-feminist' moment, which the shows enable for their female characters and audience. Where *Poldark* presents a straightforward inscription of a desiring female gaze at the male body, the case of *Outlander* is far more complex. In what follows, we begin to develop a concept of the *regionalised* (male) body as a figure which embodies historical and contemporary tensions around power, identity and territory through an exploration of its articulation in costume drama of the Celtic peripheries.[6]

Masculinities and Male Bodies

As Helen Wheatley argues, 'the appearance and disappearance of erotic spectacle is fundamental to the structures of television narrative and television scheduling.'[7] While there has been much discussion of the female gaze within film studies, until very recently there has been little to no attention to the question of desire and looking in relation to television.[8] Hazel Collie's work has suggested that we consider the repetition and intimacy central to television's affect in thinking about the desiring and admiring relationships women build with their smaller-screen objects of desire. Such relationships, Collie argues, in their longevity and routine, are more akin to long-term relationships than the one-night stand of the starry passions inspired by film star crushes.[9]

In her recent exploration of the erotics of television, Wheatley highlights both *Poldark* and *Outlander* as significant in a moment where erotic spectacle on television has been addressed directly to an assumed female viewer, and explores what she calls the 'brazen', if often concealed, female gaze within and at them. Such dramas epitomise a recent shift away from female bodies as the primary site of erotic spectacle, displaying naked and semi-naked male bodies as much, if not more than, female bodies, thus challenging the assumption of a male gaze and providing a space for a desiring, female look.[10] Male television characters have been objects of desire before, as Collie's research demonstrates; indeed, Robin Ellis, as the 1970s television incarnation of Ross Poldark, also achieved sex symbol status. Critically, however, that sexiness was not predicated upon the display of his partially clothed body.[11] As Gill, Henwood and McLean point out, the male body is increasingly eroticised and on display to be looked at.[12]

Consequently, much of the hype surrounding these shows has focused on the physical attractiveness of the male leads. *Poldark* became best known for 'that scene' in Episode Three, in which the camera, positioned low in the grasses, allows the audience to peer at a bare-chested Ross wielding a scythe on his land. Offering front and back views of his torso, the scene moved into slow motion as the audience is positioned explicitly with Demelza, just as they are in the previous episode in which she watches, unseen in the grass, from afar, as he swims naked in tantalisingly clear water. The lusting for Ross, the language used to express that desire on, for example, social media, and the unashamed focus on and discussion of his body is indicative of the wider hype surrounding the show but also of a significant shift to a privileging of an openly desiring female gaze which the show enables through what now appears as a knowing display of the male body. This visuality is connected to the fact that both Jamie Fraser and Ross Poldark represent recognisably active, muscular masculinities. We see Ross working the land, within the mine, swimming in the sea and Jamie on his land at Lallybroch and with the horses at Castle Leoch. Both are largely constructed as conventional romantic heroes, within the programmes and in their paratexts; extremely good-looking, physically active and handsomely attired in eighteenth-century costume.

The appropriately romantic/heroic masculinity of both leads is accentuated through contrast with a foil who is not masculine enough. In *Outlander*, Claire's husband Frank is cerebral, far less muscular, and infertile. In *Poldark* Francis fails to measure up to his cousin Ross, lacking his physicality and activeness, which is most strikingly emphasised in an alternative scything scene. Ross's energetic scything and display of his tanned, toned and muscular body is contrasted with Francis, clothed, pale, complaining of blisters and looking as if the scythe is too heavy for him.

Ross and Jamie are the embodiment of what Amy Burns has described as the 'New Hero' of the post-feminist 'chick flick' which also foregrounds a female point of view, 'clearly there to be looked at by women, creating a notable representation of the female gaze in contemporary popular culture' which challenges the conventional positioning of male subject, female object of desire.[13] Our heroes conform to the ideal post-feminist New Hero outlined by Burns, but have, in addition, the 'Alpha' capacity for violence and brutality – also critical to the heroes of adult romantic fiction, who, in contemporary forms, are often Navy SEALs or members of Black Ops teams which require them to be tough and violent with just cause.[14] In addition, as Celtic heroes, their capacity for violence can be heightened by recourse to stereotypical notions of the Celt as savage. Ross Poldark and

Jamie Fraser represent the ultimate conjunction of nostalgic, contemporary romantic and 'Alpha' hero.

At the same time the vulnerability of the romantic, Alpha hero is continually registered in both shows, most often through injury to the body on display. Ross's facial scar is evident. Jamie's body is visible as sexual spectacle but simultaneously the same body carries grievous scars from flogging by Jack Randall and at the end of Series One, Episode 16, he is raped and branded by Randall. Many topless scenes display Jamie's body for the titillation of the audience at the same time as that body is being patched up by Claire – shoulder dislocation, cuts, broken fingers. Theorisation of the spectacularised male body has focused on the textual trouble that it causes, whether displayed in its perfection or its devastation. Presented as the aestheticised object of an admiring, desiring gaze, a potentially passive, 'feminised' position is frequently disavowed by the subject's refusal to return the gaze, by picturing the male body mid-powerful action, by accoutrements of traditionally active masculinity included in the composition.[15] Where the male body has been (often aesthetically) displayed in damaged, broken form, accounts have been built around a 'post-feminist' moment, in which masculinity has been perceived to be in crisis, pictured on display and in decay, as a cipher of crumbling patriarchal power.[16] In our unabashed, post-feminist 'man candy' moment of 2016, then, while Aidan Turner and Sam Heughan with their shirts off might simply be dismissed as just the other swing of the pendulum, we argue in what follows that there is much, much more at stake for the female gaze.

Regional Identity and the Body

The wider significances of masculinity in both programmes should, we argue, be understood in relation to the landscape and locales of the emplaced bodies of their heroes. Jamie's heroic masculinity also draws upon a particular version of Scottishness which inflects how we can view his 'manliness.' His masculinity is supercharged by its association with Scottishness and, specifically, the Highlands, stereotyped as a wild, uncultivated, primal place. Maureen M. Martin argues that 'Scotland was most often defined by its supposedly wild, hyper-masculine Highlands.'[17] Although she sees this construction of Scotland developing in the

Television Costume Drama

nineteenth century, *Outlander's* twenty-first-century representation of the eighteenth-century Highlander clearly draws on this by now-familiar trope. Jamie's identity as a Highlander is continually emphasised, verbally and through costume, and enables the sexualisation of Scottishness for the female gaze. In this respect the show reflects Gabaldon's books where Claire's desiring gaze at Jamie is founded upon his sexiness and masculinity but also his Scottishness, which are entwined and mutually augmented through association. She tells the reader that 'a tall, straight-bodied and by no means ill-favoured young Highlander at close range is breathtaking.' She describes Jamie as 'an enormous red barbarian' while watching him 'smoothing the crimson fabric of his kilt across his thigh.' She even dreams of 'kilted Highland men, and the sound of soft-spoken Scots.'[18] The television version manages to replicate this through rendering Claire's gaze through the camera lens and her thoughts through her voice-over narration.

Ross Poldark's close association with the romanticised Cornish landscape is also essential to his construction as Romantic hero. The identification of the male body with the landscape, both constructed as objects of desire, plays into the touristic, political and economic colonisation of Cornwall (and the Highlands) as romantic, Celtic peripheries, inside and outside the text, raising questions about the politics of the desiring look which go beyond the merely erotic.[19] Cornwall's and Scotland's geographical peripherality (from an English or London-centric perspective), their status as liminal Celtic territories of Britain, the specificity of Scotland and Cornwall in terms of the world created by the shows and their constructions of gender open up possibilities for dissent and critique. Their distance from seats of governance is significant and related to their stereotypical characterisation as wild, backwards, strange and magical.

In the opening scenes of 'Sassenach', *Outlander*'s inaugural episode, Claire Randall (Caitriona Balfe) and husband Frank (Tobias Menzies) arrive on holiday in Inverness in 1945 to find blood daubed above the doorways. Frank suspects a Pagan ritual, Claire suggests it is lamb's blood to protect against the spirit of death roaming the streets at night, joking that she 'had no idea that Inverness was such a hotbed of contemporary paganism.' Frank tells her 'there is no place on earth with more magic and superstition mixed into its daily life than the Scottish Highlands.'

When later in the same episode Claire time-travels back to 1743 by touching a stone at Craigh na Dun, Frank's assessment is confirmed – the Highlands are a space imbued with magical potential. The wildness of both the Scottish and Cornish landscape is visually highlighted in both series. The sea in Cornwall is, for example, unpredictable; often a brilliantly blue millpond, sometimes also taker of life and wrecker of ships. The Highlands are similarly wild, remote, and Celtic people concurrently constructed as wild, unpredictable. The Scottish were characterised as possessing a 'savage essence', eighteenth century Cornwall as 'West Barbary' with a reputation for violence, rioting and wrecking.[20] Such representational discrimination justified England's aggressive attempts to control the Celtic territories encircling it, and this England-Other dynamic is present in both shows as both dramatic fulcrum and to make a space for political critique.

In *Outlander*, English enforcement of the 1707 Act of Union and fear of Jacobite rebellion is the basis of the tension in Series One and the larger story arc culminating with the battle of Culloden in Series Two. In Episode Six, 'The Garrison Commander', Claire is taken by British soldiers to meet Brigadier General Lord Thomas (John Heffernan), concerned she has been kidnapped by clan MacKenzie. In exchanges with Dougal MacKenzie (Graham McTavish) the English attitude to all Scottish people is revealed. There is no respect for Dougal's position as War Chief to the Clan MacKenzie and brother to the Laird. The military audience, in his presence, mock his clothes and his speech, and refer to him as 'savage', a 'creature.' Savage is a recurring epithet for Dougal and the Scots more generally. Scotland is 'blasted turf.' The Brigadier General longs for England's 'more civilised environs', and could return 'if only you behaved like the loyal British subjects you're supposed to be', he scolds Dougal. Here, Scotland – and the Scots – are clearly constructed as colonial territory.

In *Poldark* there is a conflation of anti-Celticism and classism. Celticness and Cornishness are located in working-class characters and, conversely, upper-class characters are identifiably English through their denigration of the working classes for their class and their ethnicity, both of which raise similar fears of savagery and unruliness. Dr Choake warns Ross that 'no good will come of being sentimental about such folk. They're a different breed sir.' Ross, though, is ascribable as Cornish rather than English through his self-alignment with the working classes and through the construction of his own nature as stereotypically 'Celtic.' He 'embodies the tempestuous nature of Cornwall', claims Emma Marriott.[21] Other characters view him as unconventional and unpredictable but his actions are driven by the inequalities he witnesses which make him profess: 'they disgust me, my own class.' Viewers may have initially felt Cornwall sequestered from England, the tensions playing internally between classes, but eventually the redcoats arrive en masse to quash illegal smuggling. Their presence is English power exercised, reminiscent of their equivalents in Scotland and a reminder that, like Scotland, Cornwall is also a colonised territory.

The denotative and connotative connections between regional identity and the male body underpin our argument in this chapter. From early anthropological photography which directly connected the human body to place – typically a place which is in the process of being explored and/or colonised – to twentieth-century tourism advertising which used the gendered body as an indicator of regional specificity, the alignment of the human form, dressed and undressed, and *territory*, has been an important, if under-attended, way in which meaning about place has been constructed, circulated and cemented.[22] Connections between body and place are made, in the production of place-image, for the gaze of a beholder who is invited to assess, censure or admire a body which becomes regionalised in its juxtaposition with a specified landscape. The female gaze inscribed within both of these texts, then, is also a gaze at region.

Both *Poldark* and *Outlander* persistently mobilise the male body to speak regionality, in paratextual material such as promotional imagery, as well as in the textual detail of the programmes. Ross Poldark stands dominant in the foreground of a Cornish landscape in which body and regional space are visually connected, the image manipulated into painterliness, making his body one with land, sea, mine and the wind which whips his hair and clothes and through colour and texture. He is pictured immersed in the landscape, wet, blown, dirtied by the land: swimming naked in the sea, shirtless working beneath the land in the mine, scything in the fields. Such visual connections are reinforced by reference to mining being 'in the blood like a vein o' copper.'

The significance of Ross's connectedness to his regional territory is pointed up by the contrast drawn between him, and one of his foils, George Warleggan. Warleggan is consistently compared unfavourably to Ross

Conflicting Masculinities

Figure 3.1 Ross in harmony with the landscape in *Poldark*.

throughout *Poldark*, and this is done through reference to his masculinity, his class status and his (lack of) relationship to Cornwall as land. Where Ross is of long-standing landed gentry and is repeatedly pictured in close relationship to the landscape, Warleggan is of new money and is shown to be lacking any such intimacy with region. A good example is his decision in Series Two to close off the old footpaths across Trenwith land which leads, ultimately, to an angry mob threatening to set fire to his home who have to be turned away by Ross. George's lack of respect for and understanding of the relationship between the land and its people is shown to be both misguided and dangerous, in contrast to Ross, whose closeness to and feeling for both is emphasised throughout. In this way, it is made clear that it would be impossible for Warleggan to permanently depose Ross as either local leader or romantic hero, despite his attempts to do so, because he does not embody regional empathy either through labour or through inheritance. In aspiring to elevated social status, he is shown to be lacking in the essential connectedness to the regional landscape upon which such success must, in the terms of these period dramas of region, be based. The romantic hero must be either sympathetic gentry or noble peasant: Warleggan is neither.

The close connection between body and landscape is highlighted throughout *Outlander* by the consistent costuming of Jamie (and Claire) in colours and textures – heather shades, rusts, muted greens, not least the

Fraser tartan – which tie them closely to the landscape; even his hair is the colour of highland cattle. The 'Highlander' as Jamie is frequently called by Frank Randall and others, is shown to be absolutely at one with his region, visually as well as politically, and his body, too, is often shown dirtied, wetted, injured by and immersed in his surroundings.

The connection between body and land is continued throughout the series; Jamie says of his father's building of Lallybroch, 'his blood and sweat are in the stones, the land', the land in which he is also buried. When Claire and Jenny track Jamie through the Highlands following his capture, they are able to follow the deep marks made in the ground by a cart, heavy 'hopefully because there's a rather large red-headed Scot weighing it down', continuing the series' trope in which the marking of territories and bodies is connected.

The factor which makes the connectedness of body and regional place so significant in these dramas – more than simply a matter of visual cohesiveness – is the contested status of the territories in which they are set. Cornwall has always been and remains at the centre of debates about its status in relation to England and within the UK – as the only Celtic region of Britain without nation status, despite its own language, flag and historical claims to separation.[23] Cornwall's economic reliance on tourism (bolstered, ironically, by the use of the county as a setting for popular television drama),

Figure 3.2   Jamie and Claire in harmony with the landscape in *Outlander*.

following the decline of the mining industry has led to enormous levels of second-home ownership and the pricing of the Cornish out of the housing market, especially in coastal areas.[24] *Poldark* charts the decline of Cornwall's fiscal, industrial independence, and Ross's attempts to ensure the Cornish economy through mining draw attention to the question of Cornwall's economic independence. The political tensions between England and Scotland are also longstanding and ongoing. *Outlander* is set in the Highlands in the lead up to the Jacobite Rebellion and the battle of Culloden which would end in the destruction of Highland culture. The programme establishes and maintains the conflict between 'Redcoats' and Highlanders through the use of colour manipulation; the red of the English soldiers' uniforms remains saturated against the desaturated monochrome of Jamie and Jenny's memories of their atrocities towards them, as does the blood on Jack's hands after the flogging. The metonymic relationship between Fraser and British officer Jack Randall highlights the tension between the regional and the national as pivotal to the drama. *Outlander* and *Poldark* plot heterosexual romance against the backdrop of the contested space of internal colonies, bringing the desiring gaze and the regionalised body directly into complicated play with each other.[25]

Colonised Territory: Looking at the Naked Male Body

A desiring, straight, female gaze has been one of the modes of looking highlighted around both of these television costume dramas, in paratextual spaces such as magazines, gifs and memes, but also as clear textual inscriptions within the programmes. The display of, and desiring look at, the male body in *Poldark* and *Outlander*, however, is anything but simple; post-feminist costume drama in the age of devolution, independence, Brexit and territorial contention mobilises the male body as a form and a surface upon which the tensions around power, region and nation can be played out.

Philippa Levine's fascinating work on the naked body and the colonial imagination is helpful in thinking through the significance of the conjunction of body and place in these dramas. Levine draws on a long history of anthropology, exploration and colonial cultures which can be adapted to the particular situations of Britain's Celtic edges in the eighteenth century. It is illuminating to think about the positioning of the internal colonies of Cornwall and the Scottish Highlands in relation to her taxonomy; while both are Caucasian cultures, they are also constantly referred to as profoundly different, other, from England, from lowland Scotland, from the rest of Britain. As Levine notes, anthropometric photography was also used to differentiate between racial groups within the British Isles, and notably to determine the superiority of the Saxon over the Celt.[26]

The kilt as a signifier of regional identity speaks loudly in this respect – a seemingly 'feminised' item of dress, it leaves the man's legs partially exposed (and gives rise to jokes about what is worn beneath, again alluding to the possibility of male nakedness beneath it). While the exposure of male flesh by the kilts in *Outlander* has certainly been appropriated as the object of the straight female gaze, the difference and potential nakedness suggested by the wearing of the kilt is a key marker of the difference, the primitiveness, the savagery of the Highland clans in the eyes of the English redcoats and contributes to the programme's construction of the region as a colonised space whose potentially naked inhabitants represent dangerous difference to the English. The substantial use of male nudity in, especially, *Outlander*, bears further pressure in this respect; Jamie is never seen in a full-frontal naked shot, unlike his nemesis Jack Randall (Tobias Menzies) whose penis is clearly visible during his attempted rape of Jenny as well as when Jamie recalls his rape by Randall. According to the logic of Levine's 'colonial imagination', this costuming strategy reverses the power dynamic at play in the coloniser/colonised binary, positioning Randall as the uncivilised savage and Fraser as the tragic, beaten hero of classical antiquity. Richard Dyer notes that 'the adventure film in a colonial setting with a star possessed of a champion or built body' is one of very few spaces where the white man has been displayed partially clothed in popular fictions. He argues that the white man's (partial) nakedness has been problematic for representation, because of its vulnerability, lack of status and prestige: 'The built body in colonial adventures is a formula that speaks to the need for an affirmation of the white male body without the loss of legitimacy that is always risked by exposure.'[27] *Poldark* and *Outlander*, set in the internal colonies of Cornwall and Scotland, can certainly be understood within Dyer's formulation, but they invert the typical hero power relation in which 'the built body and the imperial enterprise are analogous' and by locating aesthetic and moral strength with the colonised body, the man close to and identified with nature, with regionalised place.[28] Citing Leon Hunt, Dyer points out that the crucifixion imagery of epic films, echoed in *Outlander*'s final episodes, combines 'passivity offset by control, humiliation offset by nobility of sacrifice, eroticism offset by religious connotations of transcendence', in order to establish the moral superiority of the built white man.[29] In contrast, for example, Jack Randall's body, and that of Francis Poldark, which, in Dyer's taxonomy should occupy the position of the powerful white colonial benefactor/aggressor, are repeatedly shown as unbuilt, with Frank's slight paunch and flaccidity compared to the Highlander, who reads as superior in terms of white masculinity through the built musculature, which, Dyer suggests, make reference to classical art.[30]

Outlander: Body as Contested Territory

The conjunction of the female gaze, the male body and the colonised land signals a potentially possessive, touristic gaze in *Poldark* through the association between romantic hero and landscape which can be read as political; in *Outlander* that conjunction is yet more complex, troubling and conflicted.[31] The female gaze at the powerful male body is often textually inscribed in the genres of romantic fiction and melodrama but is not exclusive; herein lies a source of the trouble with the regionalised male body in *Outlander*. In the tradition of Tartanry (the over-emphasis of romanticised notions and aesthetics of Scottishness), the Highlander, in the figure of the solid, chivalrous but virginal Jamie Fraser in his swishing plaid, brooch and broadsword, fur bed covers and roaring fires, is constructed throughout as a romantic figure.[32] In this construction, and through the active and desiring gaze of the main female character, as Wheatley has argued, the straight female viewer in particular is invited to gaze unashamedly at his (often partially naked) body.[33] Yet while a desiring gaze is invited and rewarded in *Outlander*, it is also complicated, even compromised, from the beginning, as the camera insistently seeks out and focuses on Jamie's back, horrifically scarred following repeated flogging by Jack Randall, and the act of looking at it is established as a significant trope across the series. When, soon after the arrival in the seventeenth century, Claire tends to Jamie's wounded body for the first time, the camera pans down his scarred back as it is revealed by the movement of Clare unwrapping his plaid. Our point of view is aligned psychically, if not precisely optically, with hers, as we are given a high-angle view down at his scars, but to the side, and in close-up, as if we stand with her but have a closer view, and we retain this privileged viewpoint as her hands drift across his skin while he explains their origin. From this early point, a complication of the female gaze so clearly inscribed in *Outlander* is established. The desiring, eroticising look at the Highlander's body will always already mean looking at and confronting his scars, his treatment at the hands of the redcoats, and all that this represents. By positioning the viewer with Claire as she caresses his back, and then with Randall as he destroys it, the female viewer is immediately at risk of complicity with the redcoat aggressor through the very act of looking.

This complication of the explicitly desiring gaze is reasserted on a number of occasions, including during the millstream scene when Jenny's amusement turns to horror as he turns his naked back to her. On Jamie and Claire's wedding night (Episode Seven), as she tells him 'Take off your shirt. I want to look at you', the camera stays on Claire as she watches him undress and while her eyes appraise his front, we gaze at his scarred back. She circles him and the camera follows her hand as it trails across his buttocks, below the scarring which is again dominant in the frame, as it is too when they have sex. Similarly, in Episode Nine, when Claire and Jamie resolve their argument and make love, Claire's face, our point of identification in the shot, is caught in pleasure and framed over Jamie's shoulder, but the majority of the frame is filled with a close-up of his scarred back. Her sexual pleasure, our enjoyment of their passionate relationship, and our intimacy with Claire's response to Jamie in this moment is inextricably bound up, on the level of the visual, with Jamie's treatment by the British.

As the narrative progresses, and we gain access in flashback to Jamie's flogging, we become aware that our desiring gaze is shared with 'Black' Jack Randall, whose sadistic, possessive look at Jamie is as much about power as sexual desire. He likens his marking of Jamie's back as a creation of an exquisite work of art on a blank canvas, something made to be looked upon, asking to see it on a number of occasions. The potential for complicity between Claire as the woman who looks with desire at Jamie

Conflicting Masculinities

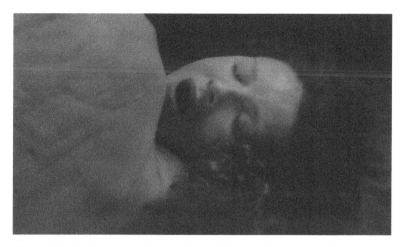

Figure 3.3 Jamie's scarred back as object of the female gaze in *Outlander*.

(and her counterpart, the viewer) and Randall, is made explicit in the final episodes of the first series, when it becomes apparent that Randall 'played' Claire to Jamie during his rape by letting down his long hair and trailing it across the Highlander's body, and Jamie, in his semi-conscious, traumatised state, repeatedly confuses Claire with Randall, aided by her disguise in breeches, a man's shirt and tied-back hair. As we see her face merge with Randall's through Jamie's eyes, the gazes of the desiring woman, the audience, and the sadistic representative of the English army, align.

In her discussion of England's colonisation of Scotland, Maureen Martin draws on Hechter's concept of 'internal colonialism' which 'in its evocation of an imperialist relationship, succinctly captures both England's economic, political, and cultural domination of the British Isles and its ability to incorporate Scotland into an enlarged sense of its own identity – an incorporation that [...] includes Scotland's supposed wealth of primal masculinity.'[34] Randall's rape of Jamie, as metonym for this colonial relationship, is, then, not only an attempt to destroy or suppress but is also a need to consume in order to possess Jamie's masculinity.[35]

Clearly, such discourses are at work in *Outlander*. In the context of the power play set up between Jamie and Randall, the connection between body and regional space, the highlighting of colonial discourse and the linking of the red uniforms with Highlanders' blood across the series' development, it is inevitable that the Highlander and the Officer will function metonymically. This makes available a reading which understands Jamie's scarred body and rape as symbolic of the destruction of Highland culture (and possibly also its touristic romanticisation and exploitation), a reading encouraged by the organisation of the text, regardless of the actual nuances of historical narrative. As Claire travels from Castle Leoch as healer with the Highlanders, the regional and political significance of Jamie's scars are made clear. Dougal, addressing a drinking crowd in untranslated Gaelic, rips off Jamie's shirt and exposes his scarred back soon after uttering the word Sassenach, using it as a spectacle of English cruelty towards the Scots to drum up support and finance for the Jacobite cause, to replace a Scottish King on the British throne and protect and maintain regional ways of life and land rights. As this spectacle is re-enacted, night after night, on their journey, eventually we simply hear the shirt rip, followed by a shot of Claire looking, and turning her gaze away and here, already, we have an intimation of the political shame associated with looking at his body. Jamie's scarred back is the ultimate expression of the colonised body, painfully and permanently marked by the aggressor and, later, to be branded with his seal. It resembles a relief map of a territory, with ridges, rivers and trails etched upon it. His body has literally become a landscape.

Conclusion

Poldark and *Outlander* are period dramas in which masculinity is articulated through the picturing of the relationship between male body and regional territory. While, conventionally, similar connections are articulated between female characters and landscape, we argue that in this socio-political, historical moment it is the male body, and definitions of heroism, which are at stake in these romances of region. While this is perhaps to be expected, in the wake of increased attention in both popular and academic discourse to questions of masculinity and visibility, the connection between the desirable body and landscape, we suggest, is best understood in relation to ongoing contestations around regional space. In *Poldark*, our erotic look at the romantic hero is also a touristic gaze which encapsulates the problematic romanticisation of a contested, de-industrialised territory still battling for recognition of its regional identity.

Viewed through the lens of regionalisation and in relation to the female gaze, these costume dramas demonstrate an increasing awareness of the politics of place, in the context of contemporary and ongoing re-organisations of territory. While *Poldark* makes visible critical questions around romanticisation and the tourist economy, the invitation to admire the regionalised male body in *Outlander* insists upon an acknowledgement of colonial brutality. In casting a desiring gaze, we are repeatedly reminded of the political significance of the erotic look at an/other.

Notes

1. Andrew Higson, 'Re-presenting the national past: nostalgia and pastiche in the heritage film', in L. Friedman (ed.), *Fires Were Started: British Cinema and Thatcherism* (London, 1993), pp. 109–29.
2. Stella Bruzzi, 'Tempestuous petticoats: costume and desire in The Piano', *Screen*, 16/3 (1995), pp. 257–66; Claire Monk, 'The British heritage-film debate revisited', in C. Monk and A. Sargeant (eds), *British Historical Cinema* (London, 2015), pp. 176–98; Helen Wheatley gives a succinct overview of the trends in scholarship in *Spectacular Television: Exploring Televisual Pleasure* (London, 2016), pp. 49–51.
3. Both leading men have experienced war, are wrongly accused of crimes, get caught up in duels and face the redcoats as antagonists. Although Ross himself is seen wearing the redcoat uniform when we first encounter him, his decision to join the army was to escape the law for various minor crimes. He divests himself of his uniform as soon as he returns to Cornwall and is henceforth an opponent of, rather than identified as, a redcoat.
4. Gemma Goodman and Rachel Moseley, 'Why academics are interested in the male body in *Poldark* and *Outlander*', *The Conversation*, 2 June 2015. Available at https://theconversation.com/why-academics-are-interested-in-the-male-body-in-poldark-and-outlander-42318 (accessed 18 September 2016).
5. Pam Cook, 'Masculinity in crisis? Tragedy and identification in *Raging Bull*', *Screen*, 13/3–4 (1982), pp. 39–46; Anne McClintock, *Imperial Leather: Race, Gender and Sexuality in the Colonial Contest* (London, 1995); Sue Harper, *Women in British Cinema: Mad, Bad and Dangerous to Know* (London, 2000); Ginette Vincendeau, *Stars and Stardom in French Cinema* (London, 2000); Goodman and Moseley, 'Why academics are interested in the male body in *Poldark* and *Outlander*', n.p.
6. We have primarily restricted our discussion here to the first series of *Poldark* and *Outlander*, as the later series of each show raise further complex issues around identity which we do not have scope to deal with here.
7. Wheatley, *Spectacular Television*, p. 191.

8. Laura Mulvey, 'Visual pleasure and narrative cinema', *Screen*, 16/3 (1975), pp. 6–18; Lorraine Gamman and Margaret Marshment, *The Female Gaze: Women as Viewers of Popular Culture* (London, 1989); Jackie Stacey *Star Gazing: Hollywood Cinema and Female Spectatorship* (London, 1994); Rachel Moseley, *Growing up with Audrey Hepburn: Text, Audience, Resonance* (Manchester, 2002).
9. Hazel Collie, '"I've been having fantasies about Regan and Carter three times a week": Television, women and desire', in R. Moseley, H. Wheatley and H. Wood (eds), *Television for Women: New Directions* (London, 2017), pp. 223–40.
10. Wheatley, *Spectacular Television*, pp. 213–18.
11. Rachel Moseley, '"It's a wild country. Wild ... passionate ... strange": *Poldark* and the place-image of Cornwall', *Visual Culture in Britain*, 14/2 (2013), pp. 218–37.
12. Rosalind Gill, Karen Henwood and Carl McLean, 'Body projects and the regulation of normative masculinity', *Body and Society*, 11/1 (2005), p. 37.
13. Amy Burns, 'The chick's "new hero": (Re)constructing masculinity in the postfeminist "chick flick"', in J. Gwynne and N. Muller (eds), *Postfeminism and Contemporary Hollywood Cinema* (Basingstoke, 2013), p. 132.
14. In a specifically post-feminist, post-9/11 context, the return of the Alpha male, Susan Faludi has suggested, has particular significance, in *The Terror Dream: What 9/11 Revealed about America* (London, 2007).
15. Richard Dyer, 'Don't look now: The instabilities of the male pin-up', *Screen*, 13/3–4 (1982), pp. 61–73; Steve Neale, 'Masculinity as spectacle', *Screen*, 24/6 (1983), pp. 2–17.
16. Cook, writing on *Raging Bull* (1980), reflected on the 'sadistic pleasure in the spectator's pitying look at Jake at the end of *Raging Bull*, partly explained by the space opened up for female desire when the powerful male is brought low' and while she complicates this position considerably in this piece, the construction of the damaged male body in relation to feminism remains important. Pam Cook, 'Masculinity in crisis', p. 46; Susan Faludi, *Stiffed: The Betrayal of the American Man* (London, 2000); Yvonne Tasker, *Spectacular Bodies: Gender, Genre and the Action Cinema* (London, 2012).
17. Maureen M. Martin, *The Mighty Scot: Nation, Gender, and the Nineteenth-Century Mystique of Scottish Masculinity* (Albany, NY, 2009), p. 2.
18. Diana Gabaldon, *Cross Stitch* (London, 1994), p. 271; *Dragonfly in Amber* (London, 1994), p. 240 and p. 50.
19. Rachel Moseley, '"It's a wild country"'; Ella Westland, 'The passionate periphery: Cornwall and Romantic fiction', in I. A. Bell (ed.), *Peripheral Visions: Images of Nationhood and Contemporary British Fiction* (Cardiff, 1995), pp. 153–72.
20. Bernard Deacon, '"The hollow jarring of the distance steam engines": images of Cornwall between west barbary and delectable duchy', in E. Westland (ed.), *Cornwall: A Cultural Construction of Place* (Penzance, 1997), pp. 7–24.

21. Emma Marriott, *The World of Poldark: The Official Companion to the BBC Television Series* (London, 2015), p. 30.
22. Philippa Levine, 'States of undress: Nakedness and the colonial imagination', *Victorian Studies*, 50/2 (2008), pp. 189–219.
23. At the moment of writing, an argument rages about the dissolution of the border between Devon and Cornwall in the creation of a 'Devonwall' Parliamentary constituency. For example, Richard Whitehouse, 'Devonwall would be "unlawful and a travesty", councillors say as plans are confirmed', *West Briton*, 13 September 2016. Available at http://www.westbriton.co.uk/unlawful-and-a-travesty-the-damning-verdict-of-plans-for-a-devonwall-mp/story-29710514-detail/story.html (accessed 20 September 2016).
24. Philip Payton, *Cornwall: A History* (Fowey: Cornwall Editions), p. 217.
25. Michael Hechter, *Internal colonialism: The Celtic fringe in British national development, 1536–1966* (Berkeley, California, 1977).
26. Levine, 'States of undress', pp. 189–90, pp. 204–5.
27. Richard Dyer, 'The white man's muscles', in R. Adams and D. Savran (eds), *The Masculinity Studies Reader* (London, 2002), p. 263.
28. Ibid., pp. 270–1.
29. Leon Hunt, '"What are big boys made of?": Spartacus, El Cid and the male epic', in P. Kirkham and J. Thumim (eds), *You Tarzan: Masculinity, Movies and Men* (London, 1993), p. 73.
30. Richard Dyer, 'The white man's muscles', p. 264.
31. John Urry and Jonas Larsen, *The Tourist Gaze 3.0* (London, 2011).
32. Colin McArthur, *Brigadoon, Braveheart and the Scots: Distortions of Scotland in Hollywood Cinema* (London, 2003).
33. Wheatley, *Spectacular Television*, p. 215.
34. Maureen M. Martin, *The Mighty Scot: Nation, Gender, and the Nineteenth-Century Mystique of Scottish Masculinity* (Albany, NY, 2009), p. 3.
35. Ibid., pp. 8–9.

4

Power and Passion: Seventeenth-Century Masculinities Dramatised on the BBC in the Twenty-First Century

Sarah Betts

'All hail Louis the Phwoarteenth' cried one reviewer of *Versailles* (Canal+, 2015–), 'it's not (quite) all about sex.'[1] Created by French Canal+, the series was written and performed in English by British writers and actors with an eye on international exportation, particularly the well-respected period drama platform of the BBC. The much-anticipated gratuitous sexual (and violent) content has been widely and disparagingly compared to *The Tudors* (Showtime, 2007–10) and HBO's *Game of Thrones* (2011–) – both notorious for similar content, but hugely successful internationally – sparking controversy in press and parliament over the drama's quality and suitability for screening on the publically funded channel.[2] In the past 20 years, the proliferation of commercial channels, the universality of digital television and the development of online viewing has loaded increasing pressure upon the five 'public service' channels in Britain. This has been particularly the case for the licence fee-funded BBC, expected to 'inform, educate and entertain', providing higher quality and culture without alienating (or being judged to be morally corrupting) their 'tax-payers'.[3]

The response to *Versailles* therefore needs to be viewed within the context of these existing anxieties about quality programming. Although sex and violence appear regularly in high-profile BBC shows like *Eastenders* (1985 –), Jerome de Groot's observations about 'historical drama' as a genre posit a useful explanation for the particular hysteria around such scenes in 'period' pieces. Long linked with 'heritage' adaptations of classic literature, such works, he writes, 'are generally associated with an educated, middle-class audience [… with a tendency …] towards cultural conservatism.'[4] In 'dumbing down', the BBC are perceived to be rejecting that core audience expecting an 'authentic' vision of the past that conforms to their own educated preconceptions (allowing them to spot inaccuracies and bemoan poor-quality programming that panders to viewers seduced by the superficialities of sex and violence). This guarding of an ideal about BBC costume drama has clearly been heightened in response to the notoriety of *The Tudors*, reaction to *Versailles* focusing far more upon 'pornographic' eclipse of informative or quality drama than did the mostly positive reception of the thematically similar *Charles II: The Power and the Passion* (BBC) back in 2003. Interestingly, although frequent, sex is by no means the only, or even the dominating, theme of *Versailles*, whilst it was a constant presence throughout *Charles II*, ranging from smouldering frisson to a scene involving fellatio performed upon a corpse, something surely more jarring to modern sensibilities than the homosexual activity of *Versailles*.

Charles II did face some criticism for historical inaccuracy, with key moments of the drama being ones of 'pure fiction.'[5] Although the writer and producer emphasised that their focus was on drama and a 'convincing' historical feel over 'accuracy', the BBC clearly took the educational opportunity of the show's run more seriously, producing two tie-in documentaries and publishing biographical briefings on key historical figures.[6] Likewise the corporation have screened several accompanying programmes on 'the real Versailles', and produced an extensive website delineating historical and fictional characters. Thus the BBC emphasise their educational credentials in showing these dramas, whilst also recognising that the period portrayed is less familiar to viewers than stories of Henry VIII, his family or even the Reformation. Both de Groot and Ronald Hutton have noted that, in spite of the period's dramatic tumult, the seventeenth century has been relatively neglected on screen.[7] Lacking the familiarity of the sixteenth century, the association with popular fantasy dramas of the medieval period, the great literary references of the nineteenth century or the empathy and nostalgia of the twentieth century, it has perhaps been judged less marketable as 'period' television. Adrian Hodges, writer of *Charles II*, disagrees, arguing that 'if you are looking in a historical subject for contemporary resonance, [...] certain aspects of the history of that period chime with our own to an extraordinary degree.'[8] This chapter explores the modern relevancy of theme and character on five rare occasions when the seventeenth century *has* been dramatised on the BBC. More specifically it examines some of the tropes of masculinity portrayed, using the five examples to highlight remarkable consistency of portrayal in spite of varying source material and intended audiences, and arguing that they demonstrate a juxtaposition of contemporary notions of manhood, sex and sexuality with perceptions of historical gendered conventions. Whilst de Groot is right in arguing that the BBC of the twenty-first century has increasingly 'courted controversy' to boost ratings, this chapter shows that the use of both sex and violence is not merely gratuitous, but an essential apparatus in both conveying and interpreting these powerful and passionate tropes of masculinity.[9]

Seventeenth-Century Drama on the BBC

The five dramas discussed here vary in terms of both source material and target audiences. Screened in six short instalments in the Sunday afternoon/early evening slot in November/December 1998, *Children of the New Forest* (BBC) was intended for a family audience and was adapted from Captain Frederick Marryat's 1847 novel. Although less prolific than in earlier generations, the tale of the four orphaned Beverley children who fell on the losing (royalist) side of the English Civil War and had to flee to the forest until restored to position and fortune at the Restoration is a well-known (and loved) Victorian classic, that would seem to be traditional fare for BBC 'highbrow' costume drama. Unlike traditional 'period' adaptations, however, the novel adapted is not contemporaneous with the times it portrays, so is essentially twice removed from historical 'authenticity'. The plot also deviates wildly from that of the original novel, although the essential themes remain. Two years later in 2000, another adaptation of a nineteenth-century novel, this time R. D. Blackmore's 1867 *Lorna Doone* (BBC), was more faithful. A feature-length drama, broadcast as a highlight of the BBC's Christmas schedule, the wild Exmoor setting, as well as the more 'rustic' time period, language and behaviour, added a sense of adventure to the well-loved formula of costumed, literary romance adaptation.

Charles II was not an adaptation but an original piece based upon the life of Charles Stuart (1630–85), son of the executed King Charles I (1600–49), restored to the throne after more than a decade in exile. The high-profile, four-part BBC One series followed Charles from the end of his exile to death. It would be another decade before BBC drama again turned to the seventeenth century, and this time, the action was set across the Channel. Turning once more to classic nineteenth-century literature, *The Musketeers* (BBC, 2014–16) was based upon Alexandre Dumas's *The Three Musketeers* (1844). Unlike earlier adaptations, however, *The Musketeers* was not a contained one-off series. Designed to replace long-running weekend primetime fantasy-adventure favourites *Robin Hood* (BBC, 2006–9) and *Merlin* (BBC, 2008–12), it was created with an eye on future annual series with storyline potential moving beyond the parameters of the original novel without the huge passage of time (and change of principal characters) that propelled Dumas's readers into the lesser-known sequel adventures. It was also what de Groot termed a 'semi-adaptation', taking the period and literary 'feel' of the setting, combined with an element of name-recognition/association, to stamp a sense of quality and authenticity onto original stories unconfined by the chronology or finality of the source book.[10] The open-ended multi-series has become the winning and now standard 'historical' drama format, in the wake of the success of *The Tudors*, *Game of Thrones* (HBO, 2011–), and especially ITV's *Downton Abbey* (2010–15), and is also the approach taken by the makers of *Versailles*, which ended its first run on a cliffhanger and was commissioned for a second series (broadcast in 2017). The only one of the five not directly a BBC production, and the only one not to air on BBC One, *Versailles* nonetheless provides rich comparison, not least because of the crossovers of theme and character. *Versailles* revolves around the character and reign of Charles II's first cousin and contemporary, Louis XIV of France (1638–1715), son of Louis XIII and Anne of Austria, both major characters in *The Musketeers*. In spite of reviews dismissing the flimsy superficiality of its context, plot and characters, the show actually presents far more varied and complex masculinities than simply a thoughtless voyeuristic and gratuitous display of the sexual mania of one man in period costume.

In spite of the varied sources, formats and intended audiences for these dramas, there are marked similarities in both the nature of the masculine powers and passions presented in each, and the dramatic devices used to evoke them. This is not coincidental. Three of them (*Lorna Doone, Charles II* and *The Musketeers*) were created by Adrian Hodges, and all five were created to appeal to BBC audiences. Partially, therefore, they reflect a received pronunciation of masculinity within the BBC's public and commercial tone. Inherent in this, in keeping with the Corporation's educational remit, is an acute awareness of historical setting, and whilst absolute historical accuracy is neither aspired to nor achieved, all incorporate elements of research into historical scholarship, so, consequently, models of masculinity portrayed do owe something to seventeenth-century sources. However, as touched on above, these dramas are also increasingly created as culturally taxable and commercial *products*, and so some of these tropes and dramatic devices recur because of their potential for ratings and sales. Despite criticism that recent historical dramas have become too 'soap opera', the resilience and mass-audience appeal of these programmes in the spiralling competition of post-millennium ratings means that the BBC and other channels have seen a commercial relevance in pursuing such 'soap' themes and formats in traditionally 'high-brow' historical dramas.

Coming of Age

All five dramas feature moments or storylines revolving around the 'growth' of a character from boyhood to manhood. This process invariably involves not only maturation but also masculinisation, each acknowledged as inherent within the other. Except legally, when inheritance was involved, seventeenth-century children were not generally culturally distinguished as masculine or feminine, but merely as infantile, lesser to, or less developed than, adult. Distinct moments and traditions, involving increased emphasis on masculine traits and ideals, marked passage from infant, to boy, to man. Examples included 'breeching' (literally a boy's first pair of trousers/'breeches' to distinguish him from the unisex gowns of infanthood), apprenticeship, establishment of an independent household and marriage.[11] Although twenty-first-century Britain has a distinctly (and commercially) gendered view of children, as well as a clearer sense of the legal and socio-cultural selfhood of children, contemporary drama still largely presents a neutrality towards child characters, often little more than accessories or appendages to the personalities and/or storylines of their parents. This is best observed in long-running dramas such as soap operas where a child character may exist for decades but whose personality and gender are essentially irrelevant until the onset of the character's first romantic and/or sexual experiences, when they will begin to display established tropes of masculinity and femininity. This is frequently underlined through recasting, replacing a child actor with an older, more physically developed artist (often older than the character portrayed) for the specific purpose of handling these more 'adult' or 'hard-hitting' storylines. None of the dramas discussed in this chapter have the longevity of soap operas and do not recast their leading characters, however, they do all demonstrate a comparatively gender-neutral attitude towards children, and all identify key experiences whereby their characters become 'men.'

Pitched towards a more juvenile audience, and revolving around eponymous child protagonists, *Children of the New Forest* might be expected to buck this trend. However, Marryat's novel is a classic coming of age tale, and the adaptation, in spite of drastic deviation from the novel, does maintain a definite sense of this, actually accentuated by its significantly condensed timeline, for the development of its hero Edward. It is not a tale of childhood, but of the progression of Edward's impending, advancing and finally accomplished manhood. This is signposted at the beginning when, to the consternation of his father, Colonel Beverley, a puerile Edward absconds from preparations for a royal visit and is found by the King poaching and 'dressed as a peasant' in the Forest. Embarrassment is compounded by the revelation that the King, as a favour to the Colonel, is to appoint Edward 'Keeper of the Forest' that very evening, an act intended to usher him into an adult position as head of the household when his father departs for war the next day. Edward's new status is emphasised by his redressing into the classic 'Van Dyck' ensemble of formal court dress with pointed lace collar and cuffs, mirroring that worn by the King, the Colonel and the other adult Cavaliers, by his presence at the King's feast (which his younger siblings watch from a balcony), and by an immediate upgrade of his sleeping quarters.

Power and Passion

In spite of these outward signs, Edward does not fully mature until the end of the series following a series of sobering experiences – the death of his father, the loss of his home, the hardships of self-sufficient forest life, knighting, defeat of nemesis, Abel Corbould – as well as the awakening of his sexuality through his rescuing of, and romance with, Patience Heatherstone. By contrast, Edward's brother Humphrey remains very much a child and at the end is allowed with his sisters to live quietly in the forest awaiting safer times, whilst Edward, now a wanted *man*, has outgrown this simple life in hiding and departs for a separate life in a (quasi) political limelight as *Sir* Edward Beverley and finally formally attired in full Cavalier court-dress. This echoes the more *longue durée* plot of the novel, in which Edward, having matured through bitter experience of a disastrous battle at Worcester under his own name is no longer able, *or suitable*, to return to the forest and goes to join the King in exile to become yet more manly through military experience before returning to finally reclaim his property and position, and marry Patience. Humphrey and his sisters, however, are safe to remain living quietly in England, protected by the innocence of their youth and consequent lack of politicised identity and significance.

Although played out over many more hours, across three series, *The Musketeers* in many ways acts as a coming of age story for the four principal characters, especially, and in keeping with the novel's ethos, that of D'Artagnan, whose initial motivations in the opening episode spring from witnessing the death of his father and becoming independent both in terms of owning property and of starting a new life of which he himself (and not his father) is master. The show tracks this early independence, his professional training, and his receiving a commission as a fully fledged 'King's Musketeer' (complete with the trademark badge). At the end of the second series he marries and establishes a new and more mature identity as husband and head of household, and in the final series, Athos watches on knowingly as D'Artagnan passes on his expertise to young cadets, echoing his own training back in Series One. As the three senior musketeers all graduate in their own way at the end of the series – Athos to fatherhood, Porthos to marriage and position as General of the Army, and Aramis to high governmental office – D'Artagnan is promoted to Captain, coming full-circle as he goes from homeless recruit, to head of the garrison both as a household and as a professional body.

Conflicting Masculinities

Father-son relationships are a recurring theme within this trope. As mentioned above, the deaths of their fathers act as traumatic severance of their childhoods for Edward Beverley and D'Artagnan. Likewise, *Lorna Doone*'s hero, John Ridd, abruptly becomes the head of his household following his father's murder at the Doones' hands. Central characters, Charles II and Louis XIV, are haunted by the untimely deaths of their fathers, as is Louis XIII in *The Musketeers*, and all three display anxieties about following paternal example. Fatherhood is also a formative experience. In the seventeenth century, siring children, particularly sons, was a public confirmation of maturity and securing of the patriarchal structures of legacy and inheritance associated with social status. It is still something which carries such connotations in twenty-first-century culture. Rebecca Feasey observes that male characters in popular television 'earn their reputations and derive their self-esteem' through fatherhood.[12] Charles II's masculinity remains unchallenged by his childless marriage because of the brood of acknowledged bastards he fathers. The opening episode of *Versailles* revolves around Louis's impending fatherhood (followed by the consequent shielding of his emasculating status as cuckold when a mixed-race baby is delivered), whilst Louis's younger brother, Philippe, feeling belittled and frustrated, expresses a desire to father his own son to reaffirm his position and identity. Although, even now, characters play towards a cultural assumption that having a son is particularly special for a man, in modern dramas, even those with an historical setting, fathering daughters is also portrayed as identity-affirming. As Feasey argues, popular television dramas are largely and increasingly preoccupied with 'issues of paternity.'[13] This is reflected in *Versailles*, where consternation and identity crises for all three occurs when Henriette, Philippe's wife and Louis's lover, falls pregnant, unable to determine which brother is the father. It is also played out as a major and recurring theme across all three series of *The Musketeers*, after a secret liaison with Aramis results in a much-longed-for royal pregnancy.

Both Aramis, who is increasingly frustrated by the impossibility of openly acknowledging his son, and Louis XIII, are transformed (masculinised and matured) by their feelings of love and responsibility towards the baby. When Louis realises the baby is Aramis's he regresses to petulant puerility, before, in the final series, mentally overcoming and accepting the issue of biological paternity to focus upon the dual goals of practical parenting, and maintenance of public acknowledgement of the prince as his son and heir. Aramis, meanwhile has to sacrifice his paternal rights whilst Louis lives to parent the boy, but, once Louis is dead does ultimately become first minister for the new king, assuming quasi-parental responsibility for his child even though their biological relationship cannot be openly acknowledged. The weaknesses of both characters, particularly callous selfishness in Louis, and sexual irresponsibility in Aramis, are mollified and even subsumed by their reactions to fatherhood. This clearly reflects what Feasey recognises in soap operas as an acknowledgement of the reconstructed nature of modern families; a theme reiterated when Porthos marries a young widow and wholeheartedly accepts her baby as his own, naming 'our daughter' himself to show that he accepts her as his own child.[14] It is practical and affectionate acts rather than biological conception within wedlock which formulate true character-forming and masculinising fatherhood.

Reaching maturity, the transition from the anonymity and powerlessness of youth to the responsibilities and autonomy of manhood is of course most clearly defined in the characters of Charles in *Charles II* and Louis in *Versailles*, magnified on the much wider stage of Kingships and Kingdoms. *Versailles* explores the new freedoms (and dangers) which Louis faces now that he is independent of his childhood regency as a result of both obtaining his majority and the death of his mother. He builds his palace to symbolically and physically contain his governing nobles within a household of which he is now head. *Charles II* also demonstrates the interrelationship of manhood and power, with Charles humiliated in early scenes by his poverty and dispossession, frittering his life away on other's generosity, unable to support or control his subjects or friends, and unable to bed the woman of his choice, Barbara Villiers/Palmer, who openly taunts him that she finds the notion of a man and especially a king without power, 'pathetic.' Restoration matures and hardens Charles as a character reversing these positions, now master of his own destiny, and the series director, Joe Wright, envisaged it as 'the story of a man, becoming a man, learning how to be a man.'[15]

Passion

Correct domestic hierarchy was essential to a seventeenth-century man's reputation, whilst challenging these 'sexist' conventions and double standards of the past, and embracing the dramatic opportunities they pose, has appeal to present-day writers. Louis XIV's outrage at his wife's adultery in *Versailles* contrasts with his own open extra-marital affairs, but he is challenged into proving himself the modern man by sparing and providing for the Queen's bastard child. In *The Musketeers*, Louis XIII's neglect of his wife and open affair with Milady de Winter renders Anne and Aramis's affair more wholesome, with Aramis cherishing and respecting her rather than simply betraying duty and faith by seducing another man's wife. Seventeenth-century male reputations were also dependent on parental authority, especially for daughters who were expected to be subservient to their father's will and advantage. Whilst parental authority is still expected in modern society, the terms in which it is exercised have changed. Patience Heatherstone verbally challenges her father, in stark contrast to her demure behaviour in the nineteenth-century novel, and he, though emphasising his authority, does not physically enforce this and in fact amends his own attitude in line with her opinions. In *Versailles*, Dr Masson becomes cumulatively frustrated with his daughter, Claudine, frequently questioning and outshining his medical knowledge. Emasculated as a father, man and professional by his daughter's superior skill and higher royal favour, he is rendered increasingly ridiculous, blustering and even physically attacking her before finally being gruesomely murdered and ultimately replaced by her as court physician. In contrast, Louis's character is enhanced by his rational recognition of Claudine's skill.

High estimation of a woman's talents is clearly prized in male characters. As with Ararmis and Anne, D'Artagnan's initial adultery with Constance is semi-justified by his egalitarian treatment of her in comparison with her husband. In *Versailles*, Louis trusts the negotiating skills of three of his lovers and each time is rewarded with his desired outcome. Whilst this correct sort of passion for a woman glorifies and enhances the character of the male lover, sexual and emotional passions can also emasculate, power transferring to the woman and male judgement becoming impaired and manipulable. Louis's negotiating women succeed in manipulating the passions of their targets towards them, and, in turn, Louis's security is threatened when his protector Marchal is blinded by passion for conspirator, Mme. De Clermont. In *Charles II*, the royal mistresses, particularly Barbara Villiers, take advantage of what starring actor Rufus Sewell describes as a gullible 'blindspot' for people who 'happened to have breasts.'[16] John Ridd responds erratically and petulantly when he believes that Lorna has moved on, whilst Humphrey Beverley teases Edward for being distracted by thoughts of Patience. This theme is especially strong in *The Musketeers*, with Milady seducing and manipulating Athos, D'Artagnan, Louis and Richelieu. Aramis's judgement is impaired by his infatuation with the Queen, and D'Artagnan's feelings for Constance, and Athos's for Sylvie both distract them and are easily harnessed against them by various villains they encounter. Meanwhile throughout the series, *Musketeers* Captain Treville's strength and purpose remains impenetrable to feminine wiles.

Lack of restraint and respect and attempts to disempower women also have an impact on masculinity, transforming the sexually impassioned male character from sexy hero to pathetic creep and/or violent criminal. Rochefort in *The Musketeers*, Abel Corbould and Carver Doone all attempt to force unwanted sexual attention upon Queen Anne, Patience and Lorna respectively, and in all three cases knowledge that the object of their desire has a romantic relationship with another man pushes them into some level of sexual assault. This contrasts with the heroic leads who may lust after an unattainable woman but would never forego consent to make advances. Passing rapine characters are also sometimes portrayed as sexually violent in order to highlight the contrasting attitudes of the heroes. When both Alice Beverley and Constance are attacked, the response of their male rescuers underlines how such behaviour towards women is unacceptable. The performance of all of these near-rape storylines slot into binary narratives well established within contemporary drama, firstly that sexual violence against women was an everyday threat to women in history, and secondly that the issue of consent is an active, *and pro-active*, one in twenty-first-century programming. The emphasis of the dramatisations in each case is to vilify the perpetrators rather than to create victims out of the women. That the dramas' male protagonists not only rescue the women, but also help them find the strength and skill to independently defend themselves from future attack, reaffirms the rightfully empowered position of modern women, and simultaneously celebrates the anti-chauvinistic contemporary appeal of the heroes, secure in their own masculine identities that fit neatly with the types of behaviour expected of the modern man.

The passions of *Versailles*'s Philippe are more complex. Across all of the dramatisations, Philippe is the only character to actually commit full rape on screen. He is also the only regular 'hero' to do so. Such is the contradiction in this for modern sensibilities concerning rape that the actor (Alexander Vlahos) felt the need to address it, explaining that: 'At that time, women had to have sex with their partners as a duty. Obviously that scene treads a very fine line [...] one of the most difficult and most challenging scenes I ever had to do as an actor.'[17] Here the 'period' setting is used to alleviate uncomfortable moral ambiguity, and the scene is converted from straightforwardly repulsive violence to thoughtful exploration of authentic historical notions of gender relations, whilst the actor emphasised 'want[ing] to do justice' to the deeply conflicted personality and position of the genuine historical figure.[18] The royal brothers are entwined by loyalty and affection but also constant competition. Philippe, who as a child was dressed as a girl and humiliated to bolster Louis's masculinity by comparison, is frustrated by his brother's failure to entrust him with power. He vacillates between a desire to serve and outright resentment, embodying many conflicting and contrasting masculinities from physical and moral dominance to subservience according to mood and fortune. Trapped at court with little independent power or identity, and knowingly cuckolded by his brother, he is silenced by Louis in council and submissive to his male lover, Chevalier, in the bedroom. Embarrassing Louis by parading in female dress, he brutally assaults a mocking courtier before Chevalier calls him off. He is mentally, verbally and physically hostile and even abusive towards his wife. Following his longed-for battlefield experience, he lauds his newfound military virility, is more openly defiant of his brother, but is not actively disloyal and not above begging for mercy for Chevalier. His intimate relationships also change. Philippe becomes less submissive to Chevalier, returning from war to initiate an aggressive and domineering sexual encounter from which Chevalier initially recoils in shock and fear. With Henriette he reaches a sense of almost camaraderie at their shared mistreatment by Louis, and is genuinely distressed when she dies, finally determining to leave Louis and Versailles with Chevalier.

Interior and Exterior Masculinities

Articulating masculinity through dress and/or environmental setting in these series highlights common themes of interior and exterior modes of manliness. Edward Beverley's switching between Court and 'peasant' dress denotes his maturation from boy to man, in conjunction with the

Power and Passion

Figure 4.1 Following the death of his wife, Philippe storms out of his brother's court in the company of his lover in *Versailles*.

character-forming experience of forest life in sharp contrast to his cossetted previous existence. The central characters of both *Charles II* and *Versailles* have been compared to the 'glamour' of rock stars, and the 'amazing hair' of *Versailles*'s men repeatedly features in reviews.[19] *Versailles*'s Cassel and Montcourt are identified and belittled as villains through plot, dialogue and visually through their 'greasy' and less well-maintained hair in comparison especially with the royal brothers. Historically both courts were renowned for fashionable conspicuous consumption, something clearly reflected in the dramas, particularly *Versailles*, where Louis and Philippe deploy seemingly menial and emasculating attention to fashion, ballet and etiquette in order to control the nobility and redefine them within their own shadow. Both shows visually contrast the exuberant lifestyle at court with the harsh realities outside it. Charles's costume and surroundings in impoverished exile are very different to his fabulous court dress, and the piece repeatedly reminds us of his less formal, stuffy and glamorous 'real-world' experience by featuring him in an earthier, wigless and 'undressed' style for many more intimate scenes, revealing the real man beneath the kingly façade. In *Versailles*, the Philippe of the battlefield is very different; there is not a hint of femininity to him, he is dirty, strong and gritty, and is seen confidently urinating outside as he surveys the battlefield, a world away from the palace's rigorous formality and refinement. The experience gives him a new self-confidence, but also fosters a natural affinity with the veteran soldiers building Versailles. When Louis later tries to capitalise on this with an award ceremony, Philippe is unable to stomach the superficiality of the King's connection with his people in comparison to his own brotherhood in arms.

The Musketeers also contrasts Court and battlefield, with Louis the only male character consistently portrayed in flamboyant court dress. Leather is used extensively to define masculinities in other characters. Each Musketeer has their own distinct style with the exclusive use of leather and regiment badge being the unifying factors. Their garments are both glamorously attractive and practical for the many action scenes, for which the four lead actors received extensive training in riding, weapon-handling and fight choreography to look more natural in the parts. The satisfying eroticism of the sound of caressing or removing leather, and the defensive armour-like look and sound of their costumes in action increase the sex-appeal and 'real' outdoor credibility of the characters in contrast to Louis.[20] They are men of action who ride forth rather than skulking in offices and palaces like kings and cardinals, insulated from everyday tribulations. When Louis does venture out of the palace, once in 'peasant dress' and once defending himself with a musket in an ambush, he is out of his depth in roles the musketeers perform daily, terrified, lazy and cowardly in the first instance and boyishly over-excited by the thrill of the second.

Lorna Doone also uses leather and interior/exterior styles of costume to demarcate masculine 'types'. The novel's John Ridd is an archetype of Victorian muscular Christianity. The casting of Richard Coyle, some felt, lacked the 'physical presence' required.[21] However, the contemporaneous familiarity of Coyle to BBC audiences from the hit sitcom *Coupling* (2000–4) in fact aids the perception of Ridd as an approachable and fairly 'ordinary guy' hero, adding to the rustic simplicity of his informal attire and pastoral life. This contrasts with depictions of court and society life far away in London's corridors of power, and also with the appearance of the Doones who, with long hair, plaits and pony tails, and leather jackets, are essentially reminiscent of a 1990s 'biker gang'. Their flouting of social and legal codes confirmed contemporary cultural expectations of violent gangs. Local Justice Baron de Whichehasle's failure to stand up to, and cowardly collaboration with, the Doones, is highlighted by his impractical, fashionable, court-style clothing and re-emphasised by his effeminate son Marwood. Portrayed by Jesse Spencer, familiar to UK audiences as

Neighbours (Seven/Network Ten/Eleven, 1985–) teen-heartthrob Billy Kennedy, Marwood's amusing accent, long wig and prominent beauty spot combine with his father's appearance to reveal both as hopelessly out of their depths with both the leather-clad outlawed Doones and the honest farming community of the Ridds.

Conclusion

This chapter has highlighted some of the many and inter-related images of seventeenth-century masculinity that have been dramatised on the BBC in the last 20 years. It has demonstrated that there are many similarities in terms of both tropes of masculinity, and of perceptions of seventeenth-century society across this period. However, differences in the delivery of these themes can be discerned both in line with variation of target audiences, and with broader trends in the production and marketing of television drama. Obviously the 'adult' content is toned down in those productions aimed at a family audience. Likewise, there are inherent differences between those adaptations based on novels and the two biopic-style original dramas focusing on the two Kings, Charles II and Louis XIV. Although *The Musketeers* is not a one-off adaptation, and although both it and *Children of the New Forest* digress significantly from the source novel in comparison to *Lorna Doone*, all three series do maintain the feel of an adventure romp, and the genuine historical figures portrayed are essentially slotted into roles which highlight the natures of the central fictional characters. Violence in these cases is sanitised, not just by time-slot regulations, but by the clearer delineation of 'good' and 'bad' inherent in the fantasised historical setting. In contrast, the central characters of *Charles II* and *Versailles* are more problematic and the tones of both dramas somewhat darker by virtue of their serious non-fictional setting. There is also a noticeable evolution in dramatic style across the 20-year period. The open-ended, longer-term formats of *The Musketeers* and *Versailles*, progress the overall story-arcs much slower than the earlier dramas, and make greater use of wider ensemble casts and subplots, as has become standard in popular television. The serial nature of *The Musketeers*, in particular, has lent itself to relatively self-contained, issue-led episodes familiar to viewers from other, well-established serialised dramas, buying into the proven popular dramatic appeal of such storylines

Conflicting Masculinities

whilst at the same time fulfilling the BBC's necessary 'public service' character by reflecting and debating contemporary social concerns. The historical setting seemingly negates the need for many of the content warnings and helpline numbers advertised around traumatic or emotive issue stories in the BBC channels' regular flagship dramas, but at the same time adds an educational tone by highlighting the juxtaposition of present-day and historical values. In all five shows this marrying of modernity and history has been central to the drama, and increasingly so. Although the most notable previous dramatisation of the seventeenth century on the BBC, *By the Sword Divided* (1983–5), definitely drew upon contemporary issues and television formats, most notably the increasing vogue for social and class history and the popularity of writer/producer John Hawkesworth's previous hit, *Upstairs, Downstairs* (BBC, 1971–5), the style and presentation of history within the series was more formal than any of the new-millennial dramas. The language was more archaic, and some of the dialogue was lifted directly out of seventeenth-century documents and testimonies central to traditional historiography. The five shows discussed here have a universal, and increasingly, contemporary feel. Language and costumes have been modernised and action has become more fast-paced.

Significantly for this current study, social issues have been progressively and consciously tackled with reference to modern attitudes. This is exemplified in the portrayals of masculinities discussed in this chapter, where depictions of interpersonal relationships drive an understanding, acceptance and/or rejection of male characters, and consequent engagement with the dramas, through reflection of modern sensibilities concerning family, authority, gender, sexuality and violence, in line with contemporary television, and in spite of, or even accentuated by, historical setting. The accessibility of these themes is increased through the use of familiar devices such as plot, set and costume which confirm and consolidate the audiences' recognition and interpretation of them. On the BBC, this feeling of familiarity is particularly strong, and feeds an impression of the maintenance of production quality by the use of popular and established figures from across their programming, on both sides of the camera. Writers, producers and directors build reputations across decades of work in different mediums, often exclusively for the BBC, and even attempts to 'beef up' the educational and home-grown credentials of *Versailles*, through the accompanying documentaries, relied upon the presenting weight of historians and regular

Power and Passion

BBC pundits Lucy Worsley and Kate Williams, and popular *Horrible Histories* (BBC, 2009 –) expert Greg Jenner. Cast are able to import a preknown sense of character, whether from different drama genres like Richard Coyle or Jesse Spencer, from similar works, such as Santiago Cabrera (who went from *Merlin*'s Sir Lancelot to Musketeer Aramis), or from previous and prestigious period pieces, such as Rufus Sewell. Although not a BBC original production, *Versailles* also participates in this culture; head writer Simon Mirren has written for hit BBC shows (as well as for the US market), thus volumising the export potential of the show, whilst in Britain it did not go unnoticed that Philippe actor Alexander Vlahos would be known to BBC viewers as troubled anti-hero Mordred from *Merlin*.[22] The response to *Versailles* also highlights this exportability of period character, with George Blagden's suitability for the regal charisma of seventeenth-century kingship likened to a 'young Rufus Sewell.'[23] Over the 20 years spanned by these five dramas the preconceived masculine personas and sex appeal of the lead actors has become increasingly more important for engaging viewers with the characters and themes of period drama. These powers and passions are not merely superficial publicity hooks, but essential devices in conveying and interpreting the complex blend of historical and contemporary masculinities in BBC period drama.

Notes

1. Sam Wollaston, 'Versailles review – all hail Louis the Phwoarteenth', *Guardian*, 24 July 2016. Available at www.theguardian.com/tv-and-radio/tvandradioblog/2016/jun/02/versailles-review-louis-the-phwoarteenth-is-a-lot-of-fun (accessed 24 July 2016).
2. Unity Blott et al., 'Sex scenes are a turn off for prudish Brits as Versailles' viewers switch channel during the raciest moments of the BBC drama', *Daily Mail*, 3 June 2016. Available at http://www.dailymail.co.uk/femail/article-3623370/Viewers-switch-sauciest-scenes-Versailles-drama.html (accessed 11 July 2016); Jack Shepherd, 'Versailles: Conservative MP outraged by BBC drama with "most graphic sex scenes in British TV history"', *Independent*, 13 March 2016. Available at http://www.independent.co.uk/arts-entertainment/tv/news/versailles-conservative-mp-outraged-by-bbc-drama-with-most-graphic-sex-scenes-in-british-tv-history-a6928651.html (accessed 9 July 2016).
3. Phil Redmond, 'Public service content: the conditions for creativity', in D. Tambini and J. Cowling (eds), *From Public Broadcasting to Public Service Communications* (London, 2004), pp. 74 – 7.

4. Jerome de Groot, *Consuming History: Historians and Heritage in Contemporary Popular Culture* (London, 2016), p. 223.
5. Ian Burrell, 'BBC defends taking liberties with the life of Charles II death', *Independent*, 12 November 2003. Available at www.independent.co.uk/news/media/bbc-defends-taking-liberties-with-the-life-of-charles-ii-death-77957.html (accessed 12 July 2016).
6. *Charles II: The Power and the Passion* DVD material, 'The Making of Charles II'.
7. Ronald Hutton, 'Why Don't the Stuarts Get Filmed?', in S. Doran and T. S. Freeman (eds), *Tudors and Stuarts on Film: Historical Perspectives* (London: 2009), pp. 246–58. Jerome de Groot, '"Welcome to Babylon": Performing and Screening the English Revolution', in M. T. Burnett and A. Streete (eds), *Filming and Performing Renaissance History* (London, 2011), pp. 70–1.
8. *Charles II: The Power and the Passion* DVD material, 'The Making of Charles II'.
9. de Groot, *Consuming History*, p. 231.
10. Ibid., p. 235.
11. Elizabeth Foyster, *Manhood in Early Modern England: Honour, Sex, and Marriage* (London, 2014), pp. 39–40.
12. Rebecca Feasey, *Masculinity and Popular Television* (Edinburgh, 2008), p. 17.
13. Ibid., pp. 16–17.
14. Ibid., p. 17.
15. *Charles II: The Power and the Passion* DVD material, 'The Making of Charles II'.
16. Ibid.
17. Jessica Earnshaw, '"It treads a very fine line": Versailles' Alexander Vlahos on THAT Henriette rape scene', *Daily Express*, 10 August 2016. Available at http://www.express.co.uk/showbiz/tv-radio/698718/Versailles-final-Alexander-Vlahos-rape-scene-Henriette (accessed 5 June 2017).
18. Ibid.
19. *Charles II: The Power and the Passion* DVD material, 'The Making of Charles II'; Jasper Rees, 'Versailles: sex, intrigue, and great hair – review', *Telegraph*, 2 June 2016. Available at http://www.telegraph.co.uk/tv/2016/06/01/versailles-sex-intrigue-and-great-hair-review/ (accessed 4 June 2016).
20. *The Musketeers* (Series One) DVD material, 'Extras'.
21. *Lorna Doone* Reviews and Ratings, Internet Movie Database. Available at http://www.imdb.com/title/tt0259786/reviews?ref_=tt_urv (accessed 17 June 2016).
22. Vanessa Thorpe, 'Raunchy French TV epic Versailles enlists British Actors to usurp Wolf Hall's Crown', *Guardian*, 30 April 2016. Available at https://www.theguardian.com/tv-and-radio/2016/may/01/french-tv-versailles-enlists-british-stars-bbc2 (accessed 27 July 2016).
23. Ryan Gilbey, 'George Blagden on dressing up for Versailles', *Guardian*, 30 May 2016. Available at https://www.theguardian.com/tv-and-radio/2016/may/30/versailles-george-blagden-playing-louis-xiv-bbc2-interview (accessed 27 July 2016).

PART II

Visions of the Nineteenth Century

5

A Post-Feminist Hero: Sandy Welch's *North and South*

Sarah E. Fanning

'It's hard [...] to imagine a world of "romantic fiction" without *Pride and Prejudice*',[1] answered Sandy Welch when asked to what degree the legacy of Andrew Davies's *Pride and Prejudice* (BBC, 1995) influenced her scripting of *North and South* (BBC, 2004). Critics and scholars have widely acknowledged that Davies's six-part mini-series was a game-changer for the classic novel serial. It gave us 'Darcymania', and prompted a factory-speed succession of film and television adaptations of Jane Austen's novels in the 1990s, memorably known as 'Austenmania'. Beyond the craze for the dark-haired brooding hero in a cravat, however, Davies's *Pride and Prejudice* demonstrated that the power of bringing British classics successfully to small screens for a new generation of viewers in a new age of television rested largely with the hero. While Davies has often been hailed for being 'the man who put sex into the Victorian novel'[2] and 'the man who made Colin Firth a sex god',[3] he deserves far more credit for bringing into focus the complexity of the nineteenth-century hero. The new practice that Davies perhaps unwittingly developed through *Pride and Prejudice* would become a model for subsequent adaptors such as Sandy Welch, whose characterisation of Elizabeth Gaskell's hero, John Thornton, in her widely acclaimed adaptation *North and South* forms the subject of this chapter. While it is difficult, as Welch says, 'to imagine a world of "romantic fiction" without *Pride and Prejudice*', it is impossible to examine classic novel heroes in twenty-first century television without first identifying the degree of influence Davies's mini-series had in shaping new adaptation practices at the turn of the century.

'The Darcy Model': Andrew Davies's *Pride and Prejudice*

The classic novel serial in the twenty-first century owes much to the BBC's 1995 landmark adaptation of Austen's classic novel *Pride and Prejudice* (1813). As I have suggested, part of what made the serial different from what had come before was Davies's characterisation of Darcy (Colin Firth). 'I wanted to make the adaptation very pro-Darcy', he asserts, 'so I thought, "Let's start with him and Bingley galloping along on their horses – nobody has ever done that before."'[4] This seemingly small decision to foreground the male characters, particularly Darcy, not only inverted the male gaze of classical Hollywood cinema into the female gaze of classic/period television,[5] but it also marked an important transition in the way the classic novel hero was presented on the small screen and how we would come to engage with men in period television more broadly.

Part of the success of *Pride and Prejudice* and the revival of the classics overall has much to do with the shifting landscape of television itself: advancements in technology, including the use of film instead of videotape, location filming, heritage film aesthetics, National Trust buildings and mobile cameras, as well as changing styles of performance. Together, these variations helped audiences better engage with the televised classic novel at the end of the twentieth century. Most importantly, it was Davies's script and, of course, Firth's portrayal of Darcy that brought new visibility to a figure who had been habitually depicted as stuffy and stifled, and whose purpose often amounted to little more than serving the romance plot. Firth's Darcy was tantalisingly good-looking, but in addition to this his laconic arrogance, psychological depth and unwavering love for the heroine, Elizabeth Bennet (Jennifer Ehle), would later generate what Davies calls 'the Darcy model'.[6] Although Davies maintains that he 'never intended to spark Darcymania'[7] with the now-famous pond scene, there was something about the depiction of Darcy's 'humanness' that enthralled audiences.

Beyond the sexual ingredient, however, Davies also seems to have registered an awareness of the cultural anxieties that were reshaping concepts of masculinity and redefining ideals of heterosexual romance at the close of the twentieth century. Firth's Darcy encompassed a level of humanness that had not been seen to the same extent in prior classic serials. Darcy's predicaments, namely his excruciating attraction to Elizabeth, his troubled past and his personal and social plights, centralised the male experience in ways that were unprecedented in classic novel serials. Thus, the adaptation not only contributed a fresh alternative to the conservative literariness that had come to characterise many British literary serials,[8] but it also brought a new afterlife for televised classic men by showing them to be at once vulnerable, conflicted and 'unbuttoned' (quite literally in the case of Darcy). By both eroticising the nineteenth-century male body and developing the figure through a focus on his human complexities, Davies's *Pride and Prejudice* proved that men in the classic serials had the raw power to reinvigorate the classic serial for a new generation of consumers.

The Evolution of Post-Feminist Masculinities in the Televised Classic Novel

Since *Pride and Prejudice* was first broadcast, depictions of nineteenth-century masculinities have evolved largely in response to Firth's Darcy, a figure who is, arguably, based in part on a cultural response to shifting concepts of gender in the final decades of the twentieth century. Notably, Firth's portrayal of Mark Darcy in the *Bridget Jones* trilogy (2001; 2004; 2016) is not simply an updated version of Mr Darcy; it is a cultural reference to the nineteenth-century hero made famous by his performance. By the 1990s, systems of patriarchy, as well as traits that were traditionally purported to embody dominant norms of masculinity, such as stoicism, virility and machismo, were being outmoded and vilified by the reverberative achievements of second-wave feminism. While positive in effecting a new culturescape of empowered femininity at the close of the twentieth century, this cultural shift also compelled new prescriptions of masculinity. The cultural changes necessitated by the late twentieth-century women's movement helped to create what is now commonly referred to as the post-feminist man of the twenty-first century. This figure, argues Stephanie Genz and Benjamin A. Brabon, emerges from the 1990s' 'crisis of masculinity', a period that witnessed 'a process of seepage between the categories or types of men' as many men were trying to 'come to terms with the shifting social and economic environment and grapple with conflicting varieties of masculinity.'[9] The post-feminist man is, they explain, best conceptualised in terms of 'a melting pot of masculinities, blending a variety of contested subject positions, as well as a chameleon figure still negotiating the ongoing impact of feminism on his identity.'[10] This fusing of different strands of masculinity has effectively obfuscated the tradition of a collective male identity whereby popular images of manhood have essentially become amalgams of different, and often conflicting, characteristics.

In response to these evolving shifts, a large majority of male protagonists in today's popular British and American television drama series have become so hybridised that they are now expected, as Lauren Thompson contends, to 'remain "masculine" while also acquiring the emergent traits of being caring, soft, aestheticised and domesticated.'[11] In 2014, *Salon* magazine noted a new trend in American and British popular television, observing that men can no longer be easily identified as heroes, anti-heroes or villains; they must be something indeterminate, figures who can straddle both camps of good and evil (think *The Blacklist* (NBC, 2013–), *True Detective* (HBO, 2014–), *Dexter* (Showtime, 2006–13) or *The Night Manager* (BBC, 2016)).[12] The new male protagonist, if he is, indeed, theorised under the umbrella of post-feminism, must therefore occupy a range of identities, being everything and nothing all at once. If the scope of masculinity is broadening and becoming more ambiguous and diversified in popular television, it is also annexing other niches like period drama, including the televised classic novel.

As many of the authors of this collection richly illustrate, contemporary period television has duly responded to this ever-changing culturescape of manhood. The different chapters in this book show that such tensions have had, and are continuing to have, an impact on the manner in which topics like wartime/postwar masculinities are depicted in shows like *Downton Abbey* (ITV, 2010–15), *Mr Selfridge* (ITV, 2013–16) and *Peaky Blinders*

A Post-Feminist Hero

(BBC, 2013–), the ways in which the presentation of the eroticised male body in series adaptations such as *Poldark* (BBC, 2015–) and *Outlander* (Starz, 2014–) has become a site of political conflict, or the way the domestication of the 'career man' is negotiated in the neo-Victorian thriller *Ripper Street* (BBC/Amazon, 2012–16). What these period dramas have in common, however, is a nuanced awareness of the tenets of post-feminism which allow for historical men to be reinterpreted as objects of the female gaze, but also to become emotionally expressive, vulnerable, self-aware and sensitive to women. Significantly, it becomes clear that not only have contemporary dramatists maintained a conspicuous awareness of the 'female-friendly' new man of the late twentieth century, ensuring a politically acceptable ideal of masculinity – a gentleman for the modern age – but they have also evoked current notions of a fluid construct of manhood that conflates traditional and modern values of gender into a new category of hybridised masculinity.[13]

Although post-feminist criticism is largely oriented around the concept of a backlash to the second wave or 'denunciations of feminism',[14] assumptions that point to divisive frictions between men and women, my intention is to engage more colloquially with the notion of post-feminism and the ways in which the representation of the nineteenth-century hero has been impacted by ongoing debates about masculinity. This chapter therefore considers how the cultural influences of post-feminism offer an alternative vision of Victorian masculinity that transcends the ubiquitous figure of the classic romantic hero in the twentieth century. It suggests that practices in adaptation have evolved in response to these cultural shifts as evidenced by portrayals of a more complex, sympathetic and nuanced image of nineteenth-century masculinity.

This chapter takes as its focus the depiction of the ambiguous hero, John Thornton, in the BBC's 2004 production of Elizabeth Gaskell's classic novel *North and South* (1854–5). The character of Thornton, a self-made man, master of Marlborough Mills, family patriarch and lovelorn suitor, provides multiple angles from which to explore anxieties concerning modern masculinities. Thornton's relationship with the women in his life, the pressures imposed on him by his social position, the tensions that exist between his public and private lives, his relationships with masters and workers, his emotional transparency and his sense of isolation provide fertile ground for a post-feminist reinterpretation of the novel.

The incentive to write this chapter was motivated partly by the fact that adaptation scholarship has tended to focus on depictions of the heroine and, consequently, on issues of femininity, which ignores the central position men and masculinities have occupied in small-screen British classics since the mid 1990s. The palpable absence of Austen films in recent years coupled with a trend that now seems to favour darker classics, including the works of the Brontës, Thomas Hardy and George Eliot, bears testimony to such transference. It is my hope, then, that this chapter will offer a fresh perspective on how we are able to engage with concepts of masculinity in the twenty-first-century televised classic novel, and to suggest that the depiction of classic men is part of a wider cultural response to ongoing debates about masculinity, and how such discourses are being negotiated through contemporary period drama.

Moreover, this chapter has also been informed by discussions with the serial's writer Sandy Welch. Welch's first globally acclaimed classic novel serial, an adaptation of Charles Dickens's novel *Our Mutual Friend* (BBC, 1998), earned four BAFTAs and several other nominations, and cemented Welch's reputation as a literary dramatist. But it was *North and South* that catapulted her career, making Welch one of British television's leading literary adaptors, with a repertoire that now includes *Jane Eyre* (BBC, 2006), *Emma* (BBC, 2009), *The Turn of the Screw* (BBC, 2009) and *Romeo and Juliet* (Lux Vide, 2014).

Moving Beyond Darcymania: A Hero in His Own Right

Far from the hero portrayed by Patrick Stewart in the BBC's 1975 serialised *North and South*, scripted by David Turner and made by an all-male production team, the depiction of John Thornton in the 2004 serial is very much a product of a collective, trans-historical female imagination. He is born out of the mind of a Victorian woman novelist, and then re-imagined through the mind of a contemporary woman screenwriter who herself is implicitly influenced by the culture of post-feminism. The casting, portrayal and reception of Richard Armitage (*The Hobbit* films (2012–14); *Berlin Station* (2016–)) as Thornton also indicates that while there is a continuing impulse to eroticise the male

A Post-Feminist Hero

body in the serialised classic novel, the nineteenth-century hero has more or less transcended the boundaries of 'the Darcy model'. Like Firth's Darcy, Armitage's Thornton is chivalrous, brooding and 'dangerously good looking',[15] but the serial moves beyond this paradigm by foregrounding Thornton as intrinsically complex, morally conflicted, emotionally expressive, vulnerable, sensitive to women, self-improving and paternally competent. Crucially, where Davies began by bringing the figure of the nineteenth-century hero into clearer focus, Welch sharpens it and, to an even greater extent than Davies, develops the nineteenth-century hero in his own right. Where adaptors of Austen are limited by the fact that never in the novels do we see men outside the sphere of women, and therefore they must sometimes invent scenes that portray men only, Welch's *North and South* profits from the fact that Gaskell regularly places her hero in situations that exclude the heroine, Margaret Hale. Chapters such as 'Masters and Men', 'Men and Gentlemen' and 'Mother and Son', as well as Thornton and Margaret's debate about the gentleman and the 'true man',[16] demonstrate Gaskell's interest in exploring changing concepts of Victorian masculinities, and having her protagonists engage with such discourses.

Other discrepancies between *Pride and Prejudice* and *North and South* (2004) are accounted for by the periods in which the serials were made. Almost a decade separates the two productions, enough time to witness significant changes emerging in the culture, including a new generation that was expanding concepts of gender and negotiating changing landscapes of sexual politics. On some level, the qualities that Gaskell uses to characterise Thornton, such has his emotional transparency, vulnerability and humility, are qualities that our culture values in men today. Therefore, the idealisation of Thornton's masculinity in Gaskell's *North and South* finds an echo in the twenty-first century where benevolence, thoughtfulness and the ability/willingness to express sensitive emotions are now culturally considered to be new virtues of manhood. As Welch opines,

> It's easier to imagine Thornton as a modern man, more emotionally in tune with his feelings, than Darcy ever would be [...]. It's difficult to imagine Darcy beyond the last paragraph of *Pride and Prejudice* [...] what does he do with his time? Whereas it's very easy to

imagine Thornton getting to work on the mill, not fettered by his 'obligation' to Margaret, and them living together happily and productively.[17]

North and South (2004): Thornton's Re-inscription as a Post-Feminist Victorian Hero

When the fourth and final episode of *North and South* aired on BBC One in Britain in December 2004, fans were rewarded with the long-awaited kiss culminating in the romantic union between Thornton and Margaret (Daniela Denby-Ashe). In fact, the anticipation was so intense that fan flurry crashed the BBC's online message boards in a matter of minutes. The incident has since become 'enshrined in fangirl lore as "the infamous night that period drama fans broke (a small part of) the BBC (dot com).'"[18] The adaptation rivalled the then-unprecedented popularity of the BBC's *Pride and Prejudice*, earning *North and South* the accolade for Best Drama of 2004 with a staggering 49.43 per cent of the vote,[19] and Armitage the award for Best Actor with 53 per cent,[20] a degree of popularity that quickly displaced 'Darcymania' with the 'Armitage Army'.

Apart from the obvious sex appeal of Armitage's brooding physicality, Thornton's character is a man of great substance. He is entangled in a labyrinth of unbelonging; he is presented in liminal terms as he grapples with several identities at once – master, colleague, son, brother and suitor – and the conflicting expectations each one affords. He is also plagued by the iniquitous 'sins of the father', an inheritance that categorically defined and shaped his life, and forced him to 'become a man [...] in a few days.'[21] Despite Gaskell's sympathetic positioning of Thornton in the novel, the serial does not immediately present him in this way.

Unlike his character in Turner's 1975 serial, who gives the impression of being the quintessential gentleman, Thornton's first appearance in the 2004 version shows him to be a harsh and unsympathetic master. Inside Marlborough Mill, Margaret witnesses Thornton beat a worker, John Boucher, for smoking in the carding room. This apparent abuse of his class privilege and position is swathed in a savage display of violence that initially seems to place him on par with Emily Brontë's Heathcliff. Although some critics found the scene 'shocking' and 'needlessly violent'[22] Welch has defended her decision by arguing that without something to concretise

Margaret's animosity towards Thornton, her character 'risks coming across as a bit of a snob', as she does in the 1975 serial, for not liking him 'simply because he [is] a northern industrialist.'[23] Welch's answer to this was to make Thornton initially appear 'very ambiguous' and 'as brutal as possible' so that viewers would better accept Margaret's hostility towards him.[24]

As Thornton is increasingly portrayed outside Margaret's *focalised*[25] subjectivity, his complexity and probity quickly come into view and 'we see a respectable man suffer from the vicissitudes of trade.'[26] Margaret's upper-middle-class, southern sensibilities predispose her to calculate Thornton's industrial masculinity in entirely deficient terms: 'a gentleman wouldn't use his fists', she later chastises when reprimanding him about beating Boucher, to which he sharply retorts, 'I dare say a gentleman is never to see three hundred corpses laid out on a Yorkshire hillside as I did last May.' Welch's dramatic invention of the 'Boucher beating'[27] lends understanding to Thornton's severe reaction towards the worker because it underscores the disturbance he felt in witnessing the bodies of workers killed in a fire at a neighbouring mill. Margaret's sense of the physical inferiority of the working-class man and the superiority of the leisured man gestures towards the chasm that exists between the hero and heroine. For Margaret, her repulsion lies not only in the violence he enacts on the worker's body, which she feels is wholly unjustified, but also in the fact that his behaviour does not, in her estimation, exude that of a gentleman.

While Margaret's framing of Thornton's masculinity in the novel is bound up with her class prejudice and conflicting ideas about shifting concepts of masculinity in the early Victorian period, particularly regarding the self-made man, the adaptation evokes similar tensions about the condition of masculinity in contemporary culture. While Margaret routinely berates Thornton for his 'ungentlemanly' conduct, her opinion that he is 'not quite a gentleman' or a 'lady's man' is in many ways construed in the adaptation as a positive force of Armitage's/Thornton's post-feminist masculinity. Although the self-made man was an ambiguous figure in early Victorian England,[28] Thornton's entrepreneurship, social mobility and personal suffering in the serial are instead implied to be the very things that have made him honest and integrous, and that have set him apart from other men who have either inherited their positions or acquired them through class privilege. For Thornton, rather, the concept of the gentleman is nothing more than a superficial social construct that says very little about what he deems a 'true man'.[29] It is this measure of honesty and rejection of a categorical definition of manhood that distinguishes him from other men of his class and valorises his self-made/self-defined masculinity to a modern audience.

Men as Men: Male Community

One of Welch's greatest deviations from dominant adaptation practices in the late twentieth century is the communal space she affords men in *North and South*. Throughout the serial, Welch advances the masculine narrative by regularly positioning Thornton in the company of other men. In such scenes, the heroine's subjectivity is implicitly rendered inconsequential and, to a great extent, distorted. There are comparatively few scenes in prior classic serials that depict men outside the sphere of women. Adaptations, however, are intrinsically free to *interpret* not only the novels on which they are based but the history from which they originated, including the implied situations and contexts that are beyond the scope of the main narrative. Davies, for instance, advanced adaptation practices when he invented scenes depicting Darcy shooting, riding, fencing, bathing and, of course, swimming. Welch's serial also profits from such licence, particularly in a scene she reformulates from a conversation in the novel between Margaret and mill worker Bessy Higgins[30] into a dinner scene between Thornton and the other masters who debate, among other things, the salubrious conditions of their mills. The scene is constructed to position Thornton 'as the sympathetic "outsider"'[31] and to show how he differs from other mill masters.

Part of the neo-Victorian logic of this adaptation is the valorisation of particular capitalist ideologies, such as social mobility and economic opportunities gained through hard work, self-determination and self-sacrifice; however, Thornton's self-making in both the novel and the serial contributes to his ambiguity, and becomes a site of social contention in the narrative. The scene differs markedly from the one in Turner's version, where Thornton's power, leadership and emotional distance are emphasised through a sequence of long shots. In Welch's scene, rather, as the masters discuss topics like cotton purchasing and mill conditions, Armitage's thoughtful performance coupled with the script show viewers that Thornton has a strong moral conscience that governs, and often conflicts with, his business acumen. 'Thornton's as straight as they come', remarks one master, 'he won't risk Marlborough Mills in any risky enterprise, even if it means passing up the chance to speculate.' While the other masters read this characterisation as Thornton's conservatism and unwillingness to hazard capital or credit, the narration depicts a man who is morally driven and, consequently, conflicted about his responsibilities as both master and man. While Thornton's reservations portray him ostensibly as a cautious industrialist, Armitage's performance shows a man whose views are more ambiguous and not fully aligned with those of the other men. The camera intimates Thornton's conflicted conscience with interweaving close-up shots that isolate him in the frame and *focalise* his interiority, combined with a performance limned chiefly through expressions. Though he never says it in this scene, we know from a later episode that his greatest reason for not speculating is driven by a moral code not to 'risk the livelihoods of my men', a decision that is likely prompted by the memory of the 'miserable circumstances'[32] surrounding his own past.

The scene also signals Thornton's humanity by electing to have him be the only master who has implemented modern technology to improve working conditions in his mill: he admits to the men that he has installed a ventilation wheel to remove 'fluff'[33] (i.e., cotton effluvia) from the air, thus producing a safer environment for his workers. The other masters, who 'can't see profit in [a wheel]', are rendered dubious and immoral in their miserly refusal to provide humane conditions for their employees. Thornton, on the other hand, at once subverts their logic and tacitly exposes their cold mercenary nature by speaking to the economic advantages of having workers whose 'lungs don't clog so easily' because they and their children are able to 'work for me longer.' His reasons are here presented ambiguously as he projects the expected hard-boiled exterior that signals economic demurral, while the narration gestures to a higher moral conscience that is in strict conflict with the (unconscionable) avarice attached to being a master.

Wounded Masculinity: Male Emotion

If Thornton does not belong to the conventional man's world, neither can he breach the feminine realm. In a scene that recalls Darcy's tortuous proposal to Elizabeth Bennet in Davies's *Pride and Prejudice*, Thornton's clumsy proposal to Margaret in *North and South* is marred by a similar misreading of the heroine's character. Margaret's pre-emptive plea for him not to 'continue in that way; it's not the way of a gentleman' prompts a defensive retort: 'I'm well aware that in your eyes, at least, I am not a gentleman but I think I deserve to know why I am offensive.' This repeated reference to his ambiguous status as 'not a gentleman' throws into question the wider condition of his masculinity. Thornton's offence, while complex for Margaret in its multiplicity, here materialises into what she sees as his patriarchal 'duty to rescue my reputation' and have her for his 'possession'. Thornton's passionate corrective – 'I don't wish to possess you! I wish to marry you because I love you!' – evokes the language of equality that has permeated decades of feminist discourses so that Thornton's qualifying 'because I love you' self-consciously divests any vestiges of a patriarchal nature. Furthermore, the camera displaces Thornton's internalised indignation in the novel – 'He loved her, and would love her; and defy her, and this miserable bodily pain'[34] – with disjointed shots that emulate feelings of rejection and pain with music that punctuates his deeply wounded masculinity. This ejection of his masculine potency, though cinematically effective for romance purposes, evokes feminist/post-feminist discourses that challenge prescriptive sex roles. As a result, Thornton's masculinity is rendered increasingly ambiguous as the serial maintains his 'heroic' status while simultaneously reminding the audience of the ongoing dismantling of men's social and cultural dominance.

Moreover, this sense of disempowerment is repeated when Thornton watches Margaret leave for London after her father's death. The camera *focalises* our gaze onto Thornton as he desperately utters to himself, 'look back ... look back at me.' The issue, however, is not whether Margaret looks back at him (we know by his reaction that she does not) but to ensure that our counter gaze aligns sympathetically with Thornton's sense of loss and impotence. This scene marks a shift in classic serial practices since the 1990s: although it elicits the female gaze, the purpose is not to eroticise Thornton's body but to foreground his emotions and evoke sympathy for him. The scene is, in some ways, an example of what J. E. Adams terms a 'parade of pain', an emotional exposition that denotes 'instances in which masculine identity is realised through a regimen of solitary but emphatically visible suffering, which claims the authority of manhood'.[35] Although I do not interpret this scene as necessarily robbing Thornton of his masculine prowess, it is the prioritising of the emotional display of his deep interior subjectivity and wounded masculinity that humanises his suffering and becomes a central means of connecting him to contemporary discourses of the post-feminist man.

While Thornton's sympathetic qualities are finely nuanced across the four episodes, he is portrayed at his most vulnerable in scenes with his mother, played by the formidable Sinéad Cusack. Unlike Margaret, who discloses little personal information to her parents, Thornton openly confides his feelings to his mother. The delicate handling of their relationship allows us to infer that to the same degree Mrs Thornton is financially dependent on her son, Thornton is emotionally dependent on his mother. He shares with her his practical concerns about the strike and the financial situation of Marlborough Mills, but he also looks to her for comfort and advice when he is plagued by personal conflict. After the riot scene, for instance, Mrs Thornton mistakenly leads her son to believe Margaret loves him, to which he innocently replies, 'but Mother – I daren't believe that such a woman could care for me.' Later, when Margaret has rejected his proposal, he admits only to his mother that 'I was not good enough for her'. In both scenes, Thornton kneels at his mother's side while she affectionately strokes his face. This composition places him so that he is physically inferior to Mrs Thornton, indicating a shift in power dynamics that, in some ways, infantilise him. A sequence of tight close-up shots, combined with music, low-key lighting and sensitive performances, create a texture of emotional vulnerability that we begin to associate with Thornton. Furthermore, the image of his loosened cravat provides a visual reference to his emotional vulnerability, which becomes a motif throughout the serial. The image shows that he is comfortable and unguarded with his mother, and is 'opening up' in the wider scheme of the narrative. Interestingly, the character of Mrs Thornton becomes a vehicle through which Thornton is able to channel his sympathetic emotions. And it is a testament to his re-inscription as a post-feminist man that he allows himself to be vulnerable with, and take emotional direction from, a woman.

Homosocial Bonding: John Thornton and Nicholas Higgins

Conversely, one of the most efficacious ways Gaskell, and by extension Welch, reveals Thornton's sympathetic qualities and, consequently, counterpoints his masculinity against other masters in the narrative is through his burgeoning relationship with mill hand Nicholas Higgins (Brendan Coyle). Curiously, the portrayal of their relationship in the 1975 serial sits at the periphery of the narrative, a creative choice that, I would argue, further isolates Thornton and stagnates his character. In Welch's adaptation, however, this relationship is essential both to the masculine narrative she foregrounds and to the manner in which Thornton's moral character is fully revealed. The delicate handling of 'the Thornton/Higgins arc', which Welch describes as 'one of the most satisfying in the serial',[36] comes across as one of the most powerful dramatic strands of the final episode. In fact, it is the moment when Thornton crosses over into the slums of Milton in search of Higgins that 'our sense of the scope of the film changes from period romance to something greater'.[37] Thornton's conversion from an obdurate industrial master to a humbled, self-reflexive 'true man' sensitive to the plights of the working class registers what David Kelly calls the hero's 'egalitarian impulses'.[38] The serial reaches an equilibrium when Thornton finally eschews the façade of cold-hearted master and begins to connect with his workers, to 'speak to them, man to man',[39] and thus reconnect with this past self, on a human level. Welch exploits this arc by embellishing and inventing scenes throughout the final episode that depict Higgins and Thornton on 'equal' terms, such as when they square their differences, become friends and join forces to devise a plan to buy food wholesale to feed the workers in the community. The dramatisation of what is only alluded to in the novel becomes a powerful narrative of male communion in the serial. As Kelly argues,

> depths of character are revealed which offer glimmerings of such a reconciliation [of social tensions], and which thereby point to the possibility of human community in which fragile sensibilities are protected and nurtured and human effort – master and worker – is put to the service of humane ends rather than naked profit.[40]

A Post-Feminist Hero

Figure 5.1 Thornton is comforted by his mother after he is rejected by Margaret in *North and South*.

Although it is 'through Margaret's influence that [Thornton] begins to unbend and have a proper dialogue with his men',[41] only viewers are made privy to the bond of friendship that develops between Thornton and Higgins. In a gesture of male camaraderie, for instance, Higgins invites Thornton to join the workers for dinner. In every dinner scene thus far, Thornton has persistently occupied the head position at the table, a social practice that has been a reminder to the audience of Thornton's privileged position as both patriarch and master, while it points more subtly to his isolation and unbelonging. Conversely, the framing of Higgins and Thornton sitting side-by-side in the outbuilding at Marlborough Mill equalises their masculine experience, collapses polarities and consolidates the 'male concerns' that now unite rather than divide them. This trope of homosocial bonding is repeated throughout the final episode with various scenes depicting Thornton and Higgins engaged in private conversation or nodding knowingly to one another across the mill yard. This focus on a shared male experience becomes a defining feature of the adaptation, and a potent way of softening and broadening Thornton's masculinity beyond the borders of a romantic hero.

Post-Feminism and the Father Figure

Similarly, one of the most original ways this adaptation relocates the novel's presentation of masculinity to accord with ideologies of the twenty-first century is through Thornton's paternal benevolence. Welch introduces the character of 'young Thomas', Boucher's orphaned son. After Boucher commits suicide, Higgins assumes responsibility of Thomas and his siblings as a means of atoning for his actions against Boucher. In Turner's serial, Thornton agrees to employ Higgins to help him support Boucher's children, but sees them as 'children, that's all' and feels no affinity towards them. The character of Thomas in Welch's serial, however, has strong implications for Thornton. Welch explains that the invention of young Thomas 'will have reminded [Thornton] of his own helplessness [...] after his father's suicide, and it will be part of the building blocks to his feeling like a father/protector for all his workers' after he, presumably, reopens Marlborough Mills'.[42] Therefore, Higgins's self-appointed responsibility for the boy's welfare not only functions as an appeal to Thornton's humanity, reminding him of his own abandonment, but the child becomes a symbol of male unity that registers a post-feminist prescription of the 'role-broadening view of men'.[43]

Political organisations in Britain and America at the turn of the twenty-first century introduced new narratives of fatherhood into the cultural lexicon. New-leftist political structures in both countries, for instance, demonstrated an attempt to 'rework and renegotiate the image of fatherhood'[44] so that men became more involved in 'the *care* of children',[45] including the implementation of paid paternity leave, shared parental leave, and shared custody of children. These changing political discourses gave rise to a 'postfeminist cultural logic [...] mak[ing] fatherhood not only culturally negotiable, but also an attractive and desirable conceptualisation of masculinity'.[46] The emphasis Welch places on Thornton's concern for young Thomas as well as the homosocial bonds she develops between the men demonstrates a new trend in classic serials that transcends the assumption that romance is the primary means of defining men in period drama and points, instead, to an evolving concept of masculinity in the twenty-first century as multifarious, fluid and meaningful beyond the scope of the female experience.

A Post-Feminist Hero

Figure 5.2 Thornton and Higgins sitting to dinner together in the mill outbuilding in *North and South*.

Conclusion

North and South demonstrates that the displacement of modern tensions of masculinity onto an ambiguous nineteenth-century hero like Thornton helps to refocus some of the concerns that plague concepts of masculinity in our post-feminist culture onto the past. By transferring contemporary issues into an historical setting, *North and South* shows that period drama offers a space in which to remediate cultural tensions through the safe space of a fictional history. Throughout the twentieth century, adaptations of nineteenth-century novels were frequently oriented around reinforcing men's patriarchal privilege and hardening their masculinities while simultaneously asking women to accept such men as romantic heroes, as is the case with the 1975 adaptation. As I have suggested, it is significant that *North and South* was adapted by a woman; it is, to my knowledge, the first time that a woman screenwriter has adapted the novel. It is tempting to say that the focus on male emotion, male experience and, crucially, men in their own right has become a woman's issue; however, the origins of the novel are rooted in Gaskell's conspicuous interest in the mind of men. In discussing his views on Gaskell, Armitage has said that to him, she 'is probably the most exciting of the Victorian novelists. Unlike others, she manages to get inside the male mind. The male is usually only a fantasy figure. The idea that this male mind was written by a female writer [is] brilliant.'[47] And while Welch engages with Gaskell's vision of Victorian manhood, she does not offer any real solution to the 'problem' of masculinity in the twenty-first century. Instead, she offers an alternative to what has long been considered a genre dominated by male writers with a persistent focus on women and female subjectivity. As a result, Welch breathes new life into Gaskell's hero, giving the figure of Thornton a chance to be relocated within a contemporary culturescape of manhood. This transposition of a beloved Victorian hero opens up an opportunity for the figure to transcend the limiting label of romantic hero, to become three-dimensional rather than iconographic, to have significance beyond the female gaze and to be part of the wider narratives of conflicting masculinities.

Notes

1. Email correspondence between author and Sandy Welch (7 October 2016).
2. John Walsh, 'Andrew Davies: The man who put sex into the Victorian novel', *Independent*, 16 April 2004. Available at http://www.independent.co.uk/news/people/profiles/andrew-davies-the-man-who-puts-sex-into-the-victorian-novel-56380.html (accessed 1 November 2016).
3. Susie Mesure, 'Andrew Davies: the man who made Colin Firth a sex god', *Independent*, 19 February 2011. Available at http://www.independent.co.uk/news/people/profiles/andrew-davies-the-man-who-made-colin-firth-a-sex-god-2219985.html (accessed 1 November 2016).
4. Nicholas Barber, '*Pride and Prejudice* at 20: the scene that changed everything', *BBC Culture* (22 September 2015). Available at http://www.bbc.com/culture/us (accessed 2 September 2016).
5. See Laura Mulvey, 'Visual pleasure and narrative cinema', *Screen*, 16/3 (1975), pp. 6–18.
6. Email correspondence between author and Andrew Davies (28 May 2016).
7. Barber, '*Pride and Prejudice* at 20'.
8. See Robert Giddings and Keith Selby, *The Classic Serial on Television and Radio* (Basingstoke, 2001), chapters four and five.
9. Stéphanie Genz and Benjamin A. Brabon, *Postfeminism: Cultural Texts and Theories* (Edinburgh, 2009), p. 136.

10. Ibid., p. 143.
11. Lauren Thompson, 'Mancaves and cushions: marking masculine and feminine domestic space in postfeminist romantic comedy', in J. Gwynne and N. Muller (eds), *Postfeminism and Contemporary Hollywood Cinema* (Basingstoke, 2013), p. 151.
12. Sonia Saraiya, 'The year in TV: how shows of 2014 remade "masculinity" on television', *Salon*, 16 December 2014. Available at http://www.salon.com/2014/12/16/the_year_in_tv_how_the_shows_of_2014_remade_masculinity_on_television/ (accessed 3 July 2016).
13. Genz and Brabon, *Postfeminism*, pp. 132–44.
14. Angela McRobbie, 'Post-feminism and popular culture', *Feminist Media Studies*, 4/3 (2004), p. 257.
15. David Kelly, 'A view of *North & South*', *Sydney Studies in English*, 32 (2006), p. 88.
16. Elizabeth Gaskell, *North and South* (Oxford, 2008), p. 164.
17. Email correspondence between author and Sandy Welch (7 October 2016).
18. Sarah Seltzer, '10 years later, "North and South" remains the greatest period-drama miniseries of all time' (2014), *North and South 2004*. Available at northandsouth2004.com (accessed 24 June 2016).
19. Anon., 'Drama: best of 2003', *BBC Drama*, 28 October 2004. Available at www.bbc.co.uk/drama/bestof2004/best_drama.shtml (accessed 1 July 2016).
20. Sarah Wootton, *Byronic Heroes in Nineteenth-Century Women's Writing and Screen Adaptation* (Palgrave, 2017), p. 121.
21. Gaskell, *North and South*, p. 84.
22. Margaret Harris, 'Taking bearings: Elizabeth Gaskell's *North and South* televised', *Sydney Studies in English*, 32 (2006), p. 71.
23. Email correspondence between author and Sandy Welch (4 September 2016).
24. *North & South* (region one) DVD material, 'commentary'.
25. The term focalisation refers to the perspective (camera, character, narrator, etc.) through which the narrative is presented. See Gérard Genette, *Narrative Discourse: An Essay in Method* (Ithaca, NY, 1983).
26. Sarah Wootton, 'The changing faces of the Byronic hero in *Middlemarch* and *North and South*', *Romanticism*, 14/1 (2008), p. 30.
27. Email correspondence between author and Sandy Welch (20 September 2016).
28. Catherine Barnes Stevenson, 'Romance and the self-made man: Gaskell rewrites Brontë', *Victorian Newsletter*, 91 (1997), pp. 10–16.
29. Gaskell, *North and South*, p. 164.
30. Ibid., pp. 101–2.
31. Email correspondence between author and Sandy Welch (28 September 2016).
32. Gaskell, *North and South*, p. 84.
33. Angus Easson, 'Introduction', *North and South* (Oxford, 2008), p. xxii.
34. Gaskell, *North and South*, p. 207.
35. J. E. Adams, *Dandies and Desert Saints: Styles of Victorian Masculinity* (Ithaca, NY, 1995), p. 16.

36. Email correspondence between author and Sandy Welch (20 September 2016).
37. Kelly, 'A view of *North & South*', p. 91.
38. Ibid., p. 91.
39. Gaskell, *North and South*, p. 177.
40. Kelly, 'A view of *North & South*', p. 91.
41. Email correspondence between author and Sandy Welch (20 September 2016).
42. Email correspondence between author and Sandy Welch (28 September 2016).
43. Jonathan Scourfield and Mark Drakeford, 'New Labour and the "problem of men"', *Critical Social Policy*, 12/4 (2002), p. 632.
44. Donna Peberdy, *Masculinity and Film Performance: Male Angst in Contemporary American Cinema* (New York, 2011), p. 123.
45. Scourfield and Drakeford, 'New Labour and the "problem of men"', p. 624.
46. Hannah Hamad, 'Hollywood Fatherhood: Paternal Postfeminism in Contemporary Popular Cinema', in J. Gwynne, N. Muller and H. Radner (eds), *Postfeminism and Contemporary Hollywood Cinema* (New York, 2013), p. 102.
47. Rita Sherrow, 'Lie back and think of England', *Tulsa World*, 2 July 2005. Available at http://www.tulsaworld.com/archives/lie-back-and-think-of-england/article_b1476763-205b-5285-9378-9a24255d7428.html (accessed 21 July 2017).

6

'Because my daddy would protect them': *Ripper Street*'s Edmund Reid and the Competing Demands of Home and Public Lives

Jessica Saxon

Ripper Street (BBC/Amazon, 2012–16) centres on detective work in Whitechapel in the years after the Ripper murders, but beneath the police and morgue work lurks the troubling spectre of home and hearth, especially for Edmund Reid (Matthew Macfadyen). His home life, specifically problems with his wife Emily (Amanda Hale) and daughter Mathilda (Anna Burnett), informs and disrupts his work as a detective. Research on and histories of working-class Victorian men is scant, as Stephen Heathorn argues; therefore, *Ripper Street*'s writers and audiences draw on assumptions about masculinity that have come down through the decades, namely that men of the time were 'practically removed from the household economy.'[1] While domestic scenes are rare in *Ripper Street*, the household economy, from which Reid is supposedly detached, is inseparable from his detective work. Scholarship on neo-Victorian male characters is similarly scant: 'While multiple studies in essay or book form have attended to issues of gender and sexuality in the representation of female characters and feminist self-construction, engagement with neo-Victorian masculinity has been sparse.'² *Ripper Street* is not an adaptation of a nineteenth-century text; instead, it is an original neo-Victorian creation, pulling on people and events of the late nineteenth century and fictionalising them for a twenty-first-century television audience. Representations of masculinity in *Ripper Street* are complex and layered; they draw on historical depictions of men in late Victorian England, on twenty-first-century assumptions about late Victorian men and on twenty-first-century views of contemporary men. Reid embodies these competing visions of what it means to be a 'good' man. In *Ripper Street*, he is characterised as 'a man apart', and, as such, Reid becomes a vessel for twenty-first-century assumptions about Victorian men and a reflection of modern views and anxieties about masculinity. While nineteenth- and twenty-first-century constructions of masculinity are complex and varied, those constructions are often reduced in popular culture to stereotypes of 'manly men' who are consumed by work and removed from family concerns; Reid's embodiment of masculinity works within and against such assumptions.

Reid, ever the liminal figure in *Ripper Street*, is neither a fully working-class nor a fully middle-class man: he straddles the boundary between the two. Reid's liminality is present even in the casting of Matthew Macfadyen as Reid. Before *Ripper Street*, Macfadyen was perhaps best known for his role as Darcy in *Pride and Prejudice* (2005). Darcy, a quintessential Romantic hero, morphs, via Macfadyen's portrayal, into a seedier version of the Romantic hero in Reid – lower in socio-economic standing, lower in prestige, a more rough-and-tumble man yet also still a heroic ideal of masculinity. In *Ripper Street*, Reid's education, his detective-inspector rank and his home mark him as middle class, but his physical work in Whitechapel as well as the men with whom he associates mark him as working class. *Ripper Street* is a neo-Victorian rewrite of assumptions about nineteenth-century masculinity, one that reinserts the man into the household and that makes domestic troubles central to the man's workplace and identity. As John Tosh notes in his analysis of nineteenth-century masculinity, 'More fundamental [to the construction and enactment of masculinity] was the clash between work and home. In which sphere was a man really himself?'³ *Ripper Street* seeks to reinstate the man in the home while also allowing him to maintain his public presence. However, Reid cannot maintain both public and private order. His home world, especially in Series One and Two, continually falls apart in spite of his triumphs in the public sphere, and by the end of Series Three, Reid gives up his career in order to rebuild his family life. Reid's home is both a personal hell (a lost daughter and an estranged wife) and an idealised paradise (a found daughter and a family, at least partially, reunited).

Other scholarly projects on *Ripper Street* have explored the show's plotlines about prostitution, violence against women and the homosocial bonds among Reid, Homer Jackson (Adam Rothenberg) and Bennett Drake (Jerome Flynn);[4] considered the ways in which the series borrows from a wide variety of television genres;[5] or read the series as a critique of neoliberalism.[6] This chapter explores the tensions between the home and the street, between the family man and the career man, as seen in Reid's character, and the ways in which the home is destroyed and reconstructed over the show's first three series. Reid eventually becomes both parents for Mathilda, taking the maternal role from the doubting (and later drunken and even later dead) mother while also asserting his role as community and home protector. Moreover, before Mathilda can return to the Reid household she must pass through the challenges of Whitechapel's crime-ridden streets – challenges that her unworthy mother could not survive. Mathilda moves from captivity through madness and nearly into prostitution. She emerges unsullied, despite having identified so deeply with the Ripper victims in her madness that she dresses like them and follows their paths through Whitechapel – and it is this journey that marks her as the true daughter of Reid, who is likewise ultimately untarnished by his work. The notion of 'separate spheres' for men and women crumbles upon closer inspection; as Tosh notes, the 'constant emphasis on the "separation of spheres" is misleading, partly because men's privileged ability to pass freely between the public and the private was integral to the social order.'[7] However, the concept of 'separate spheres', of men belonging to the public and women belonging to the domestic, has become a popular assumption about Victorian lives. *Ripper Street* uses these assumptions about 'separate spheres' as a means of exploring masculinity. For Tosh, 'Charting the ebb and flow of men's commitment to domestic life, whether in the working class or the bourgeoisie, has much to reveal about the dynamics of masculinity – then and now.'[8] Reid's enactment of masculinity is neither fully of the nineteenth century nor fully of the twenty-first century, but his enactment of masculinity is tied to both his public and private roles.

Losing His Home: Series One and Two

Over the course of the first series, the audience slowly learns about Reid's family. His work as a detective is readily apparent: he is driven by the failures of the Ripper case to make Whitechapel safer. While the tension between Reid and his wife Emily is clear from the first episode, the source of the marital discord is not. After several episodes, the audience learns that their daughter is missing and presumed dead, that Reid's actions as a detective contributed to her disappearance and that her disappearance now drives much of Reid's work in H-division. Series One is set in 1889. The previous year, in the wake of the Ripper murders, Reid spotted a Ripper suspect while out with daughter Mathilda; he chose his role as detective over his role as father and followed the suspect, Victor Silver (David Oakes), onto a boat with his daughter in tow. The steam-powered boat exploded and sank. Neither Mathilda's nor Silver's body was recovered from the wreckage; Reid's body was badly burned in the explosion. Reid is the only one who believes that Mathilda is still alive. His continued insistence that she is merely missing and not dead chips away at both his relationship with Emily (who wants to complete the mourning process with him) and his credibility as a detective (because he can neither recover his daughter nor believe the most likely and logical explanation that she has not been found because she is dead).

The loss of his daughter ultimately makes him a better public servant but a worse husband. In his search for Mathilda, Reid manages to solve several difficult cases, especially those involving children; however, his attention to these investigations frequently stems from his belief that they are linked to Mathilda's disappearance – that is, from a personal rather than professional motive. One of his child-centred cases also leads to an act of adultery with Deborah Goren (Lucy Cohu). Goren, who runs an orphanage, works with Reid to protect a young teen from accusations of murder in Episode Two of Series One, and their relationship becomes adulterous in the final episodes of the same series. It is notable that, as Emily becomes less maternal and domestic via her charitable work outside

'Because my daddy would protect them'

of the home, her absence from the home compels Reid to turn to Goren, a woman who embodies maternal ideals. Goren's buxom and soft body becomes the one Reid seeks. The sharpness and gauntness of Emily's body connotes her religious values of self-sacrifice and self-denial whereas Goren's body becomes a refuge for the world-weary Reid. Moreover, his affair with Goren stems directly from a conflict with Emily: when Emily insists they clean out Mathilda's room in order to conclude their mourning process, Reid, unable to cope with his wife's belief that their daughter is dead, turns to Goren for comfort and support. Reid is not condemned in the series for his adultery – instead, the framing of the affair is designed to elicit sympathy for Reid. Reid's adulterous affair is, unlike Jackson's, also an emotional affair – sex for Reid is seemingly a by-product of his need for emotional comfort.

In Series Two, set one year later, Emily has become mad and fled from the home. She eventually dies, but her descent into madness, her exodus from the home and her death are not shown onscreen. Interestingly, in a storyworld filled with broken and dead women whose deaths and bodies are frequently shown on-screen, Emily is ultimately so unimportant that neither her death nor her body is shown – her physical self simply disappears. While the loss of his daughter devastates Reid and drives his investigations, the loss of his wife simply frees Reid to pursue his daughter more actively; once Emily has delivered Mathilda into the world, her work is complete, and it is Reid's duty to redeliver Mathilda into the world of the living. Moreover, during her breakdown and subsequent drunkenness, Emily is living in the streets and only half-clothed, which places her under Reid's professional – as well as domestic - jurisdiction. Yet he is powerless to return his own wife to the home. Emily has proven herself the less worthy parent: she refuses to believe her daughter is alive, she refuses to trust or obey her husband's word, and she has doubly fled from the domestic via her work and her madness. Therefore, Reid must become both father and mother to Mathilda.

Regaining His Home: Series Three

Series Three is set in 1894, five years after Series One. While Series One and Two are filled with Reid's professional triumphs and personal failings, Series Three allows Reid to reclaim the domestic (and by the finale, the pastoral) ideal by reclaiming his daughter. The final episodes of the series suggest that Reid must lose not only his professional identity but also a part of his physical self to reclaim Mathilda. By the finale, Reid has been shot during an attempt to find Mathilda, and his injuries have resulted in a pronounced limp. His career is put aside in the finale's closing scene: Reid and Mathilda are seen playing by the ocean as Reid's obituary is read to the audience. The obituary, the idyllic pastoral scene of father and daughter reunited away from the death and decay of London and the finale's title, 'The peace of Edmund Reid', work together to suggest that, while Reid is still very much alive, a part of him – his professional persona – has died, has been sacrificed to the domestic ideal. Given the traumas endured by both father and daughter, remarkably, no sign is given that either has been emotionally scarred by their ordeals – and it is only Reid, not Mathilda, who is physically scarred.

Ripper Street aligns Mathilda with the Ripper victims – with sexually active and sexually available women. This alignment with the Ripper victims also helps to blur the distinction between Reid's professional and personal duties: where he failed to help the Ripper victims, he can save his own daughter. The price of regaining his daughter is a high one. In the course of finding Mathilda, Reid murders Horace Buckley (Charlie Creed-Miles), the man who had been keeping Mathilda in a cell in his shop's basement and whom Reid (incorrectly) believes abused her. Buckley was misguidedly, in fact, doing his best to protect Mathilda from her father because Buckley believed that Reid had molested Mathilda, and Long Susan Hart (MyAnna Buring), brothel madam and Jackson's wife, later hides Mathilda from Reid for the same reason. In previous series, Reid was neither the most violent nor the most sexually active of the detective trio; those roles fell to Drake and Jackson, respectively. Yet both Buckley and Susan construct Reid as one of the most violent and sexually deviant criminals imaginable: a paedophilic incestuous rapist. Reid becomes a criminal, both an imagined one as Mathilda's alleged abuser and an actual one as Buckley's murderer.

Reid is able, with Drake's help, to track Mathilda to a brothel where a pimp has taken her. Having lost Mathilda again after the brothel raid, Drake and other police search for her in the streets, but Reid returns to his home to find Mathilda there, safely returned to the familial sphere after her dangerous adventures in the streets. Mathilda finds her own way home:

'Because my daddy would protect them'

Reid does very little to secure the return of his own daughter, but her return is framed by the show as a success for Reid. Reid's vigorous search for her is ultimately an impotent search, and his power as a detective is diminished by his search: not only does he not find his daughter, but he also commits a host of crimes in his attempt and loses his job. By the end of Series Three, Reid is a domestic man, but *Ripper Street* presents this domestication (perhaps even this professional castration) as a personal and professional triumph for Reid.

Reid and Neo-Victorian Representations of Masculinity

Discussions of masculinity in neo-Victorian works are complex due to the intersection of Victorian history, post-Victorian assumptions about the era and contemporary culture; in short, neo-Victorian masculinity is an accurate portrayal of neither Victorian nor twenty-first-century constructions of masculinity. Rather, explorations of masculinity in neo-Victorian texts are both backward-looking (to the realities of and assumptions about nineteenth-century Britain – with all of the complexities of boiling down a century into generalities) and forward-looking (to the realities of and assumptions about British and American cultures – with all of the complexities of viewing those cultures as monoliths). Ann Heilmann and Mark Llewellyn define the neo-Victorian as 'texts (literary, filmic, audio/visual) [that] must in some respect be *self-consciously engaged with the act of (re)interpretation, (re)discovery and (re)vision concerning the Victorians*.'[9] While all neo-Victorian texts are post-Victorian texts, only those post-Victorian texts both set in the nineteenth century and critically re-imagining the nineteenth century are neo-Victorian texts. Via its portrayal of Reid, *Ripper Street* works to (re)interpret, (re)discover and (re)envision late nineteenth-century masculinity through a twenty-first-century lens. Additionally, neo-Victorian texts frequently contain 'the appropriation of genuine historical figures – people who actually lived – as characters in fiction in an act of imaginative boldness that, through simple attrition, readers of contemporary fiction have come to take entirely for granted.'[10] Adding to the complexity of Reid's portrayal in *Ripper Street* is the existence of the historical Edmund Reid. The historical Reid, like his fictional counterpart, was a detective-inspector in Whitechapel's H-division during and after the Ripper murders, and this historical Reid was also married to a woman named Emily and retired to live by the sea. While these facts are seemingly the extent of the similarities between the man and the character, *Ripper Street*'s appropriation of historical figures like Reid as well as its appropriation of historical events recasts and adapts history (including representations of men) for a modern audience. Joachim Kersten, in his work on modern masculinities and violence, notes that modern definitions of masculinity revolve around three core tenets: 'procreation', 'protection' and 'provision' – that is, on a man's ability to ascribe to and enact heteronormative hegemonic masculine traits of cis-gendered heterosexuality, of physical prowess and control and of economic production, consumption and power.[11] Reid embodies a 'softer' version of these hegemonic masculinity traits – neither the bully nor the pushover, neither hyper-masculine nor feminised, Reid's enactment of masculinity is at once familiar to the modern audience yet also, perhaps given his historical setting, slightly strange.

Further complicating such discussions is the relatively short history of scholarly engagement with masculinity. In *Cable Guys: Television and Masculinities in the twenty-first century*, Amanda D. Lotz argues that 'the performance of professional duties has primarily defined the [. . .] male characters [. . .]. Such shows may have noted the familial status of these men but have rarely incorporated family life or issues into storytelling in a regular or consistent manner.'[12] However, scholars such as Heilmann and Llewellyn have noted the ways in which male characters in neo-Victorian texts (including television programmes) have resisted these male character types. Such scholars are attuned to the ways in which neo-Victorian male characters are an amalgam of assumptions about nineteenth-century masculinity and of ideals and fears about twenty-first-century masculinities. Explorations of the complex ways in which masculinities are constructed – let alone the use of the plural form of masculinity – are relatively new, and the role of the working father is often central to these explorations.

Lotz argues that in dramas the working father's family life is background material; his work life, not home life, is key to his identity. However, *Ripper Street* frequently offers a more complex vision of the working father (and by extension of the family itself). The series

'Because my daddy would protect them'

'de-mythologises the patriarchal and nuclear family ideal, centred on the heterosexual married couple with offspring.'[13] *Ripper Street* works to portray a fuller vision of the working father: a man whose public and private lives inform each other, a man who is competent in both spheres. Yet that idealised balance is consistently beyond Reid's reach: early in the series, his professional triumphs are at the expense of his home life, and later in the series, his home life requires the sacrifice of his professional life. Because Reid repeatedly insists on being both family man and career man, he must continually shift between the two – never completely at home in either sphere. While his character is shaped equally by his public and domestic roles, the show also echoes twenty-first-century anxieties about the competing demands of work and home. Reid, like so many men (and women) in the twenty-first century, struggles with having both a complete home life and a complete work life. The mythic work-life balance remains a myth even in the fictional world of *Ripper Street*.

Shows such as *Ripper Street* and characters like Reid operate at the intersection of history and fiction, of the nineteenth and twenty-first centuries: we look back to the Victorian era and overlay our contemporary concerns onto it. As Margaret D. Stetz notes, 'Neo-Victorian works never merely "show" the nineteenth century, nor do they recreate it; they create it, fashioning the past that their authors require – often, for the didactic purpose of enabling and encouraging cultural change in the present.'[14] Unfortunately, much of the neo-Victorian scholarship produced in recent years has focused on the roles of women in neo-Victorian texts and frequently overlooked men's roles:

> The afterlife of Victorian men may be stymied as much by the conventions of our period as their own. In light of the challenges of modernity, the advancement of feminism and a changing professionalised context for gender relations in the twentieth and twenty-first century, Victorian ideals of masculinity may be deemed to have been eradicated (and therefore not be noticeable or worth considering) [...]. The more documented Victorian male, equally stereotyped as uptight gentleman or loose-moraled villain, has potentially proved more difficult to re-envision. Yet this critical lacuna is at odds with some of the contemporary cultures in which a recourse to nineteenth-century models of masculinity, or their parody, are prevalent.[15]

Reid, neither 'uptight gentleman' nor 'loose-moraled villain', represents many of the re-envisioning problems outlined by Heilmann and Llewellyn. In his profession, he continually crosses between being an ideal detective and a corrupt detective. In his home, he continually crosses between being an ideal husband and father and a terrible husband and father. Moreover, his professional and personal lives are inextricably entwined – his shortcomings and his successes as a detective are bound to (and sometimes even caused by) events in his personal life, and his shortcomings and his successes as a father and husband are bound to (and sometimes even caused by) events in his professional life. Heilmann and Llewellyn argue 'neo-Victorianism has undertaken some efforts to queer the notion of the masculine-feminine dichotomy, blurring the boundaries to provide a reflection on the performativity of male identity.'[16] They also caution that 'too often consideration of the Victorian male had primarily involved focusing on masculinity in relation to gendered questions around male erotics rather than masculinity as lived and enacted.'[17] While Reid is by no means an asexual character, given his affairs with at least two women over the course of the series, his enactment of his sexual desires is not as important as his construction as a detective and as a family man. Yet the equal weight given to his professional and domestic selves works to create a queered performance of male identity – one that straddles the boundaries of masculine and feminine identity constructions.

Reid is, to borrow Stetz's terminology, a 'Neo-Man.' Stetz theorises the Neo-Man as the neo-Victorian realisation of the Victorian 'New Man'. The Victorian New Man was the counterpart to the Victorian New Woman; however, the New Woman and the New Man were separated by 'the "Newness Gap" [...]. Women [...] had evolved further and faster, achieving a higher degree of idealism, moral awareness, and self-development, while men had not kept pace; the latter were, to put it bluntly, not "New" enough.'[18] Stetz's Neo-Man is, therefore, the twenty-first-century realisation of the nineteenth-century ideal. Stetz argues: 'In neo-Victorian literature, however, not every man seems to have been made. A few appear to have been born "New", without obvious cause and without effort, and to have arrived in their Victorian settings fully evolved as progressive, modern thinkers on gender issues.'[19] Reid is one of these few men – readily progressive but without explanation of how or why he is so progressive. While his colleagues repeatedly express concern about how

'Because my daddy would protect them'

Reid's private life impacts his work, Reid sees the intersection between the two as natural, and when his career and fatherhood come into conflict with each other, he willingly chooses fatherhood over his job. Yet *Ripper Street* never offers an explanation of why Reid is different from other men presented in the series, of how he became a Neo-Man. Instead, this Neo-Man state seems to be his natural state. With all his flaws and failures, Reid represents an ideal (twenty-first-century) masculinity: protective, caring, intelligent, upwardly mobile, educated, independent, violent only when circumstances 'call' for violence and law-abiding unless the laws are unjust or stand in the way of justice. In many respects, his colleagues are surrogates for Reid's baser nature: Drake is Reid's blunt instrument when violence is needed, and Jackson's overt sexuality is a foil for Reid's less obvious sexual desires.

Stetz's theory of the Neo-Man and Reid's character fit in with Nickianne Moody's view of 'new men' in twenty-first-century television. For Moody, these new male characters exemplify 'a set of developing constructions of masculinity that (in the wake of shifts in the terrain of sexual politics and the rise of lifestyle marketing) eschewed traditional "armour-plated" machismo in favour of a more emotionally literate masculine ideal.'[20] Reid embodies this 'emotionally literate masculine ideal', and *Ripper Street* sets Reid in opposition to the 'traditional "armour-plated" machismo' as embodied by Jackson (a philandering criminal) and Drake (a former solider and a boxer). In her analysis of *Ripper Street* and two other neo-Victorian detective shows, Claire Meldrum notes: 'The domestic sphere is therefore not only antithetical to the investigative sphere, but actually works to reinforce the appeal and emotional significance of the detective's professional and homosocial connections.'[21] Yet Reid's masculinity and his domestic life are not antithetical – they are entangled and inextricable. His devotion to home and his ability to become father and mother to Mathilda signal his position within Moody's construction of 'new men'. Reid's professional identity and homosocial bonds are cast aside at the end of Series Three (at least temporarily) in favour of fatherhood.

Daddy/Detective

Reid is a hybrid character. He moves from one role to another: father, supervisor, employee, husband, lover, colleague, friend – but such moves are not easy; the demand of fulfilling each of the roles is too great a weight to be sustained. Unlike the male leads Lotz analyses, Reid is neither fully of the home nor fully of the public. While Reid is cast as an enlightened and progressive character, Meldrum argues that Reid and other characters like him are perhaps not as progressive as they may initially appear. She argues 'the models of gender and gender roles presented within these programs are far from progressive, depicting a reductive gendered essentialism whose underlying ideology betrays an overt, and troubling, misogyny at odds with their anachronistic interest in scientific "progress" and rational thought.'[22] Meldrum continues:

> Reid and Corcoran [the lead character in *Copper* (BBC America, 2012–13), another neo-Victorian detective series] have lost young daughters as a result of their work obligations [...]. Their daughters are young and sexually immature. They are the only female characters for whom they admit to having an emotional connection with [...]. This, I would argue, is directly related to the daughters' age and sex: prepubescent, their non-existent sexuality doesn't threaten the homosocial order that envelops their fathers. It also reinforces and normalizes the importance of patriarchal protection and the role of the father as protector, suggesting that girls must be protected both from society as a whole as well as the nefarious influence of their own mothers.[23]

While Mathilda's age or sexual maturity in the first three series does not disrupt Reid's homosocial order, her disappearance does. Moreover, it is not that Mathilda needed to be protected from Emily's 'nefarious' influence – rather, Mathilda needed, at least as far as Reid was concerned, more maternal influence. The young Mathilda needed to be protected from her father's obsessive desire to solve a case, a desire that led him to take his child with him as he pursued a suspect. Mathilda's disappearance was a result of Reid's inability to separate his home and work, just as her recovery is a result of his inability to separate his home and work.

It is notable that Mathilda chooses to return to the Reid home because she believes that her father would protect her from the outside dangers and that the Ripper victims should have also sought refuge in the Reid household under her father's protective wings. Mathilda even explicitly states that the Ripper victims should have fled to the Reid household

'Because my daddy would protect them'

'because [her] daddy would protect them' there – but protection, in Mathilda's construction, is limited by the walls of the Reid house. Reid as father can protect, according to Mathilda, the women in his house, but her statement implies that Reid as detective cannot protect them outside of the home. The protection Mathilda wanted for the Ripper victims was impossible – as impoverished whores, they had no place in the Reid household. Yet for Mathilda the grime and sins of the streets are easily washed off once she returns home, revealing the still pure young girl. In the moment when Mathilda responds that her 'daddy would protect them', Reid's home and work merge into a single unit. While Reid is sworn to protect them (or at least bring their killer to justice), he is not their 'daddy' – only Mathilda's. Mathilda's blindness to the limitations of her father's protection illuminates the narrow range in which Reid exists. During the nineteenth century, 'a man's occupation in life was his "calling", often seen as subject to the workings of Providence. The idea that what a man did in his working life was an authentic expression of his individuality was one of the most characteristic – and enduring – features of middle-class masculinity.'[24] However, Reid is not a nineteenth-century man – he is a nineteenth-century man re-imagined for the twenty-first century, and as such, Reid's 'calling' is both professional and domestic. His job defines and consumes him, and he attempts to build a stable home as a refuge from his work. However, his job contaminates his home with the violence and filth of the street and costs him both his daughter and his wife.

Much as *Ripper Street* reflects current anxieties about crime and violence, it also represents current anxieties about gender and gender roles. 'Daddy' in the home and at work, Reid strives to protect those who cannot protect themselves. Drake and Jackson also fail at domesticity. Drake craves a domestic refuge and pines for a 'lost' woman, although Drake's 'lost' woman is not a daughter but a prostitute he hopes to 'save' by marrying her. Jackson frequently flees from his home and wife, although by the end of Series Three Susan's pregnancy seems to have reignited Jackson's desire for home and hearth. Reid and his colleagues exist in a homosocial and patriarchal context, one that values their public roles and devalues their domestic desires. The women in Reid's life – most notably his wife – who do not put themselves under his protection meet terrible ends. Paradoxically, his construction and enactment of masculinity requires others, namely women, to be sacrificed. As he takes on the 'feminine' role as the primary caregiver in the home, there is no need for other women in his home other than his daughter. Reid's family is always a broken family, lacking either wife/mother or daughter. The lost daughter in Series One and Two is a constant source of anguish for Reid, but the lost wife/mother is barely mourned by either Reid or Mathilda in Series Two and Three. Apparently, Reid is 'man enough' to be all the family Mathilda could ever need.

Conclusion

Unlike twenty-first-century constructions of masculinity, which often centre on men's physical strength and prowess, 'for the most part, the Victorian code of manliness made scant acknowledgement of the body.'[25] However, in *Ripper Street*, men's bodies become another means of representing masculinity. While the show frequently frames Reid as an intellectual, Reid is also physically tough, especially in his capacity to bear and recover from the boat explosion and the gunshot wounds. At the end of Series Three, while Reid is still limping from his gunshot wound and still has burns on his body from the explosion, Mathilda is physically untouched despite having survived an explosion, imprisonment, abduction, and attempted rape. In the Series Two premiere episode, Reid was mocked by an opponent as being 'pure as the driven snow', yet in order for the daughter to return to the home she must be 'pure.' In a show littered with 'impure' women, most of whom die, the only good daughter – the only daughter worthy of being reincorporated into the home – is a pure daughter. While Mathilda is rescued from the dangerous public world and re-ensconced in the domestic world, Reid can straddle the public and domestic spheres; he can be the tender and loving father and his body is able to bear the wounds inflicted by a dangerous outside world.

Twenty-first-century re-imaginings of nineteenth-century masculinities, like those found in *Ripper Street*, combine the yearning for the fictional 'good ol' days' of masculinity as a monolith of manly men with the view that gender is always a complex performance. The viewer is, of course, not getting a historically accurate image of nineteenth-century masculinity, nor is the viewer getting a purely twenty-first-century vision of masculinity. Instead *Ripper Street*'s portrayal of Reid is a pastiche: it draws on fantasies of older forms of masculinity and on current gendered values. The show also

'Because my daddy would protect them'

provides a form of safe passage through the dangerous waters of gender – it guides the audience through the complexities of manhood in a fictionalised nineteenth-century context and gives the audience a space to contemplate how to navigate such complexities in the twenty-first century.

Notes

1. Stephen Heathorn, 'How stiff were their upper lips? Research on late-Victorian and Edwardian masculinity', *History Compass*, 2/1 (2004), p. 2.
2. Ann Heilmann and Mark Llewellyn, 'Introduction: To a lesser extent? Neo-Victorian Masculinities', *Victoriographies*, 5/2 (2015), p. 98.
3. John Tosh, 'What should historians do with masculinity? Reflections on nineteenth-century Britain', *History Workshop*, 38 (1994), p. 188.
4. Claire Meldrum, 'Yesterday's women: The female presence in neo-Victorian television detective programs', *Journal of Popular Film and Television*, 42/4 (2015), pp. 201–11.
5. Elke Weissmann, 'Troubled by violence: Transnational complexity and the critique of masculinity in *Ripper Street*', in J. Leggott and J. A. Taddeo (eds), *Upstairs and Downstairs: British Costume Drama Television from* The Forsyte Saga *to* Downton Abbey (Lanham, 2015), pp. 275–86.
6. David McWilliam, 'London's dispossessed: Questioning the neo-Victorian politics of Neoliberal austerity in Richard Wardlow's *Ripper Street*', *Victoriographies*, 6/1 (2016), pp. 42–61.
7. John Tosh, 'What should historians do with masculinity?', pp. 188–9.
8. Ibid., p. 189.
9. Ann Heilmann and Mark Llewellyn, *Neo-Victorianism: The Victorians in the twenty-first Century, 1999–2009* (Basingstoke, 2010), p. 4 (emphasis in original).
10. John Dee quoted in Heilmann and Llewellyn, *Neo-Victorianism*, p. 20.
11. Joachim Kersten, 'Culture, masculinities and violence against women', *The British Journal of Criminology*, 36/3 (1996), p. 383.
12. Amanda D. Lotz, *Cable Guys: Television and Masculinities in the 21st Century* (New York, 2014), p. 10.
13. Marie-Luise Kohle and Christian Gutleben, 'Introducing neo-Victorian family matters: Cultural capital and reproduction', in M.-L. Kohle and C. Gutleben (eds), *Neo-Victorian Families: Gender, Sexual and Cultural Politics* (Rodopi, 2011), p. 10.
14. Margaret D. Stetz, 'The late-Victorian "New Man" and the neo-Victorian "Neo-Man"', *Victoriographies*, 5/2 (2015), p. 119.
15. Heilmann and Llewelyn, 'Introduction', pp. 98–9.
16. Ibid., p. 102.
17. Ibid., p. 101.

18. Stetz, 'The late-Victorian "New Man" and the neo-Victorian "Neo-Man"', p. 107.
19. Ibid., p. 114.
20. Moody quoted in Lotz, *Cable Guys*, p. 43.
21. Meldrum, 'Yesterday's women', p. 210.
22. Ibid., p. 202.
23. Ibid., p. 209.
24. Tosh, 'What should historians do with masculinity? Reflections on nineteenth-century Britain', p. 186.
25. Ibid., p. 182.

7

'Pleasure and pain, again and again' — Between Monstrosity and Inner Turmoil: The Representation of Masculinity in *Penny Dreadful*

Caroline Langhorst

Introduction: 'Not a girl's heart. A man's heart'

In the neo-Victorian TV series *Penny Dreadful* (Showtime/Sky, 2014–16), created by John Logan,[1] gender is self-reflexively exposed as a cultural construct. Additionally, it is also portrayed as an outspoken Butlerian performative masquerade,[2] providing a certain disruptive queer potential and a distinct aesthetic. As Andrew Smith and William Hughes proclaim, queerness 'in Gothic terms is [...] seemingly to adhere to one and yet to desire [...] the other. It is to juxtapose the familiar and the unfamiliar, the rational and the supernatural, the past and the present, the acceptable and the condemnable.'[3] All of this, and more, may be located in *Penny Dreadful*. By means of its fin-de-siècle London setting and occasional encounters with the shadowy, supernatural 'demimonde', its explicit references to iconic literary texts such as Mary Shelley's *Frankenstein* (1818), Robert Louis Stevenson's *Strange Case of Dr Jekyll and Mr Hyde*

(1886), Oscar Wilde's *The Picture of Dorian Gray* (1890) or Bram Stoker's *Dracula* (1897), the hybrid series combines a nineteenth-century period setting with a decidedly contemporary interpretation of gender and sexuality. On top of this, gender and related sexual desire are linked to an – albeit complex – monstrosity throughout the entire series, which spans three seasons. Despite the recurrent use of gore effects and the relentless Gothic drives of Eros and Thanatos, *Penny Dreadful*'s sincere look at troubled, solitary and rather ambiguous outcasts who deviate from the norm in different ways, and to varying degrees, is, however, not demonising but notably sensitive and understanding. Furthermore, it may be stated that the series' focus on homosocial interaction, its queer potential and ambivalent and nuanced depiction of monstrosity also bring to mind Ardel Haefele-Thomas's remark that 'Gothic narratives can help us call into question the monolithic ideas we might have about Victorian culture and Victorian attitudes [...] these texts transgress monstrosity in the sense that they help interrogate the very idea of what is monstrous.'[4]

While the potentially threatening monstrous-feminine is captivatingly embodied by several female characters, such as the antagonistic witch Evelyn Poole (Helen McCrory) and her daughters, or the show's central female protagonist, the enigmatic yet highly troubled and clairvoyant Vanessa Ives (Eva Green), a closer glance at the series' depiction of monstrous yet simultaneously fragile forms of masculinity seems equally rewarding; especially, although not exclusively, due to the carefully reflected casting choices. Accordingly, the male actors surrounding Eva Green's convincing rendering of Vanessa Ives's torment also lend another layer to the series due to their different role biographies and constructions of masculinity. These still resonate to some extent in their *Penny Dreadful* characters: Welsh veteran actor Timothy Dalton (Sir Malcolm Murray), for example, is famous for portraying James Bond in a comparatively brooding and darker manner as well as playing 'tall, dark and handsome' and highly conflicted Brontëan characters such as Mr Rochester and Heathcliff. The young Josh Hartnett was publicly regarded as an attractive and charismatic teen heartthrob before embarking on darker roles, such as that of Mr Chandler, whereas Reeve Carney (Dorian Gray) has previously played a torn character leading a double life when he starred in the leading role in the Broadway musical *Spider-Man: Turn Off the Dark* (2011).[5] Prior to the subsequent close examination of masculinity in *Penny Dreadful*, the series' specific take on Victorian Gothic will be explored briefly in the next subchapter.

'When you transform a life, you're making it anew': *Penny Dreadful* and Victorian Gothic

In the wake of the twenty-first century, the medial representation of the Victorian age has, irrespective of its status as generally popular and seasoned fare, undergone a significant resurgence. Recently, there have been several cinematic and televisual outputs similar to *Penny Dreadful* that place certain emphasis upon troubled and pathologised masculinity, such as Joe Johnston's Gothicised 2010 remake of the Universal horror classic *The Wolf Man* (1941)[6] or ITV's *The Frankenstein Chronicles* (2015–), which is examined in Chapter 8 by Katherine Byrne.

Due to *Penny Dreadful*'s resurrection of iconic characters such as Victor Frankenstein and his creature, Dorian Gray and Dracula, it comes as no surprise that most scholarship on the series so far has concentrated on its construction of Victorian London as well as its employed models of adaptation.[7] *Penny Dreadful* therefore does not only employ rich literary allusions, it also unabashedly comments upon various strands and moral views of Victorian life while at the same time 'the very notion of "period" is radically destabilised'[8] on account of its assemblage of literary texts from different eras. Thus, various Victorian discourses are reflected upon by the series to a varying degree, such as urbanisation and industrialisation and the related technological progress, medicine and science or empire, and their potential association with gender, corporeality and sexuality. Most significant in this regard would be the circulation of theories of degeneration and the resulting pathologisation of deviant conduct, physicality and sexual orientation. This will also be of particular importance for *Penny Dreadful*'s representation of masculinity. Accordingly, sensation fiction's 'excessive codification of the body, which often turn[s] characters into spectral or liminal figures hovering between the realm of the living and the dead'[9] and Victorian pulp fiction's emphasis upon violated corporeality can also be detected in the series: gore and physical violation are self-reflexively underscored and put on display in performative terms by the foreshadowing Grand Guignol performance of 'The Transformed Beast' in the episode of the same name in Series One,

Conflicting Masculinities

and the Putney's waxwork cabinet, with its horror chamber of gruesome recreations of Jack the Ripper-echoing crime scenes, seen in Series Two. Victorian sensation fiction also articulated 'a variety of anxieties around such questions as class mobility, changing marital legislation and the multifaceted nature of identity.'[10]

Additionally, it is also important to note that the contemporary view of the Victorian age may at times be clouded by reductionist readings. Jarlath Killeen's term for the repressive nature of Victorian society, the so-called 'Dr Jekyll and Mr Hyde view',[11] critically questions the clichéd notion that the members of Victorian society were 'monsters of perversity who lived public lives of staid conformity but who came out of the closet nightly to perpetuate the most horrific versions of abuse.'[12] Nonetheless, the male characters in *Penny Dreadful* are all to a certain extent haunted by an inwardly torn Jekyll-and-Hyde personality, yet the series tries to eschew a simplistic good-and-evil binary model, leaving enough room for ever-shifting in-between positions. The intricate link between monstrosity and humanity is therefore not only constantly upheld throughout the series as the characters are shown in their darker, brutal as well as most vulnerable and helpless moments, but often even conflated by means of acts of utmost monstrosity that are yet deeply human. As a result, the characters' contradictory nature and their conflicting feelings of pain and desire evoke a similar audience reaction that is marked by an oscillation between (Blakean) attraction and repulsion, understanding and rejection of certain moral stances and actions such as, for example, the Creature's murder of Van Helsing (David Warner), Victor Frankenstein's selfish killing of the consumptive Brona (Billie Piper) and his betrayal of Ethan Chandler's confidence or Dorian Gray's equally cold-blooded murder of his transgender lover Angelique (Jonny Beauchamp).[13] *Penny Dreadful*'s episodic narrative similarly alternates between Victorian daily life and encounters with the seemingly always lurking supernatural demimonde, between different classes, milieus and London boroughs such as Sir Malcolm Murray's upper-class Westminster manor, Grandage Place, Dorian Gray's opulently decorated home and the more humble abodes of Victor Frankenstein and Ethan Chandler.

Furthermore, despite the Gothicised 'blurring of the real with the unreal',[14] the series combines two central modes of Victorian Gothic: the domestic and the urban.[15] At the same time, it also makes a foray into the

Representation of Masculinity in *Penny Dreadful*

adventure-oriented, and at times monstrous,[16] imperial Gothic in Series Three, by means of its additional temporary settings in colonised (Africa) or formerly colonised (the American Wild West) territory, and the character of the manly explorer and hunter, Sir Malcolm. The sphere of the domestic Gothic is characterised by an innate ambiguity, and it also 'represents a particular manifestation of the uncanny in which the "home" now becomes [...] the site of troubled sexual secrets, so that [...] the domestic becomes the space through which trauma is generated.'[17] This may be said of Vanessa Ives's childhood and the witnessed illicit sexual encounter between her mother and Sir Malcolm, a primal scene, which marked the beginning of her inner conflict, and her present substitute home at Grandage Place. Having lost her family, listened to the whispering, dark voice and been hunted and desired until her eventual death while fighting her own combat against her inner demons, there is no ultimate safety to be found anywhere, not even in her new abode.

The male characters are likewise all outcasts in their own way: the imperious and reckless Sir Malcolm has lost his son and eventually loses his daughter-turned-vampire Mina (Olivia Llewellyn) by shooting her himself and his estranged wife, while under Mrs Poole's spell, commits suicide. At the end of Series Two, his loyal African manservant Sembene (Danny Sapani) is accidentally killed by the rugged, womanising Westerner and deeply troubled American Werewolf in London, Ethan Chandler. The uprooted and melancholy Mr Chandler, in turn, is on the run from his patriarchal father (Brian Cox), who has set some bloodhounds on his trail, and from the obstinate and crippled Scotland Yard inspector Bartholomew Rusk (Douglas Hodge) who has sworn to bring him down, following him everywhere with an unyielding compensatory fanatic obsession that echoes Captain Ahab. The notion of home and safety has likewise been contaminated for the physically effeminate, cerebral yet poetry-loving Victor Frankenstein by his mother's early death. The solitary, gentle-hearted yet revengeful Creature/Caliban/John Clare's attempts at finding a home, acceptance and security are repeatedly and cruelly thwarted. Even his temporary reunion with his wife and sick son in Series Three has a calamitous outcome, the death of his son, which eventually places him again on a barren and lonely shore. The eccentric, ambiguous and closeted queer Egyptologist Mr Lyle (Simon Russell Beale) intends to emigrate in Series Three since he does not feel truly accepted in Victorian society. The sexually open-minded, narcissistic dandy Dorian Gray is also predestined to solitude and caught in his compensatory hedonistic cycle of ephemeral interests and transgressions, whereas Dr Jekyll (Shazad Latif), who only makes a brief appearance in Series Three as one of Victor Frankenstein's old school friends, obstinately strives for respect and admiration in order to compensate for his existence as a colonised and seemingly Othered foreigner in imperial Britain. Believing in mankind's innate duality, he aspires to create his own self, ultimately inheriting his despised father's aristocratic, and potentially corrupting, title, Lord Hyde.[18]

While the London streets are often foggy and dark, Sir Malcolm's London estate also seems at times rather unsettling, being frequented by either vampires in Series One or witches in Series Two. Consequently, 'the generally staid and calm manor house of Victorian fiction'[19] and the related bourgeois Victorian idealisation of domesticity, which John Ruskin (1865) famously regarded as a perfectly tranquil place and ultimate refuge,[20] turn into a vulnerable site of potential – and actual jeopardy – and lasting emotional strife. In *Penny Dreadful*, the male characters are likewise situated within the domestic sphere as it is not restricted to their female counterparts. Living in a predominantly homosocial environment, some of the male characters such as Sembene or Ethan Chandler even take care of the domestic tasks, while Vanessa Ives, in comparison, does only very little housework. In Series Three, Grandage Place even shortly falls to decay when a lonely and depressed Vanessa feels abandoned by the men and does not clean the almost derelict house for weeks. Ultimately, however, as Mr Chandler, for whom the manor similarly serves as a surrogate home, remarks rather aptly, the only temporary shelter for the principal characters is 'the people we trust.'[21] But even the bonding of the small group that at times takes on the appearance of an alternative family[22] does not find much rest in the ongoing battle against outer evil forces and their own inner conflicts.

'For the monster is not in my face, but in my soul': The Portrayal of Conflicted Gothic Masculinity in *Penny Dreadful*

As the following analysis will demonstrate, the series' male characters are endued with considerably different character traits. As a result, they

Representation of Masculinity in *Penny Dreadful*

embody differing forms of masculinity (e.g., imperial masculinity, dandyism) or cross-overs (gentleman/predator as in the case of Dr Sweet/Dracula) and monstrosity – a certain degree of contradictoriness being their principal common denominator. These at times highly differing individuals become incidentally acquainted with each other and their evolving social interaction is predominantly characterised by a homosocial bonding and understanding as well as potential conflicts arising from their different tempers. The community surrounding Sir Malcolm and Vanessa Ives that is initially brought into existence on account of his missing daughter consists of him, Vanessa, Ethan Chandler, Victor Frankenstein, Sembene and later, on several occasions, Mr Lyle. Each of the characters of the core group interacts with other characters whose storyline, in spite of not being a part of the inner circle, is closely connected to one or several members of the group surrounding Sir Malcolm (e.g., the Creature or Dorian Gray).

Penny Dreadful's male characters are not only defined by monstrosity and inner torment. Given the series' exposure of gender performativity and actual fragility of hegemonic masculinity, a certain paradoxical coexistence of non-heteronormative traits and patriarchal conduct may be noted. Thus, even the proponents of a comparatively more deviant masculinity such as, for instance, Victor Frankenstein, whose physically delicate stature is often juxtaposed with Ethan Chandler's physical prowess, have their patriarchal moments. This is paradigmatically exemplified by his wish to turn the suddenly more emancipated and, from his point of view, therefore contaminated Lily into an obedient and domesticated Victorian woman before realising rather late that his intention might be wrong. Similarly, Dorian Gray attempts to reimpose his patriarchal authority when he murders the young Justine (Jessica Barden) who had been rescued by him and Lily from an abusive past and a destitute existence, deeming her to be brain-washed and too presumptuous and radical in her hatred of men. Both men want to stay in control.

Moreover, in true dandy fashion, the androgynous, playful yet easily bored Gray, yearning to be noticed by others, enjoys making a spectacle of himself,[23] by means of which his performative, artificial identity is underscored. His character also articulates dandyism's 'complex playing-off of manliness and effeminacy',[24] which additionally made it more difficult to distinguish the dandy from the gentleman. The elusive, seductive and manipulative Dracula, who makes his entrance in his human incarnation as the refined zoologist Dr Alexander Sweet after having lurked in the shadows, unites the soft-spoken, sophisticated appearance of a gentleman and a domineering patriarchal demeanour as master of the vampires. With regard to his beloved Vanessa Ives/Amunet/Mother Evil, he behaves as predatory and possessive as the obsessed and jealous Victor does with regard to Lily: thus, he does not only claim her to be 'his', but he even tells his obedient vampires to wait for the moment when she is defenceless and begs for his seduction. During their eventual sexual encounter, however, Vanessa does not easily succumb to him, but remains dominant, thereby complicating the scene and Dracula's planned entrapment. Yet her presence as Mother of Evil is significantly reduced in the last two episodes of Series Three[25] as the male characters return to the wasteland previously known as London and set out – in vain – to rescue her.

Heteronormative, imperial masculinity as embodied by Sir Malcolm, then, is not only repeatedly criticised by other, both male and female characters, but also unmasked by himself on several occasions, either by a display of emotions (e.g., his breakdown after the tour-de-force of the séance in the eponymous episode of the first series) or verbal acknowledgement (his realisation that one has ceased to be the hunter and become the prey). In Series Two, Sir Malcolm then actually ends up as prey as he falls victim to Evelyn Poole's seductive and highly manipulative spell. Moreover, virile manhood is even more radically subverted when Ethan Chandler ends up spending an absinthe-infused night with Dorian Gray, articulating the multifarious nature of desire, the underlying queer potential of homosocial bondings and the constructed, fragile nature of hegemonic masculinity. At this point, one may recall Smith's and Hughes's claim regarding the initially stated queer potential of the Gothic, which primarily emanates from its inherent liminal position and potential transgression of cultural and moral boundaries.[26] The supposed patriarchal authority is further dismantled by means of possessed Vanessa's brutal exposure of the male character's weaknesses (e.g., Victor Frankenstein's sexual repression) and sins (e.g., Sir Malcolm's egocentric behaviour, his failings as husband and father and his monstrous colonial misdeeds that consist of violent bloodshed and lustful sexual gratification abroad).

Representation of Masculinity in *Penny Dreadful*

The master/servant and related coloniser/colonised model are similarly disclosed as utterly volatile as Sir Malcolm's conscientious, observant and rather taciturn manservant Sembene is not afraid to openly speak his mind, telling him that they are not the same and that Sir Malcolm might err in thinking his daughter could still be saved. Similarly, Ethan Chandler's other potential surrogate father, the Native American and werewolf Kaetenay (Wes Studi), who develops a bond with Sir Malcolm in Series Three after Sembene's death, is likewise able to stand up to the English explorer. Dracula's and Renfield's (Samuel Barnett) master-and-servant relationship is equally fragile due to Dr Sweet/Dracula's transgression of the gender dualism as *Penny Dreadful*'s Dracula aligns both patriarchal and feminine traits.[27] Dr Frankenstein's and the Creature's creator/created relationship, or, as the Creature describes it in the episode 'Fresh Hell', their eternal 'wheel of pain', is also highly unstable as each reciprocally inflicts pain upon the other. At the same time, this ongoing vicious cycle echoes Eve Kosofsky Sedgwick's well-known claim that Shelley's *Frankenstein* is predominantly centred upon the struggle between two men who relentlessly hunt each other.[28] At least in this regard, and in terms of the 'circulation of the position of monstrosity',[29] the insistence upon 'the discomposure of masculinity, on the troubled and troubling representation of the male body'[30] and the omnipresence of the Creature in Victor's thoughts, *Penny Dreadful* evokes Shelley's novel to a certain extent.

As mentioned before, *Penny Dreadful* thus comments upon the Victorian age's allegedly patriarchal order by presenting different instances of masculinity in crisis. Simultaneously, Judith (now Jack) Halberstam's statement regarding cinematic depictions that Gothic monstrosity has undergone a transformation in the twentieth century into 'Gothic masculinity'[31] may be said to become manifested in *Penny Dreadful* on account of its many tormented male characters, which outnumber their by no means less troubled female counterparts. In spite of being a twenty-first-century and televisual text, *Penny Dreadful* combines Halberstam's nineteenth-century (determined by a fear of monstrous bodies, which was intricately interwoven with signifiers of class, race, sexuality and nationality) and twentieth-century model (primary emphasis upon gender and sexuality)[32] by means of its aforementioned representation of Victorian Britain from a self-reflexive and post-colonial

Figure 7.1 'All the broken and shunned creatures' – Victor Frankenstein, his Creature/John Clare and their ongoing painful struggle in *Penny Dreadful*.

twenty-first-century perspective. The transsexual character of Angelique and Dorian Gray's sexual orgies and their at times fetishistic bondage gear, for example, have a very modern appeal. While Oscar Wilde's general adaptability to the twentieth, but also the twenty-first, century, has often been noted,[33] Elisa Glick's reading of the modern queer subject and dandy as 'embodiment of capitalist modernity's constitutive contradictions (public/private, work/play, appearance/essence)'[34] proves particularly rewarding with regard to *Penny Dreadful*'s Dorian Gray. Ethan Chandler's troubled and charismatic persona then combines different character types: the twentieth-century construction of the cinematic melancholy, fatally doomed and (self-)destructive werewolf, which has repeatedly been read as an expression of troubled masculinity,[35] is combined with that of the outlawed Westerner. Additionally, Ethan's composite character displays traits of a Romantic – that is, more specifically, Byronic – tormented masculinity as the enigmatic American is likewise burdened by the enormous weight of his past and misdeeds. Contrary to the classical depiction of the hopeless fight against the lycanthropic 'beast within', Ethan Chandler, acting in his assigned role as Lupus Dei, finally succeeds in transcending his cursed existence by killing Vanessa Ives, with whom he had formed a very close bond defined by mutual trust, understanding and love, on her request. Her death may seem to reinforce Victorian conventions and gender roles at first sight, yet Vanessa's central role as an intermediary between the men, their hesitant rebonding after her death or their general inner torment and the series' deconstruction of heteronormative masculinity add a more ambiguous layer to the matter.

Due to its specific perspective, *Penny Dreadful* thus articulates Cyndy Hendershot's remark that Gothic texts tend to expose the fragility of traditional manhood by revealing the discrepancy between 'the actual male subject and the myth of masculinity.'[36] Haefele-Thomas supports this by stating that the Gothic is often employed 'to interrogate and subvert Victorian hegemonic ideals regarding sexuality, gender identity, race, empire and nation.'[37] Thus, it permits 'authors to look at social and cultural worries consistently haunting Victorian Britain even as the official discourse worked tirelessly to silence those concerns.'[38] Ultimately, it then exposes 'the real monstrosity [...]: the triumvirate of homophobia, transphobia and xenophobia.'[39] The series also responds to the fin-de-siècle fear of endangerment by sexual deviancy and the emergence of the 'New Woman', which were susceptible to being pathologised and Othered due to their incompatibility with heteronormative gender constructions.[40] As Kelly Hurley notes, this correlates with nineteenth-century medicine's and science's desire to explain instances of alleged monstrosity or abhumanity through the use of scientific terminology.[41] Thus, the supposedly scientific discourse itself displays a slightly Gothicised monstrosity to a certain degree. In *Penny Dreadful*, the proponents of science, Dr Frankenstein, Dr Jekyll and Professor Van Helsing themselves, are at times presented as being monstrous, the former two are partly depicted as selfish Victorian 'unethical experimenter[s]'[42] and Victor unsuccessfully tries to categorise Vanessa's possession as a psychosexual disorder.

As Andrew Smith highlights, however, not only emancipatory or allegedly hysterical women and same-sex desire tended to be pathologised and subjugated to the potentially monstrous scrutiny of the male, medical gaze (as Vanessa is repeatedly, although ultimately in vain, in *Penny Dreadful*); accordingly, even 'dominant masculine scripts came to be associated with disease, degeneration and perversity.'[43] Writings by Samuel Smiles, Charles Kingsley and Edwin Lankester, for instance, all connect the state of the diseased male body with notions of national decline and failure.[44] The series responds to this prevalent notion by presenting male characters whose initial self-composure soon begins to crumble, exposing men who are, in true Gothic fashion, haunted by their past and their various personal obsessions, desires and addictions. As a result, the Foucauldian medical gaze and the cinematic male gaze are eventually inverted as the male characters' torment and weaknesses are laid bare. Consequently, they mainly oscillate between deluding themselves to be in control of their lives and past and feeling helpless and haunted by it, often yielding to temptations and addictions. By this means, they also comment upon Smiles's and Kingsley's constructed 'versions of the male subject which suggest that subject's inability to resist the temptations of a range of moral vices',[45] whether it be Dorian Gray's seemingly infinite list of moral and sexual transgressions, Mrs Poole's successful enticement of Sir Malcolm, who believes himself to have regained his youth after symbolically shaving his sign of rugged virility, his moustache (Series Two) or Ethan Chandler's brief embrace of his dark side and succumbing to Hecate Poole (Sarah Greene) (Series Three). Mr Chandler, for example, is described by Vanessa on their first meeting as a nonetheless troubled 'man who [...] has given himself to excess and the unbridled pleasures of youth.' Desire and temptations are also particularly associated with predatory masculinity: both Sir Malcolm and Ethan Chandler shortly serve as devil incarnates in Vanessa's presence, the former even addressing her by seductively reciting the line 'Darkling I listen [...]' from 'Ode to a Nightingale'. As pleasure and pain go hand in hand with regard to all characters, for the lovesick, repressed and pretentious man of science, Victor Frankenstein, life's painful tragedies and alluring temptations seem more frightening than death. As a result, he becomes increasingly addicted to his chosen antidote to his largely self-inflicted emotional pain: morphine. Unlike the men, Vanessa Ives, on the other hand, is on her guard, with the exception of occasional moments of boundary transgression such as her passionate sexual encounters with Mina's fiancé or Dorian Gray (Series One) or her eventual acceptance of Dr Sweet/Dracula's seductive wooing (Series Three). Being likewise torn between mind and desire, she tells Dorian that 'there are things within a soul that can never be unleashed [...] They would consume us.' The male characters, in turn, tend to be consumed by their inner demons, their frustrated male desire as well as external temptations and dangers.

'You're a very young man. I've long since learnt that the truth is mutable': Troubled Father and Son Relationships

Actual father/son conflicts such as between Sir Malcolm and Peter or Ethan Chandler and his father and similarly complicated surrogate father/son constellations such as Sir Malcolm and the rivalling 'siblings' Victor Frankenstein and Ethan (or Ethan and his three father figures Jared Talbot, Kaetenay and Sir Malcolm) are central to the series' representation of masculinity. As previously indicated, the relationship between the male characters is equally determined by conflict, differences and homosocial bonding. Vanessa's central role as the bond that keeps the heterogeneous group together is particularly expressed in the Series One episode 'Possession'. Here the male characters of the Sir Malcolm squad are forced to interact with each other while caring for the possessed Vanessa, being restricted to the increasingly claustrophobic confinements of Grandage Place. Their male bonding and simultaneous disagreements and accusations that emanate from the tense atmosphere and unnerving daily rituals of assisting Vanessa to fight her demons, their feelings of helplessness and their confrontation with their own misdeeds are visually articulated by several means: conversations between characters reveal a distance between the men as they are often positioned separately while one of them is occasionally presented out-of-focus. Furthermore, the characters – and this applies not only to the men – are repeatedly shown in framed shots, thereby accentuating their inner prison and alienation. During one conversation, Sir Malcolm, Victor and Ethan are placed in different positions in the dimly lit library: Sir Malcolm, the potential surrogate father figure for both, is presented sitting in the middle on a chair, Victor is positioned on a book ladder while Ethan, seemingly worried yet not ready to give up, is depicted in the foreground. The characters' complicated relationship is thus comprised in one shot: their differences, shared concerns, feelings of guilt and loss, mutual suffering, anger and critique of the other's respective misconduct, although they are similarly flawed. Sir Malcolm's heinous deeds in Africa are, for instance, compared to Ethan's bloody involvement in the Indian Wars, which still haunts him.

Sir Malcolm's and Victor Frankenstein's contradictory personalities are also repeatedly juxtaposed to stress both their differences and similarities.

Figure 7.2 Sir Malcolm and his boys: between male bonding, anger and despair in *Penny Dreadful*.

In one scene, for example, Victor gives advice to the older explorer regarding their newly gained responsibility for the vampirish Fenton (Olly Alexander), which simultaneously mirrors his ongoing struggle with the Creature. In another relevant scene of the episode 'Possession', he accuses Sir Malcolm, who initially uses Vanessa as bait to rescue Mina, but who later implicitly 'adopts' her, to have 'not a shred of decency left.' In contrast to the former, however, who comes to terms with his guilt and tries to be more human, Victor himself grows more monstrous throughout the next two series and behaves similarly immaturely, ruthlessly and selfishly and acknowledges his wrongdoings rather late. Moreover, Victor's and Sir Malcolm's encounter in the homosocial atmosphere of a gentleman's club at the beginning of the first series and their shared hallucinations of a confrontation with their conscience in the shape of their enraged families in the finale of Series Two illustrate their differences and parallels. At the beginning, both talk about their respective obsessions: hunting and exploring (Sir Malcolm) and transcending the threshold between life and death (Victor). Victor's rational and at the same time poetic use of language and Romantic hyperbole,[46] a manner which is echoed and surpassed by the Creature, is confronted with Sir Malcolm's more practical conduct. What both men have in common is their ruthless willingness to sacrifice almost everything to reach their personal goals.

Sir Malcolm's martial disposition and apparently strong-willed virility, his bonding with Sembene and his shortcomings as husband and father are paralleled by Dr Frankenstein's cold-bloodedness (that arises from both calculation *and* emotional despair), his hypocrisy and his double life. This reflects the critical interrogation of fatherhood, the role of the husband and even the medical profession at the fin de siècle[47] and demonstrates that 'reconfigurations of masculinity compensated for the loss of traditional, more assured forms of masculine identity and authority.'[48] As becomes especially apparent in the figure of Sir Malcolm and his compensatory preference for action, conquest and trophies such as the stuffed animals in his manor, 'British manliness [...] was also, however, deemed recuperable by way of the empire in the form of physical adventure and homosocial bonding.'[49] Additionally, Sir Malcolm's and Ethan Chandler's father's virile behaviour bear a certain resemblance as Jared Talbot equals Sir Malcolm in terms of overbearing conduct and irascibility. The latter, having learned his lesson from his failures and the destruction of his own family, resents being explicitly connected with Mr Talbot, who cannot forgive his son for the annihilation of his family. As a result, Sir Malcolm shoots Talbot to spare Ethan the guilt of parricide and to be able to move on personally.

Conclusion

In the series' finale, the characters' fates are then realigned. Vanessa Ives's death, which puts an end to her painful struggle, exposes the sudden void left behind by her absence and stresses, once again, her central role regarding the community's social cohesion: without her, the male characters of the Sir Malcolm squad seem at first grief-stricken and adrift. After a while, they hesitantly try to rebond with each other as is hinted at by Ethan's potentially staying with Sir Malcolm since both have lost their families. The 'immortals', the Creature/John Clare and Dorian Gray, both realise that they have to endure the pains of lasting solitude while Dracula simply vanishes. Whereas the heartbroken Creature, who claims to embody both technologised modernity while simultaneously finding solace in (Romantic) poetry, kneels before Vanessa's grave, Dorian Gray comes to terms with his actual inner emptiness, comparing himself to the lifeless portraits in his mansion. As the preceding analysis has demonstrated, the representation of masculinity in *Penny Dreadful* is marked by various contradictions, homosocial bonding and a blurring of the demarcation line between monstrosity and humanity. Moreover, the contradictory elements such as monstrosity and inner turmoil, or deviancy from heteronormative norms and patriarchal conduct, are defined by a coexistence of (supposedly) progressive and reactionary traits. They also encompass modernity and Romanticism (as in the case of the Creature/John Clare) as well as compensatory, escapist excess and actual realisation of one's misdeeds. The series both draws and comments upon prevalent notions of Victorian manhood such as imperial masculinity, while at the same time radically interrogating and deconstructing them by means of its exposure of gender as a cultural, performative construct, and its queer Gothic aesthetics and stance. Its nuanced depiction of ambivalent monstrosity in a thoughtfully constructed (neo-)Victorian setting, the characters' depth, and their special social interaction, make *Penny Dreadful* stand out from other period dramas and representations of monstrous Gothic masculinity. More specifically, the embodiment of troubled masculinity is rendered in such a way that the male characters, who may also – as has been pointed out – partly echo a few of the actors' previous roles, turn out to be still very appealing to a twenty-first-century audience. It therefore comes as no surprise that the sudden ending of the series was considered too abrupt and met with mixed feelings, ranging from blank astonishment or disappointment and sadness to outright criticism.

Notes

1. For further information regarding *Penny Dreadful*'s relation to the terminologically problematic penny fiction genre, see Benjamin Poore, 'The Transformed Beast: *Penny Dreadful*, Adaptation, and the Gothic', *Victoriographies*, 6/1 (2016), pp. 63–6.
2. See Judith Butler, *Gender Trouble: Feminism and the Subversion of Identity* (Abingdon and New York, 2014; originally published in 1990), pp. 163–80.
3. Andrew Smith and William Hughes, 'Introduction: Queering the Gothic', in A. Smith and W. Hughes (eds), *Queering the Gothic* (Manchester, 2009), p. 2.
4. Ardel Haefele-Thomas, *Queer Others in Victorian Gothic. Transgressing Monstrosity* (Cardiff, 2012), pp. 4–5.
5. Additionally, Christian Camargo (Dracula) already slipped into the role of an albeit vegetarian vampire in *The Twilight Saga: Breaking Dawn – Part 1* and *II* (2011/2012) and also took on the role of Henry Wotton in Duncan Roy's *The Picture of Dorian Gray* (2007). Rory Kinnear (the Creature/John Clare),

in turn, portrayed both Hamlet (2010) and Iago (2013) in stage productions of *Hamlet* (2010) and *Othello* (2013) for the National Theatre (which were broadcast across cinemas), and Harry Treadaway (Victor Frankenstein) played Joy Division drummer Stephen Morris alongside Sam Riley's inwardly torn Ian Curtis in Anton Corbijn's elegiac *Control* (2007).

6. The iconic character of the Wolf Man is also explicitly referenced in *Penny Dreadful* via the character of Ethan Chandler whose real name is revealed as Ethan Lawrence Talbot.
7. While Lauren Rocha's essay 'Angel in the House, Devil in the City: Explorations of Gender in Dracula and Penny Dreadful', *Critical Survey*, 28/1 (Oxford, 2016), pp. 30–9, for instance, pays attention to gender issues with regard to the series' construction of urban London, Chris Louttit, 'Victorian London Redux: Adapting the Gothic Metropolis', *Critical Survey*, 28/1 (2016), pp. 2–14, Sinan Akilli and Seda Öz, '"No More Let Life Divide...": Victorian Metropolitan Confluence in Penny Dreadful', *Critical Survey*, 28/1 (2016), pp. 15–29 and Dragos Manea, 'A Wolf's Eye View of London: Dracula, Penny Dreadful, and the Logic of Repetition', *Critical Survey*, xxviii/1 (2016), pp. 40–50, concentrate on the show's urban aspect and *Penny Dreadful*'s liberated take on adaptation.
8. Poore, 'The Transformed Beast', p. 72.
9. Smith and Hughes, 'Introduction', p. 7.
10. Carol Margaret Davison, 'The Victorian Gothic and Gender', in A. Smith and W. Hughes (eds), *The Victorian Gothic. An Edinburgh Companion* (Edinburgh, 2012), p. 132.
11. Jarlath Killeen, *Gothic Literature 1825–1914* (Cardiff, 2009), p. 9, quoted in Smith and Hughes, 'Introduction', p. 2.
12. Ibid.
13. It may further be noted that the constant vacillation between extreme inner states of mind, ranging from the displays of monstrosity to instances of emotional instability and the resulting inner turmoil of the male characters, is repeatedly linked to recurrent self-reflexively employed references to poets and poetic works such as John Milton's *Paradise Lost* (1667), William Wordsworth's and Samuel Taylor Coleridge's *Lyrical Ballads* (1798), John Keats's *Ode to a Nightingale* (1819), Percy Shelley's *Adonais* (1821), John Clare or Alfred Lord Tennyson. Poetry also functions as a special means of communication between characters (e.g., the Creature/John Clare and Vanessa Ives).
14. Smith and Hughes, 'Introduction', p. 5.
15. Ibid., p. 3.
16. See James Procter and Angela Smith, 'Gothic and Empire', in C. Spooner and E. McEvoy (eds), *The Routledge Companion to Gothic* (London, 2007), p. 95.
17. Smith and Hughes, 'Introduction', p. 4.
18. This is at the same time also an apt example of *Penny Dreadful*'s liberated and innovative take on its literary sources.

19. Davison, 'Victorian Gothic and Gender', p. 127.
20. Ibid.
21. In the episode 'Possession' (Series One).
22. See Poore, 'The Transformed Beast', p. 67.
23. Catherine Spooner, *Fashioning Gothic Bodies* (Manchester, 2004), p. 95.
24. Ibid.
25. Yet Vanessa mockingly critiques and defies patriarchal notions of docile Victorian womanhood at several instances throughout the series. At the end of Series Two she even rejects the deceitful offer of leading a bourgeois life full of lasting domestic bliss with Ethan Chandler.
26. Smith and Hughes, 'Introduction', p. 3; Haefele-Thomas, *Queer Others in Victorian Gothic*, pp. 2-3.
27. This is in accordance with Stoker's novel, see, for instance, Lisa Nystrom, 'Blood, Lust and the Fe/Male Narrative in Bram Stoker's Dracula (1992) and the Novel (1897)', in J. E. Browning and C. J. Picart (eds), *Draculas, Vampires, and Other Undead Forms: Essays on Gender, Race, and Culture* (Lanham, 2009), pp. 63-76.
28. See Judith Halberstam, *Skin Shows: Gothic Horror and the Technology of Monsters* (Durham, 1995), pp. 19-20.
29. Bette London, 'Mary Shelley, Frankenstein, and the Spectacle of Masculinity', PMLA, 108/2 (1993), p. 255.
30. Ibid., p. 262.
31. Halberstam, *Skin Shows*, p. 108.
32. Ibid., p. 16 and p. 4.
33. See, for instance, Joseph Bristow's edited collection *Oscar Wilde and Modern Culture* (Athens, OH, 2008).
34. Elisa Glick, *Materializing Queer Desire: Oscar Wilde to Andy Warhol* (Albany, NY, 2009), p. 7.
35. See Chantal Bourgault Du Coudray, *The Curse of the Werewolf: Fantasy, Horror and the Beast Within* (London, 2006), p. 66. She also highlights that the notion of the melancholy and self-destructive werewolf builds 'upon the familiar culture-nature, human-beast, civilized-primitive dichotomies underpinning nineteenth-century thought.' Ibid.
36. Cyndy Hendershot, *The Animal Within: Masculinity and the Gothic* (Ann Arbor, MI, 1998), p. 4.
37. Haefele-Thomas, *Queer Others in Victorian Gothic*, p. 2.
38. Ibid., p. 3.
39. Ibid., p. 7.
40. See Davison, 'The Victorian Gothic and Gender', p. 126 and p. 136.
41. Kelly Hurley, 'Science and the Gothic', in A. Smith and W. Hughes (eds), *The Victorian Gothic. An Edinburgh Companion* (Edinburgh, 2012), p. 172.
42. Smith and Hughes, 'Introduction', p. 12.
43. Ibid.
44. Ibid., pp. 14-32.

45. Ibid., p. 23.
46. He uses expressions such as 'deep bottom of the sea' or 'top of the highest mountain' in his passionate speech.
47. Smith, *Victorian Demons*, p. 2 and p. 7.
48. James Eli Adams, *Dandies and Desert Saints: Styles of Victorian Masculinity* (Ithaca, NY, 1995), p. 5.
49. Davison, 'The Victorian Gothic and Gender', p. 138.

8

Pathological Masculinities: Syphilis and the Medical Profession in *The Frankenstein Chronicles*

Katherine Byrne

Damaged, depressed and haunted by the loss of his wife and child, John Marlott, the central character of *The Frankenstein Chronicles* (ITV, 2015–) seems to fit neatly into a long tradition of British television detectives in shows with settings both historical and contemporary. From the eponymous *Luther* (BBC, 2010–) and *Wallander* (BBC, 2008–) to the subject of Jessica Saxon's chapter in this book, *Ripper Street*'s (BBC/Amazon, 2012–16) Edmund Reid, it is now commonplace for the lead in police dramas to be tortured by demons from their past, and by dangerous mental states which both disrupt and enhance their work. To be a male television detective is to be deeply troubled, either messily divorced or widowed, often addicted to either drugs or alcohol, and frequently grieving for the tragic loss of a child.[1] We might add, of course, that this is only part of a wider trend by which, 'since the 1990s, men have increasingly appeared across a range of social and aesthetic practices as troubled subjects, with Western masculinity reported to be in a critical state': this is one of the themes this book as a whole sets out to address.[2] If the television detective is in personal crisis, however, his work is compensation for his personal suffering. Trauma, addiction and mental illness, in these shows, makes the central character more perceptive, gifted with what was once known as 'female' intuition, and more emotionally astute while more psychologically disturbed. Indeed, the blurring of the line between the mental states of villain and hero is frequently what enables the latter's success in catching the former.

All this is true of the bereaved and tormented detective in *The Frankenstein Chronicles*, played by Sean Bean, whose unwavering commitment to his work stems from his guilt over the loss of his family, and whose frequently altered mental state points him in the right direction in this, his first murder case. In this regard, Saxon's argument about Edmund Reid – that 'the loss of his daughter ultimately makes him a better public servant' – is also true of Marlott: it seems that men on contemporary television are never allowed to 'have it all' in terms of personal and public success. Indeed, as I will discuss, the acquisition of power and knowledge in this show destroys families, as well as corrupting the (inevitably white, middle- and upper-class) men who already possess it and will do anything to keep it. Far from being trustworthy patriarchs, the politicians and doctors who fill this drama will betray colleagues, patients, servants and sisters to achieve their ends: the plot offers a soberingly cynical view of the establishment figures society is meant to trust.

Monstrous Doctors and the Legacy of Mary Shelley's *Frankenstein*

The Frankenstein Chronicles is especially interesting for its preoccupation with nineteenth-century disease and medicine, as it is set in the years leading up to the 1832 Anatomy Act, and hence explores the attempted legitimisation of the medical profession at an important moment in its history.[3] This connection between science, crime and the body will form the focus of this chapter, which locates the show's portrayal of masculinity in relation to contemporary television's ongoing fascination with the diseases, physicians, and especially the pathologists, of the past. It is notable that there are also important themes in other series like *Ripper Street, Penny Dreadful* (Sky/Showtime, 2014–16), and the recent *Jeykll and Hyde* (ITV, 2015), all of which feature doctors as central characters and are preoccupied with the damage which malevolent – and always male – medical knowledge can inflict on the human body. Despite the huge medical advances that have taken place since the periods in which these shows were set, they seem to reflect and reinforce an underlying distrust of medical professionals which persists today. This is after all a traditionally male profession which has a great deal of power over the rest of society, and which has long been regarded as exploiting that power.[4] Recent media coverage about doctors as sexual predators have further damaged the reputation of a profession whose ethics have been viewed with suspicion since the eighteenth century.[5]

With this in mind it is appropriate that the show functions as a loose postmodern adaptation of one of the first and most famous critiques of medical power and its practitioners: Mary Shelley's *Frankenstein: The Modern Prometheus* (1818). This is a novel which famously warns about the dangers of playing God, a 'myth [which] incorporates an unresolvable ambiguity about the work of the scientist at its most exciting and most dreadful'.[6] The characters here are inspired – or corrupted – by Shelley's novel, like her Victor attempting to recreate life with destructive consequences. One of *Penny Dreadful*'s plotlines operates on a similar principle with its version of the *Frankenstein* story, one which also draws attention to the flaws of its male scientist and the havoc he unleashes through his experimentation. As discussed in Caroline Langhorst's chapter of this book, however, that version of Victor is rather more troubled and hence more sympathetic than the unambiguously evil and unrepentant doctor-villains represented here. This six-part series opens with the horrific discovery of a child's body assembled from body parts, and follows the process by which Bean's detective tracks down the murderer/scientist. With this use of well-established detective tropes, *The Frankenstein Chronicles*, in many ways, feels as familiar as its famous source text, and indeed its fundamental premise is a popular one in contemporary period dramas like *Penny Dreadful*. As a *Guardian* review pointed out, this is just

> the latest drama that uses out-of-copyright literary characters in a new interpretation or setting, following on from *Penny Dreadful* and the current ITV *Jekyll and Hyde*, with the trend about to be extended by BBC1's *Dickensian* [...] it is also financially canny to plunder the vaults of out-of-copyright books.[7]

Pathological Masculinities

It is hence part of a recent trend in which television, instead of adapting classic literature in a more straightforward way, uses literary history as a starting point for new narratives. It is becoming increasingly commonplace, for example, to base shows around the further adventures of fictional creations: BBC One's hugely popular *Sherlock* (2010–) is perhaps the most well known of these. *The Frankenstein Chronicles* builds on this idea through the character of Marlott, who, in a further postmodern twist, is himself a version of another fictional creation: the hero of Bernard Cornwell's *Sharpe* novels, Richard Sharpe, as I will discuss. Furthermore, borrowing perhaps from shows like *City of Vice* (Channel 4, 2008) in which Henry Fielding is a detective, or even *Doctor Who* (BBC, 1963–89; 1996; 2005–) which over the years has had several appearances from Shakespeare and Dickens as characters,[8] this drama also features famous nineteenth-century writers like Mary Shelley, Charles Dickens and William Blake. In this metafictional Gothicism, 'this gory drama was rather like Frankenstein's monster itself, constructed from stitched together elements of *Sharpe, Sherlock, Oliver Twist, Ripper Street* and *Penny Dreadful*.'[9]

This show *is* unusual, however, in its gritty and grimy mise-en-scène, which is the polar opposite of the glossy appearance of something like *Penny Dreadful*:

> At times, the show feels like it was filmed in the end-days of the dinosaurs, when ash clouds blocked out the sun. You get the feeling that there are no shiny surfaces because absolutely nobody wants to see their own reflection, with old-fashioned clothes (even for the period) that might have been up-cycled from dish cloths, and faces so etched in dirt and by the hard lives they've led [...].[10]

Even more exceptionally, its hero is afflicted by syphilis, the least glamourous of nineteenth-century diseases, and it is this which is responsible for his mental illness and for the destruction of his family (his wife commits suicide after the death of their daughter from the congenital form of the disease). Other recent period dramas may portray the psychological problems attendant on modern and proto-modern masculinity, but they usually celebrate and objectify the male body, nonetheless. As Goodman and Moseley discuss in Chapter 3, the damaged body of the lead in shows like *Outlander* (Starz, 2015–) and

Poldark (BBC, 2015 –) serve to stress 'the vulnerability of the romantic, Alpha hero', not to undermine their appeal. Mental and even physical illness or disability are not usually allowed to interfere with physical attractiveness. Jamie Fraser's torments are offered up to the female viewer, after all, just as Ross Poldark's distinctive facial scar only serves to make him more desirable to his legions of fans, and even *Downton Abbey*'s (ITV, 2010 – 15) Matthew Crawley still looks personable in his wheelchair. In contrast Marlott's declining, chancre-scarred body displays a new and more gruesome development in the portrayal of damaged masculinity on the small screen, and one which seems to do away with the promise of romance usually offered by the period drama: it seems there can be no love interest for someone dying of a transmissible venereal disease. Here, we have come a long way from the virile Mr Darcy emerging clean, refreshed and desirable from his lake.

A gritty and realistic portrayal of disease is in keeping with the themes of the show, however. *The Frankenstein Chronicles* is also interested in public health, and uses its medical plot as a lens through which to question some of the most controversial, divisive and topical aspects of medical science today: abortion, sexually transmitted disease, human embryo research and plastic surgery. Of course the choice of *Frankenstein* as a source text is essential for a show which wishes to explore these concerns, given that Shelley's novel is 'our first and still one of our best cautionary tales about scientific research [...].'[11] The questions which surround medical ethics are unchanged whether the science in question is galvanism in the nineteenth century or stem cell research in the twenty-first: this is why this novel remains a timeless and endlessly popular and much-adapted text. 'Mary Shelley asks, if y had been achieved by whatever means, what would be the moral consequences?':[12] this show invites the contemporary viewer to do the same.

An Unlikely 'Hero': Marlott and Syphilis

These modern anxieties mostly find their expression through *The Frankenstein Chronicles'* hero, his illness, and his 'treatment'. Bean's Marlott, struggling with the shame and stigma of his sexually transmitted disease, invokes for the viewer many of the contemporary prejudices which have surrounded HIV/AIDS. Marlott is portrayed as a social and sexual pariah, trying to keep his disease secret from others and constantly anxious about its most visible symbol, the chancre on his hand. This need for secrecy is justified in the final episode when his illness becomes known to his colleagues and is used against him by those he suspects. As a result he is deemed no longer capable of doing his job and his – entirely justified – suspicions are disregarded as syphilitic madness by his superiors and employees alike. Even his sidekick Nightingale judges him harshly when he learns of the disease: 'Why do you wear these gloves, sir? I know what *it* is ... I'd like to take Flora back to my lodging ... I'm thinking of her. Her safety, sir. I need that gun too [...].' No longer deemed fit either to be Flora's guardian or to be in possession of a weapon, Marlott's personal and professional life is over. This onscreen discrimination reminds us of the ways in which those afflicted with HIV/AIDS were stigmatised in the late twentieth century, and the prejudices they may still face today, both in the developing world and in the West, where there is currently controversy about the cost of drugs which prevent transmission of the disease.[13] This is unusual subject matter for even the edgiest period television, but it is only one of several themes in the show which invite debate about the most pressing issues associated with the modern body and the role of modern medicine.

Marlott's cure, too, opens up discourse about science and ethics in a way appropriate to Shelley's novel and to our own society, while criticising the professionals who take their responsibilities lightly. The medicine we see practised on the show is a mix of traditional approaches, accurate for the time, and more exciting, if somewhat anachronistic, proto-modern experimentation, mostly by the show's doctor-villains. The plot reminds us of the old-fashioned, brutal prescription of mercury for syphilis, and shows us futile attempts at galvanism and (even more anachronistically, for it was not practised until the 1930s) a futile attempt at early CPR: all of which are used to condemn the arrogance and ignorance of the medical profession who blindly experiment with their patients' lives. It also, however, displays the unconventional talent of Lord Hervey, a doctor of alternative (very alternative, as it turns out) therapies, who is considered 'a quack' by the medical establishment, but whose unorthodox methods are ahead of his time. He practises highly efficient and safe abortion methods – Flora is up and about the same day after she chooses to end her pregnancy – and what is presumably meant to be early stem cell research (we are told that Flora's foetus is the source of the experimental drug which he administers to Marlott, and which in the final episode brings him back from the dead). Hervey is highly skilled, but he takes and gives life with the arrogance of Victor Frankenstein, and with even fewer scruples, given that the bodies he uses for experimentation are still alive. He is, however, only one of several abusive, dangerous doctors in the drama. The father of Flora's child, Garnet Chester, is a sexual predator; Sir William Chester is a murderer, and both are deeply contemptuous of their working-class patients: 'Inbreds. If it weren't for us they'd all be wallowing in scrofula', as Garnet remarks. Of course, it is not only physicians who are monstrous here: almost all the male characters are corrupt, from the pimp Billy Oates to the ruthless Home Secretary Sir Robert Peel himself, who blackmails his political rivals in order to have his bill passed.

This drama does, then, make a fascinating comment on the nature of recent televisual masculinities: whether contaminated and contaminating like Marlott, or manipulative and dangerous like the power-hungry physicians and politicians he investigates, the men in this show are inherently and inevitably pathological. This is further displayed by the chaos which follows Marlott as he investigates this crime. Like late Victorian social investigator W. T. Stead (infamous author of 'The Maiden Tribute of Modern Babylon' in the *Pall Mall Gazette*) he penetrates the London Underworld to save children from harm, but despite his best intentions endangers them along the way. His unofficial ward, Flora, is repeatedly placed in danger by his care: firstly she is placed with Hervey as an unwitting spy, then she nearly dies after being used as bait to trap a group of white slave traders, and eventually she is murdered in order for Hervey to frame Marlott for the crime. Indeed, the viewer is left uncertain about who has in fact killed her. It is clear that Marlott has been set up, but less clear whether his hand has still committed this deed, albeit under the influence of forcibly administered drugs. In fact, either way he is responsible for her death, as he, paranoid and angry, has previously imprisoned her in his house, and hence exposes her to danger. The whole concept of the 'hero' is thus questioned in this show. Only the appropriately named Nightingale is authentically good – gentle, religious and compassionate, if quick to judge and condemn Marlott's immorality, as we have seen – but he is also the most ineffectual of all the characters. He falls in love with Flora, but he is constantly thwarted in his attempt to make a family with her by other men, who impregnate her, abort her child, abduct her and finally murder her just before their wedding, leaving him powerless at every point. Perhaps because he is the only black character in the drama, Nightingale lacks the authority to intervene in the actions of the rich white men he polices, and decent though he may be, he always is just too late at every point. Hence his failure to intervene in time contrasts unfavourably with the other men in the series. In this world, to be 'manly', able and successful is to be morally questionable. Hervey is a sociopath, but he is also a genius. The Home Secretary is corrupt and manipulative, but he is also powerful and driven. And Marlott, dangerous, unbalanced and even violent though he might be, does in the end solve the mystery and frees the imprisoned abducted child Alice.

Power and Education

If this drama is cynical in its portrayal of masculinity, it is even more severe about the wealthy and privileged in society. There are some working-class criminals here, but they tend to be motived by poverty, rather than being actually evil, and as a result are not at the centre of the plot. The real villains in this rather anti-establishment show belong to the highly educated professional classes, and it is they who must be policed and punished by the lower-class and less educated Marlott. Julie Anne Taddeo's chapter on the televisual representation of World War I indicates a shift in focus from the officers – who once would have been at the heart of the narrative – to the humble Private in recent period drama, and we could say that this newly democratic interest in the hero from humble origins extends to this series too. Initially a member of the Thames River police until he is unexpectedly promoted by Peel, Marlott is perhaps not quite working class, but has neither wealth nor a sophisticated education. His skills are earthy and based on observation and experience: he knows the patterns of the tides, for example, but performs basic empirical experiments of his own to determine the source of the body. He is able to read and write but his literary education is limited: he has never heard of William Blake, nor of Mary Shelley's famous novel, and so we see him reading it – perhaps like the viewer after watching this series – for the first time. (By the end of the series, of course, so immersed is he in this Gothic world that he has become a character: the Creature itself.) We can see here the evolution of his literary education, but he never really progresses to middle-class status, constantly oppressed by his social superiors and finally dying upon the scaffold alongside the humble criminals he had previously captured.

However, this lack of social mobility is not only the reason Marlott is constantly underestimated by his bosses in the Home Office, but is probably a positive attribute in a rather anti-intellectual series which seems to distrust the upper classes, and in which education and knowledge is constantly seen to be malevolent. Almost every middle- or upper-class character has something to hide: Mary and Percy Shelley's pursuit of knowledge is responsible for the untimely death of James Hogg; the aristocracy represented by the Hervey siblings are immersed in secrets and lies; and from the Home Secretary downwards, the politicians here are corrupt and will resort to anything, including blackmail, to achieve their ends. Only working- or lower-middle class characters like Nightingale or Flora are intrinsically 'good': even the deeply religious Lady Hervey is implicated somehow in her brother's crimes. Marlott has been used throughout by those with the money and power he lacks, and his final fate is a consequence of the arrogance of one whose education and status make him feel entitled to use and exploit the working-class body as he wishes. For a programme which demands a certain literary knowledge in its viewer, *The Frankenstein Chronicles* seems determined to uphold the 'ordinary' working man against those more educated, more sophisticated, more healthy and even more handsome members of the upper classes. Hence the final scene of the last episode is a significant one: Marlott, after stabbing his jailer (Hervey's implausibly loyal valet, surely a subversive reference to *Downton*) is shown running away from Hervey's beautiful country house where he has been imprisoned, in a rejection of the subject matter of conventional 'heritage' period drama. Instead of a focus on nostalgia, the stately home here has become a source of corruption and death, and instead of being charmed by the lives of the rich, we see the sinister abuses of power that lie behind their privilege.

Changing Masculinities: *Sharpe* for the New Millennium?

Throughout I have been arguing that this show offers an interesting evolution of the 'classic' period drama, grittier and more corporeal than we are accustomed to seeing on our screens. In this regard it shares an

Pathological Masculinities

approach with some other recent historical fictions discussed in this book, namely *Banished* (BBC, 2015) and *Peaky Blinders* (BBC, 2013 –), but, with a diseased hero as well as dangerous medical villains, the view of masculinity it offers is even darker and more pathologised. This has much to do with the important casting of Sean Bean in the lead role. Bean has a long history in period drama, and one which is notable for his working-class, Northern Otherness from the kind of old Etonian actors who usually play these parts.[14] One of his first roles was Mellors in the BBC's *Lady Chatterley's Lover* (1993) and the rake Lovelace in *Clarissa* (BBC, 1991) but he really found fame in the 1990s through his portrayal of Richard Sharpe in the popular long-lived ITV adaptation of Bernard Cornwell's novels. As Sian Harris points out, 'it is now more than 22 years since Bean first appeared as Sharpe, but the character retains a powerful hold on his reputation.'[15] Harris suggests that even the major HBO show *Game of Thrones* (2011 –) makes reference to *Sharpe* (ITV, 1993 – 2008), and certainly *The Frankenstein Chronicles* deliberately and repeatedly does so. Bean is shown unpacking his old uniform, which is the distinctly green – rather than red – uniform of the 95th Regiment of Foot (Rifles) (made famous by his former self in the earlier show) in one scene, and in another a character hums its theme tune, 'Over the Hills and Far Away'. This intertextuality is not simply there as an in-joke for period drama fans, as some critics have assumed:[16] rather it complicates the characterisation in the drama. Their name may have changed, but Marlott seems to function here as Sharpe 20 years later, a sad, disillusioned and aging version of his young and dynamic televisual alter ego. Cornwell's hero began his existence, in 'Sharpe's Rifles' (1993), as a handsome but working-class Sergeant in the Army during the Napoleonic wars who is unexpectedly field promoted to Lieutenant for saving the life of a superior officer. As Harris puts it, 'At a time when officer ranks were usually the preserve of the socially and financially privileged, Sharpe is a working-class outsider who gains his promotion through merit and bloodyminded determination.'[17] His intelligence, courage and unorthodox methods ensure his continued success over both his snobbish and prejudiced fellow officers, as well as the French he is fighting. Marlott, we are told, served in the same regiment, but brings back something much more sinister than medals from the war: he says his syphilis is 'contracted [...] during the Peninsula Campaign' (and he can thus be regarded as another of the men damaged by warfare, of which there are many in this book). He, too, is frustrated frequently by his struggles with the British upper classes, of course, and despite his personal qualities, has rather less success overcoming discrimination than Sharpe: humble origins can be forgotten, perhaps, but a sexually transmitted disease cannot. Indeed, the evolution of this character indicates interesting changes in the period drama, and particular in the hero, in the 20 years that have passed. As Richard Sharpe, Bean was handsome and vibrant: if too working-class to be Mr Darcy, his appearance in the uniform of the Napoleonic wars was at least reminiscent of the kind of officer the younger Bennet sisters might have pursued in *Pride and Prejudice*. Bean has played more rugged and unconventional leading men in middle age, however (perhaps best summed up by his appearance as facially scarred Bond villain Alec Trevelyn in *Goldeneye* (1995)) and as Marlott he offers a very different version of masculinity for the new millennium. Here, he is, as one critic notes, 'quite shorn of his Sharpe good looks and allowed to just get on with being a good actor.'[18] This does not go quite far enough, for in fact the camera seems determined to display his body in a highly unflattering light. In keeping with the gritty theme of the series, his clothes look scruffy and grubby, and when he is viewed without them, his slightly flabby body is far from the toned physique he displays in his other roles. And, of course, his desirability is further compromised by the disease which makes his sexuality so pathological, and which is empathised rather than disguised by the stained bandage on his hand. If he is a version of Sharpe, it is Sharpe ravaged by time, illness and grief.

This series, then, seems to resist what we might term the *Poldark* formula for success: from Colin Firth's emergence dripping from the lake in *Pride and Prejudice* (BBC, 1995) onward, period drama frequently ensures its popularity by offering up a handsome male lead to the female or homoerotic gaze. Sean Bean may be, in the wake of *Game of Thrones*, still a desirable and bankable star, but there is a deliberate attempt here to undermine his physical appeal, as Benjamin Ross, the director, acknowledged in an interview while writing the drama:

> About a year ago, I was having a discussion about this new project, and I said that it could be quite exciting to use a very famous English star. One of the things I want to do with the main character,

however, is to rot him over the course of the film. He's a kind of a gangster character, and then he has maybe syphilis, and bits of him keep dropping off, he loses his hair, he loses a bit of his nose, there are all these things that come out [...] It's kind of slightly comic and it's horrible at the same time. And at the end, he's just a bit of worm, really.

And I thought that it was quite good having a star doing it because if you do have a star in that role, people will be attracted and they'll go see him. And you can push him – and the audience – into more extreme situations. Of course if it's somebody beautiful whom they love, are attracted to or want to identify with, you have it even more. That to me seems a creative use of a star [...][19]

In the final version of the show the grotesquely comic possibilities of syphilis were not exploited in quite the same way as Ross anticipated. The patient tragically suffering from the tertiary form of the disease who we are introduced to in Episode Three is missing their lips and nose, and hence is a horrifying reminder of Marlott's future appearance: there is no dark humour here. And Bean's character does 'rot', in mental and moral as well as physical terms, over the course of the production. In this his body is reflective of the slowly industrialising London in which the drama is set, which as critics have noted looks 'visibly decaying, as though the city itself is a great bloated, rotten corpse full of noxious gasses and ripe for autopsy or expulsion.'[20] He could hardly be a more bleak symbol of a masculinity in crisis: a former soldier who once had his place and is now alone and adrift in a dark and rapidly changing world. The same could perhaps be said of Ross Poldark, of course, but that is where the similarity ends.

There is some light at the end of the tunnel for Bean's Marlott, however. Condemned to a life of celibacy by his infectious disease, he is nonetheless pursued throughout by the lovely Lady Jemima Hervey (Vanessa Kirby) who even from their first meeting is inexplicably attracted to him in a way which disregards their class and age differences and his downtrodden and indeed pathological appearance. It is as if she, in some metafictional way, seems able to recognise his former existence as a heartthrob, or his potential to become one again, as we will see. And, indeed, her patience is finally rewarded – as is Bean's fanbase! – by his bodily transformation in the final episode. After death on the scaffold and resurrection by Lord Hervey, Marlott's 'new' body is revealed, naked, to himself and the viewer.

His torso is crisscrossed by culturally familiar Frankenstein-style scars from the surgery he has undergone, and it is unclear how much of the body he now possesses is made up of parts of another, but it is nonetheless more youthful, more muscular and more conventionally desirable (as well as healed from his syphilis) than his former self. The moment when he is first confronted with himself in front of a mirror, supported by his doctor, recalls the 'big reveal' of a contemporary 'makeover' show, and hence in this way it comes to function as a powerful metaphor for perhaps the most controversial of modern medical practices: cosmetic surgery. In this way the series plays around with our contemporary ideas about beauty, for here nature's decay is improved upon by the surgeon's skill. In this the viewer who might desire Bean, and who at any rate is certainly pleased at his salvation, is implicated in the activity of the show's villain. Like Jemima, we might be appalled at Hervey's murderous methods, but we presumably approve of his results, which have restored Marlott not only to life, but to all that is more valued by the modern world: youthfulness, desirability and the promise of a romantic relationship. The show, then, is clear in its condemnation of doctors, but is less morally certain about the medicine they practice. And, it both critiques and reinforces the conventions surrounding the hero of period drama. Hervey's 'makeover' feminises and infantilises Marlott, who is aligned with his previous victims, young girls, and who like them is violated, objectified and finally reduced to his body. Several scenes of him being spoon-fed by Hervey and Jemima reinforce this further. In the drama's final scenes, however, this is reversed: Marlott forms an alliance with (and passionately kisses) Jemima, kills his jailer and escapes. His compromised masculinity is seemingly restored, and in these regards at least he finally becomes a more conventional hero, with the promise of a future both sexual and actual – thanks to the nefarious practices of modern science.

Conclusion

Visiting Marlott in jail before he is hanged in Episode Six, Lord Hervey explains his accusations as the result of syphilitic paranoia: it is a common feature of the disease that 'the patient misconstrues his doctor as the source of all his agony.' Hervey's remark is ironic, for *The Frankenstein Chronicles* does place the blame for much that is wrong with this world on its

Pathological Masculinities

Figure 8.1 Marlott resurrected from the dead by Hervey in *The Frankenstein Chronicles*.

professional classes generally and its physicians in particular. Wealthy, educated and powerful, these men have the ability to impact the poverty and squalor which we see in every scene of the drama, but instead they bring death and devastation to the poor. This is most clearly symbolised by the political change which forms the backdrop to the plot: the 1832 Anatomy Act has been interpreted by left-wing critics (then and now) as an attack on, and punishment of, the poor, who from this point on risked dissection by a medical profession which valued progress and knowledge over humanity. This anxiety about medical and scientific discovery was, of course, also articulated by Mary Shelley's novel: as one critic notes, 'the fundamental flaw that the text makes so manifest is science's lack of humanity [...] [It] creates a power not only alien to and lacking in human values but also capable of their effacement.'[21] These questions about the ethics of medicine – and the morality of those who practise it – have never really gone away: that is why *Frankenstein* remains such a popular and much-adapted text. Furthermore, they are accompanied in Britain by debates about the role of an NHS frequently under attack about its efficiency and effectiveness while constantly threatened by austerity, continued public spending cuts and fears surrounding privatisation. In other words, public health has become a site of political struggle, argued over by (still) predominantly male and predominantly upper-class politicians. Hence it is difficult not to read this drama of, in Marlott's words, 'monstrosity [which] reaches to the very heart of our government' as an anti-establishment parable, representing not so much a crisis in masculinity as the lengths the middle- and upper-class male will go to hold onto his power. Saving this society from its upper classes, however, is Marlott, an unusually asexual central character who is damaged and violent, and yet functions as a kind of Christ-like figure, defined throughout by the wound on his hand. Marlott becomes a martyr oppressed and rejected by the dark and evil world he inhabits, finally dying – on the scaffold if not on a cross – for his convictions and rebellion, and then finally reborn, scarred by modernity, as a new type of hero, perhaps appropriate for a new age of period drama. As well as being part of a recent trend to 'reanimate' the classic novel adaptation, this show seems determined to reassemble and transform the male lead. Bean's character is part monstrous Creature, part anti-establishment detective and part fallen sex symbol. And, as *The Frankenstein Chronicles* has just returned for a second series amid widespread praise for his performance, this latest formula for televisual masculinity seems to be a successful one.

Notes

1. See also Rustin 'Rust' Cohle in Series One of *True Detective* (HBO, 2014–), Martin Rohde in *Broen/Bron/The Bridge* (SVT1, 2011–), and Hank in *Stranger Things* (Netflix, 2016–).
2. Fintan Walsh, *Male Trouble: Masculinity and the Performance of Crisis* (Basingstoke, 2010), p. 2.
3. This was the Act of Parliament (under consideration since 1828 and finally passed in 1832) which allowed doctors and medical students access to the corpses of the workhouse poor for dissection, to discourage the illegal trade in cadavers. While this provided more opportunity for medical practice and progress, it was highly unpopular because it was regarded as effectively a punishment for poverty. For further discussion see Ruth Richardson, *Death, Dissection and the Destitute: The Politics of the Corpse in Pre-Victorian Britain* (Chicago, 1987).
4. Most famously the case of Harold Shipman, the Leeds GP who killed more than 200 of his patients, and most recently, disgraced surgeon Ian Paterson, jailed in 2017 for performing unnecessary surgery on hundreds of women.
5. See, for example, the scandals reported by the BBC at http://www.bbc.co.uk/news/uk-england-cambridgeshire-30273548 and http://www.bbc.co.uk/news/uk-england-stoke-staffordshire-32819187 (accessed 6 November 2016).

6. Andrew Spicer, *Typical Men: The Representation of Masculinity in Popular British Cinema* (London, 2003), p. 61.
7. Mark Lawson, 'Frankenstein TV: what happens when literary classics drop out of copyright', *Guardian*, 16 November 2015. Available at https://www.theguardian.com/tv-and-radio/tvandradioblog/2015/nov/16/frankenstein-tv-what-happens-when-literary-classics-drop-out-of-copyright (accessed 21 July 2017).
8. Ben Lawrence and Catherine Gee, '*Doctor Who*'s best historical figures', *Telegraph*, 7 September 2012. Available at http://www.telegraph.co.uk/culture/tvandradio/doctor-who/9528099/Doctor-Whos-best-historical-figures.html (accessed 21 July 2017).
9. Michael Hogan, '*The Frankenstein Chronicles*, Review', *Telegraph*, 11 November 2015. Available at http://www.telegraph.co.uk/culture/tvandradio/tv-and-radio-reviews/11989543/The-Frankenstein-Chronicles-review-eerily-effective.html (accessed 21 July 2017).
10. Carl Wilson, '*The Frankenstein Chronicles* Series 1, Episode 1 – "A World Without God"', *Popmatters*. Available at http://www.popmatters.com/review/the-frankenstein-chronicles-series-1-episode-1-a-world-without-god/#ixzz4HPZQO37ehttp://www.popmatters.com/review/the-frankenstein-chronicles-series-1-episode-1-a-world-without-god/ (accessed 16 November 2015).
11. Robert Wexelblatt, 'The Ambivalence of *Frankenstein*', *Arizona Quarterly*, 36 (1980), pp. 101–17.
12. James Rieger, 'Introduction', *Frankenstein, Or the Modern Prometheus: The 1818 Text* (Chicago, 1982), p. xxvii.
13. The availability of new prophylactic drugs like PrEp for HIV has stirred up debate and revealed strong public prejudices about the role of medicine in sexually transmitted disease, especially regarding the cost to the NHS. For further discussion, see the report of a recent High Court ruling at http://www.bbc.co.uk/news/health-36946000 (accessed 25 July 2016).
14. For discussion of Bean's working-class roots and 'outsider' status, see interview with him at http://www.compleatseanbean.com/mainfeatures-104.html (accessed 10 November 2016).
15. Sian Harris, 'Sharper, better, faster, stronger: Performing Northern Masculinity and the legacy of Sean Bean's Sharpe', *Journal of Popular Television*, 4/2 (2016), p. 247.
16. Wilson, 'A World Without God'.
17. Harris, 'Sharper, better, faster, stronger', p. 240.
18. Euan Ferguson, 'The week in TV: *The Frankenstein Chronicles; London Spy; Peep Show; Unforgotten*', *Guardian*, 15 November 2015. Available at https://www.theguardian.com/tv-and-radio/2015/nov/15/week-in-tv-frankenstein-chronicles-london-spy-peep-show-unforgotten (accessed 2 November 2016).

19. Henri Béhar, 'Interview with Benjamin Ross on "The Young Poisoner's Handbook"', *Filmscouts*. Available at http://www.filmscouts.com/scripts/interview.cfm?File=ben-ros (accessed 15 August 2016).
20. Wilson, 'A World Without God'.
21. Fred Botting, *Making Monstrous: Frankenstein, Criticism, Theory* (Manchester, 1991), p. 164.

PART III

Masculinities from World War I to the Cold War

9

'The war is done. Shut the door on it!': The Great War, Masculinity and Trauma in British Period Television

Julie Anne Taddeo

As Emma Hanna notes, television has long been the main provider of visual interpretations of World War I (1914–18), feeding the popular perception of the war as 'a conflict which was fought for reasons no one could remember, resulting in Britain losing her brightest and best, a lost generation which would never be replaced.'[1] Since the 1960s British period drama in particular has relied heavily on this standard narrative, reinforced by Alan Clark's 'lions led by donkeys' thesis, the re-discovery of Wilfred Owen and other 'Soldier Poets' and memoirs and histories that have tended to prioritise the experience of the upper-class, highly literate male officer.[2] The pessimism and anti-establishment mood of the 1970s set the tone, for example, of the fourth series of *Upstairs, Downstairs* (ITV, 1971–5) in which aristocratic son, James Bellamy (Simon Williams), gallantly volunteers only to return home shell-shocked, bitter and in desperate need of countering the lies of government propaganda, a theme that played well to an audience commemorating the 60th anniversary of the war and who still remembered loved ones who had taken part in it. Determined to leave behind a written testament of his experiences should he die at the front, James tells his family, 'there can't be any dispute, any argument, that's worth so many lives [...] the dead died for nothing [...] slaughtered like cattle and for what? A few yards of mud.' By the time of *Blackadder Goes Forth* (BBC, 1989), this oft-repeated narrative of youthful idealism drowned in the mud of the Western Front seemed ripe for parody (Hugh Laurie's aristocratic character, the naïve Lt. The Honourable George Colthurst St. Barleigh, describes himself and his classmates as 'the last of the leap froggers from the Golden Summer of 1914 [...] crashingly superior fellows, fine, clean-limbed'), but the mocking tone of *Blackadder* did not negate what for viewers and critics alike was 'the whole terrible horror of war, the waste, the finality, the absurdity.'[3] Indeed, even *Blackadder* ended its series on a sombre note, with the gang going 'over the top' as the final scene faded to a field covered in red poppies. Writing in the *Guardian* in 1999, Desmond Christy concluded: 'What with Wilfred Owen, *Oh! What A Lovely War* and *Blackadder*, we know what to make of World War I. Upper-class twits running the show, the ordinary, dispensable soldier suffering the bullet, the shell and the bayonet and dying in the muddy, rat-infested trenches.'[4]

Historians have exhaustively documented the eagerness with which so many upper-class men volunteered in 1914, representing, at least in part, the culmination and triumph of Victorian ideals that equated manly behaviour with patriotism, courage and sacrifice. Oscar Wilde's son Cyril, for example, asked 'nothing better to end in honourable battle for my King and Country'[5] (he died in May 1915 at Neuve Chappelle). But did *all* men, such as the 'ordinary dispensable soldier', or for that matter, even those among the elite officer class, express such sentiments and aspire to such a demanding ideal of masculinity? What of those who resisted out of pacifism or fear or were denied service due to age or infirmity? On the British side alone five million men served in the armed forces, all from different backgrounds, education and ages; men served for varying lengths of time in different roles and not all were wounded or killed; in short, 'not all men experienced the same war in the same way.'[6] Samuel Hynes adds that during this war the Victorian ideal of the 'soldier hero' inevitably adapted to the horrific conditions of the trenches because 'once the soldier was seen as a victim, the idea of the hero became unimaginable';[7] to be 'manly' and 'heroic', therefore, sometimes only required 'endurance' and survival.[8] Furthermore, the war prompted the emergence of other male

'The war is done. Shut the door on it!'

identities, with no clear division among any of them: '[T]he martial jostled for space with the coward, the frightened boy, the conscientious objector, and the shell shock victim.'[9]

In recent years, as historians move beyond the notion of a 'universal wartime masculinity',[10] so, too, is the period drama attempting a more 'bottom-up' approach, to include previously ignored perspectives and experiences, particularly those of working-class men in and out of the trenches. While *Upstairs, Downstairs*' footman Eddie suffered from shell shock, the series was dominated by aristocratic James's trauma, and the soldiers of the other most prominent war-themed TV drama, *Testament of Youth* (BBC, 1979) were all public school graduates, musicians and poets among them. Privates remained largely absent or silent in period dramas, or, as in *Blackadder Goes Forth* (which parodies period dramas about the war), were represented by the clueless cockney Baldrick, who didn't seem to mind the flooded trenches and in fact made coffee out of their very mud! The current crop of television programmes produced in the wake of the war's centenary, including *Downton Abbey* (ITV, 2010–15), *Peaky Blinders* (BBC, 2013-), *Mr Selfridge* (ITV, 2013–16), among others, occasionally fall victim to the long-held popular obsession with 'mud, blood, and poetry'[11] (even hardened gangster Thomas Shelby in *Peaky Blinders* twice quotes 'In the Bleak Mid-Winter' when faced with death, co-opting a narrative usually reserved for upper-class officers). These newer TV series, however, complement recent historians' efforts at a more nuanced examination of 'the effects of war on masculine ideals',[12] imagining the multiple ways in which British men – soldiers *and* non-combatants – struggled with masculine identity and coped with trauma (physical and emotional), often long after the war ended.

Uniforms and Masculine Authority

In *Upstairs, Downstairs*, Richard Bellamy (David Langton), the master of 165 Eaton Place, and a Conservative MP who espouses many liberal sentiments, refuses to toast Britain's declaration of war against Germany: 'I refuse to drink to war. From battle and murder and death, Good Lord deliver us.' He echoes what many viewers in 1974 were surely thinking, knowing in hindsight that Lord Bellamy's son was not in for 'a great adventure' after all. Forty years later Julian Fellowes returns to this moment in another aristocratic household. In Series Two, Episode Three of *Downton Abbey*, Lord Grantham (Hugh Bonneville) observes, 'The world was in a dream before the war but now it's woken up... and so must we', warning the audience that the Edwardian age they had come to mythologise (with the help of *Downton*'s shamelessly nostalgic first series) is over and to prepare for tragedy. In *Edwardians on Screen*, Katherine Byrne argues that *Downton* offers a 'particularly modern' view of the war as 'futile',[13] a view consistent with the narrative promoted by memoirists and historians since the 1920s (and by earlier period dramas like *Upstairs, Downstairs*), and which continues to resonate with twenty-first-century audiences who themselves have witnessed far too many 'futile' wars in recent memory. Nevertheless, the declaration of war inspires more patriotic reactions among the residents of Downton than those expressed at Eaton Place. Even Isobel Crawley (Penelope Wilton), usually the most progressive thinker at Downton, proclaims, 'I don't want my son to die either, but this is a war and we must be in it together, high and low, rich and poor' and insists that any eligible male servants still not in khaki sign up immediately. The grand size of Downton, with its larger family and staff than the London townhouse of *Upstairs, Downstairs*, allows Fellowes to present the full spectrum of male participation (and lack of) in the war, from the heir of the estate who proudly volunteers to those who, according to Mrs Crawley, shirk their manly duty.

In her study *Men of War: Masculinity and the First World War in Britain*, historian Jessica Meyer argues that no event has more affected our 'social and cultural understanding of what it was to be a man' than the Great War, with popular culture during and since the war prioritising 'the authority of the man who was there.'[14] Overnight, by donning khaki, boys were transformed into men, as we see in the opening episode of *The Passing Bells* (BBC, 2014), when working-class lads of 18 exit the registration office in their new uniforms and are hailed by onlookers as England's heroes. Fellowes, however, compels his audience to contemplate the experience, indeed the emotional trauma, of men who, accustomed to having authority before the war, now, due to reasons of age or lack of 'fitness', will be excluded from this 'sphere of masculine attainment.'[15] Lord Grantham, already late middle-aged, eagerly dons his old uniform but soon realises it will be only 'for show', lamenting that 'it appears they (the army) don't want me.' Mr Grove (Tom Goodman-Hill), *Mr Selfridge*'s

'The war is done. Shut the door on it!'

fatherly store manager, also recognises that 'war is a young man's game' but even he, by the last year of the war, will serve at the front, fulfilling the definition, according to Lord Grantham, of 'a *real* soldier.'[16] TV veterans of previous wars share this sentiment; in the finale of *Poldark*'s (BBC, 2015–) second series, the hero (Captain Ross Poldark played by Aidan Turner), now a 'settled' man with a successful mine and family, unearths and lovingly caresses his old uniform from the North American colonial war, contemplating a return to his regiment to fight against the French on the continent. As the head of the estate, Lord Grantham likewise calls his own manliness into question as he witnesses the new type of service being performed by his male staff: 'So both my footmen have gone to the war while I cut ribbons and make speeches [...] I envy their self-respect and I envy their ability to sleep at night', and, perhaps even more shamefully, he witnesses the bustling activity of his wife and daughters as they transform part of the Abbey into a convalescent home for officers. Surrounded at home, once his domain of power, by people in uniform – of the soldier and nurse – Lord Grantham eventually seeks refuge in a flirtation with a maid yet he has become so impotent that he cannot bring himself to consummate his desire for her. As Byrne notes, depression and the loss of identity due to *non*-service, such as that experienced by Lord Grantham, represent forms of trauma usually ignored in period dramas (and histories) about the war.[17]

The World War I nursing drama *The Crimson Field* (BBC, 2015) echoes Lord Grantham's anxieties about the uniform as the only true signifier of British masculinity. In Episode Six, a minister tells the recovering soldiers in the field hospital ward that, when they return home, it is their 'God-given duty' to tell any man they see *not* in uniform that 'he has no right to call himself a man.' But this task is already being performed back home, not by other men in uniform, but by women. As historian Nicoletta F. Gullace notes, women played an active role in the recruiting campaign, wielding 'the language of sexual shame to coerce young men into military service'.[18] *Downton* employs what has by now become a familiar image of this type of shaming power, when women at a hospital benefit hand out white feathers to the male servants who have just waited on them, as Lady Edith (Laura Carmichael), concurs, 'it's hard to watch healthy young men do nothing.' When handed the feather, William Mason (Thomas Howes), who has been itching to sign up but whose father has been withholding permission, innocently asks, 'What is it?', and for any viewer who still doesn't know, the woman explains, 'a white feather, of course – coward.'

When Mason finally does enlist, he appears proudly in his new uniform, to the admiring praise of his fellow servants below stairs. Serving dinner upstairs one last time, he beams when the visiting general tells him, 'there is no livery so becoming as a uniform.' Mason tells Daisy (Sophie McShera) that his uniform makes him 'a real soldier' and, by implication, a real man, as he demands she 'let a Tommy kiss his sweetheart when he's off to fight the Hun' (he never before felt bold enough to take such liberties with her). William's demand for a kiss resembles Michael's insistence in *The Passing Bells* that now that he has signed up for war, he cannot possibly die a 'coward', but to fully be a man, he mustn't 'die a virgin' either and his fiancé obliges before he leaves for the front.

Not all men had such anxiety about being labelled cowards for their refusal (or inability) to sign up but they inevitably faced intense scrutiny and possible punishment. The British government and public believed 'there was nothing more effeminate and cowardly than a man willing to stand up for his beliefs when the nation was mobilised behind the war effort and behind the very essentialised construct of the citizen soldier's masculinity.'[19] Another recipient of a white feather at the Downton charity

Figure 9.1 The white feather as symbol of cowardice in *Downton Abbey*.

'The war is done. Shut the door on it!'

event, Irish chauffeur Branson (Allen Leech), blithely points out to its giver, 'I'm *in* uniform' and laughs off the accusatory response that his is 'the wrong kind.' Branson has repeatedly stated he will not support England's war but his attempts to object officially become pointless when he fails the military physical due to a heart murmur. Curiously, after receiving his diagnosis, Branson, a supposedly staunch Irish nationalist, repeats Lord Grantham's words, with a touch of disappointment in his voice: 'the Army doesn't want me.'

Fellowes won't allow any real 'conchies' at Downton, and as Lucy Brown's chapter indicates, the conscientious objector, true to the sentiments at the time, rarely epitomises masculinity in period dramas. One potential exception is the Bloomsbury drama *Life in Squares* (BBC, 2015), in which the artists and homosexual lovers (already socially marginalised male figures due to their career choices and sexuality), Duncan Grant (James Norton) and David Garnett (Jack Davenport), are shown working on a farm, as the song 'Johnnie Get Your Gun' plays and Vanessa Bell's (Phoebe Fox) young sons 'play at war.' Vanessa insists that Duncan show his blistered and swollen hands to visitor Clive Bell (Sam Hoare) and boasts that Duncan toils '12 hours a day' for the war effort. Nevertheless, the men's pacifism has translated into government-mandated hard labour, and therefore as a form of manliness, remains suspect. Even Duncan, who does not deny the physically exhausting nature of his war work, replies with embarrassment in his voice, 'Still, it's hardly the Somme.'

Hysterical Men

Even for those who served at the front, and perhaps survived a battle as deadly as the Somme without any *visible* injuries, the removal of the uniform before the war's end still called their manhood into question, even more so if they were discharged on psychological grounds. According to Elaine Showalter, shell shock (also referred to as 'war neurosis' but now known as post-traumatic stress disorder, or PTSD) represented 'a crisis of masculinity and a trial of the Victorian masculine ideal'; its symptoms resembled those of female hysteria and as such, Showalter suggests, signaled an unconscious protest 'not only against the war but against the concept of "manliness" itself.'[20] Officers suffered the highest rates of shell shock – four times that of privates – but the latter 'often displayed more "physical" symptoms (as opposed to officers' mental or "nervous" symptoms), such as uncontrollable spasms, "wobbly legs" and mutism.'[21] Perhaps that is why in *Downton* the ailment is given not to the heir but to one of the servants, as the physical manifestation of shell shock makes for greater dramatic effect as it drives home to viewers just how emasculating the war experience could be. Henry Lang (Cal MacAninch), the new valet at Downton in Series Two, suffers nightmares and such trembling hands that he cannot seem to avoid dropping plates. He senses that 'people look at me and wonder why I'm not in uniform', a suspicion confirmed when fellow servant Ethel (Amy Nuttall), watching him sew, sarcastically wonders aloud: 'However can you make those big hands do such delicate work?' Lang's condition is proof that trench warfare 'could destroy as well as make men.'[22] He finds champions in his new master, Lord Grantham, himself feeling less than manly – 'you've been in the trenches and I have not. I have no right to criticize' – and in the usually mean-spirited lady's maid, Miss O'Brien (Siobhan Finneran), who tells Lang her favourite brother had shell shock before he died.

Such awareness of and sympathy for sufferers of 'war neurosis', however, was not typical among the general population, and certainly less so among the military establishment, despite its prevalence.[23] The actual number of cases of shell shock among British soldiers alone has been estimated to be between 80,000 and 200,000 men, but even these figures are based only on those formally diagnosed and treated for shell shock while many men likely never sought medical attention and suffered nightmares and other traumatic symptoms long after the war's end.[24] Not until the 1922 *Report of the War Office Committee of Enquiry into 'Shell-Shock'* was shell shock, still regarded as a form of 'cowardice' by the military, at least recognised, in special cases, as 'beyond the individual's control.'[25] Doctors, even when they designated shell shock a legitimate ailment, believed it was curable, so that 'those who continued to suffer symptoms [...] were cast not as sufferers of wartime traumas but rather as lazy indigents' and their claims for disability pensions were usually rejected by the state.[26] Lang, after embarrassing himself, and his employers, at a dinner party for a prominent general (that same dinner party where William Mason serves his last meal in his new uniform), is finally dismissed from service, and though he is promised a generous severance – and a letter of recommendation *if* he recovers – his future livelihood remains uncertain.

'The war is done. Shut the door on it!'

Introduced as a temporary character at Downton, Lang likely won't be missed by the family or staff (or viewers), but the plight of *Mr Selfridge*'s Henri LeClair (Grégory Fitoussi), whom viewers have known since the start of the series, concerns everyone, especially the store's owner, who offers LeClair his old job as a path to regaining normalcy. While Byrne has previously described this series as a conservative celebration of patriotism,[27] *Mr Selfridge*'s third series offers a surprisingly nuanced depiction of failed postwar masculine recuperation. When LeClair returns from France in the opening episode, it soon becomes obvious that he is no longer the dapper, carefree man everyone knew before the war. At a store event in the next episode, a fashion designer says, with surprise audible in his voice, 'Mr LeClair, such a handsome young man ... what happened?' Indeed, his good looks have faded, and as the crowd cheers 'our war hero', the camera's flashing bulb drives him from the store. But worse than Henri's tarnished looks is his insomnia, reliance on alcohol, visions of dead men, and seething anger; his wife Agnes (Aisling Loftus), who has thrived at work in his absence, struggles to understand what is wrong with him: 'I lie next to you every night. I hear you crying in your sleep, and when I hold you, you hold onto me, but when you wake up you push me away.' Henri has experienced some of the worst moments of the war, details of which he cannot bear to share with Agnes, or even say aloud to himself. When her friend, and former store employee, Victor Colleano (Trystan Gravelle), explains, 'he was at Verdun', Agnes replies (speaking for the audience, too), 'I don't know what that *means*!' After much pressing from Agnes, Victor describes the conditions Henri, in charge of his own regiment, likely encountered: his men gassed, starved, freezing to death, as 'bodies, mounds of them, piled up left there to rot [...] hell on earth.' Since Henri cannot function at work and earn a living until he recovers, Agnes decides to whisk him away from the noisy city and return with him to his boyhood home; as she cradles him in her lap, she tells him she will make him better. Henri, who had once been her mentor and Agnes his 'protégé' at work and in the bedroom, has become the child, dependent on her to make all the decisions and heal his wounds.

Her husband's trauma has made Agnes aware that the other men she loves who served in France may also be scarred, though in less visible ways. She finally asks her brother George (Calum Callaghan), who seems unfazed by his past service, 'Are *you* all right?' and he surprises her with his honest answer: 'Some days I hardly think about it, others, everything around you looks the same, it's like it's not real, it'll break apart any minute.' George, like his best friend Victor, now a successful nightclub owner, appears to have managed what Tommy Shelby urges his brother Arthur in *Peaky Blinders* to do, to accept that 'the war is done, shut the door on it.' (As Meyer notes, the truth was that most men, though 'pushed to the limits of their endurance [...] *did* endure',[28] but those are not the stories of which compelling period dramas are made.) A similar phrase is used by Harry Selfridge (Jeremy Piven), but with a very different meaning, when he explains to his Deputy Manager, Mr Grove, that they can't 'shut the door' on Henri; instead, they must get him to talk about his experiences so he can begin to heal. Harry's statement, while in sync with more modern efforts to destigmatise PTSD, also captures how, at the time, class difference shaped attitudes about and treatments for the shell shocked; while officers underwent 'talking cures' (psychoanalysis) to address their feelings of guilt, working-class privates were treated, often quite cruelly, mainly for their physical symptoms (for example, electric shock therapy to induce speech). Endurance, of course, does not necessarily mean that men forgot or fully recovered emotionally from their experiences at the front. Unfortunately, in sending men like Lang and LeClair away to heal off-screen, these dramas prompt viewers to 'move on' and forget their plight, a plight which even the seemingly blasé Victor Colleano acknowledges 'never ends.'

The Manly Death, Shirkers and Disabled Bodies

Although government propaganda initially valourised 'masculinity through service', the realities of the multitude of shell shocked soldiers prompted a revised discourse that prioritised the 'manly death' over mere endurance and survival.[29] In *The Crimson Field*, all of the action takes place in a field hospital – we see nothing of battle, only the aftermath, of mangled bodies and blood stained bandages – but even in this drama, it is rare for any of the characters to actually *die*. And so the death of a major character in *Downton* comes as a shock but is necessary to drive home the full impact of the war. Before the war, William Mason, as a servant, could not claim full masculine authority and even had he reached the age of 21, without his own household to head, he would be disenfranchised; his quest for masculinity, therefore, can be rewarded only in the most extreme ways:

'The war is done. Shut the door on it!'

in battle and his subsequent deathbed marriage to Daisy. Ignoring Daisy's protests, he tells her he wants to leave her with a war widow's pension; unable to be her breadwinner while alive, he will do so when dead. His is a life cut short, but as a true hero his name will later be inscribed on the village war memorial in Series Five. Dying in battle 'marked men out as the best of men',[30] a sentiment best expressed by Horatio Bottomley, editor of *John Bull*, in 1917: 'Every hero of this war who has fallen on the field of battle has performed an act of Greatest Love, so penetrating and intense in its purifying character that I do not hesitate to express my belief that any and every past sin is automatically wiped from the record of his life.'[31]

Though perhaps not a 'sin', Mason's class status, however, is a temporary obstacle to his manly death and underscores the lie behind Isobel Crawley's earlier quoted statement about the 'equality of sacrifice.' Mason served as valet to Isobel's son, Matthew (Dan Stevens), at the front, and though he is mortally injured protecting the heir to Downton, he is denied admission to the village hospital, which is for officers only. Dr Clarkson's (David Robb) hands are tied; as he says, 'the answer is – and must be no.' Fortunately, the benevolent Granthams step in and move Mason to a family bedroom at Downton where he is nursed by none other than Lady Edith, atoning for her earlier remarks about young men who 'do nothing.'

And what of the other men that Lady Edith once criticised for 'doing nothing' – the 'shirkers' – or those who enlist, or are conscripted after 1916, but long for, and manoeuvre, an escape from the front? Mr Moseley (Kevin Doyle), who Isobel Crawley tried to pressure into enlisting, convinces Dr Clarkson that he has already been declared unfit for service; it's obvious that he is afraid and the doctor takes pity on him. In *The Crimson Field* the same actor, Kevin Doyle, portrays the kindly field surgeon, Lt. Col. Brett, who is accused by his superior of being too soft ('toughen up, you're not their father') and who orders Brett to send the 'cowards' (those Brett says have shell shock and should be sent home) back to the front: 'If they can walk and shoot, then back out they go.' In *Downton*, Matthew tells Lord Grantham that his men 'pray to be spared, of course, but if that's not to be, they pray for a bullet that kills them cleanly.' Thomas Barrow, however, thanks God for his 'deliverance' as he raises his hand above the trench wall, clutching his cigarette lighter, and prays to be wounded by a German sniper; his prayer answered, he returns to

Downton, not in shame, but still in his corporal's uniform and put in charge of the estate's hospital ward. Barrow escapes the more likely fate of a soldier in *The Crimson Field* whose self-inflicted wound will result in his court martial. The Matron (Hermione Norris), urging compassion for the soldier, points out that 'some men just aren't soldiers. You can't condemn them for not being soldiers', but the truth was that some men *had* to be condemned in order to reinforce ideals of martial masculinity that were already threatened by conditions at the front.

The emerging notion of 'endurance' as a masculine ideal (albeit one that was less valourised than dying in battle) was an inevitable product of the war that dragged on well beyond the expected deadline of Christmas 1914. Victorian and Edwardian models of masculinity had emphasised self-control, and were thus incorporated into martial masculinity, so that 'men who endured were those who controlled their emotions not only in the moment of fear and stress but also when confronted with the on-going horrors of warfare.'[32] Matthew Crawley is no aristocrat – he's a middle-class lawyer – which perhaps explains the refreshing absence of him writing poetry in the trenches or while on leave. He appears, at first, as the epitome of British 'pluck', shown in charge of his regiment whom he affectionately refers to as his 'chaps', and tosses off such stiff-upper-lip quips as, 'I've had bloody enough of this for one day', as he dodges sniper fire and explosions. But Matthew's case illustrates how precarious endurance can become, when faced with the potential threat of disability. In another episode he leads a charge over the top, armed with – what else – just his bayonet, leaving him for the remainder of Series Two wheelchair bound from spinal damage. Rather than letting the series enter *Lady Chatterley* terrain, Fellowes has Matthew nobly release his fiancé Lavinia from her commitment since he may not be able to give her children (he later miraculously recovers – ironically only to die in a car accident immediately after the birth of his own heir, with his wife Mary, in Series Three). When a possible usurper appears among the wounded officers at Downton posing as former heir Patrick Crawley, who should have died on the Titanic in Series One, and is now so disfigured that no one can recognise him, Matthew wryly notes that, 'He's not very pretty but he can walk around the estate on his own two legs and sire a string of sons to continue the line.' When Matthew walks again, Dr Clarkson reassures him, 'You *will* have a normal life'; Matthew has endured physical injury and

'The war is done. Shut the door on it!'

almost literal emasculation, and his reward will be a restoration of full masculine privilege: work, marriage and children.

And so, too, will the current Lord Grantham return to his 'normal' life at the war's end when he can remove his sham of a uniform – and his surviving servants exchange their khaki for livery – when masculinity will no longer be solely a martial identity. He tells his wife and daughters, whom he expects to resume their largely decorative role at Downton, 'Before the war I believed my life had value. I suppose I should like to feel that again.' But not all gentlemen of his class returning home will feel that putting on their old clothes will restore them to their pre-war authority, nor will the clothes fit their now disabled bodies as they once did. Matthew's fear of being 'impotent, crippled, stinking of sick' is realised in the story line of *The Crimson Field*'s Major Crecy (Rupert Graves), who has lost both legs and attempts suicide rather than disappoint his wife. Indeed, she's not very understanding when she first sees her husband, once 'a giant of a man', but who now lies helpless in bed, with two bandaged stumps where his legs once were: 'He's a hunting man ... the outdoors belonged to him ... the house was mine. It will be different now.' She insists he forget about the front – 'you're not a soldier anymore Eddie' – but he doesn't know how he will physically resume his duties overseeing his large estate and without his uniform he assumes he is 'nothing'. The happy ending (as short-lived as it is) for Matthew Crawley is not afforded to the seriously wounded like Major Crecy. His body, cut off below the waist, is a horrific and permanent reminder of 'the inability of military masculinity to withstand modern technological warfare.'[33] Likewise, Lady Edith's fiancé, Sir Anthony Strallan, returns from France with a paralyzed arm, and fearful that he will be saddling Edith with a burden, abandons her at the altar. Even though physically disabled veterans were presented as war heroes in official discourse after 1918 and financially compensated for their injuries while their shell shocked comrades were not, as the following chapter illustrates, some men themselves, and their families and local communities, inevitably regarded their disability and enforced passivity as emasculating.[34]

The Veteran's Anger

Even when the war ends and the glamour of the Jazz Age sets in, these period dramas demonstrate that there would always be some men left behind, unable to 'shut the door' on their physical and emotional traumas and return to work and their families with ease. The British government made a concerted effort to memorialise the dead and encouraged employers to hire veterans – a sentiment expressed by Lord Grantham, who urges at the end of *Downton*'s second series, 'Let us remember the sacrifices that have been made and the men that will never come back and give them our thanks.' The unpleasant truth soon emerged, however, that it was much more difficult to honour the sacrifices made by those men who actually *returned*. Furthermore, not only were all returning soldiers not employable, but as *Mr Selfridge* daringly illustrates in its third season, not all veterans were 'heroes' or even 'good' men. The assault on one of the store's favourite employees, Kitty Hawkins née Edwards (Amy Beth Hayes), by the drunken vets (interviewed earlier and plied with that very alcohol by her journalist husband, Frank) underscores the resentment some soldiers felt towards women who remained in the workforce even after 'the duration'. Ironically, when war was declared at the start of Series Two, the staff at Selfridges had shouted, 'Three cheers for King, Country and Miss Kitty Hawkins!' but Kitty's success during and after the war angers those outside the store's doors. As Lucy Bland notes in her study of the postwar 'modern woman', when soldiers returned home to see women like Kitty made 'head of department' (as well as many rewarded with *the* marker of masculine privilege, the vote) while they faced unemployment and homelessness, many lashed out at women, often assaulting them on the streets.[35] This TV series, which has always trumpeted the ethos of self-help, refuses to have us take pity on such men. Walking through the alleyway and observing just how many men have been left behind by the postwar recovery, Kitty, in a rare moment of empathy, says 'it makes you wonder where their families are, their friends' – until she's reminded that her attacker 'was always a bugger' and donning a uniform for four years failed to alter that fact. Meanwhile, Harry Selfridge discovers that his 'home for heroes' project is based on a lie and will likely never be built.

Finding heroes among the Shelby brothers, who with their gang of 'Peaky Blinders' rule the dirty, violent streets of postwar Birmingham, proves equally problematic. We first learn of gang leader Tommy Shelby's (Cillian Murphy) war record from a photograph of his younger, more naïve looking self that is now part of a police file on his postwar criminal

'The war is done. Shut the door on it!'

activities. That same photo is framed and sits atop Tommy's desk through the first three series of *Peaky Blinders*, perhaps a reminder to him and anyone who enters his office, of his service to King and Country, a record he both tries to forget and uses for his own convenience. In the opening episode of the series, the camera pans from the police file to Tommy in his bed, using opium to drown out his recurring dreams of the tunnels where he and his mates confront bayonet-wielding Germans who literally burst through the dirt walls. Some nights he lies awake hearing shovels picking and scraping behind his wall. It's only when he makes love with Grace (Annabelle Wallis) that he finally feels free, as he tells her, 'I don't hear the shovels against the wall' and asks her to help him, 'with everything ... the whole fucking thing' – a rare moment of vulnerability for a man who has learned to kill with such ease. His older brother Arthur (Paul Anderson), however, can find no respite from his 'Flanders Blues' – no amount of alcohol and cocaine, sex, and later religion, seems to help him forget. Likewise, their friend Danny Whizzbang (Samuel Edward-Cook) cannot stop his headaches and rage: 'I left my fucking brains in the mud [...] the shit, the shit that we got told to do' and he makes Tommy promise not to bury him anywhere there is mud. When the friends discuss their time in France they reflect how, as tunnellers, they were turned into animals, like rats (the rats we never see

Figure 9.2 'The war is done. Shut the door on it, like I did': Tommy to Arthur Shelby in *Peaky Blinders*.

in any of these dramas), but the worst part, they conclude with self-contempt, is that 'we fucking volunteered'.

For Tommy, the war has made him even more aware of his class, how 'those bastards [...] politicians [...] lords and ladies [i.e., the class to which the Crawleys of *Downton* belong] [...] will never admit us to their palaces [...] because of where we came from.' He does, however, manage to manipulate Isobel Crawley's belief in the 'equality of sacrifice' to his advantage; because he 'bloody fought for the King' he can lord his two medals 'for gallantry' over his superiors. When dealing with his rival, Chief Inspector Campbell (Sam Neill), whom we learn did *not* serve in the war, Tommy says with contempt, 'Now why would I shake the hand of a man who didn't even fight for his country?' When Campbell reminds Churchill (Andy Nyman), who has hired Tommy as an assassin, that 'Thomas Shelby is a mongrel, murdering gangster' and a 'gypsy' (the Shelbys are of Roma descent), Churchill replies, 'and yet, the tunnels were built beneath our feet to silence the guns pointed at our hearts.'

Peaky Blinders, often described as a 'gritty' and 'anti-*Downton*' period drama, privileges the perspective of the working-class male who does not reside below the stairs of a great manor house or owe his employment to the benevolence of a wealthy storeowner. These veterans, even the decorated Tommy, would likely find no welcome in Harry Selfridge's idealised 'homes for heroes' but that does not mean that their trauma, and even their guilt, triggered by their wartime actions, is no less relevant (Arthur, who appears to be the most brutal of killers, says at one point, 'it gets to the point where you can't walk into a room without bringing a load of them [the dead] with you'). What makes the Shelby brothers so different from the other men we typically encounter in period dramas is that they have no desire to return to their pre-war lives (when they were merely petty criminals); instead, the war has unleashed their rage and violence and there is no turning back. They have been liberated by what Graham Dawson has termed 'the pleasure culture of war'.[36] As veterans, the skills they acquired at the front – digging and killing – keep them gainfully employed (of sorts); in Series Three Tommy orders the seven remaining men from his regiment (there were once 50) to Birmingham to help him tunnel beneath an estate, to steal treasure from White Russian enemies. Previously ordered to kill 'for the King's shilling', his brothers

'The war is done. Shut the door on it!'

and mates now kill for Tommy, for whom his younger brother John (Joe Cole) says they act as his 'toy soldiers' as they wage their own 'little war in a little place'; in short, Birmingham has become the Shelbys' new front.

Conclusion: Memorialising Male Sacrifice

Peaky Blinders' postwar Birmingham often looks like a war zone, with gun fire, explosions and occasionally corpses littering its streets, a far cry from the idyllic village in *Downton Abbey* that erects its memorial to the war dead in Series Five (aired during the first year of the Great War's centenary). The earl and his butler Carson (Jim Carter) butt heads over location and other details of the memorial, but at the end, all petty squabbles are resolved as the household joins the rest of the town in the village square; bugles play and the memorial is unveiled as the camera pans the sombre crowd. Lord Grantham has even arranged a special plaque to commemorate the death of his cook's nephew – accused of treason for going AWOL. During the war about 3,000 British soldiers were convicted of cowardice, desertion or other crimes and 306 of them were executed for cowardice or desertion specifically.[37] In Series Two we learned that the nephew of Mrs Patmore (Lesley Nicol), Archie Philpotts, was one of those shot for cowardice, although his only 'crime' was shell shock-induced fear. The question of how to deal with this uncomfortable legacy of the war (shooting men for being scared) has surfaced, and Lord Grantham's solution is almost a century ahead of its time (in 2006, Britain issued a blanket pardon for soldiers executed for cowardice and desertion in World War I and they received their own memorial, the 'Shot at Dawn Memorial' in Staffordshire in 2001). Still, the plaque for Archie is some distance from the memorial honouring the true heroes of the town: 'It is just as it should be', a servant comments, reaffirming the good judgement of the lord of the estate and the need to maintain a hierarchy of male sacrifice. In 1925 a journalist observed of the construction of war memorials that 'our true task is to make sure the memory is a *right memory*'[38] and *Downton* demonstrates how period dramas still struggle to present the 'right memory' of war and male sacrifice.

War, as many scholars have argued, was and still largely is one of the 'seemingly "natural" homelands of masculinity',[39] with the dominant narrative focusing on those who fought. The Great War, however, was unique in that 'the infantry soldier in the trenches was more often the victim than the perpetrator of violence.'[40] Any notion that the war would be as depicted in government propaganda – a great adventure, a form of sport, a chivalric event – soon clashed with the realities of modern technological warfare which left one in eight British soldiers dead and one in four wounded by war's end.[41] Even as the military and government tried to establish a hierarchy of service and sacrifice – prioritising and rewarding some forms of injury or death over others – men's actual experiences and self-perceptions defied neat categorisation.

Period dramas have been praised, rightly so, for recovering lost or marginalised voices of the past – women, colonised subjects, homosexuals – and no less significant is the genre's recent efforts to offer a diverse representation of men in wartime, not just of men who 'were there' but, equally important, those who were not, those who objected and those whose fear equated them at the time with cowardice. But, just as popular culture once romanticised the upper-class 'soldier poet', so now must it be careful to avoid romanticising and universalising the figure of the 'ordinary soldier' and of continuing a narrative of 'disillusionment and fatalism',[42] a nod to which we see in the Remarquian ending of *The Passing Bells* when the two young (and working-class) protagonists, one English, the other German, both die in battle at the very moment the Armistice is signed. The story line of the damaged soldier will likely always hold a 'grim fascination'[43] for TV writers and audiences, who since the 1970s when *Upstairs, Downstairs* first aired, have become all too familiar with the persistent failure of governments to adequately address the needs of veterans. When Isobel Crawley, once a patriotic supporter of the war, asks 'are we doing enough for them [i.e., veterans]?' she speaks not just for the men at the Downton hospital but for all survivors of war.

Indeed, it is the postwar stories of the living, of those who endured and survived, that period dramas are now eager to tell, with interesting differences among them, from men who seem barely touched by their time at the front, to those who struggle to readjust to civilian and domestic life. The dramas discussed above underscore the contradictory behaviours and identities that the war imposed on men, as they were required, temporarily, to unleash violence that had once been contained by Victorian and

'The war is done. Shut the door on it!'

Edwardian norms of self-restraint. Still, as Michael Roper observes, the war also simultaneously encouraged 'a softer conception of masculinity', producing 'a body of men with an enormous need for care and reassurance' but who also, 'having experienced the depths of human need' became 'practised carers' themselves.[44] Thomas Barrow may have shirked his duty at the front but even this hardened character comes to cry for one of the wounded and dying under his care at Downton. Likewise, the Shelbys maintain a brotherhood of mates born in the trenches, protecting each other long after the war has ended. Men as 'carers' is a trope present in many recent period dramas that feature veterans of wars other than World War I. Ross Poldark, for instance, nurses his wounded cousin Francis back to health with skills he learned in the Revolutionary War and *Call the Midwife*'s (BBC, 2012–) Dr Turner's (Stephen McGann) brief spell in a military psychiatric hospital near the end of World War II has only made him a more empathetic caregiver to the poor women of London's East End. In all of these cases, we are shown how masculinity is shaped by and responds to war and when faced with unbearable conditions is both fragile and resilient.

In the final episode of *The Passing Bells* a young private comments (reflecting the self-awareness of these series produced during the centenary): 'A hundred years from now and none of us will be here, and all this will be ancient history. I wonder what they'll make of it.' As historians uncover more and more diaries, letters, and other records of men's experiences during the war, the period drama has a role to play in giving these men a voice, too, and in helping audiences not only understand an event 100 years in the past, but to question the role that violence and war continues to play in constructions of masculinity.[45] Rather than shutting the door on the war or prioritising one experience over another, period dramas like *Downton Abbey* and *Peaky Blinders* – seemingly worlds apart aesthetically – can help us understand the many ways in which men bore, and continue to bear, witness to traumatic events.

Notes

1. Emma Hanna, *The Great War on the Small Screen: Representing the First World War in Contemporary Britain* (Edinburgh, 2009), p. 8.

2. Alan Clark, *The Donkeys: A History of the British Expeditionary Force in 1915* (London, 1961). For a discussion of the war in relation to the upper-class male experience, see Paul Fussell's now classic text, *The Great War and Modern Memory* (Oxford, 1975) and Michael C. Adams, *The Great Adventure: Male Desire and the Coming of World War I* (Bloomington, IN, 1990).
3. Unnamed television critic quoted in Hanna, *The Great War on the Small Screen*, p. 133.
4. Desmond Christy, 'Fighting Blackadder', *Guardian*, 30 October 1999. Available at https://www.theguardian.com/books/1999/oct/30/historybooks1 (accessed 31 May 2016).
5. Cyril Wilde quoted in Alan Sinfield, *The Wilde Century: Effeminacy, Oscar Wilde and the Queer Movement* (London, 1994), p. 126.
6. Jessica Meyer, *Men of War: Masculinity and the First World War in Britain* (Houndmills, Basingstoke, 2009), p. 10.
7. Samuel Hynes, *A War Imagined: The First World War and English Culture* (New York, 1991), p. 215.
8. Meyer, *Men of War*, p. 142.
9. Hynes, *A War Imagined*, p. 214.
10. Meyer, *Men of War*, p. 10.
11. Hanna, *The Great War on the Small Screen*, p. 116.
12. Tracey Loughran, 'Masculinity, Shell Shock, and Emotional Survival in the First World War', *Reviews in History*, August 2010. Available at http://www.history.ac.uk/reviews/review/944#f2 (accessed 7 July 2016).
13. Katherine Byrne, *Edwardians on Screen: From* Downton Abbey *to* Parade's End (Houndmills, Basingstoke, 2015), p. 82.
14. Meyer, *Men of War*, p. 2.
15. Ibid., p. 1.
16. Emphasis added. Lord Grantham is about 50 at the start of the war, which would not necessarily disqualify him from service, and in the last months of the war the extension of the Military Service Act 1916 made men up to the maximum age of 56 liable for call-up.
17. Byrne, *Edwardians on Screen*, p. 84.
18. Nicoletta F. Gullace, 'White Feathers and Wounded Men: Female Patriotism and the Memory of the Great War', *The Journal of British Studies*, 36/2 (1997), p. 180.
19. Lois Bibbings, 'Images of Manliness: The Portrayal of Soldiers and Conscientious Objectors in the Great War', *Social & Legal Studies*, 12/3 (2003), pp. 335–58.
20. Elaine Showalter, 'Rivers and Sassoon: the inscription of male gender anxieties', *Behind the Lines: Gender and the Two World Wars*, in M. Higgonet et al., (eds) (New Haven, CT, 1987), pp. 61–9.
21. J. D. Taylor, '"Hysteric or Neurasthenic": The Role of Class in the Treatment of Shell Shock in World War I', *The Drowned and the Saved*, 29 April 2013.

'The war is done. Shut the door on it!'

Available at https://drownedandsaved.org/2013/04/29/hysteric-or-neurasthenic-the-role-of-class-in-the-treatment-of-shell-shock-during-world-war-one/ (accessed 1 June 2016).
22. Meyer, *Men of War*, p. 3.
23. It has taken an entire century of wars, most notably after the Gulf War, for war-induced PTSD to finally gain recognition by military authorities (and society in general) but the stigma persists, preventing some veterans from seeking treatment.
24. Tracey Loughran, 'Masculinity, trauma and "shell shock"', *The Psychologist*, 28 (March 2015), pp. 250–1. Available at https://thepsychologist.bps.org.uk/volume-28/march-2015/masculinity-trauma-and-shell-shock (accessed 31 May 2016).
25. Report cited in Mo Moulton, 'Watching *Downton Abbey* with an Historian: Cowardice, Shellshock, and a Right Memory', *The Toast*, 20 January 2015. Available at http://the-toast.net/2015/01/20/watching-downton-abbey-historian-right-memory/ (accessed 30 May 2016).
26. Meyer, *Men of War*, pp. 98–9.
27. Byrne, *Edwardians on Screen*, p. 106.
28. Meyer, *Men of War*, p. 165 (emphasis added).
29. Ibid., pp. 82–3. An official letter of condolence, for example, offered grieving parents the comforting knowledge that 'even in your sorrow, feel proud of your son's gallant end, for he played his part like a man.'
30. Ibid., p. 83.
31. Bottomley quoted in Moulton, 'Watching *Downton Abbey* with an Historian'.
32. Meyer, *Men of War*, p. 142.
33. Suzannah Biernoff, '*Flesh Poems: Henry Tonks and the Art of Surgery*', *Visual Culture in Britain*, 11/1 (March 2010), pp. 25–47.
34. Other than the imposter in *Downton* (whose facial wounds are concealed by bandages and who is a minor character), none of these war-themed dramas give soldiers the more extreme, yet common, injuries that made re-entry into civilian life so difficult (loss of all limbs, missing jaws or eyes, for example). Shell shock or a vague spinal injury allow a wounded soldier like Henri or Matthew to remain handsome since viewers might be put off if the physical injuries of their favourite characters look too 'realistic'.
35. Lucy Bland, *Modern Women on Trial: Sexual Transgression in the Age of the Flapper* (Manchester, 2013).
36. Graham Dawson, *Soldier Heroes: British Adventure, Empire and the Imagining of Masculinity* (London, 1994).
37. Moulton, 'Watching *Downton Abbey* with an Historian'.
38. Quoted in ibid. (emphasis added).
39. Meyer, *Men of War*, citing Stefan Dudink, p. 1.
40. Michael Roper, *The Secret Battle: Emotional Survival in the Great War* (Manchester, 2009), p. 4.
41. Ibid., p. 4.

42. Meyer, *Men of War*, p. 165.
43. Loughran, 'Masculinity, Shell Shock and Emotional Survival in the First World War'.
44. Roper, *The Secret Battle*, p. 305.
45. At the time of writing this chapter, the association between masculinity and violence dominate political discourse (such as the aggressive posturing of Donald Trump and many of his male supporters in the USA).

10

Pride versus Prejudice: Wounded Men, Masculinity and Disability in *Downton Abbey*

Claire O'Callaghan

Dominant conceptions of masculinity have long been intertwined with ideals of physical 'normalcy'. As the disability scholar Jenny Morris puts it, 'the social definition of masculinity is inextricably bound with a celebration of strength [and] perfect bodies' because 'to be masculine is not to be vulnerable.'[1] In this questionable gendered equation, notions of hegemonic masculinity – that is, a culturally idealised form of manhood that celebrates men's dominance and apparent 'natural' toughness – govern understandings of the male gender, with able-bodiedness and physical strength perilously accepted as *the* benchmark by which all masculinities are validated. Consequently, both historically *and* in the present day, disabled men and 'non-normative' expressions of maleness are rendered as Other, derided as inauthentic and supposed weak. How and in what ways, then, do men with physical differences negotiate the seemingly oppositional categories of 'masculinity' and 'disability'? And how is this experience represented in British costume drama?

With their focus on historical representation, period dramas are often caught in a quandary between representing the past authentically, which may mean reflecting questionable ideals and pejorative attitudes, particularly towards issues such as disability, while speaking to more 'enlightened' approaches to socio-cultural topics.[2] This dilemma becomes especially apparent with regards to representations of male disability onscreen. Take, for example, the inclusion of Joseph Carey Merrick (played by Joseph Drake) in BBC's *Ripper Street* (BBC/Amazon, 2012–16). Although Merrick is better known today as the Elephant Man (a phrase that emphasises his biological sex), *Ripper Street* constructs him as freakish. Merrick is feminised repeatedly by his socio-cultural positioning in London's Whitechapel, a notion emphasised when he is bullied and beaten by the ruthless Inspector Jedediah Shine (Joseph Mawle) who is keen to gain Merrick's silence as a witness to the policeman's involvement in the heroin trading taking place in and around the city.[3] Sadly, the notion of male disability as 'freakery' can also be found in BBC's *Call the Midwife* (2012–), in particular through a controversial episode in Series Three which focused on the relationship between Jacob Milligan (played by Colin Young), a young man with cerebral palsy, and his love interest, Sally Harper (played by Sarah Gordy), who has Down's Syndrome. The show poignantly rendered the tender romance between the young couple and was intended to highlight the treatment of people with physical and intellectual disabilities in the 1950s. But, also in keeping with the period setting – a time in which subjects with disability were often incarcerated in mental health hospitals – the show represents how such love has, historically, been deemed unnatural and inappropriate. Moreover, the 'inappropriateness' of this couple's love is not only emphasised through the focus on their respective disabilities, but particularly on Jacob's inability to be a 'real' man. Finally, the incompatibility between masculinity and disability has been repeatedly emphasised onscreen in the various remakes of D. H. Lawrence's *Lady Chatterley's Lover* (1928), in which the veteran Clifford, who, postwar, requires the use of a wheelchair, deems himself inadequate for being unable to satisfy his wife sexually and/or produce an heir. Interestingly, the actor who played Clifford in the BBC's 2015 adaptation, James Norton, acknowledged the gloss that is often placed on the on-screen relationship between masculinity and disability. In an interview promoting the show, Norton noted that although the public does 'hear about post-traumatic stress disorder (PTSD) in a generalised way', very rarely is any detailed insight given to the complex, gendered adjustments that take place 'when a young man comes home from Afghanistan or Iraq either with PTSD or a serious injury' or what this means in terms of the individual's experience of identity politics.[4] As Norton indicates, 'It was glossed over in Lawrence's day and it's pretty much glossed over now.'[5] Importantly, his words echo Jessica Meyer's observation that the position of ex-servicemen, especially if they are disabled, is 'not an easy one.'[6] As Meyer puts it, 'while reintegration into postwar society' is a struggle for 'all ex-servicemen', the disabled man faces 'particular hurdles as their experiences of disability often directly' challenge the 'expectations of the masculine roles they had anticipated inhabiting upon their return to civilian life.'[7]

Importantly, such politics of representation have also been a prominent feature in ITV's popular, award-winning drama, *Downton Abbey* (2010–15). Over six series, the Abbey has played host to numerous physically impaired men, mostly, like *Lady Chatterley's Lover* (1928), in the guise of ex-servicemen and wounded soldiers. Matthew Crawley (Dan Stevens), for instance, the heir to the Grantham estate, returned from World War I with a suspected spinal cord injury that confined him to a wheelchair. His paraplegia, however, which I will discuss in the course of this chapter, is temporary, since Matthew rises 'like Lazarus' from his wheelchair, suddenly able to walk again, and his injury is declared a misdiagnosis.[8] Likewise, Lady Edith Crawley's (Laura Carmichael) former fiancé, Sir Anthony Strallan (Robert Bathurst), who meanly jilted Edith at the altar, also returned from the war with permanent paralysis in his right arm. In contrast, the Abbey's malevolent footman, Thomas Barrow (Robert James-Collier) allowed himself to be shot in the hand so he could escape the trenches. More poignantly, the plight of Lieutenant Edward Courtenay (Lachlan Nieboer), a soldier whose blindness from chemical weapons and associated depression led to his suicide, provided the catalyst for the Abbey to transform temporarily into a convalescent home. During this transition, the audience also met Patrick Gordon (Trevor White), a soldier with extensive burn injuries whose facial disfigurement leads him to pass as Patrick Crawley, the rightful heir to the Abbey who was presumed dead on the sinking of the RMS *Titanic*. But it is the beloved figure of John Bates (Brendan Coyle), Lord Grantham's (Hugh Bonneville) trusted valet, who permanently required the use of a cane to support a limp arising from shrapnel wounds he gained in service, whose narrative gravitated consistently around debates concerning masculinity and dis/ability.[9]

Importantly, the show's creator, Julian Fellowes, has stated that he wrote Bates specifically as a disabled veteran to 'make him more vulnerable.'[10] In other words, Fellowes situates centrally the very concern that Morris's earlier comment made apparent: that 'disability' and 'masculinity' are at odds with one another. What, then, are the ideological and ethical implications of Fellowes's need to make Bates and the other men described above 'more vulnerable' through disability and, what conclusions does *Downton Abbey* offer on the relationship between masculinity and physical 'normalcy'?

Taking these questions as a starting point, this chapter debates the extent to which *Downton Abbey* successfully portrays the relationship between masculinity and able-bodiedness to interrogate what Russell Shuttleworth, Nikki Wedgwood and Nathan J. Wilson term the 'dilemma of disabled masculinity'.[11] Recognising that Fellowes's period drama is 'driven by a desire for [an] "authentic" and trustworthy view of the past' (in other words, nostalgia for a traditional, elitist, Conservative English society), there are limits to the diversity of gendered representations that *Downton Abbey* can accommodate.[12] However, as I have argued elsewhere, *Downton* nonetheless mirrors 'contemporary culture albeit [...] channelled through the fortunes of one family and their country house estate.'[13] Throughout the accompanying scripts to the show, Fellowes makes such connections himself, thus revealing, as Katherine Byrne has persuasively argued, how *Downton* 'self-consciously adapts and responds' for a contemporary audience 'through a range of strategies'.[14] Accordingly, in consideration of the portrayal of disabled masculinity, I contend that *Downton Abbey* not only reinforces a narrow model of masculinity defined by hegemonic masculine ideals, phallocentric logic and able-bodiedness but that it falls too often on outdated ideologies and clichéd ideas about disabled masculinities which suggest that masculinity is 'compromised' by disability.[15] While accepting that the popular period drama does – on occasion – attempt to open a discursive space to generate empathy, understanding and tolerance of masculinity and bodily difference, I argue that its political endeavour falls short of its potential value by endorsing a binary opposition between the able-bodied and disabled male subject, which privileges physical 'normalcy' as a requisite of 'real' masculinity. In unfolding this argument, this chapter begins first with an exploration of the critical issues at stake in conceptual approaches to disabled masculinities before attending to the political and ethical representation of these matters onscreen.

The Dilemma of Disabled Masculinity

As a field of scholarly enquiry, disability studies explore the way in which disability often serves as a form of social oppression through prejudice and discrimination. In this respect, disability studies shares an important corollary with feminism, which also focuses on the restriction and barriers faced by women in their campaign for equal rights, access to education and employment, and fair treatment in society and culture.[16] However, across the field there are different conceptions of what the term 'disability' means. The medical profession, for instance, binds disability to impairment by pathologising bodies in a reductive 'normal' vs. 'abnormal' dichotomy that seeks to 'correct' unusual variations of embodied normality, a perspective known as the medical model of disability. In contrast, the social model of disability articulates how society and culture socially and discursively constitute cognitive and physical difference and create social and structural barriers that disadvantage and disable those with physical impairments. Similarly, the social relational approach posits that disability is constituted differently within and across socio-cultural and historical contexts that shape experience and activity (something we shall see is important in the context of a British period drama). And, more recently, the human rights model of disability moves from viewing disabled persons as passive objects without rights by elucidating the economic and social processes that constitute disability in the first place. While this brief gloss identifies the important differences between conceptions of 'disability' and 'impairment' in disability studies, these approaches commonly articulate how the personal is political for disabled subjects. Moreover, they gesture to how disability is, for many men, often a 'lived and embodied dilemma'.[17]

Downton's preoccupation with wounded and/or physically impaired servicemen provides a useful means of analysing the seemingly competing concepts of masculinity and disability, while also revealing something important about the configuration of particular bodies as 'different'. Disability, in this context, as David A. Gerber indicates, can take many forms; it can describe those 'injured or [who] become chronically ill' in combat, but also those whose wounds constitute 'physical or mental injury or illness' beyond combat and whose service may be 'foreshortened'.[18] 'Impairment or disfigurement' and 'partial or complete loss of [bodily] function' may be a feature of masculine disability in this context, or the wounds may not be visible at all, with disability taking shape instead in more 'muted forms'.[19] Irrespective, as Tom Shakespeare explains, there is 'a particular crisis' for the able-bodied man who suddenly 'loses physical prowess', for one reason or another, precisely because 'so much of [masculinity] is constructed on the basis of strength and invulnerability'.[20]

Gerber also notes that since the twentieth century, disabled veterans have become 'a major project of the modern state, which endowed them recognition as a group worthy of continuing assistance, and with entitlements in the form of advanced medical care and prosthetics, pension schemes, vocational rehabilitation, and job placements.'[21] Sadly, this was not always the case, and with its early twentieth-century period setting *Downton Abbey* represents masculine disability at a time when gender norms were more rigidly entrenched and society less accepting of physical difference. The period following World War I, in particular, as many historians and cultural critics have demonstrated, was one in which disabled individuals not only faced 'widespread ability-based discrimination' but were discouraged from participating in society, with many being 'institutionalised'.[22] A figure like Mr Bates, then, would have been unlikely to receive employment in a country house like Downton, something vocalised when Lord Grantham sacks Bates in Series Two (temporarily) after a trial period with him as his valet.

Today, there is increased legislation to protect individuals from discrimination on the grounds of disability and a much greater cultural understanding of the effects of prejudice more broadly by the able-bodied majority. However, I suggest that period dramas like *Downton Abbey*, whose plotlines of social justice have continued relevance in the present moment, have an ethical responsibility to not only 'uncover the hidden history of disabled people' but to 'raise awareness of the unconscious attitudes and values embedded in media images.'[23] Indeed, despite the gains made in equality, access and the visibility of disabled people in society, prejudice, negativity and awkwardness towards them prevail. As a 2014 report from the UK charity Scope found, prejudice towards disabled individuals in the UK remains widespread: 67 per cent of the British public felt 'uncomfortable talking to disabled people', 36 per cent of people believed that disabled individuals are 'not as productive as everyone else', and 21 per cent of people aged between 18–34 actively avoid 'talking to disabled people'.[24] Interestingly, Scope also found that men 'aged 18–34 are the group least likely to interact with disabled people and most likely to hold negative attitudes' about disability.[25] One might ask why this is the case. Clearly, a full answer to this question is beyond the scope of this chapter, but in what follows I want to suggest that dominant ideas about men, masculinity and physical 'normalcy' set in contrast to pejorative notions of disabled male subjectivity contribute to the problem. And, as I will now show, many of these ideas can be traced on-screen in *Downton Abbey*.

'Think of me as dead': Matthew Crawley's Disabled Masculinity

Matthew's transition from elite army officer to paraplegic focuses obsessively on disabled masculinity as connoting a lack of manhood. While Dr Clarkson (David Robb) emphasises that Matthew 'will regain his health' and that disablism does not signal 'the end of his life', Lady Mary Crawley (Michelle Dockery) remains skeptical: 'Just the start of a different life', she remarks, her words foregrounding Matthew's altered physicality and its consequences; he and his life are now 'different'.[26] In Matthew's eyes, meanwhile, he is now an 'impotent cripple, stinking of sick'.[27] As he sees it, 'No one sane would want to be with me as I am now.'[28] Thus, he rejects his fiancé, Lavinia Swire (Zoe Boyle), advising her that she should 'think of [him] as dead' and to 'remember me as I was', words which dwell upon disability as an affront to masculinity and therefore life itself.[29] Underpinning Matthew's questionable view is the implicit sense that 'having a disability [is] seen as synonymous with being dependent, childlike and helpless', for seemingly, that is contrary to 'all that is embodied in the ideal male: virility, autonomy and independence', something which chimes with similar comments made by Clifford in D. H. Lawrence's *Lady Chatterley's Lover*, in which he too perceives of himself as a child-man for his dependency on others.[30] Matthew's story, then, may reflect the problematic historical truism that disabled individuals were 'discouraged from seeking relationships', but such ideas are dated and work only to reveal how the disciplines of masculine 'normalcy' are predicated on able-bodiedness and heterocentricity and 'not only enforced but internalised' by society.[31]

Sadly, this notion is likewise reinforced in the storyline surrounding Sir Anthony Strallan's abandonment of Lady Edith. Despite Edith's assurance that she loves Anthony 'in spite of your needing to be looked after', as Strallan tells Lord Grantham, it is difficult 'just... because of all this', he says, pointing to his lame arm.[32] For him, 'it's wrong' to marry Edith and be happy, 'so terribly happy', as she says, because it equates to Edith throwing 'away your life', which is something he 'can't let' happen so that she does not 'waste yourself on me.'[33] More destructively, this notion is reinforced by the Dowager Countess (Dame Maggie Smith) who tells Edith, 'Let him go. You know he's right. Don't stop him doing the only sensible thing he's come up with in months.'[34]

Downton also represents the reductive notion that masculine disability is emasculating since it equates to a lack of manhood, something implied through reference to sexuality and reproductive capacity. Matthew's perceived spinal cord injury renders him impotent, itself a clichéd screen and fictional narrative. Lord Grantham, Mary and Lavinia receive the news that Matthew may never walk again together, but Dr Clarkson draws Lord Grantham aside to speak privately. The script reads:

- *Out of the women's hearing, Robert looks shocked.*
- ROBERT: You mean there can be no children?
- CLARKSON: No anything, I'm afraid.[35]

This exchange – man-to-man – about Matthew's newfound 'lack' infers emasculation, with Dr Clarkson's use of the indefinite pronoun affirming his patient as 'less manly' because, as per narrow medical norms, penile function equates to masculinity. In the original script, Matthew's disability is also coupled with urinary dysfunction, thus doubly disqualifying Matthew as a 'real' man since his body is now an affront to masculine norms, with his physicality, genitals and sexual and psychological health all functioning 'abnormally' to the detriment of his gender. Sadly, as Aristotelis Nikolaidis points out, 'discriminatory perceptions of people with disabilities' all too frequently return to 'the idea of asexuality, sexual inadequacy or impotence', and its effect is to displace physically different

Pride versus Prejudice

individuals 'as subjects' while concomitantly fetishising them 'as objects in the context of the medical tragedy model.'[36]

But there is a secondary implication, too, at stake in Dr Clarkson's words about masculinity and disability that illuminate the gendered, class *and* cultural implications of Matthew's impairment. His reproductive incapacity means he cannot continue the hereditary line of inheritance on which aristocratic estates like Downton rely. Erectile failure and exclusion from sexual activity aside, then, Matthew is socially and culturally disabled by the tradition of heritage. In preventing Matthew from fulfilling his particularly aristocratic patriarchal 'obligation', Fellowes renders visible here the pejorative way in which dominant ideas about masculinity in relation to class are (and remain) reliant on patriarchal *and* heterosexual ideology as much as effective sexual function for meaning. Indeed, as Series Three problematically suggests, the absence of a male heir is conceived of in terms of failure such that Lord Grantham feels disabled by his own inability to provide a male heir to the Grantham estate.

This narrow conception of masculine disability also suggests that heterosexual and patriarchal ideologies are oppressive to men, too. Unsurprisingly, with regards to Matthew's impotence, the show fails to embrace (or even allude to) a broader range of sexual practices beyond traditional penetrative sex, because as Matthew tells Lavinia, 'we could never be properly married.'[37] In this way, *Downton* conceives of masculinity solely in phallocentric terms. It is hugely important, therefore, that this view is counteracted by alternative and more sensible voices of reason, and both Lavinia and Mary protest Matthew's ill-thought view. But, in the notes to the script, Fellowes explicitly rejects the idea that disabled men *can* have healthy sex lives, declaring 'You do see dramas where the suggestion is that men can be paralysed, but still sexually active. This is not true; certainly it was not true during the First World War, and we try to make that clear.'[38] Historical inaccuracy aside, Fellowes's absolutist comment endorses the false belief that disabled men are *always* 'excluded from sexual activity'.[39] Yet, as numerous disability scholars and activists have argued, while 'paralysis often impacts people's sexuality, including changes in physical functioning, sensation and response [...] the range of sexual options may be different [but] physical attraction and sexual activity are realistic expectations – no matter the level or completeness of paralysis.'[40] *Downton*'s medicalisation of masculinity through male sexual dys/function, then, is not only 'oppressive and undermining' to disabled men but distinctly archaic.[41]

Disabled Masculinity: The Case of Mr Bates

Like Matthew, Mr Bates is a wounded veteran, but while Matthew transitions from able-bodied to disabled in the course of the show, the audience meets Bates as disabled from the outset. This is important since it brings corporeality back into focus in the ideological critique of hegemonic masculine ideals. Aaron Richmond has argued that in comparison to Matthew, Bates *is* a more positive representation of disabled masculinity not least in the way that his narrative debunks many of the reductive ideas articulated through Matthew's paraplegia. But, I propose that the representation of Bates's disabled masculinity, too, is not without its problems.

Alongside a medical perspective on disability, Bates's narrative also elucidates the social model of disability; he is constructed as Other by the Crawley family and fellow servants alike. One of the first images of Bates on-screen gives primacy to his disability, with the audience following lady's maid Miss O'Brien's (Siobhan Finneran) gaze via camera angles that move from Bates's cane to his face and to his cane again. Moments later, when Bates leaves the room, O'Brien speculates, 'I can't see that lasting long', condemnatory words that reinforce Scope's finding that able-bodied subjects do not view disabled persons as effective as others.[42] Moreover, it is significant that the 'that' which O' Brien is referring to here, posits Bates's inclusion among the service staff at *Downton* as something of a temporary recipient of charity, rather than a fully fledged employee.

Via Bates, persistent attention is given to disabled masculinity as frail and limited by physical restriction, with the valet consistently negating charges of vulnerability and weakness. Mary, for example, ponders how a servant can 'do his work when he's lame?', while Mrs Patmore (Lesley Nicol), the Abbey's cook, wonders whether Bates can manage 'because we've all got our own work to do', the implication being that the able-bodied are unable to compensate for Bates's physical inabilities.[43] Bates, it is suggested, needs to support himself with minimal assistance from others. Yet, these attitudes go on to manifest more troublingly as bullying by O'Brien and Barrow.

Pride versus Prejudice

O'Brien, on one occasion, kicks away Bates's cane so that he falls to the ground as the servant staff line up outside the house awaiting the arrival of an important guest in the series' opening episode. This act is done out of pure maliciousness and designed to humiliate Bates and remind the Crawleys of his apparently 'weak' status. Meanwhile, Barrow's hostility to Bates stems primarily from jealousy at being 'passed' over for the role of valet by 'Long John Silver'.[44] In other words, Barrow's able-bodied masculine identity is affronted by the presence of disabled masculinity (something that, nonetheless, Barrow draws on to his own advantage in Series Two when he deliberately courts a German sniper to shoot his hand to be returned home from the front line). But Barrow is also suspicious of what he perceives as Bates's misplaced arrogance, his stoic masculinity in the face of physical impairment. As a result, Barrow undermines Bates by feminising him at all opportunities. He rejects Bates's offer, for instance, to help move some suitcases upstairs, telling Bates tenderly, 'I couldn't ask that of you, Mr Bates, not in your condition', a sentence that 'poses as care' but is actually 'an insult' by feminising disability.[45] Later he laughs in the valet's face when threatened with physical violence for bullying another member of staff. Barrow mocks Bates's display of violence when he throws him up against a wall, asking: 'Is this supposed to frighten me, Mr Bates? Because, if it is, it isn't working.'[46] Here, *Downton* points to the senseless idea that able-bodied men are 'naturally' superior to disabled males. Barrow's words, in both instances, reinforce the notion that Bates is not a 'real' man because he does not have access to 'natural' masculine physical strength in a conventional manner. Accordingly, *Downton* reminds us of the unjust way in which, as Tom Shakespeare points out, disabled men do not 'enjoy the power and privileges of non-disabled men'.[47] Of course, through these scenes, Fellowes rightly shows how men are not always the oppressor but can be victims, too, of oppressive gender/sex ideologies.[48] It is also interesting that despite Barrow's own wounded male body from a gunshot, Fellowes suggests that it is his homosexuality that serves to truly disable the footman. Nonetheless, the show fails to follow this up with imagery of how prejudicial attitudes towards disabled subjects can reconstitute discriminatory social structures. With regards to Bates, he is shown as attempting to 'normalise' his physical difference through the purchase of a limp corrector.[49]

Conflicting Masculinities

The device that Bates purchases is described as 'a kind of caliper, with iron struts and straps on and an adjustable foot platform at the bottom' that is 'extremely uncomfortable'.[50] But in the scenes in which Bates is shown wearing the brace, notions of male bravery and the rejection of weakness are upheld as the vanguard of masculinity. Bates is shown visibly distressed, 'breathing deeply' and crying 'out in pain' at the discomfort caused by this 'vicious implement' but he nonetheless protests that he is 'fine', words that not only deny the corporeal reality of his situation but also reject weakness, frailty and emotion and thus emasculation.[51] In the notes to the script surrounding these scenes, Fellowes comments that:

> The great moral triumph of being different, so brilliantly illustrated by the Paralympics, is to accept your difference which of course empowers you, but there is, I suspect, often a period that you have to go through when you're trying to be the same before you can get to that. I didn't want Bates to be too much of a saint on a monument. He's settling in, he likes Anna more and more and understandably wants rid of his limp [...] He wants to go back to normal. He is also brave enough to subject himself to considerable pain in his efforts.[52]

Fellowes's attitude here is overtly gendered even as he speaks ostensibly to celebrate physical difference. His comment is notably free of condemnatory language and clearly he does not seek to belittle disabled men, but the inference of a constricting binary opposition between the able-bodied and disabled male is paramount. Bravery – the archetype of the warrior – is valued as the preserve of 'real' men. Fellowes's inexplicit register privileges masculine 'normalcy', failing to accommodate the para-Olympians whose physical difference he evokes, thus reinforcing disability and specifically masculine disability as at odds with one another.

Paul Darke has questioned whether the normalisation of disability as 'different' is positive when normality and conformity are validated and disability is, as Fellowes infers above, posited as something to be overcome.[53] Sadly, *Downton Abbey* falls into this trap too. Mr Bates discards of the limp corrector by throwing it into the lake, vowing (to housekeeper, Mrs Hughes) that he will 'never again try to cure myself' and will 'spend my life happily as the butt of others' jokes and I will never mind them.'[54] The inference of this scene is that Bates 'overcomes' his seeming 'inadequacy' through moral strength and integrity. Yet Fellowes

Pride versus Prejudice

Figure 10.1 'Mr Bates, a shadow of a man?' in *Downton Abbey*

couples this with further measures to valorise Bates's masculinity, not least in how Bates is portrayed as a 'super-crip', that is, super cripple.

Coined by John Clogston, super-crip is a phrase to describe someone who is either deviant and overcomes their 'incompleteness' *in spite of* their disability, or who is idealised and romanticised for achieving 'normalcy' in the face of gendered and physical adversity.[55] Fellowes's conception of Bates encompasses both of these traits. In Series One, we learn that when Bates returned from the second Boer war he was an unhappy, injured man who was an unpleasant husband to his then wife, Vera, and whose discontent manifested as alcoholism. Recognising the error of his ways, however (and after a spell in prison), Bates sought a 'better' life for himself at Downton and 'turned his life around' by embracing the romanticised and idealised super-crip image via hypermasculinity.

Leonore Manderson and Susan Peake have explained that disabled men often perform hypermasculinity as a means to reclaim and validate their identity because sadly it helps to 'normalise' a sense of self.[56] In the show, Bates articulates hypermasculinity through heroism. Before he is romantically involved with Anna, for instance, he brings her food and flowers in secret when she is poorly to make her 'feel better' and then tucks her up in bed (thus taking on the role of romantic hero, too). Likewise, he tenderly comforts housemaid, Gwen (Rose Leslie), whom he finds crying because she fears she'll be stuck in service and fail to become the secretary she desires to be. Bates repeatedly displays honour and integrity when refusing to name Thomas as a petty thief for stealing wine from the Abbey's supplies, for example, even though he tries to set up Bates as the thief to protect himself. Later he displays honour and humility by leaving Downton of his own volition to stop Vera from exposing Mary's scandalous past to the press – that she took the Turkish Ambassador's son as a lover and he died in her bedroom. As Lord Grantham describes it, 'Bates fell on his sword to protect the reputation of my family', words which endorse a sense of chivalry in the valet's actions.[57]

Exalted by such gallant plotlines, it is unsurprising that one servant observes how 'everyone talks of him [Bates] as if he were a King', and that the women of the house should find him 'a romantic figure'.[58] Indeed, such was the effect of Fellowes's writing and Brendan Coyle's performance as Bates, that these sentiments were also echoed in the UK's popular press. The *Evening Standard* newspaper, for instance, described the phenomenon of 'The Cult of Mr Bates', with one reporter noting that

> he is 'somber', 'manly', 'dignified' – with a gorgeous speaking voice and sex appeal that goes off the scale. Who are we swooning about? Johnny Depp? Brad Pitt?
> Wrong. It's Mr Bates in *Downton Abbey*. Who would have thought a lame valet would have us all going hot under the collar? [59]

The derogatory attitude masquerading as flattery here reinforces Clogston's conception of the 'super-crip', since even a 'lame footman' can 'overcome' his disability to have sex appeal.[60]

However, to underscore Bates as 'super-crip', Fellowes situates the valet in a series of plotlines that equally constitute him in a pity-hero dichotomy. Such narratives are, in a dramatic sense, extreme, because they must pull on the audience's heartstrings so that Bates can be pitied and, latterly, applauded for his gallantry. Aptly, for much of Series Two and Three, Bates is wrongly convicted and imprisoned for Vera's murder, only to later receive a reprieve. But troublingly this dramatic device also extends to the portrayal of his wife's sexual assault in Series Four, for not only is Bates deeply tormented about the physical and emotional horror his wife is subjected to (and we see him crying after he finds out), but his disability is perniciously invoked as *the* reason that underlines such sexual violence in the first place.

Pride versus Prejudice

Anna's rapist, Mr Green, a valet to another of the Crawley's houseguests, arrives at the Abbey and quickly turns from being friendly with Anna to violent. In the scene that culminates in the attack, Green callously says to her: 'You look to me like you could do with a bit of real fun for once [...] You're not telling me that that sad, old cripple keeps you happy?'[61] Anna's reply is firm and her offence evident: 'If you must know, yes, he keeps me very happy.'[62] However, Green greets this with doubt and further aggression, 'Perhaps you've just forgotten what you're missing', he says maliciously, before violently punching Anna in the face and then assaulting her.

Elsewhere I have written of my concerns regarding the portrayal of Anna's rape in *Downton Abbey*.[63] Here, in the context of debates about masculinity and disability, it is apparent that disabled masculinity is being deployed pejoratively as a vehicle to render visible sexual violence against women. As feminist critics have vehemently argued, rape is never about sex, but about power, and here Green's words work to overpower and belittle Anna. But, with regards to masculinity and disability, there is a derogatory inference that disabled men cannot 'satisfy' an able-bodied woman because the disabled man is not a 'real' one. This false 'logic' and primetime television imagery is deeply problematic and begs the question: why should Bates's disability be invoked as symptomatic of a gendered inadequacy that provides *the* underlying 'cause' for his wife's rape? The answer, tragically, is simple. As Fellowes's comment cited at the beginning of this chapter indicates, for him, disability makes Bates 'more vulnerable' because it calls into question his masculinity, and to deploy a rape narrative in relation to Bates's wife makes him especially vulnerable.[64] The 'philosophy' underpinning this premise insinuates that disabled masculinity is not only weak and inauthentic but, as *Downton* goes on to suggest, must be reconciled through empowerment. In gendered terms this means that Bates must ascribe to hegemonic masculine ideals. Put another way, the disabled male subject must adopt a warrior persona and 'fight like a man', something, of course, Fellowes gestures to when Bates threatens to kill Mr Green.[65]

Conclusion

Tom Shakespeare reminds us that it is 'important not to buy into screen myths and models of masculinity which are inappropriate to the majority of men, let alone disabled men.'[66] Yet *Downton Abbey* fails to contribute to this endeavour by dispelling derogatory stereotypes concerning disabled masculinity.[67] Despite the ways in which *Downton* exposes many of the reductive ideas associated with patriarchal discourses of masculinity, nonetheless the period drama always seems to reach the conclusion that able-bodied masculinity *is* superior to disabled masculinity. Through its representation of the lived experience of male physical impairment, prejudice and discrimination, and the sexual politics of disability, *Downton Abbey* suggests that disabled men *can* have a life, but a distinctly different one to 'normal' men. Its plotlines conclude by suggesting that disabled men *should* compensate for their 'lack' by performing (and perhaps over perform) traditional masculine norms.

A respondent to the Scope survey cited earlier commented that: 'We need a more realistic view of disabled people – we're not all heroes or villains, even though I love stories about disabled people becoming heroes, overcoming adversity. But we all have the right not to climb a mountain!' [68] British costume drama, however historicist in truth, needs to provide more sophisticated insights into the experiences of disability and physically different men that challenge essentialist conceptions of hegemonic masculinity. Without them period dramas run the risk of impoverishing the fields of masculinity and disability studies, and therein social justice and equality.

Notes

1. Jenny Morris, *Pride Against Prejudice: Transforming Attitudes to Disability – A Personal Politics of Disability* (London, 1991), p 93
2. For more on calls for the diversity of disability onscreen see Scott Jordan Harris, 'The BBC's plans to show more disabled people on TV are good – but they should be better', *New Statesman*, 13 August 2014. Available at http://www.newstatesman.com/media/2014/08/bbc-s-plans-show-more-disabled-people-tv-are-good-they-should-be-better (accessed 29 October 2016).
3. For more on conceptions of disability and freakery in neo-Victorian period drama and especially the portrayal of Joseph Merrick in *Ripper Street*, see Helen Davies's *Neo-Victorian Freakery: The Cultural Afterlife of the Victorian Freakshow* (Basingstoke, 2015).
4. Annabelle Fenwick Elliot, 'It's 2015! People have sex!', *Daily Mail*, 1 September 2015. Available at http://www.dailymail.co.uk/femail/article-3217419/Lady-

Chatterley-star-James-Norton-defends-raunchy-BBC-adaptation-relevant-claims-encourage-youngsters-read-classics.html (accessed 29 October 2016).
5. Ibid.
6. Jessica Meyer, *Men of War: Masculinity and the First World War in Britain* (Basingstoke, 2009), p. 97.
7. Ibid., p. 97.
8. Sarah Crompton, 'Dan Stevens: Why I left *Downton Abbey*', *Telegraph*, 7 March 2016. Available at http://www.telegraph.co.uk/culture/tvandradio/downton-abbey/9765334/Dan-Stevens-Why-I-left-Downton-Abbey.html (accessed 3 June 2016).
9. As Julie Anne Taddeo's chapter describes, the Abbey also witnessed the decline of Henry Lang, a short-term valet to Lord Grantham who suffers from shell shock, or PTSD as it is now termed. Lang had been 'invalided out' from service during the war and struggles to adjust to life back home following his experience on the frontline.
10. 'The Unlikely Cult of Mr Bates', *Evening Standard*, 3 November 2010. Available at http://www.standard.co.uk/lifestyle/the-unlikely-cult-of-mr-bates-6531833.html (accessed 28 January 2016).
11. Russell Shuttleworth, Nikki Wedgwood and Nathan J. Wilson, 'The Dilemma of Disabled Masculinity', *Men and Masculinities*, 15/2 (2012), p. 174.
12. Katherine Byrne, 'Adapting Heritage: Class and Conservatism in *Downton Abbey*', *Rethinking History: The Journal of Theory and Practice*, 18/3 (2013), p. 316.
13. Claire O'Callaghan, 'The Downturn at *Downton*: Money and Masculinity in *Downton Abbey*', in H. Davies and C. O'Callaghan (eds), *Gender and Austerity in Popular Culture: Femininity, Masculinity and Recession in Film and Television* (London, 2016), p. 45.
14. Bryne, 'Adapting Heritage', p. 312.
15. Aaron Richmond, 'Disabled at Downton', in William Irwin (ed.), *Downton Abbey and Philosophy: Thinking in That Manor* (Chicago, IL, 2016), p. 71.
16. Tom Shakespeare, 'The Sexual Politics of Disabled Masculinity', *Sexuality and Disability*, 17/1 (1999), p. 54.
17. Shuttleworth et al., 'Dilemma', p. 174.
18. David A. Gerber (ed.), *Disabled Veterans in History* (Michigan, 2000), p. 1.
19. Ibid., p. 2.
20. Shakespeare, 'Sexual Politics', p. 63. Shakespeare writes eloquently in this context of the case of Christopher Reeve, who starred in a series of *Superman* films in the 1980s before becoming a quadriplegic following a riding accident in 1995. It is also worth noting here the extensive body of cultural work on male bodies and the Great War that resides alongside the field of disability studies. Joanna Bourke has examined the cultural implications of maimed male bodies on discourses of masculinity. Likewise, Lisa Herschback and Roxane Panchasi have both discussed the development of the post-World War I prosthetic limb industry that emerged for ex-servicemen that sought to

'reconstruct' the male body. Erin O'Connor has examined the development of medical discourse on the social meaning of amputations for men, although she situates her argument across the period 1851–1914. Finally, both Mark S. Mirale and Ben Shephard have discussed the discourses of emotional 'disability' – i.e., shell shock and 'war hysteria' in relation to discourses of post-war masculinity.

21. Ibid., p. 3.
22. Richmond, 'Disabled at Downton', p. 71. Also, see Jessica's Meyer's *Men of War* cited earlier.
23. Paul K. Longmore, *Why I Burned My Book and Other Essays on Disability* (Philadelphia, 2003), p. 146. This quotation is also cited in Richmond, 'Disabled at Downton', p. 71.
24. Hardeep Aiden and Andrea McCarthy, *Current Attitudes Towards Disabled People* (London, 2014), p. 3. Available at http://www.scope.org.uk/Scope/media/Images/Publication%20Directory/Current-attitudes-towards-disabled-people.pdf (accessed 20 June 2016).
25. Ibid., p. 7.
26. Julian Fellowes, *Downton Abbey: Season Two – The Complete Scripts* (London, 2013), p. 272.
27. Ibid., p. 300.
28. Ibid., p. 299.
29. Ibid., p. 285.
30. Adrienne Asch and Michelle Fine, 'Introduction: Beyond Pedestals', in M. Fine and A. Asch (eds), *Women with Disabilities: Essays in Psychology, Culture and Politics* (Philadelphia, 1988), p. 3.
31. Richmond, 'Disabled at Downton', p. 71; and Susan Wendell, *The Rejected Body: Feminist Philosophical Reflections on Disability* (London, 1996), p. 88.
32. Julian Fellowes, *Downton Abbey: Season Two*, p. 151.
33. Ibid., p. 182.
34. Ibid., p. 183.
35. Ibid., p. 272.
36. Aristotelis Nikolaidis, '(En)Gendering Disability in Film', *Feminist Media Studies*, 13/4 (2013), p. 760.
37. Fellowes, *Downton Abbey: Season Two*, p. 284.
38. Ibid., p. 273.
39. Shakespeare, 'Sexual Politics', p. 58.
40. Anon., 'Sexual Health for Men', *Christopher and Dana Reeve Foundation*, n.d. Available at https://www.christopherreeve.org/living-with-paralysis/health/sexual-health/sexual-health-for-men (accessed 15 August 2016).
41. Shakespeare, 'Sexual Politics', p. 58.
42. Julian Fellowes, *Downton Abbey: Season One – The Complete Scripts* (London, 2012), p. 18.
43. Ibid., p. 38 and p. 17.
44. Ibid., p. 21.

45. Ibid., p. 49.
46. Ibid., p. 221.
47. Shakespeare, 'Sexual Politics', p. 61.
48. William Sewell, 'A Theory of Structure: Duality, Agency and Transformation', *American Journal of Transformation*, 98/1 (1992), p. 4.
49. There is a body of literature that has examined the rise of the post-World War I prosthetic limb industry and its relationship to discourses of masculinity. As noted earlier, Lisa Herschback and Roxane Panchasi are particularly valuable in this regard.
50. Fellowes, *Downton Abbey, Season One*, p. 145.
51. Ibid., p. 145.
52. Ibid., p. 144.
53. See Paul Darke, 'Understanding Cinematic Representations of Disability', in T. Shakespeare (ed.), *The Disability Reader: Social Science Perspectives* (London, 1998), pp. 181–97.
54. Fellowes, *Downton Abbey: Season One*, p. 184.
55. See John Clogston, *Disability Coverage in 16 Newspapers* (Louisville, 1990). Sayantani DasGupta also reads Bates as representing the super-crip stereotype. See DasGupta's blog: 'Masculinity and Disability on *Downton Abbey*', *Stories are Good Medicine Blog*, 25 January 2011. Available at http://storiesaregoodmedicine.blogspot.co.uk/search?q=disability (accessed 13 July 2016).
56. See Lenore Manderson and Susan Peake, 'Men in Motion: Disability and the Performance of Masculinity', in C. Sandahl and P. Auslander (eds), *Bodies in Motion: Disability and Performance* (Michigan, 2005), pp. 230–42.
57. Ibid., p. 73.
58. Fellowes, *Downton Abbey: Season Two*, p. 17 and p. 226.
59. Anon, 'The Unlikely Cult of Mr Bates'.
60. Ibid.
61. Julian Fellowes, Downton Abbey: *Season Five*, episode four, n.p.
62. Ibid.
63. Claire O'Callaghan, 'Rape at Downton Abbey', *Feminist and Women's Studies Association Blog*, 17 November 2013. Available at http://fwsablog.org.uk/2013/11/17/rape-at-downton-abbey/ (accessed 13 June 2016).
64. Ibid.
65. Shuttleworth et al., 'Dilemma', p. 185.
66. Shakespeare, 'Disabled Masculinity', p. 63.
67. Ibid., p. 63.
68. Aiden and McCarthy, *Current Attitudes*, p. 16.

11

A Minority of Men: The Conscientious Objector in Period Drama

Lucy Brown

The conscientious objector is a familiar figure in modern perceptions of World War I. As attitudes have shifted in the century since the conflict, the CO has become as recognisable a figure as the propaganda posters featuring Lord Kitchener. However, in reality, there were only around 16,000 COs out of the millions of men who actually fought or served. When considered in this context, the representation of the CO in various period dramas seems disproportionate at best. Many modern period dramas relating to either World War I or II include a CO, or a man who aspires to be a CO. The authenticity of these representations varies in the four dramas examined in this chapter. All four, however, represent objectors unmanned in one form or another, with a complex set of values impacting the representation of their masculinity within the narratives.

Concepts of ideal masculinity were prevalent in contemporary depictions of the CO. Lois S. Bibbings highlights that: 'Both before and during the war the soldier was constructed as exemplary and aspirational in a range of cultural forms, and the characteristics which he was supposed to embody were celebrated.'[1] This construction of the soldier as an ideal form of masculinity was exacerbated by the outbreak of war. Masculinity

A Minority of Men

became inevitably entwined with the thirst for excitement and the bravery of enlistment and, for a time, this was enough to provide the number of volunteers required by the forces. Alongside this, concerted recruitment campaigns utilised dubious methods, as Ann Kramer notes:

> Images of women and children appeared on recruiting posters, urging their men to defend Britain, while some women handed out white feathers – traditional symbol of cowardice – to men not in uniform [...] The campaign reflected the public mood at the time and certainly forced some men to enlist rather than be humiliated.[2]

By labelling men who refused to enlist as unpatriotic cowards, these campaigns helped develop the language which would later be applied to those who refused conscription.

The Military Service Act of 1916 introduced conscription whilst allowing four grounds for exemption. One of these was a conscientious objection to combatant military service, a contentious clause that was hotly debated but eventually included. The initial belief of the government was that objectors could be controlled and placed into other necessary work, although some objectors refused to participate in anything connected to the war effort. Tribunals were established to deal with the conscientious objectors. These, however, were biased, as Kramer again explains:

> Baffled by conscientious objectors and feeling a duty to bring men into the army, most tribunals treated objectors with disdain and rudeness, COs finding themselves on the receiving end of questions and comments that were at best dismissive and at worst downright aggressive and bullying.[3]

The public mood encouraged the harsh treatment of COs and there was little support for their course of action. In this climate, the assertion of cowardice was coupled with the suggestion of 'unmanliness', as Bibbings notes: 'When constructed as selfish, shirking or cowards, objectors were often portrayed as representing a parasitic unmanliness, shirking responsibility and living off the efforts of others.'[4] As a consequence, the language surrounding COs was inextricably linked to their masculinity, or lack thereof.

This chapter will examine four characters in recent costume dramas and their representations of the CO. *The Village* (BBC, 2013–14) tells the story of a small Northern community beginning with the outbreak of war in 1914. Amongst the supporting characters is Gerard Eyre (Matt Stokoe), a schoolteacher who refuses the call-up. *Downton Abbey* (ITV) ran for six successful series between 2010 and 2015 with the exploits of the Crawley family from 1912 onwards. World War I was covered during Series Two, with several men leaving to actively fight. One who does not wish to is chauffeur Tom Branson (Allen Leech), who desires to be a political CO but is unfit. Echoes of World War I are also present in *Home Fires* (ITV, 2015–16) and the continuation of *Upstairs, Downstairs* (BBC, 2010–12), both of which are set in and around the period of World War II. In *Home Fires*, postman Spencer Wilson (Mike Noble) refuses to fight due to his father's suffering in the previous war, while in *Upstairs, Downstairs*, butler Warwick Pritchard (Adrian Scarborough) is revealed to have been a conscientious objector in World War I and loses a chance at romantic happiness. With the exception of Branson, all the men make their stand and are punished for doing so in one way or another. There is also a correlation between 'unmanliness' and cowardice, which is implicit at the very least, and this is explored in the reaction to the characters within the programmes. Again, Tom Branson is an exception to this, essentially escaping censure as his wish to become an objector and an agitator are unfulfilled. This chapter will examine the representation of these four men and analyse how their masculinity is called into question by their status as conscientious objectors.

'His name is Coward. His name is Shirker': Realism and Melodrama in *The Village*

The Village and *Downton Abbey* are vastly different period dramas, despite their ostensible similarities. Both take place within insular communities, *The Village* in a small rural community in the Peak District and *Downton* in the splendid surroundings of a manor house in North Yorkshire. The difference between the two is summed up in a review of Series One of *The Village* in the *Independent*: 'It was a welcome relief from those McCostume dramas (mentioning no names) that offer little more than a game of "dress-up" with a host of posh frocks and a repertoire of above/below stairs shenanigans.'[5] The reference to 'McCostume dramas' is a direct criticism of the early years of *Downton*, of which Katherine Byrne notes that: 'Popular support is not matched by critical acclaim, however. *Downton* remains a guilty pleasure for many viewers: it is eminently watchable but at times politically or ideologically indefensible.'[6] Although the tone of *Downton* darkened considerably from Series Three onwards, the first two series were representative of a paternalistic aristocracy and were essentially a period soap opera. Conversely, *The Village* is keener to expose the divisions between the classes and depict a grittier side of Northern life at the beginning of the century. This is deftly illustrated in their differing treatments of conscientious objectors.

Gerard Eyre in *The Village* is a schoolteacher who wrestles from the opening episode with his doubts over fighting, and ultimately rejects conscription. His journey, whilst not explicitly condemned by the narrative, is shown in juxtaposition to other war stories. The brutal death of villager Paul (Luke Williams) at the Front is described in graphic detail by traumatised Joe Middleton (Nico Mirallegro), himself later shot for desertion when suffering from shell shock. Eyre, on the other hand, is vilified on all sides for his stance. When he returns to the village in Series One, Episode Six, Peter (Jim Cartwright), the landlord of the pub tells him, '137 men went to fight from this village, 25 came back. And you.' Eyre, therefore, is perceived as something apart, neither one of the dead or one of the glorious. It continues to haunt him through the rest of his time in the village.

The Village depicts the precursors and reaction to Eyre's initial stance utilising real-life evidence taken from public life and tribunal decisions. For instance, in Series One, Episode Two, a virulent sermon is given by Robin Lane (Scott Handy) condemning the war which deliberately echoes real comments made by the likes of the Bishops of Chelmsford and Oxford. Eyre is seen actively struggling with his conscience in the chapel during this sermon and it forms an integral part of the stance he makes in the following episode. Equally, his tribunal experience in Series One, Episode Three is based, in part, on real-life examples. Firstly, it is questioned whether 25 is 'old enough to have a conscience', possibly in a direct reference to Harold Bing, who was told in 1916 that 18 was not old enough to possess a conscience.[7] Eyre is then confronted with a hypothetical scenario of German soldiers attacking the children in his care, of the type that was documented in some tribunals. Melodramatically, Eyre's steadfast response that he would not kill is contradicted by his pupil, Bert Middleton (Bill Jones), who had asked him the same question previously and received a favourable, if lukewarm, response. Eyre's application is therefore rejected on the unofficial evidence of his pupil and he is forcibly collected by the military. This process is also used by the writers to add authenticity to their narrative. For instance, they initially tell him: 'You will be taken at dawn to a suitable place where you will be shot by firing squad. Do you understand?' He is horrified before being told it was a sentence handed down to someone for disobeying an order. As well as being a tool for controlling Eyre, then, this also has direct echoes of the way real conscientious objectors were originally told they were going to die, as Will Ellsworth-Jones explains: 'There was a long, dramatic and intentional pause, more than enough time for all four men to realise that the sentence really was a death sentence, before the officer continued.'[8] Again, *The Village* utilises real-life examples of the military's behaviour to back up the authenticity of their fictional narrative in the same way as they have adapted real-life tribunal transcripts and motivations for conscientious objection.

The origins of Eyre's conscientious objection to service may be based on real-life examples, but the choice of Eyre as a conduit plays into the stereotypes of the CO as unmanly and feminised. As a teacher, Eyre is unlike many of the men who leave the village to fight in the Pals Battalion. They are farm labourers and factory workers, stereotypically masculine and hard-working. Eyre, conversely, is a teacher whose methods are seen from the first episode to be unorthodox and enlightened. To modern sensibilities, Eyre is in the right and the war-hungry headmaster Crispin Ingham (Stephen Walters), originally rejected from the military for being too short, is wrong. In this sense, *The Village* is as conscious of the twenty-first-century perception of World War I as *Downton* is. Indeed, in her book, *Edwardians on Screen: from* Downton Abbey *to* Parade's End, Katherine Byrne notes that: 'The British Army is not the only institution criticised by *The Village* [...] but it is the one most directly and repeatedly attacked, in the strongest terms.'[9] By highlighting the fact that *The Village* frequently attacks the military, Byrne demonstrates that the tenets of the early twentieth century are open to retrospective criticism by period dramas. *The Village*, however, is also guilty of adhering to stereotypes in its depiction of Eyre as a schoolteacher instead of any of the more traditionally masculine occupations depicted elsewhere. In reality, objectors came from many walks of life, as Ann Kramer explains: 'They were clerks, engineers, journalists, post-office workers, teachers and lecturers, watchmakers, chemists, skilled artisans, parliamentary candidates and local councillors. They included lawyers [...] builders, intellectuals, thinkers, artists, musicians and farmers.'[10] Depicting Eyre as a teacher of a mixed-sex class with a progressive viewpoint naturally provokes the later twentieth-century connotations of feminised men working with children and, therefore, suggests that he is more sensitive and open to being considered alongside predominantly women. Alongside this is the fact that Eyre is shown in such a way that the audience identifies with and respects him as the most educated man in the village and as an enlightened conscientious objector. The complexities of Eyre's representation in *The Village*, then, include a resolve to show the unvarnished truth of conscientious objection during World War I, coupled with an awareness of twenty-first-century sensibilities.

Eyre's return to the village in Series One, Episode Six marries the realistic with the melodramatic. His visit to the pub interrupts a meeting about the village war memorial. Already, then, Eyre is defined by his lack of service in comparison to the men in the pub who are injured and missing limbs. He is mocked with a chorus of 'Land of Hope and Glory' and later punched for standing up for Bert. The status he had before as an educated and respected teacher has disappeared. More significantly, Eyre is the vessel via which Spanish Flu finds its way to the village when it has been previously spared from the epidemic. He is therefore seen as a conduit for a disease that kills the village's children, a symbolic position for a teacher. It is also significant that Eyre is incapacitated by the flu in his first foray back into the classroom. At the time, his illness is undiagnosed and so, when Ingham finds him struggling, his illness and status as a conscientious objector become bound up together: 'What have we here? A teacher who can't write his own name. Why not? Shall we ask him? Why can't you do it? Is it shame? Or is it guilt? I'll tell you his name. His name is Coward. His name is Shirker.' Eyre is physically unable to teach at this time and this is linked with his perceived cowardliness. It also links with the theories of degeneration that pervaded contemporary discourse about conscientious objectors, as Bibbings notes: 'The CO was cast as an unnatural man, a pointless man, an aberration who was not only unmanly and possibly an invert, but was also less than a woman; a subhuman breed.'[11] In demonstrating that Eyre is a conduit for the flu, a danger to women and children, he is further condemned for his stance as a conscientious objector. Eyre does not die but others do, just as they did during the war while he refused to fight. Conversely, this survival may be seen as a reward for his steadfast refusal to participate in the hostilities and a confirmation of the strength which has been hitherto denied to him by his stance as a conscientious objector.

Eyre's return into the community as a teacher stretches the boundaries of the realism which *The Village* strives to portray in Series One. In reality, many conscientious objectors struggled to continue their careers, as Ellsworth-Jones explains: 'If the COs were patient and persistent they nearly always found employment in the end, but it was seldom what they hoped for.'[12] Eyre's career as a teacher should have been severely hampered by his stance and it is unlikely that he would have been accepted in the same village and school he had taught in before the war. In retaining the character of Gerard Eyre, the writers lose some of their realism, and his rehabilitation also includes an admittance of cowardice in Series One, Episode Six, in a discussion with Robin Lane: 'Everything that I say about the war and killing, I believe to be true. But I know that the stand that I took was also motivated by fear. I didn't wanna kill anyone. And I didn't wanna be killed.' Although Eyre qualifies his acknowledgement by stating that he believes he was right, he also confirms that he was scared of pain and death. Robin Lane's response further muddies the waters: 'I saw the men in this village go off to fight. I saw the courage it took for them to offer themselves up to suffering. None had the courage to reject suffering, apart from you.' Labelling Eyre's actions as courageous is a compliment, though it is laced with the implication that he valued self-preservation more than the other villagers. Through this exchange, Eyre is invited back into village life and secures his return to teaching. The tacit implication here is that Eyre can only remain once he has admitted to a degree of cowardice.

Eyre's affair with Martha Allingham (Charlie Murphy), Robin Lane's daughter, in Series Two ostensibly asserts his masculinity in comparison to the aristocratic war hero, George (Augustus Prew), who suffers due to his experiences in the trenches. He has been physically and mentally damaged by the war, while Eyre has escaped relatively unscathed and wins Martha's love. However, he is marginalised from playing an active role in obtaining her when George Allingham effectively gives his wife away to him, despite being the broken one. Even when depicted as the physically superior man, Eyre is still an outsider, with Allingham's honour, morality and self-renunciation trumping his own apparent selfishness.

The final episode of *The Village* shows Eyre and Martha fleeing the village due to her inability to obtain a divorce (through no fault of her husband's). That Eyre is once again running away from a difficult situation is compounded by the fact he is taking something that does not belong to him in the form of George Allingham's wife. By refusing to stay and fight, therefore, Eyre is framed again as a coward, and one who has alienated his closest friend, Bert, by pursuing a woman he had feelings for. Eyre leaves the village in disgrace and, it is assumed, he and Martha do not intend to return. It is notable, however, that Eyre's departure storyline is not about him. Instead of a natural progression to his status as a conscientious objector which may have included him being unable to find work and struggling to demonstrate his masculinity in other ways, he is an auxiliary to the marriage plotline of George Allingham and the greater dynamic of the Allinghams and the Middletons that pervades *The Village*.

'Mixed with sour milk': *Downton Abbey's* Idealistic CO

Unlike Gerard Eyre, Tom Branson's desired objector status in *Downton Abbey* is merely a footnote in the evolution of a character from a radical chauffeur to a son-in-law helping to steer the Crawley family through the twentieth century. He is legitimately excused from service by a health issue and his attempt at another type of stand is subsequently foiled too. He gradually develops over the rest of *Downton*'s run into one of the most sensible characters. This inability to allow Branson to publicly declare and be punished as a conscientious objector stems from two things: firstly, that the representation of a conscientious objector in *Downton* is merely to fulfil a staple of World War I fictional representation and, secondly, that the writers do not wish to lose or damage such a popular character when his progressive sensibilities fit so firmly into the twenty-first century.

Conflicting Masculinities

Branson is shown from his first appearance in Series One, Episode Four to be independently and politically minded. He shares pamphlets with Lady Sybil (Jessica Brown Findlay) about suffrage and is quietly pleased to find her more independently minded than the majority of her class. When war breaks out, he does not enlist and, in Series Two, Episode One laughs at a woman who hands him a white feather. His objector stance comes to the fore in Series Two, Episode Three when Sybil hears he has received the call-up, although he is adamant he will not fight. His analysis of what he will do is idealistic: 'I'll go to the medical, I'll report for duty, and when on parade I'll march out front and I'll shout it out loud and clear. And if that doesn't make the newspapers then I'm a monkey's uncle.' Considering that Series Two, Episode Three takes place in summer 1917, it is extremely unlikely than any such stand would be received favourably by the press. Ann Kramer explains that: 'Given the appalling war casualties by 1917, it is perhaps hardly surprising that the public attitude towards conscientious objectors was extremely bitter and in April 1917 public anger was stoked up by a deliberate press campaign.'[13] So, while *Downton* uses Sybil as a mouthpiece for the dangers Branson could face in terms of prison and a criminal record, the expectation that the *Downton* plot will feature one of the most memorable and morally recognisable characters as part of the war experience takes precedent over realism and coherent characterisation. As Julie Anne Taddeo's chapter argues, *Downton* is intent on demonstrating the spectrum of war experience through Matthew Crawley (Dan Stevens), a wounded hero who is almost maimed for life, William (Thomas Howe), a lower-class willing soldier who dies after protecting Crawley, and Thomas (Rob James-Collier), who deliberately wounds himself to be sent home. There are also supplementary plots, including Mrs Patmore's (Lesley Nicol) deserter nephew who was shot at dawn, and Mr Lang (Cal MacAninch), a valet who suffers from shell shock. While Branson is certainly the most likely candidate to be a conscientious objector, his timing and idealistic notions are extremely unlikely in the context of World War I and in light of his intellectual characterisation.

Branson's convenient diagnosis with a heart murmur precludes any tribunal experience such as that faced by Eyre or the possibility for imprisonment. His attempt to, as he says to Sybil in Series Two, Episode Three, 'get them another' way can be seen as petulant at best. The audience and several members of the household are led to the conclusion that

A Minority of Men

Branson intends to harm a general who is visiting Downton. He is frogmarched away from the dining room by Carson (Jim Carter) and Mrs Hughes (Phyllis Logan), after which it becomes apparent that he was merely going to throw a tureen of slop over the general. While this prevents Branson being depicted as a potential murderer who would have required public punishment, it also displays him as naïve and perhaps even cowardly. This is his version of taking a stand: 'Oil and ink and a bit of a cow pat, all mixed with sour milk. He'd have needed a bath, right enough, but not a coffin.' Branson's method of being a conscientious objector does not require a public stand or public condemnation. The few people who do know of his plans conceal them and he is free to continue pursuing Lady Sybil. That romantic storyline would not have been possible had Branson taken a public stand and, like Matthew Crawley's inability to walk or father a child, it is abandoned to the greater narrative arc. Branson's subsequent reformation into one of Downton's saviours and the voice of reason entirely buries his earlier anti-war stance.

On the outside, Branson's attempts to 'humiliate the British Army' could be seen as befitting his desired status as a conscientious objector. After all, the attitude of many COs was that killing another human being was against God's will and many invoked the Ten Commandments as evidence of this. Neither Branson nor Eyre use religion to back up their war stance, despite Branson being a Catholic and religious belief being an oft-cited reason for refusing conscription. Throughout the early years of *Downton*, his socialism is more prevalent than his Catholicism, and it is his Irish nationalism that partly prompts his stance. When asked by Sybil why he is 'so angry all the time' in Series Two, Episode Three and mentions the problems in Ireland, he responds, 'Not at your best? Not at your best? I lost a cousin in the Easter Rising last year.' His reason for opposing conscription is more immediately political than anything else, and it also serves, once again, to implant an historical event into the *Downton* narrative. Branson is therefore used as a dual plot device by *Downton*: he fulfils a category necessity as a conscientious objector and he is the token Irish radical disillusioned by events in his homeland. However, his desire to be a conscientious objector is soon forgotten and his evolution from radical chauffeur to Crawley family saviour is complete by the end of Series Six. Although he flirts with politics throughout his life, he becomes a widowed father whose primary concern is his daughter. While this also, in effect, unmans him, placing him in the nursery instead of the billiard room, the portrayal is heroic to modern audiences, perhaps as another example of him doing his duty in a manner recognisable to them.

'You're not the man I thought you were': Echoes of World War I in *Home Fires* and *Upstairs, Downstairs*

World War II narratives are not free from representations of conscientious objection. However, Will Ellsworth-Jones concedes that: 'The conscientious objector discovered that the process had become both easier and more acceptable.'[14] Although some of the approximately 62,000 registered COs served time in prison, lessons had been learned from World War I about how to deal with those who refused conscription. Consequently, the representations of Spencer Wilson in *Home Fires* and Warwick Pritchard in *Upstairs, Downstairs* are based more around the attitudes of their communities than any legal ramifications.

Wilson is first depicted as a rather sweet postman in Series One, Episode One of *Home Fires*. He comes to the rescue of maid, Claire (Daisy Badger), when she falls off her bicycle and later overhauls the entire machine before returning it to her. While this could be seen as a masculine response, he is feminised by his sweetness and physique. For instance, in Series One, Episode Two, Jenny (Jodie Hamblet), the woman who is trying to claim him as her sweetheart, points out that: 'Spencer's the only lad round here who doesn't reek of manure.' Although this is seen as a positive at the time, when his objector status is revealed later in Series One, Episode Four, Jenny's attitude changes: 'Even when we were stepping out, I knew he wasn't quite right. Left all decisions about what we did and where we went to me. Always backed down when we had an argument. No backbone. I should've guessed.' Here, Jenny invokes all the stereotypical qualities of a weak man, particularly when she mentions his lack of 'backbone.' The qualities which Jenny had prized him on before are suddenly unmanly and not 'quite right'. Other villagers are also quick to condemn Wilson, with Mrs Brindsley (Claire Price) warning that he and his mother are not welcome in her shop and Joyce Cameron (Francesca Annis) calling him an 'unpatriotic coward'. In Series One, Episode Five his bicycle is plastered with duck feathers and Jenny places a white feather in his buttonhole in front of the crowd. That Wilson has signed up to the auxiliary fire service ensures that he will not be one of those incarcerated and his entire negative experience of his stance comes from the reactions of his friends and neighbours. This corresponds to the experiences of Tom Branson in *Downton*, where his only censure comes from his own community. Like Branson, Wilson avoids other forms of external punishment, although he takes action in joining the auxiliary fire service while Branson's heart murmur negates any service whatsoever.

The reasons for Wilson's stance come from echoes of his father's death in World War I. Ernest Wilson walked straight into enemy fire on a suicide mission, as Wilson learned: 'Every one, he spoke of his regret at having to kill a German soldier with his bayonet. Awake or asleep, he couldn't get the man's face out of his head. The begging and screaming haunted him constantly. He was still writing about it in his last letter before he was killed.' Due to the censorship in operation for soldiers' letters during World War I, this scenario is unlikely, although it does supply a credible backdrop for Wilson refusing to fight. Like Eyre's stance in *The Village*, it also invokes a type of response in the modern audience that they are familiar with: the reluctance to fight and kill anyone. He is perceived as unmanly by Jenny and other villagers, but Claire stands by him and they ultimately marry in Series Two. Wilson's CO stance is neatly tidied away and in Series Two he gains recognition for alerting villagers to an unexploded bomb above their heads and staying near to it during the defusing process. In a programme focused on women, Wilson is represented as feminine too by his refusal to fight. The war is seen through a prism of how it affects the women in the village, from Steph's (Clare Calbraith) struggles to maintain her farm following the departure of her husband to fight to Mrs Brindsley's fears over her son joining up. Wilson is consequently seen as someone refusing to do his duty, even while the programme itself is sympathetic in its representation of his conscientious objection.

In the second series of the continuation of *Upstairs, Downstairs*, butler Warwick Pritchard finds his previous status as a CO during World War I impeding a potential relationship as World War II looms. He develops a bond with a lady's maid in Miss Whisset (Sarah Lancashire) in Series Two, Episode Five who shares his feelings. However, she is deeply conflicted when she hears that he was not unfit to fight in the earlier conflict as she had assumed. Pritchard attempts to defend himself: 'It was not an easy decision, nor one I arrived at lightly. But I had to do what I believed in.' Unlike some COs, Pritchard agreed to undertake some war work in the form of ambulance assistance and has already been appointed as an ARP warden in this conflict. However, his conscience still scuppers his relationship with Miss Whisset: 'I'm so sorry, Warwick. I feel I no longer know you [...]. You're not the man I thought you were.' Miss Whisset's absolutist attitude draws on the experiences of the earlier war and demonstrates the potency conscientious objection could still have on lives. This is, in part, based on documented experiences. Nor is Miss Whisset the only person to express disappointment. Mrs Thackeray, the cook, also comments: 'Course, to my mind, he should've been off fighting with the rest of them. But not a lot to be gained now by dwelling on the past, is there?' This comes seconds after she has proudly stated that: 'He's one in a million, our Mr Pritchard.' So, while he is considered exceptional and one of the family by those he lives and works with, the spectre of his conscience still looms large. Following Miss Whisset's rejection, teetotaller Pritchard falls into a drunken spiral, which the household endeavour to help him out of. It is clear, however, that Pritchard's inability to keep Miss Whisset's affection is a direct result of his previous actions. While Pritchard may be another example of a token CO in a period drama, his lack of a happy romantic ending is more in-keeping with real-life experiences than the other characters examined in this chapter.

Conclusion

The three men who publicly declare their conscientious objection in the period dramas analysed above suffer within their insular communities. Tom Branson, on the other hand, flourishes as a character because he cannot declare his objection publicly and, therefore, it need not affect the way other characters view him. *The Village* struggles to extract Gerard Eyre from his feminised role as an objector, and he continues to serve as a plot device during his affair with Martha Allingham. The World War I echoes evident in *Home Fires* and *Upstairs, Downstairs* demonstrate the realistic long-lasting effects of earlier conscientious objection on the later conflict. However, these dramas still play into the stereotypes of feminised men via the characters they choose to demonstrate objection through. As an alternative to this, Taddeo's chapter in this book highlights how the 2015 drama *Life in Squares* (BBC) demonstrates masculinity in objection in the form of homosexual couple Duncan Grant (James Norton, christened by the media as a 'period hunk' in the Poldark mode)[15] and David Garnett (Jack Davenport). They are shown working on a farm as part of their alternative service, although Taddeo notes that their manliness remains suspect due to the fact the government mandates their labour. It is also notable that *Life in Squares* ignores Lytton Strachey's (Ed Birch) appearance before the military board, where he jokes that he would 'come between' any German raping his sister. This real depiction of a conscientious objector risks tarring other representations of objectors with negative connotations. In order for a character to be sympathetic to the audience, their motivations cannot be wholly selfish as a realistic representation of Strachey would likely appear to be. If the trope of moral conscientious objection is common to twenty-first-century period drama, it is also notable that objectors are represented as physically unexceptional and defined, at least in part, by their perceived cowardice.

Notes

1. Lois S. Bibbings, *Telling Tales About Men: Conceptions of Conscientious Objectors to Military Service During the First World War* (Manchester, 2011), p. 90.
2. Ann Kramer, *Conscientious Objectors of the First World War: A Determined Resistance* (Barnsley, 2014), p. 21.
3. Ibid., p. 45.
4. Bibbings, *Telling Tales About Men*, p. 101.
5. Arifa Akbar, 'TV review: The Village gives viewers – finally – a proper, grown-up period drama', *Independent*, 1 April 2013. Available at http://www.independent.co.uk/arts-entertainment/tv/reviews/tv-review-the-village-gives-viewers-finally-a-proper-grown-up-period-drama-8555619.html (accessed 31 August 2016).
6. Katherine Byrne, 'New Developments in Heritage: The Recent Dark Side of *Downton* "Downer" *Abbey*', in J. Leggott and J. A. Taddeo (eds), *Upstairs and Downstairs: British Costume Drama Television from* The Forsyte Saga *to* Downton Abbey (Lanham, Boulder, New York, 2015), p. 177.
7. Will Ellsworth-Jones, *We Will Not Fight: The Untold Story of World War One's Conscientious Objectors* (London: 2008), p. 74.
8. Ellsworth-Jones, *We Will Not Fight*, p. 169.
9. Katherine Byrne, *Edwardians on Screen: from* Downton Abbey *to* Parade's End (London, 2015), p. 145.

10. Kramer, *Conscientious Objectors of the First World War*, p. 35.
11. Bibbings, *Telling Tales About Men*, p. 116.
12. Ellsworth-Jones, *We Will Not Fight*, p. 242.
13. Kramer, *Conscientious Objectors of the First World War*, p. 125.
14. Ellsworth-Jones, *We Will Not Fight*, p. 254.
15. '"Poldark made me feel inadequate!" Period drama hunk James Norton opens up!', *Woman Magazine*, n.d. Available at http://www.womanmagazine.co.uk/publication/woman-magazine/poldark-made-me-feel-inadequate-period-drama-hunk-james-norton-opens-up (accessed 29 November 2016).

12

Cads, Cowards and Cowmen: Masculinity in Crisis in World War II Television Drama

Stella Hockenhull

Home Fires (ITV, 2015 – 16) is a television drama series about the Women's Institute[1] which is loosely based on Julie Summers's 2013 book, *Jambusters: The Story of the Women's Institute in the Second World War*. Set in the Cheshire village of Great Paxford immediately prior to and during World War II, the first episode commences with a shot of an army truck full of soldiers hurtling through the countryside almost out of control. Rounding the corner, the men encounter a herd of cattle being brought in for milking by local farmer's wife, Steph Farrow (Clare Calbraith), and her teenage son, young Stan (Brian Fletcher). The vehicle halts and the soldiers honk their horn, gesture at the assemblage and shout angrily for them to move out of the way. However, despite their irritation and unreasonable behaviour, Steph is defiant and uncompromising; displayed in close-up, her features are resolute as she stares at the men and refuses to budge. In a subsequent scene the local village doctor, Will Campbell (Ed Stoppard), informs his patient, David Brindsley (Will Attenborough) that he has asthma and must be careful of a reoccurrence if he decides to enlist. David does join the navy, but with serious emotional and physical consequences when he is injured in a fire. A further setback for the male population of Great Paxford occurs when the doctor himself attempts to join up, only to be informed that he is suffering from lung cancer and is therefore unfit. Other male figures include Bob Simms (Mark Bazeley), who is the local reporter, and an abusive, yet insecure, husband who resents his wife for 'holding him back' as he puts it; he is cruel both physically and mentally, constantly insulting and undermining her. Spencer Wilson (Mike Noble), on the other hand, is a conscientious objector, and, as Lucy Brown discusses in the previous chapter, perceived as cowardly and therefore bullied by the locals as a result. Additionally, Wing Commander Richard Bowers (Philip McGinley), who is stationed nearby at the local RAF Head Quarters, is a habitual adulterer, unable to resist having affairs with young women despite being married. The above instances are only a few of the many examples of the damaged, dysfunctional or vulnerable men that feature in *Home Fires*, and there are more. Indeed, masculinity in this drama is usually impaired in some way, and men are frequently injurious towards others: often philanderers or sick individuals in need of help. I argue here that *Home Fires* features strong and positive representations of women to the disadvantage and disempowerment of men. Moreover, the series uses the historical setting of World War II as a conduit to comment on the contemporary situation regarding gender, chiming with what Kira Cochrane terms fourth-wave feminism, and with Donna Peberdy's notion of white male decline.

Masculinity in British Cinema and Television Drama

As noted, *Home Fires* is a period drama set in World War II and, unlike films made during this period, features the male population in a bad light. The hero of films made between 1939 and 1945 was represented as uncomplaining and brave, particularly when fighting at the front. As Graham Dawson suggests, 'The soldier hero has proved to be one of the most durable and powerful forms of idealised masculinity within Western cultural traditions since the time of the Ancient Greeks.'[2] Films such as *In Which We Serve* (1942) and *Nine Men* (1943) demonstrate the fighting spirit of the ordinary British soldier, the former focusing on three main characters, CPO Hardy (Bernard Miles), Shorty Blake (John Mills) and

Cads, Cowards and Cowmen

Captain Kinross (Noel Coward), who emanate from a mixture of social classes, and undertake heroic deeds and acts of bravery.[3] Representations of men during wartime existed in unchallenged patriarchy: they were viewed as capable, long-suffering and valiant. Equally, British television costume dramas postwar about World War II, specifically those made during the late 1970s and early 1980s such as *Danger UXB* (ITV, 1979) and *Piece of Cake* (ITV, 1988), also featured a predominantly male cast who were shown to be adept and proficient in their work. As A. Bowdoin Van Riper suggests, men in these dramas are 'defined by their knowledge and skills rather than by their wealth and social position. Inattentive, incompetent, and inflexible characters routinely fall and frequently die; the survivors, in turn, learn to be more focused, more skilful, and more adaptable'.[4] Both series centre on combat operations at specific periods of the war, and are representative of the notion of a triumphant Britain with their emphasis on work while introducing values such as compliance and competence. As Van Riper notes, 'the virtues of industrial capitalism and the factory floor – are everything'.[5] For him, masculinity in these television dramas is represented as heroic and proficient, and thus a product of Thatcherite Britain, embodying the ex-Prime Minister's political style and values '*because* [men] are uncompromising in pursuit of their goals, willing to defy convention and trample the sensitive feelings of others when the survival of the nation is at stake'.[6]

Andrew Spicer too documents the correlation between various versions of masculinity and social history in British cinema. In contemporary film he identifies a 'damaged men' period, whereby masculinity represents inadequacies which form 'part of the broken promise of post-war reconstruction'.[7] He traces a lineage from immediate postwar films which introduce the subject of dislocation and sexual uncertainty following prolonged absences away, to the veteran suffering from psychotic disorders. The damaged man, and indeed masculinity in crisis, is revisited in contemporary social realism commencing with films such as *Nil by Mouth* (1997) and continued in the work of Ken Loach, Shane Meadows and Duane Hopkins.[8] Donna Peberdy advances Spicer's argument, describing US cinema as containing a pervading master narrative of white male decline.[9] She argues that this is evident in various cultural media, not just cinema, and is particularly noticeable in the performance of male angst both off and on-screen. As she points out, 'it is impossible to deny the instability of the male *image* evident in the overwhelming permeation of a discourse of masculinity crisis during the 1990s and 2000s.'[10] For Brian Baker, many contemporary television dramas that represent the military past link with current events and 'renegotiate representations of masculinity, and culturally produced constructions of the soldier have clear political urgency for the contemporary period, where British and American troops have been engaged in wars in Afghanistan and Iraq'.[11]

This interrogation of masculinity not only chimes with present conflicts, but also reveals an inability to deal with feminism's continuing evolution. Indeed, Kira Cochrane notes that 'the women's movement may have been in hiding through the "ladette years", but in 2013 it has come back with a vengeance.'[12] As she elucidates:

> Everywhere you looked in the summer of 2013, a fourth wave of feminism was rising in the UK, women were opening their eyes to misogyny and sexism, and shouting back against it [...] Every day a new campaign starts, often created by women who are just discovering sexist injustice, and responding with anger, alacrity and vigour.[13]

Fourth-wave feminism is the current phrase deployed to embody women's call for equality,[14] and, according to Cochrane, they are now more active using social media because they do not have a voice in the rest of the world.[15] Fourth-wave feminism also coincides with a rise in strong roles for women in television – a point mooted by Jacquie Lawrence, who demands:

> Why is it that television produces better roles for women? According to audience research, the reason better roles have become available over the last decade is simply that as viewership fragments, men have become less important to advertisers who want to reach viewers with control over disposable income. So television creates roles that appeal to women.[16]

Home Fires also corresponds with other television period dramas such as *Land Girls* (BBC, 2009–11) and *Call the Midwife* (BBC, 2012–), both featuring strong women protagonists, a factor which might be attributed to a reconsideration of the past through period drama, albeit their focus now is mainly the twentieth century rather than the 'bonnets and breeches' historical dramas. Indeed, the trend seems to be a move away from the classic nineteenth-century adaptations towards more recent history, a point mooted by Ben Dowell, who suggests:

> Ratings dipped for BBC1's most recent costume drama, Charles Dickens' *Little Dorrit*, which sank to a low of 2.5 million viewers for one midweek episode last month. By comparison, *The Diary of Anne Frank* pulled in about 4.5 million viewers, while *The 39 Steps*, starring former Spooks actor Rupert Penry-Jones, attracted 7.3 million [...][17]

If current British television period dramas are set in the more recent past, then, as Lawrence notes, these tend to be politically radical and female-led productions. *Call the Midwife*, for example, is set in the 1960s and features a strong female cast consisting of 'Capable women, their shirt sleeves pushed up past sturdy forearms, wading through a series of gloomy interiors [...] it's like a feminist version of Das Boot'.[18] Nonetheless, *Call the Midwife* was and is popular, with viewing figures tripling those of its contemporary, *Downton Abbey* (ITV, 2010–15).

The emphasis on strong women in lead roles rather than the heroic male is continued in *Home Fires*, and where better to air this than in a costume drama that depicts a robust female organisation such as the Women's Institute (WI) during a period of male absence. Commencing in 1915 in wartime Britain, the WI in its early years presented a means for women in rural areas to temporarily leave their home tasks and socialise. In the lead-up to World War II, the organisation had expanded considerably and, as Summers points out, 'The London-based National Federation of Women's Institutes had serious lobbying powers and a reputation as a powerful force that was well organised, passionate and clear in its aims.'[19] The WI crossed class barriers, and its early members included, amongst others, those who fought for women's suffrage. With the outbreak of World War II, numbers declined considerably because women were drafted into war work, and those that remained were expected to become involved in food production and to care for evacuees. Recently, the organisation has become increasingly fashionable, and has experienced an unexpected revival,[20] a point argued by Josie Ensor who explains that 'more women are interested in learning skills such as crafting and baking thanks to the television shows *The Great British Bake Off* and *Kirstie's Handmade Britain*.[21]

Although WI women worked hard during wartime, collecting produce to make jam, knitting scarves and headwear, and cultivating vegetable patches as part of the Dig for Victory campaign, conversely it would be untrue to suggest that they were liberated: writing specifically about her grandmother's experiences, Summers in fact observes that:

> She belonged to an era before women's liberation from the slavery of the home. Husbands dominated and the social hierarchy of the village counted for a great deal. This was a time when country families had pews in church and women wore hats to go shopping. Women had less help in the house than their mothers and grandmothers had done and mod cons were still a dream for many.[22]

If the WI, therefore, offered a route out of the home for rural women, they were by no means set free from the dominance of patriarchy. *Home Fires*, on the other hand, excises this aspect of the organisation, instead mobilising a critique of masculinity and representing women to be strong and in control. This is exemplified in the first episode when, in the above-mentioned scenario, Steph is left to deal with the aggressive soldiers alone. On this occurrence and throughout the series, her husband, Stan (Chris Coghill), is rarely in sight, although he is meant to be in charge of the farm, his work protected under the legislation of farming as a reserved occupation. Frequently he is witnessed languishing in the fields and brooding about his need to do his duty and enlist. It is Steph who must be strong for both of them, as demonstrated when she points out that his indolence is unconstructive and that she supports his decision to join up for the war – and this he duly does on her advice. In an impassioned speech Steph informs her husband of her exasperation concerning his withdrawal from conversation and tells him to leave, 'because you're no bloody good to us like this', thus now asserting her position as head of the household. Although Stan's approach to the war is commendable, visually he appears slothful and depressed, a state of mind demonstrated through his facial expressions, which are sullen and morose.

Steph, in the meantime, continues to work physically hard, as displayed in Series One, Episode Three, which opens with shots of her on a tractor ploughing the fields. Not only does she labour on the farm, she is also busily employed indoors. After a day's work, and in a flurry of activity, she fills the bathtub for the lethargic Stan while he seems apathetic and worried. This mentality is evidenced when the camera slowly circles him as he lies silent and unmoving in the bathtub which Steph is busy replenishing, she appearing busy and frenetic in contrast as she carries heavy pots of hot water across the room. After his departure to the Front, she becomes even more independent, paraded through her expert firearms skills. In one episode, seen centre frame in medium-shot, she practises her aim, and a cut to a close-up of the target demonstrates her skill and expertise. Stan's 'white male decline' is therefore contrasted with Steph, who acquires equality of status and is presented as a role model and a strong female protagonist. In this relationship, and generally, the tone to the war seems to be that men are best positioned at the Front and women left to run the home and the Home Front independently.

Masculinity in crisis in *Home Fires* is connected to the effects of war, exclusion from society, sickness and displacement. This is illustrated when, in the second series, Stan, having eventually joined up, returns home on leave. According to Baker, 'A return "home" is one to a primal scene of exile, of alienation',[23] and this is true of his situation. He is clearly damaged and further mentally disturbed by his experiences, and this derangement translates into extreme and obsessive behaviour and disaffection at home. As Baker suggests, 'The traumatized male subject has become a recognizable figure across a range of cultural representations in the United States and the United Kingdom, concretized in the figure of the "veteran" or the soldier suffering from Post-Traumatic-Stress-Disorder.'[24] Stan's trauma is apparent on the first evening of his arrival home when Steph discovers him frantically searching through the kitchen cupboards to retrieve his gun. On its discovery, he subsequently elevates it, pointing it towards his wife in a threatening manner while informing her that he cannot sleep at night, his facial expression tense and anxious. Later, he is instructing young Stan on suitable places to hide weapons on the farm, his paranoia now stretching to the belief that the Germans will invade the area and that Steph and Stan must know where to locate the artillery should this occur. Steph tries to reason with him, but he is unable to think logically, and ignores her pleas. He even begins to instruct young Stan on how to kill a German: 'The only good German is a dead one' he avers, encouraging violence in the boy, while further reinforcing that he must 'Aim for the head or the chest.' His face is one of fury and angst as he explains illogically to his wife that this is all in self-defence, but she is enraged as she observes his aggressive behaviour. The above narrative strands not only create the image that women are the backbone of the community, they also point to current anxieties about terrorist invasion and contemporary xenophobia[25] in Britain and America, both countries having witnessed such recent propensities.[26]

Stan continues to prepare their guns in readiness for attack, and is extreme in other aspects as well; he places high fencing around the perimeter of the farm for fear of incursion, and images of him thrusting his bayonet into bags of straw indicate his paranoia. Even more shockingly, he also coerces his son into undertaking similar actions, believing that his family is in imminent danger. In despair over their situation, young Stan takes to stealing from his parents with the intention of selling their produce on the black market for inflated prices, and he too begins to behave in an aggressive and illogical way, thus imitating his father. When one customer queries the cost of the butter he is stealing from his family farm, he exclaims belligerently that a 'price is a price!' and refuses to waiver, demonstrating the same misguided tenacity of his father.

Later in the series, the villagers, including Steph and Stan, are forced to evacuate to an air raid shelter following a siren alert and, misguidedly, Stan stands up and makes an emotional but unhinged oratory about safety. His voice breaks as he speaks, and his facial expressions indicate that he is a deranged man, a fact which, at this point, Steph too realises. As a result, and on her bequest, Stan surrenders his guns. As though to contrast her strength with his weakness, this scene opens with an extreme close-up of a hand gun, before the camera tilts upwards to reveal it is now Steph holding the weapon rather than, as the spectator might assume, her husband. Subsequently, Stan emerges from the house carrying a rifle, and wearing a troubled yet resigned expression on his face. In a silent exchange he removes the bullets and hands the weapon to his wife. She raises her chin in a gesture of approval and decisively walks away from him towards the house carrying the armoury – she now the stronger of the two. Stan's weakness and mental instability is thus reinforced by Steph's resolution and she is instrumental in suggesting that his use of guns must be continued on the battlefield only, not the home.

Wounded Masculinity in Period Drama

Further male vulnerability occurs in *Home Fires* through the character of the local butcher's son, David Brindsley. David is subjugated by his overprotective mother, Miriam (Claire Price), who does not want her son to enlist. Despite her anxieties, he joins the navy but is reported missing, presumed dead. Miraculously he eventually returns home; however, he is psychologically and physically scarred following an act of bravery where, we are informed, he saved the lives of four of his fellow servicemen. Having been told by the doctor he will not work again as a result of his injuries, he becomes distant from his family and rebukes the advances of a local girl who is a possible suitor. He is 'damaged for life', as his doctor informs him, because his scars will always open up. Visible disfigurement such as this seems to be a new trope in period drama. For example, Captain Poldark (Aidan Turner) in *Poldark* (BBC, 2015–) has a battle scar on his face, and Jamie Fraser (Sam Heughan) in *Outlander* (Starz, 2014–) has a blemished back, and the scars ache and are sometimes re-opened following floggings. The above make for a dramatic illustration of male suffering and act as markers of past vulnerability, while also suggesting that such trauma is lasting – although sometimes they additionally indicate that the male body 'is not easily defeated or killed'.[27]

Corporeal impairment is demonstrated in *Home Fires* when, determined to prove his worth via working in his parents' shop, David attempts to carry the heavy carcass of an animal. Bodily weakness is a sign of male vulnerability, and this is mobilised when, seen in close-up, David's face is strained with exertion, the dead beast draped across his shoulders. He staggers and collapses under the strain, his body covered in blood leaving the spectator unsure whether this emanates from the open wounds which we understand will not heal, or that of the carcass. Thus, not only is David scarred emotionally by his wartime experiences, but his body also bears the marks as proof. Further, the butcher's shop and its attendant activities acts as an endorsement of the violence and carnage he has experienced at war. From then on, David must accept this emasculation and, as a result, he becomes alienated from family and friends, wandering the lanes alone and unable to communicate socially. Here, it is Laura (Leila Mimmack), the doctor's daughter, who helps him, advising that he can contribute to the war effort and help her in the observation tower.

In a similar vein to David, she too is wounded through her ostracism by the villagers following her affair and, while this new task is one that is available to both sexes, it offers him some redemption; as Fran Pheasant-Kelly suggests, although the body is violated, 'scarring marks the resealing of the taut body (and hence restored masculinity) and simultaneously signifies its ability to endure pain and suffering.'[28]

Doctor Campbell is also rendered powerless in the narrative. When informed of his lung condition at the hospital he seems ill at ease; to verify this, the right side of his face is in shadow, and his eyes are downcast and averted. Not only is he sick and therefore enfeebled, he believes that he is of no use to his country. He also relies heavily on his wife, Erica (Frances Grey) for the day-to-day running of the surgery, and it is she who protects him from the aggressive patients, such as Miriam, who are requesting certification to enable their sons to remain at home rather than go to war. Erica is also a reassurance to him concerning his disease although Will is a defeatist from the outset, wondering aloud what will happen when he is dead; as a result his wife bolsters him, stating that he must have faith in the treatment available. When his practice suffers and he begins to lose patients because of allegations against his daughter, it is Erica that saves the day, informing her husband that she will be the key provider through her pharmaceutical knowledge. She subsequently commences work, dispensing drugs for the local military.

Bob Simms, on the other hand, is not initially represented as weak, but as an insulting, violent husband towards his wife, Pat (Claire Rushbrook). When we first encounter him he is seated outside his house smoking a cigarette, his performance indicating his objectionable personality. He is clearly a difficult man, and as she departs to respond to some unreasonable request he has made of her, the camera cuts to a close-up shot of his upturned face, his eyes narrowed against the light as he draws on his cigarette. His demeanour indicates his cruel behaviour, and this is illustrated when, in the first episode, he throws his breakfast on the floor and makes Pat eat it; in a later scene he refuses to let her visit the lavatory until he provides permission; finally, he disagrees with the fact that she is in work, a fact displayed when he completes the Government forms for national registration. In fact, he puts down 'Housewife' although she is employed in the telephone exchange, thus denying her any individual status. However, Pat falls into the 'female character overcoming vulnerability through masculinised aggression'[29] category. Whereas at the beginning of the series she is weak and defenceless, as the narrative progresses she becomes confrontational and strong, dominating Bob in the process. This is what Sarah Hagelin describes as 'resistant vulnerability [which] works in two ways. It proves that vulnerability needn't be gendered female, and it suggests that we alter our basic assumption that a suffering body is vulnerable and needs our pity and protection.'[30] Pat's rising resistance begins to physically render Bob defenceless. At one point, she poisons him with fish – we presume in error although tellingly she did not partake in the meal – and he is taken to hospital. On his discharge, he limps and carries a walking stick to aid his progress. Seen in medium shot, he descends from the ambulance and Pat arms him across the road, she now appearing the stronger of the two. A little later, she agrees to speak at a Ministry of Food meeting on behalf of the WI. She informs the diegetic audience, 'Make no mistake ladies, this is our time too', thus relating to a contemporary spectator while also vicariously explaining her own circumstances; at this juncture, the camera retains focus on her within the frame for some seconds enabling spectator identification as she visibly gains confidence. Pat has also been provided with a bottle of lithium salts by Erica to dampen Bob's temper. Erica has observed Bob's treatment of his wife some time earlier and suspects him of cruelty to the woman. Pat duly administers the medicine, but she overdoses him resulting in his emergency hospitalisation.

Pat's strength gradually increases. Indeed, her representation in *Home Fires* chimes with a strengthening of sympathy towards victims of domestic violence in contemporary society. Whereas once perceived as weak and not in control there has been a shift in public consideration of the role of the victim in such situations.[31] After Bob becomes a war correspondent he is again injured and Pat visits him in hospital. When she first espies him he is being pushed through the ward in a wheelchair, but she deliberately hides from him, her hand covering her face to prevent recognition. He is asleep, however, his head lolling forwards, and his mouth wide open thus rendering him defenceless and her in control. Later, on his return home, he requests chocolate, but Pat has gained strength: 'Saying please occasionally won't kill you' she assertively responds, and, at this point the camera adopts his point of view. Bob is seated and Pat physically towers above him, and her body fills the frame. He and the spectator are aware of Pat's

Conflicting Masculinities

Figure 12.1 Injurious Men: the violent and cowardly Bob Simms in *Home Fires*.

authority, and reluctantly he obeys her request. 'Please' he replies obsequiously and one feels that she has won a momentous victory in their relationship. The camerawork registers this conquest by panning downwards to frame Bob's feet, his heavily bandaged leg filling the foreground of the frame as though to reinforce his infirmity and therefore helplessness. Gradually Pat is responding to his aggression with a violence of her own, and these actions are surely relevant within the context of the war. As Nancy Berns suggests, victim empowerment has become omnipresent in the media focusing on 'the victim's problem and how she solved it'.[32] Berns is critical of the media for encouraging women to take control in such situations and argues that this effectively discourages social action and change. Indeed, she sees the portrayal of domestic violence as distinctively framed for entertainment purposes whereby:

> complex social problems are reduced to emotion, drama and heroic tales. Stories about social problems that are shaped to be inspiring and entertaining are usually simplistic and focus on just the individuals involved, which does not reflect the complexity of the problem.[33]

In another narrative spin-off, Pat commences an affair with a Czech soldier, Marek Novotny (Alexandre Willaume), who is stationed nearby. He is chivalrous and kind, arriving at her house with a bunch of flowers as an apology for an incident where one of his men accidentally knocked her over in the street. She offers to darn his shirt for him in return for the flowers and, as he changes and removes his clothing, she observes his torso through a mirror. In Laura Mulvey's[34] terms, she subverts the dominant patriarchal position; he becomes the object of the look and she the subject of the gaze. Her voyeurism is all the more explicit when the camera focuses on her face and, from her point of view, and shown through the use of extreme close-up, Marek is witnessed in the background changing his clothes. The camera concentrates on his muscular body which is reflected in the mirror, and her facial expression indicates her arousal. Pat is thus active whereas Marek is passive – she the controller of the gaze. Although Marek is represented more positively than many of the other men, telling Pat at one point that 'not all men are like your husband', there remain few positive representations of men in the series.

It is not only the local men that are injurious to women. Wing Commander Richard Bowers, who is stationed at the neighbouring RAF camp, is a serial adulterer, unable to resist seducing his young office clerk, Laura. He is represented as predatory and lecherous, only later exposed as a cheat and a liar. When he first approaches Laura, she is in his office and the room is bathed in a soft light. Dressed in uniform, he appears tall, handsome, clean shaven, suave and charming, thus duping Laura. Later, he asks her to dinner and to stay with him in a 'top notch' hotel for the night. When news breaks of the affair, Laura is fired from her post, but her father confronts Bowers, later assaulting the man as retribution for his dalliance with his daughter. Shown from an overhead shot, Bowers is emasculated as he falls to the floor, his nose bloodied and 'probably broken', we are informed. Thus, whereas in World War II cinema, the pilot in uniform was seen 'to encode heroic "excess", affording the wearer an instantaneous aura of dignified glamour',[35] the representation of Bowers does not comply. Indeed, he is a flawed character, as demonstrated when he finally informs Laura that he is to be divorced for adultery and she is to be cited. Visibly, at this point, he appears alarmed and distressed, his unshaven appearance and his hooded eyes belying the unsavoury position in which he finds himself.

The WI Saves the Day

As aforementioned, in direct contrast to the damaged and vulnerable men in *Home Fires*, the women are represented as resilient and motivated.

One such example is the central character, Frances Barden (Samantha Bond). She is adamant that the local branch of the WI remain open for the duration of the war, despite attempts by the current Chairwoman, Joyce Cameron (Francesca Annis), to close it, and ultimately she takes over the responsibility of running it as a result. Frances also demonstrates her strength when she becomes manager of her husband, Peter's (Anthony Calf) factory on his sudden death. He, it transpires, was a philanderer and was leading a dual life, but Frances recovers and, in her new role as boss, immediately effects changes to create better working conditions for the women employees; as one measure, she advocates more windows to allow greater accessibility to sunlight, and is thus depicted as robust and a woman of changes. 'This is my factory now so I am going to run it as I see fit', she states emphatically.

While there are some positive representations of men, these only serve a purpose for the advancement of the women, and thus female characters can pose a threat as well. Nick Lucas (Mark Umbers), for example, is a handsome military man who proposes to the local schoolteacher, Teresa Fenchurch (Leeanne Best) but she is using him as a cover for her lesbianism. Conversely, he is not always moral; in fact at one point he makes overtures to the local vicar's wife while her husband is imprisoned in a Prisoner of War camp. Also, Spencer Wilson, the conscientious objector, has just reasons for not wanting to join up, but it is his fiancé, Claire Hillman (Daisy Badger) who is his defender while the town turns against him at various moments.

Conclusion

Home Fires ends with a cliffhanger when an RAF fighter plane crashes into the house of Bryn Brindsley (Daniel Ryan) while his wife is in labour; there is no indication of who survives and who perishes and the series has now been cancelled, a decision which has baffled cast, critics and fans alike. Indeed, the *Home Fires* creators were also surprised and disappointed with this decision, the writer, Simon Block, having already commenced work on the third series. No reasons were given by ITV about their pronouncement other than they wish to refresh the channel's drama portfolio. On the other hand, Clair Woodward writing for *The Express* suggests that one reason might be that the series provided strong roles for more mature women and storylines that explored inviolable subjects. As she explains,

The series showed what these women did and provided great roles for actresses in their prime, including Samantha Bond, Francesca Annis, Ruth Gemmell and Claire Rushbrook. *Home Fires* also contained storylines that explored taboo subjects for women at the time: would closet lesbian Teresa (Leanne Best) marry Wing Commander Nick Lucas (Mark Umbers)? The series wasn't all making preserves and knitting vests for Our Boys.[36]

Doubtless *Home Fires* does create strong women characters to the detriment of their male counterparts, and men are not only harmful to women but also helpless and ineffectual at a time when their strength is most needed. This might be attributable to the fact that women are the main consumers of programmes such as this and therefore are enabled identification with strong female roles, a trend noted by Lawrence who remarks on the current vogue for placing women as leading characters in other genres, particularly detective programmes. In addition, *Home Fires* chimes with the contemporary social, economic and political climate including fourth-wave feminism, and current concerns about domestic violence which are common stories in film and television and the media.[37] Moreover, the series uses the historical setting of World War II to comment on the problems with contemporary masculinity and manliness in peril, thus articulating fears about the threat of terrorism and invasion with its inevitable links with immigration and war. Indeed, the series addresses topical issues corresponding with present concerns, and also presents the WI in a favourable light. Nonetheless, a return to the screen for *Home Fires* remains uncertain in spite of the fact that it has left a legacy as a feminist period drama, achieved through its proliferation of strong female characters to the disadvantage of its male population.

Notes

1. The Women's Institute is an organisation that originated in Canada in the nineteenth century, although the first British WI was not formed until 1915. Initially it had two clear aims: to revitalise rural communities and to encourage women to become more involved in producing food during World War I. The organisation's activities have since widened to include the provision of educational opportunities for women and the chance for them to learn crafts and build new skills. Other activities include campaigning on community issues and policies.

2. Graham Dawson, *Soldier Heroes: British Adventure, Empire and the Imagining of Masculinities* (London, 1994), p. 1.
3. For further reading see James Chapman, *The British at War* (London, New York, 2000).
4. A. Bowdoin Van Riper, 'Good-Bye to All That: *Piece of Cake, Danger UXB*, and the Second World War', in J. Leggott and J. A. Taddeo (eds), *Upstairs and Downstairs: British Costume Drama Television from* The Forsyte Saga *to* Downton Abbey (Lanham, Boulder, New York, 2015), pp. 153–64.
5. Ibid., p. 155.
6. Ibid., p. 163 (emphasis in original).
7. Andrew Spicer, *Typical Men: The Representation of Masculinity in Popular British Cinema* (London, New York, 2003), p. 197.
8. See Claire Monk, 'Men in the 90s', in R. Murphy (ed.), *British Cinema in the 90s* (London, 2000), pp. 156–66.
9. Donna Peberdy, *Masculinity and Performance: Male Angst in Contemporary American Cinema* (London, New York, 2013), p. 6.
10. Ibid., p. 7 (emphasis in original).
11. Brian Baker, *Contemporary Masculinities in Fiction, Film and Television* (New York, London, Oxford, New Delhi, Sydney, 2016), p. 27.
12. Kira Cochrane, 'The fourth wave of feminism: meet the rebel women', *Guardian*, 10 December 2013. Available at https://www.theguardian.com/world/2013/dec/10/fourth-wave-feminism-rebel-women (accessed 29 July 2016).
13. Kira Cochrane, *All the Rebel Women: the Rise of the Fourth Wave of Feminism* (Guardian Book, Kindle Edition, 2013), Available at https://read.amazon.co.uk/?asin = B00H7G1DMY (accessed 30 July 2016).
14. The First Wave began with the 'Votes for Women' campaign immediately prior to World War I. Second-wave feminism commenced in the 1960s and eventually led to the Equal Pay Act of 1970 followed by the 1975 Sexual Discrimination Act. The Third Wave continued into the 1990s despite arguments that feminism was now outmoded, and the period was hailed as a post-feminist era. See Angela McRobbie, *The Aftermath of Feminism: Gender, Culture and Social Change* (Los Angeles, London, New Delhi, Singapore, Washington, DC, 2009).
15. Cochrane, *All the Rebel Women*.
16. Jacquie Lawrence, 'Hollywood still trails TV when it comes to strong roles for women', *Guardian*, 22 April 2015. Available at https://www.theguardian.com/media/2015/apr/22/hollywood-tv-roles-for-women-the-fall-house-of-cards (accessed 30 July 2016).
17. Ben Dowell, 'Lark Rise to Candleford escapes BBC costume drama cull', *Guardian*, 6 March 2009. Available at https://www.theguardian.com/media/2009/mar/06/lark-rise-candleford-escapes-cull (accessed 15 September 2016).

18. Emma Brockes, 'Call the Midwife: an Unexpected PBS hit with Another Brit Import', *Guardian*, 26 April 2013. Available at https://www.theguardian.com/commentisfree/emma-brockes-blog/2013/apr/26/call-the-midwife-pbs-hit-import (accessed 15 September 2016).
19. Julie Summers, *Jambusters: The Story of the Women's Institute in the Second World War* (London, New York, Sydney, Toronto and New Delhi, 2013), p. 10.
20. More recently, British popular culture has promoted ideas about the WI. Examples include the film, *Calendar Girls* (2003), which was later turned into a successful stage play and also a musical; the Abigail Wilson and Jennifer Saunders sitcom entitled *Jam and Jerusalem* (BBC, 2006–9) featuring Dawn French. Furthermore, the WI came to the fore in 2000 when, in an error of political judgement, Tony Blair tried to use their national conference in Wembley as a platform to reposition Labour as a party of traditional values in a changing world. The audience of 10,000 women responded first with sporadic heckling, then slow handclapping and finally undisguised jeering from sections of the hall. See John Carvel, 'Heckled, Jeered Booed – Blair Bombs at the WI', *Guardian*, 8 June 2000. Available at https://www.theguardian.com/politics/2000/jun/08/uk.labour3 (accessed 18 October 2016).
21. Josie Ensor, 'Much More than just jam', *Telegraph*, 13 January 2013. Available at http://www.telegraph.co.uk/women/9797917/Much-more-than-just-jam-waiting-list-for-new-look-Womens-Institute.html (accessed 16 September 2016).
22. Summers, *Jambusters*, p. 294.
23. Baker, *Contemporary Masculinities*, p. 26.
24. Examples include *The Deer Hunter* (1978), *Coming Home* (1978) and more recently *The Hurt Locker* (2008). Baker's book focuses on the damaged soldier and the secret agent in the Bond films and the Bourne film series including *The Bourne Identity* (2002), *The Bourne Supremacy* (2004) and *The Bourne Ultimatum* (2007). Ibid., p. 2.
25. In existence at the time that the series was aired and exacerbated by the June 2016 vote to leave the EU. See Maya Goodfellow, 'Britain's raging racism calls for more than symbolic safety pins', *Guardian*, 1 July 2016. Available at https://www.theguardian.com/commentisfree/2016/jul/01/britain-racism-safety-pins-brexit-migrants-xenophobic (accessed 16 September 2016).
26. Richard Wolffe, 'Britain allowed its populist right to rise: America should heed the warning', *Guardian*, 24 June 2016. Available at https://www.theguardian.com/commentisfree/2016/jun/24/britain-right-wing-brexit-america-trump (accessed 19 September 2016).
27. Peter Lehman, *Running Scared* (Philadelphia, 1993), p. 63.
28. Fran Pheasant-Kelly, *Abject Spaces in American Cinema: Institutional Settings, Identity and Psychoanalysis in Film* (London and New York, 2013), p. 164.
29. Sarah Hagelin, *Reel Vulnerability: Power, Pain and Gender in Contemporary American Film and Television* (New Brunswick, New Jersey, London, 2013), p. 3.

30. Ibid., p. 4.
31. Nancy Berns, *Framing the Victim: Domestic Violence, Media and Social Problems* (New Brunswick, New Jersey, 2009), p. 28.
32. Ibid., p. 78.
33. Ibid., p. 102.
34. Laura Mulvey, 'Visual Pleasure and Narrative Cinema', *Screen*, 16/3 (1975), pp. 6–18.
35. Gill Plain, *John Mills and British Cinema* (Edinburgh, 2006), p. 64.
36. Clair Woodward, 'Why Extinguish ITV's Home Fires?', *Express*, 22 May 2016. Available at http://www.express.co.uk/comment/expresscomment/672669/ITV-cancelled-series-Home-Fires (accessed 18 October 2016).
37. This is evident in the recent episodes of the long running British BBC radio serial, *The Archers* (1950–) featuring a plotline about domestic abuse. Paul Kerley and Claire Bates examine this in detail. See Paul Kerley and Claire Bates, 'The Archers: What effect has the Rob and Helen story had?', *BBC News Magazine*, 5 April 2016. Available at http://www.bbc.co.uk/news/magazine-35961057 (accessed 22 June 2017).

13

'Have you seen Walliams' Bottom?': Detecting the 'Ordinary' Man in *Partners in Crime*

Louise FitzGerald

In his review of David Walliams's 2013 stage performance of Bottom in *A Midsummer Night's Dream*, theatre critic Henry Hitchings described the actor as simultaneously a 'camp cravat wearing thesp' and a 'strappingly masculine presence'.[1] Hitchings appears to have difficulty aligning the two models of masculinity, suggesting that to be camp and powerfully muscular at the same time is so incongruous that it warrants discussion. Hitchings is not alone in highlighting Walliams's apparently incompatible configuration of manhood: much has been written in the tabloid press and in online forums about his multifaceted masculine persona and, by extension, his sexuality on- and off-screen. And Walliams, aware of the discourses that circulate around him, playfully reinforces the complexity of his male identity. Additionally, academic interest in Walliams's ability to do gender differently, realised especially in the British comedy sketch show *Little Britain* (BBC, 2003–6), is beginning to suggest that Walliams might be read as a discourse shifter. As a man who presents himself as gay, camp, straight, heroic, manly, virile, vigorous amongst others, Walliams's embodiment of manhood is explicitly constituted by conflicting male signifiers and dualisms that have traditionally, and for so long, been employed to consolidate the myth of hegemonic masculinity.

This chapter considers how the multiplicity of incongruous and contradictory signifiers of masculinity embodied in Walliams might impact on his portrayal of sleuth Tommy Beresford in BBC's drama series *Partners in Crime* (BBC, 2015). I am interested in the construction of male gender identity within the Cold War context of this programme and the way that Tommy both reflects and refracts the national story about men. Walliams's performance was not received favourably by critics, however, and I will suggest that his interpretation of Cold War British masculinity hints at the potentiality of what Butler describes as an 'assertion of alternative domains of cultural intelligibility, i.e. new possibilities for gender that contest the rigid codes of hierarchical binarisms'.[2] I am particularly interested in the way that the term 'ordinary man' permeates the narrative and the manner in which it is aligned with Cold War discourses of the everyman/common man. I will argue that *Partners in Crime* opens up a new cultural space for the articulation of an ordinary masculinity that is constituted by ambiguity, complexities and instabilities that are traditionally associated with Otherness. And I will suggest the convergence of Otherness and 'ordinariness' embodied in Tommy Beresford offers a model of masculinity that is distinctly *not* in crisis. I conclude this chapter by considering the political potential of the construction of an inclusive male identity presented in *Partners in Crime*.

Gender and Genre

It is worth noting that reviewers of *Partners in Crime* had difficulty defining its generic category. This is an important point; scholars such as Yvonne Tasker have argued that expressions of gender should be explored in conjunction with the history of the genre from which they appear.[3] In combining the conventions of detective genre with an adventure story, an espionage narrative within thriller conventions and an adaptation of two Agatha Christie stories, clear genre definition is rendered as particularly complex. Despite the slippery nature of genre, a thematic focus on masculinity is foregrounded in each of the genres that constitute the programme. For example, Joseph A. Kestner shows that the subject of male identity is implicit in the adventure story that constitutes as he notes, 'a cultural product which reveals to young men or old a discourse about a process which involves most men'.[4] Masculinity is also a key theme of the detective genre, which as Philippa Gates notes systematically maintains its ideological function to 'scrutinise the hero's masculinity throughout the investigation of crime'.[5] Similarly British espionage narratives, which found their zenith in the Cold War period, have been described as a response to the renegotiations of gender identity and national identity in the context of decolonisation. Scholars have shown how such renegotiations were played out within popular culture especially through the ultimate Cold War ideal masculine fictional figure of James Bond, whose heterosexuality was often juxtaposed with the more effeminate and sometimes asexual villains of the Bond films as a way of shoring up his masculine credentials.

Analysis of *Partners in Crime* is made all the more complicated because it is constituted by two three-part stories: 'The Secret Adversary' is aligned with the detective genre and adventure story although there are elements of espionage throughout; 'N or M' is situated as espionage story. Moreover, director Edward Hall suggests each story should be seen as a separate entity – 'individual screenplays which both have two very different backdrops'.[6] For the sake of clarity, consistency and as a response to the scope of this chapter my analysis will focus on 'The Secret Adversary'.

Camp David, Camp Criticism and Otherness

During July and August 2015, BBC One broadcast two stories, 'The Secret Adversary' and 'N or M?' based on Agatha Christie's less well-known short stories about a married sleuthing couple, Tommy and Tuppence Beresford (Jessica Raine). The Sunday-night drama garnered decent weekly viewer figures of 6.5 million[7] and was appreciated by reviewers for its production values, which the *Independent*'s Ellen Jones argued 'had much more visual style than ITV ever managed'.[8] Indeed, the period detail, glorious lighting and gorgeously stylish costumes were 'beyond high'.[9] Praise for Raine's sparky and feisty performance of Tuppence Beresford was a common feature of analyses; however, reviewers were much less impressed with Walliams's performance, which was described as a 'tentative and dismal portrayal of 1950s masculinity'.[10] Michael Hogan of the *Telegraph* bemoaned Walliams for being the 'least convincing sleuth in screen history. As the camp comic played hapless, bumbling and buttoned up beekeeper Tommy Beresford, he couldn't witness violence without wincing, enjoy the attentions of a floozy without flinching or slug some Scotch without spluttering.'[11] *Daily Mail* critic Christopher Stevens said Walliams's acting style left him cold – he looked, said Stevens, 'as if he been working on an expression of repressed discomfort, like a man at a job interview who has sat on a drawing pin and doesn't like to mention it',[12] and the *Huffington Post* argued Walliams was not the right man for straight drama, accusing him of 'leaning back on the broad, camp approach that's worked so well in everything from *Little Britain* to the *Britain's Got Talent* panel'.[13]

This is not the first time *Partners in Crime* has been adapted for television, nor the first time it has been referred to as camp. In 1984, James Warwick and Francesca Annis played the Beresfords in an ITV adaption described as having a 'wonderfully campy feel to it'.[14] The 1984 version of the show was set in the Roaring Twenties, which might account for the reference to the camp excesses of the adaptation. Indeed Warwick's portrayal of Tommy as ostentatious, affected and exaggerated is associative of a camp sensibility, but it is also a long way off Walliams's depiction of Tommy, whose bumbling amiableness and display of domestic contentment are defined as his central characteristics. The 'accusation' of campness in the 2015 adaptation was however not levelled at Tommy's characteristics or the sensibility of the adaptation; instead it was aimed at Walliams's masculinity, drawing overtly from ideas about his male persona outside the programme.

Susan Sontag's exposition of camp, whilst defining it in relation to the consumption of popular/low culture and notions of bad taste, also situates camp as a method of breaking down hierarchies – a process of contesting unyielding regulations of hierarchies and systems.[15] In her response to Sontag's conceptualisation of camp, Kim Michasiw argues that the political task of camp is also tied to the 'self-approximation of what one is not'.[16] Michasiw's definition of camp – to approximate that which one is not – might have some bearing on responses to Walliams's performance as Tommy. Reviewers' use of camp is derogatory, and it counteracts the very political potential of camp to break codes of masculinity because it actually reinforces the rigidity of gender binaries that camp has the very potential to destabilise. In other words the use of camp in this instance ensures that

Walliams's male identity can only be understood in terms of what it is not – heteronormative.

But perhaps it is not surprising that reviewers fell back on using the term camp because it already circulates around Walliams and is played out in the twin narratives of his life and work. Walliams rose to fame in 2003 in the British sketch show *Little Britain* (which he co-wrote with Matt Lucas) where he played a whole host of characters. The most interesting, and possibly most contentious, of the *Little Britain* ensemble of characters, was Edward 'Emily' Howard – an unsuccessful transvestite who tries to pass as a Victorian lady. Edward's inability to pass as Emily showcases what Ellie Kennedy argues was a representation of 'inflexible gender bending' employed to 'confound stereotypical expectations based on sexuality and gender'.[17] In *Come Fly With Me* (BBC, 2010–11), a mockumentary co-written again with Lucas, Walliams plays Moses Beacon, an effeminate passenger liaison officer, and Ian Foot, a racist chief immigration officer. Both characters employ catchphrases that are empty of meaning and, in so doing, highlight the ludicrous and often empty nature of language. In 2008, Walliams played the role of English comedian and comic actor Frankie Howerd in the BBC Four film *Rather You Than Me* which documented the impact of Howerd's homosexuality on his career. Walliams has also written a number of books for children; the most successful of these, *The Boy Who Wore a Dress* (2008), was adapted for BBC television in 2014. Drawing from his own childhood experiences of wearing dresses, the book was described by the *Telegraph*'s Tim Martin as a 'gleefully democratic and politically acute drama'.[18] And Walliams's presence on the *Britain's Got Talent* (ITV, 2007–) panel raised eyebrows across the British press when he flirted with Simon Cowell and inferred they shared an intimate relationship.

I am not suggesting that his portrayal of homosexual, transvestite, cross-dressing characters bears any relation to Walliams's sexuality or male persona but it is clear that the roles he plays destabilise ideas about masculinity, identity, sexuality and language. Indeed Walliams has been always open in voicing his discontent about being 'locked in a box of forced masculinity',[19] and whilst he has not claimed to be bisexual, he has made it clear that he would just as happily marry a man if he found the right one. However Walliams's personal reference to campness in his biography *Camp David* (2012) and the rhetoric of campness and non-heteronormative masculinity that surrounds him on- and off-screen sits in contrast to a number of other markers of maleness that he embodies.[20] Cast as an action man after completing the 140-mile Thames swim in 2011 and a channel swim for *Sport Relief* in 2006, Walliams consolidated a more traditional model of masculinity which was then reinforced when he married model Lara Stone in 2010 and became a father in 2013. And whilst the tabloid press blamed his subsequent divorce from Stone in 2015 on his penchant for cross-dressing, his 'maleness' was quickly redeemed and re-set in reports about subsequent relationships with other women. This brief account of Walliams's performance of masculinity on- and off-screen suggests that he actively embodies multiple signifiers that complicate gender binaries; as such Walliams destabilises hegemonic heteronormative masculinity through his overt openness to otherness.

I argue then that reviewers' earlier recourse to the word camp in reference to Walliams's performance in *Partners in Crime* suggests that his personal openness to difference and otherness and his unfixed performances of maleness are perceived as threatening; their rhetoric reveals an underlying 'fear of the changeable, the multiple' which test the 'myths of masculine legitimacy'.[21] The notion of Otherness as threatening is also deeply significant to the historical context of *Partners in Crime* where the Other – constituted as it was by non-adherence to gender norms and sexuality – was perceived as a figure of threat to national security. As historian Marilyn Michaud notes, 'In the Cold War context, those residing outside the centre assume a submissive, feminine role – they were seen as being soft, limp and possibly homosexual and ultimately a threat to national security.'[22] In America especially but also in Britain, homosexual men and effeminate men were perceived to be as dangerous as Soviet Russians because it was assumed that their 'deficient' masculinity rendered them ineffective in protecting the nation. Historian Robert Nye reiterates this argument when he writes,

> the conflation of 'red scare' with 'lavender scare' was at least in part a consequence of the great publicity that had been given to Kinsey's sexual identity rating system which reinforced that any man, not simply an effeminate one, might be a homosexual and thus eligible to blackmail from foreign agents.[23]

With all of this in mind, the remainder of this chapter explores how Walliams's performance of detective Tommy Beresford conflates and embodies Otherness and 'ordinariness' as a stable model of masculine identity within the confines of a narrative set in a period of time where the ideology of gender dualism was explicitly tied to masculinity and to national security.

The Two Tommys: *The Secret Adversary* and Models of Male Identity

A common concern about adaptation is that of fidelity to the original text, however in this case I am not so concerned with issues of faithfulness, rather I want to explore how the 1922 and 2015 portrayals of Tommy Beresford coalesce with historical discourses of masculinity circulating at the time each version was set. Both narratives represent moments in British history where questions of gender, national identity and social and national stability were most urgent. Of course, the fact that the 1952-set adaptation was made in 2015 raises questions about the relevance of the model of masculinity showcased in this version of *Partners in Crime*. I return to this later in the chapter.

The Secret Adversary was written in 1922 but set in 1916 just after the sinking of the Lusitania. Tommy has been de-mobilised after being injured in the Mesopotamia campaign, a campaign that famously saw large numbers of British and Indian soldiers injured and killed. Tommy was also injured in service in France where 1,400,000 soldiers were killed and more than 4,300,000 men were wounded. The casting of Tommy as an injured solider assigns him a heroic and patriotic status, characteristics that coalesce with the national story about British masculinity circulating during World War I. Tommy is vigorous, he has a sporty physique, he is audacious and possesses a bulldog tenacity; 'His face', writes Christie, 'was pleasantly ugly – nondescript, yet unmistakably the face of a gentleman and a sportsman.'[24] Tommy cannot secure a job and after meeting up with his old university friend Tuppence, they decide to set up in a joint business venture as private investigators and The Young Adventurers Ltd is born.

Christie's description of Tommy's key characteristics demonstrates the importance of recognising that imagined masculinities are contingent on historical and geographical markers: Tommy is a war hero, he embodies what Nye suggests was a model of maleness that 'emphasized physical strength, muscular development, the stiff upper lip, adventure, fortitude and action'.²⁵ By coding Tommy as a university graduate and as a vigorous, sporting man Christie draws attention to two of the most significant movements that impacted on representations of World War I idealised masculinity: the introduction of schools and the development of armies which 'inculcated evangelical values designed to confirm the superiority of the Englishman'.²⁶ Tommy's role as a sleuth is a reflection and continuum of the stories of bravery, action and intellect that were aligned with soldiers of World War I – his sleuthing adventures, physicality and toughness consolidates his maleness which is fused with models of masculinity that were tailored to fit the national story of the period.

Walliams's representation of Tommy also reflects the national story of Cold War masculinity. The duo's investigative capers take place against a backdrop of '1950s Britain rising from the ashes of World War II into the political landscape of the Cold War',²⁷ where Tommy and Tuppence become amateur detectives and find themselves stumbling into the world of murder and Cold War conspiracies. The series paid close attention to creating characters and settings that moved away somewhat from the traditional rendering of Agatha Christie stories. The drama of *Partners in Crime* takes place in the 'couple's suburban house and London bombsites and bombed out buildings with rat runs and little side streets where you could get in trouble'.²⁸ Episode One begins in 1950s Paris with the couple boarding a train to London; they encounter a distressed woman, Jane Finn (Camilla Marie Beeput) who suddenly leaves the train carriage and does not re-appear. Tommy isn't terribly interested in the missing woman, but Tuppence is concerned and decides to investigate the disappearance. Their investigations bring them into contact with her uncle, Anthony Carter (James Fleet) who works for the government's Third Floor. Carter informs them that Jane Finn was carrying a secret recording that would reveal the identity of a Soviet assassin, Mr Brown. Tommy and Tuppence must discover Mr Brown's identity in order to locate and rescue Jane; the story ends with Tommy's successful rescue of her.

Director Hall claims that moving the story to early Cold War Britain offered

> [a] wonderful backdrop to set our series. The year we placed Partners in Crime was the year Casino Royale was published for the first time, James Bond and the whole spy culture was just beginning

to come out of the Second World War and Russia was instantly on the offensive with America with the arms race going on. There is a changing of the social and political landscape of spies, espionage and information.[29]

Whilst Hall highlights the significance of the political and cultural landscape he does not refer to the shifting ideals of masculinity that had been affected by World War II – a glaring omission given his claims in interviews that he also aimed to 'refract the male figure in different ways'.[30] After World War I, attitudes about preferred modes of maleness shifted away from the sort of 1920s masculine traits embodied in the novel's Tommy. The dreadfully high number of deaths and terrible injuries incurred by soldiers in World War I impacted on the national story of masculinity that had been propagated throughout the inter-war years. As Elaine Showalter has shown, the sight of men's bodies literally torn apart affected the way that maleness had been discursively constructed, leading to a 'crisis in masculinity'.[31] Nye illustrates how pre-World War I 'physical culture movements' played 'an important role in cementing the link between manliness, physical fitness and patriotism in inter-war Britain', but these models and ideas of nation were associated in the main with a middle-class worldview.[32] Andrew Spicer suggests that the evacuation of the working-class man from this paradigm of masculinity and of nation had to be altered in a way that democratised the idealised model of manliness, which in turn would help co-opt working-class men to enlist. Thus emerged the idea of the heroic common-man whose

> figure formed part of the discourse of the People's War – a new everyman, a masculine ideal of stoicism, steadiness and modest hopes for the future- associated with a gradual change in masculinity – not a radical new image of masculinity but a renegotiation of the debonair ideal, a democratized version of the same values.[33]

Although the shift in ideological markers of masculinity as outlined above took place much earlier than the Cold War period, it is relevant here because the figure of the common/everyman/ordinary man begins to emerge and these are the very same terms associated with Walliams's 1952 version of Tommy when he refers to himself as 'an ordinary man who likes to wear slippers and make honey'. This 1950s Tommy is not trained for the dangerous world that he enters and as such he reflects Spicer's description of the everyman as 'trained for nothing but ready for anything'.[34] Tommy's ordinariness is also reinforced in his role as husband and father, two models of masculinity that 'were dominant motifs of social reconstruction'.[35] It is worth noting here that framing Tommy as a father and a husband marks another change from the original source: Tommy and Tuppence are not married until the end of 'The Secret Adversary' and their three children do not appear until later in the series. These adaptations might be understood as a reflection of the contemporary emphasis placed on paternalism as the indicator of a fully formed masculine identity and of good citizenship, a discourse that has been ramped up by British and American governments particularly since 9/11 and has permeated popular culture. However, Claire Langhamer has shown how 'gender roles were differently configured in the Cold War period where economic developments, the changing nature of work and technology, demographic shifts, postwar patterns of immigration and rising standards of living' impacted on ideas of masculinity.[36] In an attempt to mediate a 'crisis in masculinity', the male role of 'bread winning and paternity' was culturally sanctioned.[37] This discursive strategy of mediation is evidenced in Tommy's role in the family; he cooks dinner for the family, his business endeavours are a means to support his wife and child and he is a loving father.

This model of manliness – domestic and paternal – is rarely seen in the detective genre. In foregrounding the Beresfords as a couple and as a family, the programme reflects postwar cultural discourses that lauded the married family man as the ideal form of masculinity for health and security of the nation. Thus, when Tommy is aroused by Tuppence dressed in a blonde wig and disguised as a maid in Episode Two, it is not just a moment of comedy arising from sexual jealousy. Instead, Tuppence becomes the regulator of heterosexual desire that was so necessary to the national story of heteronormative masculinity of this period.

Importantly whilst Tuppence appears to be the more adventurous of the two, it is Tommy who puts his life in danger when he eventually traces Jane Finn's whereabouts. Tommy's disguise as a gangster fails when he infiltrates a crime syndicate whom he believes is holding Jane captive. Interestingly, although the style of his clothing (suit, tie and hat) and his physicality appear to be accepted by the criminals, Tommy's rejection of the attentions of one of the prostitutes, his inability to play poker properly and his middle-class mannerisms cause suspicion amongst the men. This might suggest that the fluidity that I argue is embodied in Walliams's performance of Tommy Beresford does not extend to class – this is an issue I will return to later. Tommy's failure to pass as a working-class criminal results with him being held captive and beaten by the criminals. Tommy's inability to successfully infiltrate the gang might be seen as undermining his masculine credentials; however, the casting of a black woman to play the part of the programme's damsel in distress serves as a way to rescue Tommy's flailing masculinity. De-colonisation impacted deeply on race relations in 1950s Britain and led to heightened nationalism that excluded those from the former colonies from the national story. Wendy Webster notes that de-colonisation led to a crisis of white masculinity with the demise of the British adventurer and the end of his exertion of power.[38] By rescuing Jane, Tommy also rescues, redeems and reinforces his male status as the white British adventurer – a trope that harked back to the days of the colonial adventurer. On the surface then, Tommy embodies the masculine ideal of the Cold War period and of the national story, but a closer examination of the opening scene of the first episode might suggest a contradictory reading.

Of Bees and Men: Gender Dualism and the Detective Figure

The opening scene begins with Tommy carefully carrying a small box while Tuppence carries their luggage to their train carriage. Once seated Tuppence teases Tommy about the box he is holding which contains a queen bee that he intends to use to begin his honey making business. Tuppence enquires whether Tommy has read a bee-keeping manual as preparation, Tommy replies he hasn't and Tuppence looks at him warmly but admonishingly. This exchange is played for comedy and it showcases the couple's companionable relationship; however, Tommy's lack of preparedness becomes a recurring motif throughout the three episodes (although his beekeeping enterprise does save the day). It is important to note at this point that the original story does not include reference to bees or bee-keeping or honey throughout, but I suggest the incorporation of

Conflicting Masculinities

Figure 13.1 Tommy as a gangster in *Partners in Crime*.

bee-keeping in the 1952 story serves two ideological purposes. When Tommy tells Tuppence that 'plenty of people don't know about Queens' he is of course referring to the biology of his queen bee. But another reading might suggest a queering of Walliams's portrayal of Tommy, of his masculine identity and of the genre.

Bee-keeping tends to be a hobby that is associated with domesticity: most beehives are kept at the end of a garden and bee-keeping is in the main an isolated and male activity. The beehive is symbolic of civilised society – one that is headed by a female; indeed, across ancient religions and belief systems a number of goddesses are represented through the image or language of the bee because a connotation of female nurturance is tied to the production of honey for human consumption. It is this symbolism of femininity tied to the motif of bees and of bee-keeping that Sabine Vanacker picks up on in her feminist study of Sherlock Holmes, a male detective figure who, much like Walliams, has been discussed in terms of his ambiguous representation of heteronormative masculinity. Vanacker points to the antepenultimate of the Holmes's stories, 'His Last

Bow' (1917), wherein Holmes moves away from the trenches of World War I and retires to an isolated small farm on the Sussex Downs where he takes up bee-keeping. Vanacker suggests that in so doing, Holmes demonstrated that he was at odds with the ideological conventions of masculinity presented in the national story of World War I.[39]

Holmes's bee-keeping activities have also been aligned with the demise of the hegemonic gentlemanly detective figure from 'a stable, Victorian influenced masculinity of order to one that is destabilised and disorderly'.[40] Although masculinity and order have been correlated from the earliest of the detective genre, this begins to break down when Holmes refuses to engage in the national story about masculinity; 'the correlation becomes much more complicated as competing discourses of masculinity begin to proliferate.'[41] In framing Tommy Beresford as a novice bee-keeper from the beginning, *Partners in Crime* already suggests that the myth of hegemonic masculinity and the narrative of the hegemonic detective will be destabilised.

Throughout the three episodes the audience discover that Walliams's Tommy failed at university, and he didn't get to go to war. In stark contrast to the original Tommy, who was injured in active service – twice – the adaptation's Tommy was hit by a catering van on his first day as a soldier. The symbolic resonance of a catering van, associated as it is with femininity or, at least, as less masculine than an army tank, as the cause of Tommy's injuries and emasculation compounds anxieties about his masculinity that are expressed in the show. Although Tuppence insists that Tommy was very brave (because the catering van was driven by a maniac), her mediation of a story that negotiates his manliness also infantilises him. Indeed, Tommy's male identity is called into question again when Tuppence reminds him how to behave in an interview; 'sit up straight', she says, 'and don't interrupt the employer.' And his inability to articulate his sexual desire for Tuppence (when she is dressed in disguise) speaks to a performance of masculinity that teeters between male repression, emasculation and queered masculinity. Tommy is also fully domesticated; in Episode Two, when Tuppence and Tommy are in the kitchen, Tuppence discusses the case and how to use a gun whilst Tommy, dressed in a cooking apron, is more concerned with carrots, celery and cutlery. Although the characterisation of Tuppence suggests the possibility of a feminist inflected narrative, I argue she actually functions to mark out Tommy's diminished manliness.

Conflicting Masculinities

Tommy is less adventurous than Tuppence; he is, as he says, a stay-at-home man – an ordinary man who likes to make honey. His catch phrase 'leave it to the man' is persistently undermined by his clumsiness, ineptitude and failed business endeavours which, Carter notes, combined, makes him an 'unsuitable candidate' for detective work. Tommy's unsuitable masculinity is further reinforced in a scene in Episode One when he enters Carter's office where the older man is listening to a game of cricket on the radio. Carter motions for Tommy to enter the room but to remain quiet until the match is finished. Excited at the England win, Carter looks at Tommy and says, 'The Aussies might trout, but you can't beat an Englishman with a cricket bat.' Turning to Tommy, Carter asks, 'You follow?' – at which Tommy looks away and shakes his head. Tommy's admission that he is not interested in cricket causes Carter a moment of concerned contemplation and the silence between the two men lingers a little bit longer than is comfortable. As noted earlier, sport became an essential marker of masculinity and cricket 'was one of those coded gestures which made men Englishmen'.[42] Pragmatically, though, cricket was also seen as 'an occasion for dramatising gender segregation and affirming heterosexual sexuality' and a means of 'exhausting school-boys in the hope that they would drop off to sleep before masturbating'.[43] By rejecting the world of cricket, Tommy also rejects historical models of British heteronormative masculinity. Indeed the programme's rejection, or at least, complication of its presentation of the heteronormative male figure is reiterated by the decision to give Tommy a Cary Grant look – an aesthetic that was picked up on by a number of critics of the show and was used by Tuppence when she tells her husband that he 'looks like Cary Grant' in a moment of intimate reconciliation. Whilst Tommy's style serves to frame him as a desirable male figure, it cannot be coincidence that Cary Grant was widely rumoured to be a bisexual.

The show's complex rendering of 1950s masculinity sits in contrast with discourses circulating throughout the Cold War period which cast 'deviant' male sexuality as a threat to national security. Deviant male sexuality was constituted through a system of gender dualisms which, as Michaud argues, 'became a way of configuring failed masculinity and were structured as hard vs. soft; manly vs. effeminate'.[44] Popular culture served as a vehicle for the expression of these binaries in double or doppelganger narratives which spoke to 'masculinity in crisis' through the male's 'self condition of rupture, disjuncture and fragmentation'.⁴⁵ The double narrative (especially evident in detective films and espionage narratives) constructed 'a masculine duality that recounts the enforcement of gender prescription and proscription'⁴⁶ so that the double served as an example of failed masculinity. As Michaud argues: 'In post-war culture, gender dualism and the double paradigm served to test the sustainability of masculine identity in an increasingly polarised post-war world.'⁴⁷

Michaud's analysis draws from principles of maleness as set out by American social critic and historian Arthur Schlesinger in his infamous book *The Vital Centre* (1949), where he unconditionally situated domesticated 'softer' forms of masculinity as the result of emasculated masculinity of the mid-twentieth century. ⁴⁸ Robert Nye argues that, in its conservative form,

> This ideology imagines and constructs a narrative identity that lends coherence to the self by ruling out certain ways of imaging and acting in the world. In the Cold War complex of gendered dualisms, those residing outside the centre assume a submissive, feminine role; they are soft, limp, possibly homosexual and ultimately a threat to national security.⁴⁹

Rather than adhering to the binaries as outlined by Nye, Tommy embodies the gendered dualisms that determined idealised masculinity. Tommy is manly *and* effeminate, hard *and* soft, submissive *and* proactive. But *Partners in Crime* is not a doppelganger narrative that positions Tommy's masculine identity as problematic and conflicted; indeed after his sleuthing adventures throughout *The Secret Adversary*, Tommy is returned back to the domestic space where he celebrates the fact that he can 'get back to normal'. In this instance 'normal' is aligned with being a husband, a role that is consolidated by the return of his wedding ring lost at the beginning of his investigative capers. As the episode draws to a close Tommy agrees albeit somewhat reluctantly to return to sleuthing as long as he can 'have the weekend off'. Tommy is not forced to choose one model of masculinity over another; he can be father and detective, husband and sleuth, courageous and scared, strong and limp – all of these combine to render him as a successful model of manhood. And as a model of successful masculinity Tommy does not pose any threat to national security. Indeed, Tommy is instrumental in maintaining national security; this is especially evident in 'N or M?', where he is asked to work alone on a secret mission to uncover the identities of two Russian spies. Although Tuppence eventually joins Tommy on his mission, it is still Tommy who outwits the Russian spy and deactivates a bomb that was aimed to destroy the British people. Yet, despite his heroism and agency the closing scene of the episode sees Tommy returning to his more cautious, domesticated self. Having been offered a paid role as private detectives, Tommy and Tuppence disagree about the sort of cases they might be asked to take. Tuppence is excited by the thought of protecting the nation whilst Tommy suggests that they could 'carve a nice little earner out of domestic disputes'. In this sense, Tuppence demonstrates a sense of national loyalty that was so central to the construction of Cold War masculinity whilst Tommy turns away from the nation to the domestic sphere – and his closing words, 'I must re-new my library card' – re-places him from Cold War hero to an ordinary man. Tommy does not entertain any sense of guilt for what were perceived transgressions of manliness in the 1950s because he does not perceive them to be transgressive. Instead the construction of masculinity on offer in *Partners in Crime* appears to be inclusive: Tommy still bears the markers of fortitude, strength and courage, but he also embraces submissiveness, softness and effeminacy as signifiers of ordinary, everyman maleness.

Conclusion

By way of conclusion I want to return to the idea of the inclusive nature of Tommy's male persona to see how it might bear some relation to shifting ideas about contemporary masculinity. It is often the case that nostalgic renderings of male identity foregrounded in genres like the costume drama tend to function as a way of resolving a contemporary crisis in masculinity. For example, much has been written about the costume drama *Mad Men* (AMC, 2007–15) as recuperating a particularly nostalgic form of masculinity within a post-feminist political and cultural environment. However, reading *Mad Men* as a deeply conservative text, an accusation often levelled at costume dramas, denies the possibility of recognising its potential to destabilise and critique the very form of masculinity foregrounded in the show. This suggests then that the costume drama has the potential to destabilise and to dismantle ideas about hegemonic masculinity. As such, the costume drama engages with politics of camp by offering a proactive social commentary through its use of nostalgia. As I have shown, *Partners in Crime*'s social commentary resides in its destabilisation of Cold War ideas about hegemonic masculinity. The presentation of Tommy Beresford, who embodies the very same gendered binaries that were used to differentiate ordinary men from Othered men, is noteworthy because of its inclusive approach to masculinity. And by casting Walliams, whose identity extends to and includes heteronormativity and non-normative, queer masculinity, *Partners in Crime* reiterates its ideological schema of dismantling the idea of hegemonic masculinity.

The notion of inclusivity played out in *Partners in Crime* suggests that the hierarchical stratifications of masculinities that have historically produced, reproduced and sustained hegemonic male identity are now irrelevant. Eric Anderson would agree with this line of reasoning; his 'inclusive masculinity theory' argues that hegemony has been replaced by heterogeneity, and Anderson sees this as a result of diminishing homophobia that frees heterosexual men to act in more feminine ways without threat to their masculinity.[50] As such, inclusive masculinity theory cancels out any recall to masculinity in crisis discourse.

On the surface then, inclusive masculinity theory offers a hopeful narrative about masculine identity and men, and I suggest this optimistic approach is reflected in *Partners in Crime* and explicitly expressed in Walliams's own performance of masculinity on- and off-screen. However, the optimism is somewhat mediated by the rather homophobic references reviewers made about Walliams's campness, suggesting that the shifts in attitudes towards homosexuality or queered masculinity might not be as widespread as Anderson proposes. Furthermore, the theory's emphasis on heterosexual masculinity as the foundational and privileged identity is problematic, because it maintains a hegemonic position which enables privileged white men to choose, appropriate and enact multiple signifiers of male identity as and when required. This suggests that transgressive forms of masculinity are not transgressive at all when appropriated by white, heteronormative men; rather they actually serve to shore up masculinity. As such Tommy's masculinity in *Partners in Crime* is not a contravention of hegemonic masculinity because white, cis-gendered males have the privilege of choice.

Moreover, inclusive masculinity theory does not take in to account issues of class and race and in so doing maintains the hegemony of cis-gendered, white, middle-class male identity. Anderson's lack of consideration of the relationship between masculinity, class and race is reflected in criticism of Walliams's personal, political and cultural presentation of manhood. Deborah Finding, in her essay 'I can't believe you just said that: Figuring gender and sexuality in *Little Britain*', argues that despite that show's political potential for masculinity, the comedy resides in reinforcing Otherness, constituted as it is by class, race and femininity.[51] Walliams might offer a representation of masculinity that is multifaceted but it is one that reinforces hierarchical stratifications of race, class and gender. And whilst Tommy has the potential to be read as challenging the Cold War scripts of ordinary and everyman manliness, he does so with impunity. His contraventions of masculinity do not break the rules of inclusive masculinity because it relies on appropriating transgressive forms of masculinity to extend the reach of the hegemony of white masculinity. In this way, whilst the camp nature of *Partners in Crime* might allow for provocative and enlightened social commentary about male identity, the show actually functions to reinforce and maintain the conservatism of hegemonic masculinity that it purports to destabilise.

Notes

1. Henry, Hitchings, 'Award for comedy: David Walliams', *Evening Standard*, 19 November 2013. Available at, http://www.standard.co.uk/goingout/theatre/london-evening-standard-theatre-awards-2013-how-we-chose-the-winners-8948507.html (accessed 3 August 2016).
2. Judith Butler, *Gender Trouble: Feminism and the Subversion of Identity* (New York and London, 2011), p. 185.
3. Yvonne Tasker, *Spectacular Bodies: Gender, Genre and the Action Cinema* (London and New York, 1993), p. 55.
4. Joseph Kestner, *Masculinities in British Adventure Fictions, 1800–1915* (Farnham and Burlington, 2010), p. 13.
5. Phillipa Gates, 'Detectives', in M. S. Kimmel and A. Aronson (eds), *Men and Masculinities: A Social, Cultural and Historical Encyclopaedia: A-J* (Santa Barbara, Denver, Oxford, 2003), p. 215.
6. Edward Hall, 'Agatha Christie's *Partners in Crime*', Press Release, p. 26. Available at http://downloads.bbc.co.uk/mediacentre/partners_in_crime.pdf (accessed 7 July 2016).
7. Niall Johnson, 'Agatha Christie drama Partners in Crime tops Sunday viewing', Mediatel Newsline, 27 July 2015. Available at http://mediatel.co.uk/newsline/2015/07/27/agatha-christie-drama-partners-in-crime-tops-sunday-viewing (accessed 7 July 2016).

8. Ellen Jones, 'Partners in Crime, BBC 1: TV review', *Independent*, 26 July 2015. Available at www.independent.co.uk/arts-entertainment/tv/reviews/partners-in-crime-bbc1-tv-review-excellent-leads-just-lack-that-spark-of-sexual-chemistry-10416626.html (accessed 7 July 2016).
9. Ibid.
10. Ibid.
11. Michael Hogan, '*Partners in Crime*: episode 2: "jolly good show"', *Telegraph*, 2 July 2015. Available at http://www.telegraph.co.uk/culture/tvandradio/tv-and-radio-reviews/11776285/Partners-in-Crime-episode-2-review.html (accessed 11 July 2016).
12. Christopher Stevens, 'Sorry Walliams but you can't wince as well as Arfur Daley', *Daily Mail*, 16 August 2015. Available at http://www.dailymail.co.uk/tvshowbiz/article-3200229/Sorry-Walliams-t-wince-Arfur-Daley-CHRISTOPHER-STEVENS-reviews-weekend-s-TV.html (accessed 3 July 2016).
13. Caroline Frost, 'Partners in Crime review', *Huffington Post*, 27 July 2015. Available at http://www.huffingtonpost.co.uk/2015/07/26/partners-in-crime-tv-review-david-walliams_n_7875534.html (accessed 3 July 2016).
14. Paul Mavis, 'Agatha Christie's Partners in Crime: The Tommy and Tuppence Mysteries', *DVD Talk*, 29 January 2013. Available at http://www.dvdtalk.com/reviews/58818/agatha-christies-partners-in-crime-the-tommy/ (accessed 15 July 2016).
15. Susan Sontag, 'Notes on "camp": camp, queer aesthetics and the performing subjects', in *Against Interpretation and Other Essays* (New York, 1961), p. 277.
16. Kim Michasiw, 'Camp, masculinity, masquerade', *Differences: A Journal of Feminist Studies*, 6/3 (1994), p. 148.
17. Ellie Kennedy, 'But I'm a lady: undoing gender bending in contemporary British radio', in Gaby Pailer, Andres Bohn, Stefan Horbacher and Ulrich Sheck (eds), *Gender and Laughter: Comic Affirmation and Subversion in Traditional and Modern Media* (Amsterdam and New York, 2009), p. 236.
18. Tim Martin, 'The boy in a dress: review', *Telegraph*, 26 December 2014. Available at http://www.telegraph.co.uk/culture/tvandradio/tv-and-radio-reviews/11310500/The-Boy-in-the-Dress-review-witty-and-heart-warming.html (accessed 3 July 2016).
19. Lisa McGarry, 'Has the reaction to David Walliams and Lara Stone's split been homophobic?', *UnrealityTV*, 27 July 2015. Available at www.unrealitytv.co.uk/britains-got-talent/has-the-reaction-to-david-walliams-lara-stones-split-been-homophobic (accessed 15 July 2016).
20. David Walliams, *Camp David* (London, 2012).
21. Gill Plain, *John Mills and British Cinema: Masculinity, Identity and Nation* (Edinburgh, 2006), p. 16.
22. Marilyn Michaud, 'The double as failed masculinity in David Ely's Seconds', *eSharp: Identity and Marginality*, 6/1. Available at http://www.academia.

edu/893747/The_Double_As_Failed_Masculinity_In_David_Elys_Seconds (accessed 2 July 2016).
23. Robert Nye, 'Western masculinities in war and peace', *American Historical Review*, 112/2 (2007), p. 427.
24. Agatha Christie, *The Secret Adversary* (New York, 1922), p. 9.
25. Nye, 'Western masculinities in war and peace', p. 428.
26. Plain, *John Mills and British Cinema*, p. 19.
27. Hall, 'Agatha Christie's *Partners in Crime*', p. 26.
28. Ibid.
29. Ibid.
30. Ibid., p. 27.
31. Elaine Showalter, *The Female Malady: Women, Madness and English Culture, 1830–1980* (New York, 1985).
32. Nye, 'Western masculinities in war and peace', p. 428.
33. Andrew Spicer, *Typical Men: The Representation of Masculinity in British Popular Culture* (London and New York, 2011), p. 43.
34. Ibid., p. 44.
35. Ibid., p. 46.
36. Claire Langhamer, 'The meanings of home in post war Britain', *Journal of Contemporary History*, 4/2 (2005), p. 343.
37. Ibid., p. 344.
38. Wendy Webster, *Imagining Home: Gender, 'Race' and National Identity, 1945–1964* (New Jersey, 1998), p. 67.
39. Sabine Vanacker, 'Sherlock's progress through history: feminist revisions of Holmes', in S. Vanacker and C. Wynne (eds), *Sherlock Holmes and Conan Doyle: Multi-Media Afterlives* (Basingstoke and New York, 2013), pp. 93–108.
40. Lisa M. Cuklanz, *Rape on Prime Time: Television, Masculinity and Sexual Violence* (Philadelphia, 2000), p. 19.
41. Ibid.
42. Nye, 'Western masculinities in war and peace', p. 427.
43. Ibid.
44. Michaud, 'The double as failed masculinity in David Ely's Seconds', p. 6.
45. Ibid.
46. Ibid.
47. Ibid.
48. Arthur Schlesinger, *The Vital Centre: Politics of Freedom* (Boston, 1949), p. 9.
49. Nye, 'Western masculinities in war and peace', p. 428.
50. Eric Anderson, *Inclusive Masculinity: The Changing Nature of Masculinities* (Abingdon and New York, 2009).
51. Deborah Finding, 'Figuring Gender and Sexuality in Little Britain', *Media@LSE*, EP13 (2008). Available at http://www.lse.ac.uk/media@lse/research/mediaWorkingPapers/pdf/EWP13.pdf (accessed 10 September 2016), pp. 1–29.

14

'No Need to Matronise Me!': *The Crown*, the Male Consort and Conflicted Masculinity

James Leggott

At the end of the seventh episode of *The Crown* (Netflix, 2016–), there is a striking exchange between Britain's young new monarch and her perpetually sulky yet mischievous prince consort. It is late in the day, and the Queen asks him where he has been. It transpires that while Elizabeth has been busy preparing herself for an (ultimately cancelled) encounter with the American president, and building up the courage to give her prime minister a matronly dressing-down for failing to inform her of his indisposition, Prince Philip has been involved – off-screen – in a football match for one of his philanthropic organisations, and also undertaking dangerous 'spins and rolls' on the airfield where he is speedily training to become a pilot. Following her new-found expression of confidence in herself and the role of constitutional monarchy, Elizabeth II seems 'taller', somehow, to him, and their conversation takes a flirtatious turn. Telling her to cancel her planned meeting with her Private Secretary, Philip perches expectantly on his bed, and offers her two alternative options: 'either I get some stilts so I can reach the heights of my new, tall woman. Or ... [a suggestive pause] she could get on her knees.' Elizabeth smiles appreciatively, and there is a disarming – and in the circumstances, strangely suggestive – close-up of her elderly male secretary's hands clasping on top of her 'red box' (i.e., her file of paperwork from government ministries).

For the observant viewer of Peter Morgan's leisurely paced series, set around the run-up to and aftermath of Elizabeth's 1953 coronation, this erotically charged proposal is evidently a specific reference to the plotline in an earlier episode involving Philip's hostility at bending his knee to her at the ceremony: 'I will feel like a eunuch', he had protested, 'an amoeba kneeling before his wife.' Across the course of its first ten episodes, *The Crown* sketches a canvass wide enough to accommodate not only the arc of Elizabeth's growing self-assurance in the face of personal and constitutional conflict, but also Philip's escalating sense of resentment and emasculation. *The Crown* gives ample time to other characters in the Queen's orbit undergoing comparable crises of agency – for example, Princess Margaret and Peter Townsend's doomed romance, and Winston Churchill doggedly clinging on to his symbolic role as 'father to the nation'. However, the show, like many of its commentators, seems particularly invested in Philip's adjustment from his life as a naval officer to, as the character puts it, 'grinning like a demented ape while [the Queen] cuts ribbons'. Andrew O'Hagan's long review for the *London Review of Books*, for example, begins with the suggestion that: 'Prince Philip is a pure catch for a dramatist. Imagine nearly seventy years in the mellow afterglow of someone else's radiance, two steps behind, a man infantilised beyond belief, provided with everything in return for being a constant second.'[1] Philip's apparent invitation to his wife to undertake a very specific sexual act gives support to those reviewers who have noted a 'sort of misogynistic dickishness'[2] to his attitude and behaviour in *The Crown*, and unquestionably ammunition to those who consider the real Duke to be 'everyone's least favourite hoary old racist [...] best known for his fatuous comments about strippers and Indians'.[3] But it also encapsulates to some degree his place in the British popular imagination as, in the words of his impersonator (Matt Smith) in the show, a 'maverick',[4] famed as much for his buffoonish outspokenness and irritability as for his charitable work and, when younger at least, physical prowess and appeal. In May 2017, the announcement of his 'retirement' at the age of 95 resulted in a number of critical opinion pieces in the UK press. For some he was the 'very id of England', acting as a kind of safety valve against political correctness;[5]

'No Need to Matronise Me!'

for others he was 'a charmless man' made 'fantasy figure', exposing not only class deference but double standards with regards to gender roles.[6] Writing in the *Guardian*, Terence Blacker argued that 'Philip has often been gushingly praised for doing what countless wives of public figures do unnoticed every day – putting their own careers second to that of their spouse and keeping him company as he works.'[7] Within this context, the suggestion of royal fellatio, even off-screen, is just one way that *The Crown* expresses its own 'maverick', outlier credentials as a prestigious and costly, yet non-genuflecting rendering of living members of the royal family. Commissioned by the online streaming site Netflix, and with a rumoured budget of £100 million,[8] *The Crown* may well have not featured such as a moment – nor two glimpses of Philip's bare bottom, or the scene where George VI, soon after coughing blood in a lavatory bowl, delivers a raucous limerick including the word 'cunt' – had it aired on its 'most natural home, the BBC'; not least because the BBC typically uses a senior executive as liaison officer with the monarchy for programmes relating to the royal family.[9] Given that *The Crown* aligns Philip with forces of modernity, and – as part of the show's meta-commentary on representational strategies and symbol-making (alongside Winston Churchill's destruction of a commissioned portrait that dares to enfeeble him) – makes him a strong advocate for the televising of the Coronation as a means to humanise the royal line, it is perhaps foreseeable that he becomes such a sympathetic and intriguing character here.

This chapter deals with how the representation of Prince Philip – as husband, father and prince consort – chimes with how the male consort of British monarchical history and representation is typically understood as a compromised, emasculated figure. But *The Crown* also bids us to consider Philip's crisis of identity as indicative of evolving perceptions of ideal masculinity in the postwar, social democratic era. Just as the Philip of *The Crown* is sensitive to the mythological function of the family he has married into, so the show itself offers scope for an exploration of historical drama's complex relationship with shifting ideals and definitions of hegemonic masculinity.

The Feminised Monarchy and Melodrama

The Crown follows a long and often prestigious tradition of popular film and television portrayals of British monarchs undergoing conflict or crisis, from *Victoria the Great* (1937) to *The Queen* (2006).[10] Significantly, it is Britain's queens – particularly the iconic trio of Elizabeth I, Victoria and Elizabeth II – that have tended to dominate. As Mandy Merck notes, the prominence of such figures offers plentiful leading roles to women as 'representatives of an institution deemed to have become increasingly feminised'.[11] Furthermore, the 'longevity of Victoria and Elizabeth II, the idealisation of the maternal wife and her influence and the presumed amenability of women contributed to this feminisation, and to the "depoliticisation" of the royal role.'[12] Unsurprisingly, such figures would provide 'rich narrative opportunities for royal screen fictions in the genres of romance, costume drama and melodrama, with their ready-made female following'.[13] The fictionalised royal 'biopic' has taken various forms, from the plethora of low-brow romantic dramas made by US television, to the 'post-national and post-historical' populism of *The Tudors* (Showtime, 2007–10).[14] If the 'collision between the public and private figure'[15] is a fixation of many biographical dramas, this is particularly so for monarchical narratives, with their dramatisation of high-stakes tensions between public duty and personal desire, or between constitutional and human loyalty. Such stories, with their emphasis upon the interior struggles of conflicted or suffering characters, invite interpretation as 'melodrama', a term that Merck uses to describe how *The Queen*, also written by Peter Morgan, generates sympathy for Elizabeth II in the wake of the death of Princess Diana – not least through the 'star power' gained through the casting of Helen Mirren.[16] In a similar way, *The King's Speech* (2010) takes a melodramatic approach to its subject of the stammering George VI, to 'evoke sympathy for the strain the royal role places on the monarch as private individual'.[17] On the one hand, his determination to overcome a speech impediment to enable him to speak publically is emblematic of the 'violent imposition of duty over private desires that characterises the melodramatic terrain',[18] but there is also a familial melodrama at work in the evocation of a 'underdog' son traumatised by an inability to match the expectations of his father; similar territory is explored by the one-off TV drama *Bertie and Elizabeth* (ITV, 2002), charting his evolution from awkward young man to stately king via speech therapy and the support of his 'commoner' wife. If George VI has been defined by the historian David Cannadine as the 'ultimate castrated male'[19] – the epitome of the 'emasculated' constitutional monarchy – it is

'No Need to Matronise Me!'

no surprise that representations of him tally with those of protagonists in female-oriented biopics, which typically find 'suffering and therefore drama in a public woman's very inability to make her decisions and discover her own destiny'.[20]

In various ways, *The Crown* exemplifies yet also complicates this web of established associations between royal representation, genre and gender. Following a first episode concerning the King's ailing health from 1947 onwards, the remaining nine episodes (each approximately an hour in length) concentrate on the three years following the Queen's ascension in 1952, although there are flashbacks to incidents in previous decades. Individual episodes typically focus upon a specific incident or dilemma that is illustrative of the 'desire versus duty' or 'symbol versus self' dilemmas of those in power; many of these involve Elizabeth making decisions against the preference of her husband and sister. But *The Crown* – like ITV's *Victoria* (2016–), which was premiered in the United Kingdom at roughly the same time – is distinct from many of the royal representations mentioned thus far in having the potential to be a long-running serial drama. At the time of writing, a second series has been commissioned, again to be written in its entirety by Peter Morgan, an *auteur* of distinctive dramas for film, television and theatre based around confrontations between famous political and media figures; in particular, *The Crown* expands the scope of *The Queen* and his stage play *The Audience* (2013), which imagines a series of encounters between the monarch and successive prime ministers. Although the scale, budget and casting of the show positions it within a tradition of 'quality' or 'heritage' drama, it is not unreasonable to describe Morgan's ambitious yet theoretically open-ended project as akin to televisual soap opera, a form historically associated (particularly in its UK variant) with matriarchal figureheads, female address and a multi-perspective approach to narrative. But the royal drama, as a subset of the broader biographical drama, carries a particular charge when devised for television, as its 'deconstruction of public and private spheres' overlaps with the *modus operandi* of the small screen to 'bring the public sphere into the privacy of the home'.[21] As we will see, it is no small irony that, in *The Crown*, it is Prince Philip – whose narrative arc can be summed up as a resistance of domestication – who becomes an advocate for the televising of his wife's coronation, an occasion that famously boosted television ownership and viewing in Britain.

Furthermore, the potentially open-ended storytelling of *The Crown* allows the show to function as a kind of meta-narrative, encompassing developments in British political, social and media history already dealt with by other sources and representations: for example, Morgan's writing ranges over terrain already covered by contemporaneous films and television dramas such as *A Royal Night Out* (2015), *Churchill's Secret* (ITV, 2016) and *W. E.* (2011).

The Male Consort: Malcontent and Moderniser

Although *The Crown* obviously follows a lineage of British and international royal (melo)drama, its commissioning by Netflix – and thus its status as non-mainstream but prestige television – arguably shifts its position on the spectrum of 'quality' television towards the kind of contemporary, made-for-cable TV dramas like *Breaking Bad* (AMC, 2008–13) and *The Sopranos* (HBO, 1999–2008) that, as Amanda Lotz has observed in detail, share a preoccupation with 'men struggling to find their place in the early twenty-first century'.[22] To place *The Crown* within such a context may seem counter-intuitive, but I would suggest that the programme gives as much, and perhaps even greater, attention to the 'problem' of masculinity in the postwar period, than to Elizabeth's status as (proto)feminist challenging the patriarchal order – which coincides with the programme's complex, transnational positioning between British 'heritage' and American 'quality' traditions. In his study of the 'masculinity in crisis' trope of Obama-era 'quality' US television – which offers more artistic risk than traditional network broadcasting – Michael Albrecht notes how the 'bravado-infused masculinity of the Bush years resulted in an anticlimactic ending to two wars and a weak economy that was typically painful to men'.[23] With the 'effete' Obama himself standing in 'synecdochally for the ostensible crisis and the complicated constructions of masculinity' manifest during his presidency, it is no coincidence that 'legitimating certain shows as Quality carries with it certain gender implications'.[24]

Of course, *The Crown* revolves around the lives and dilemmas of an extremely select group of characters, although their symbolic significance has received much popular and academic attention. Charles Beem and Miles Taylor note how the male consort position – typically defined as the husband or wife of a reigning monarch – has traditionally been a 'much better fit for a woman, whose primary job was to be a good wife and bear the heirs that perpetuate the dynasty'.[25] Whereas the function of queen consort has usually been recognised as an integral aspect of monarchy – which is commonly interpreted in terms of a dual position of a king and his consort jointly reigning and producing heirs – male consorts have historically struggled to inhabit a public role that is not merely 'female gendered' but 'ambiguous, contested, and *de facto*'.[26] Furthermore, in recent times, and particularly in the case of Britain, it has been argued that the 'presence of a female monarchy, and the attendant ambiguity surrounding the place of the male consort, has led to the "emasculation" of the monarchy, and deprived it of its chief roles, now restricted to ceremony and philanthropy.'[27] The most famous male consort in British history is arguably Queen Victoria's husband, Albert, who overcame both xenophobic attitudes to his German origins and an early popular perception of his 'want of manliness'.[28] As Karina Urbach has observed, Albert was able to transcend his position of relative powerlessness – particularly so in a male-dominated age where the idea of the consort was an abnormality – through a sensitivity to the 'new rhythm of the epoch'[29] and a recreation of the royal family as a 'national model for bourgeois respectability';[30] this story is central to the BBC's 2001 mini-series *Victoria and Albert*, and introduced early in ITV's *Victoria*.

Like Albert, who was the co-organiser of the 1851 Great Exhibition, Philip would be recognised as an advocate of new science and technology, a 'modernizer who wished to adapt the monarchy to the changing political and social economy'.[31] The plotline in *The Crown* concerning Philip's orchestration of the coronation demonstrates the way in which his 'egalitarian' vision meets resistance among the 'grey old men' (in his words) who dominate politics and the court:

> We have a new sovereign, young and a woman. Let us give her a coronation that is benefitting of the wind of change that she represents: modern and forward-looking at a moment in time where exciting technological developments are making things possible we never dreamt of!

But as his biographer Tim Heald observes, his persona was also that of a 'sporting prince', whose image projected an 'unrelieved tough masculinity'.[32] His patronage of various organisations – such as the National Playing Fields Association and the Duke of Edinburgh award scheme – promoting the physical, mental and moral values of sporting and youth activities, can be understood in terms of an evolving 'welfare monarchy'. Yet such endeavours clearly draw upon 'dominant codes of masculinity', and correspond with definitions of sport as a 'site of cross-class and cross-generational male bonding where masculinity is constructed and affirmed'.[33]

At the same time, Philip's work and activities, specifically within the postwar context, might be read as characteristic of what the gender historian Sonya Rose has described as the age's ideal of 'tempered masculinity', a concept grounded upon an understanding of hegemonic masculinity as fundamentally unstable and contingent upon definitions of others.[34] Thus, the 'aggressive and belligerent' masculinity of World War I had been superseded by a 'quieter, more domestic, and anti-heroic style'.[35] The outbreak of World War II predictably brought a return to 'martial' values, and a kind of re-masculation of the nation[36] but this was 'tempered by a cult of stoic good-humoured ordinariness which matches the role of civilians on the home front':[37] hence, 'good citizenship and masculinity were virtually the mirror images of each other.'[38]

This concept of restrained masculinity certainly resounds with the representation of Philip in *The Crown*, his rugged sporting, team-playing and military credentials expressed early in sequences of him rowing and socialising with his crew in Malta – his naked torso glistening in the sun a direct contrast with surrounding scenes of a poorly king in a gloomily lit palace. The first episode introduces a contrast between Philip's robustness and longevity (which are of course known extratextually by audiences, invited to sympathise with his 'life sentence' of royal duty), and the chain-smoking, cancer-ridden king, seen in flashbacks throughout the series. Although Philip's care for his body might seem to suggest a 'modern' attitude, it is made clear that his wife's protective injunctions against him smoking in her presence are read by him as illustrative of his dwindling agency. The sequence in which, whilst on a Kenyan safari, he protects his wife and others from being charged by an elephant is a near-parodic expression of Philip the action hero, as is the depiction of him striding manfully towards his aircraft. These scenes, among others, prompted the historian Hugo Vickers to accuse the programme of vulgar and misleading 'sensationalism',[39] to which Andrew O'Hagan adroitly responded in his own review: 'it was simply time, in that particular episode, for Philip to stare down an elephant, the kind of event for which poetic license was surely invented.'[40]

But in keeping with Rose's notion of the ideal masculinity of the era being a compromise between the 'solider hero' and the humble team-player, *The Crown* also establishes that, despite having 'won the greatest prize on earth', Philip is at ease in a variety of company; as shown by his bond with local children on his Commonwealth tour, and his mocking rejection of fine dining rituals: 'don't they realise we're savages? Good for nothing but school dinners and nursery food!'. His 'ordinariness' and anti-authoritarian stances are unquestionably relative, but are manifest in his 'outsider' status among the British establishment as someone who (in his words in the show) 'left Greece in an orange crate', his propensity for swearing, his railing against the establishment, and his bellwether sensitivity to the capricious mood of the British people.

The Crown seems alive to the ways that the kind of masculinity Philip embodied might be alluring to those at the time, and to the present time too, despite its problematic elements. At the start of the first episode, when asked by him whether she would have preferred someone other than a 'homeless Charlie Kraut', Elizabeth responds, amusedly, by saying that would have been 'antiseptic', and she later confides that it was his 'pride and strength' that were 'in part, what attracted me to him'. The consensus, at least among the Windsor sisters, about the desirability of rugged 'action' types is confirmed by the opening of the 'Act of God' episode, which sees Philip striding out of an aeroplane hanger as if from a contemporaneous war movie, and Elizabeth's comment that she can understand the attraction to her sister of Captain Peter Townsend: 'he's a handsome war hero.' The programme colludes in such attitudes, to a degree, through the inclusion of a couple of scenes that debatably allow scope for the objectification of Philip and/or the actor (Matt Smith) playing him; one shows his naked torso as he rows with his crew, the other offers a brief view of his bare bottom as he jumps to the attention of the King who has suddenly appeared in his bedroom. The former is documented by the Queen on her film camera, a moment that simultaneously reinforces his sexual potency to her, and reminds the viewer of their own voyeuristic invasion of the 'private' lives and bodies of the royal family. Philip's discontent is often directed towards the emasculating commodification of his body via the 'absurd pantomime' of royal visits, wherein a 'uniform' becomes a feminising 'costume', that is, a performance, not a job of work. On a couple of occasions, as if to ward off objectification, he shares in homoerotically charged banter with his friend Michael about his clothing choices: he is told that ostrich feathers 'suit him' and that he looks 'wonderful'. Philip's 'strength', though, subverts archetypes of masculine empowerment through silence. Whereas the Queen is observed in *The Crown* to have exercised control by 'barely opening her mouth' and develops a skill for succinct yet purposeful expression in her official dealings, Philip's loquaciousness might even be defined as 'womanly', if judged according to old-fashioned stereotyping of male and female conduct.

The Crown takes an ambivalent stance on Philip's accomplishment as a father figure, perhaps mindful of the real Charles and Philip's own public statements on their 'complex relationship', including the Prince of Wales's disclosures about feeling 'emotionally estranged' from his parents, not least through being sent away to boarding school.[41] Philip is shown far more frequently than Elizabeth interacting with their children, and we see the Queen smiling from her window as she watches her husband attempting to teach the young Charles to play football, even when the hapless boy accidentally throws the ball into his crotch: 'not bloody bad, Charles!' She is also quick to defend Philip from her mother's accusation that he is 'taking out his own frustrations' on his young son, which seems like a fair reading of a scene we have witnessed (unlike her) of Philip losing his temper at Charles's failure to grasp the basics of fishing. Philip's conservative attitude to gender roles is exemplified by his exasperated diagnosis that 'our daughter's a boy, and our son is, God bless him, a girl.'

The masculinity denoted by Philip in *The Crown* is ultimately contingent upon the programme's evocations of other male characters, which are generally found wanting. The series begins with the image of King George VI spitting blood, precipitating his decline and early death; as already noted, the programme positions the sickly, stammering, increasingly splenetic King as the epitome of 'emasculated monarchy', mocked by Churchill for 'wearing rouge' in an attempt to disguise his pallor. The first two episodes also perturb the likely expectations that audiences have of the mise-en-scène of stately royal drama by including

'No Need to Matronise Me!'

close-up footage of his surgery, including the shocking image of a removed diseased lung, and a sequence in which Princess Margaret observes the embalming of his corpse. His brother, the ex-king and now Duke of Windsor, is a snarky, petulant presence, at war with a family he proclaims to despise in his letters to his wife; he is also portrayed as a literal 'mummy's boy', climbing in the bed of his (dying) mother. The political establishment are uniformly the 'grey old men' derided by Philip; Churchill's periods of incapacitation triggering a constitutional crisis, his younger successor Anthony Eden similarly unfit for duty, secretly self-administering injections that leave tell-tale blood stains on his suit. Peter Morgan's script engineers an amusing encounter between the Queen and a private tutor, employed to boost her conversational confidence with (male) leaders and to supplement her limited childhood education (the source of some friction with her mother). The professor, distinguished from the 'establishment' through his Northern (English) accent – a signifier here of regional, working-class origin – gives her a strategy for dealing with errant politicians based on an overtly Freudian interpretation of their sexual proclivities: 'Because they're English, male and upper class, a good dressing down from Nanny is what they most want in life.'

A potential quasi-father figure to Philip, Group Captain Peter Townsend wins his respect for his wartime achievements, piloting and bridge-playing, but is dismissed as 'desperately dull' and ultimately suspect as a man because of his 'breakdown' during the war. The 'Assassins' episode (the ninth) introduces a former beau of Elizabeth, the straightforwardly aristocratic but decidedly 'beta' male, Lord Porchester, to underscore the estrangement between husband and wife. 'Porchey' – his nickname alone conveying his infantilised and non-sexually threatening demeanour – is her companion and advisor for her horse-breeding hobby/work, but Philip is evidently intimidated by his closeness to the Queen, as demonstrated by his access to a private telephone to her: a privilege not extended, despite his wishes, to his own friend Michael.

The Crown and the Philip Problem

The Crown places the 'problem' of Philip front and centre by beginning with his formal renunciation of his Greek nationality, and ending its first series with his grudging agreement to undertake a five-month solo tour – 'a long time for a father to be away from his children' – as a means for him to help identify his role and overcome mounting resentment at his wife. The differing spatial configurations of these two book-ending sequences encapsulate the ways that their relationship has changed. In the first, Elizabeth – still a princess – is barred (presumably through protocol) from the room where the formal yet homosocially convivial ritual is taking place, and paces apprehensively in the corridor. At their subsequent marriage ceremony, Philip's poise – conveyed by Matt Smith through physical assuredness and a facial expression suggesting wry amusement – contrasts with Elizabeth's more jittery demeanour. By the end of the first series, however, Philip's countenance is markedly more sombre, his vocal tone incrementally sarcastic, in contrast with his wife's increasing bodily and verbal composure, and thus explaining, in part, his effective 'banishment' from the royal household.

This is a logical conclusion to a spate of clashes across the series between Philip and Elizabeth over the question of the former's agency as husband, father and royalty. When it becomes apparent that his children will not bear his family name of Mountbatten, he explodes: 'What kind of marriage is this? What kind of family? You've taken my career from me, you've taken my home. You've taken my name.' Even on one of the few occasions where Philip is able to exercise some free will, by undertaking flying lessons, Churchill becomes obsessed with stopping him, and he is 'grounded' anyway by the descent of a fog over London. Given the responsibility of chairman of the coronation board, he grumbles that this is an act of pity, a job for 'appearances sake': 'no need to matronise me!' He is seen shortly afterwards chortling at a theatrical performance involving a male comedian playing a bumbling stage-hand interrupting the performance of a ballerina: a vague parallel for his own disruptiveness in a support role to the Queen. The expectation that he should publically subjugate himself to his wife at the Coronation unleashes further disgruntlement, which comes to a head when the Queen questions his 'strength' as a man in being unable to kneel before her. Philip also rails against her commitment to fulfilling a gruelling, potentially even dangerous royal tour; while the Queen stoically subjects herself to injections to ward against a smile-induced spasm, Philip moans about the 'miserable circus' that makes him no more than a 'dancing bear', waving to crowds in his sleep as if on autopilot.

'No Need to Matronise Me!'

Indeed, Philip's words and actions become bitter and spiteful as the series progresses, their toxicity explained narratively and thematically through such challenges to his agency as a man and a husband. This also accounts in part for his tendency to disappear to homosocial bolt-holes with his frequent companion Michael, such as the Soho lunch club where political discussion (in this case, of anti-imperialist developments in Egypt) is leavened by boorish banter ('bloody natives!') and leering sexism. On a couple of occasions, we are given the Queen's perspective, from her bedroom window, of Philip and Michael – a character with no defining feature other than as a 'wing man' to the Duke – driving to and from what is evidently a lairy, alcohol-fuelled adventure; cries of 'toodle-oo' and mention of a 'snifter on route' seem part of the writer's mechanism for undercutting Philip's egalitarian charms with signifiers of loutish upper-class privilege. Similarly, his comments to his wife about her father's cancer and her motives for impressing him, prompted by her repeated requests for him not to smoke, are provocatively nasty, and cause Elizabeth to admonish and fight him.

The Crown and the Twenty-First Century

There are naturally pitfalls with any reading of Philip's behaviour in *The Crown* as consistent with a rational character arc. In interviews about the role, Smith has expressed his sympathy towards a man of 'tremendous courage', whose instinctively outspoken response to injustices, personal or otherwise, is explicable from a 'very difficult childhood',[42] and a traumatic incident – mentioned by the character in a matter-of-fact way to Townsend in a rare moment of introspection – where he saw his pregnant sister die in a plane crash.[43] The use of this 'back story' to humanise and elucidate is comparable with the programme's tendency to hold the camera on his pained facial expression following a confrontation of some kind with his wife. However, *The Crown* does acknowledge aspects of his outlook that clash awkwardly with contemporary attitudes – including his politically incorrect use of terms like 'sissying' (to describe his role in the decoration of Clarence House) – but most notably via a scene in Africa where he insults a tribesman by inferring he might have stolen his medals: a nod to Philip's formidable reputation for public 'gaffes', particularly around ethnic and cultural identity. Nevertheless, interviews with the creative personnel of *The Crown* reveal an impulse to challenge tabloid stereotyping of the 'misunderstood' Duke and reveal him to be, in the words of the producer Suzanne Mackie, 'incredibly, surprisingly vital, progressive, modernising, energetic, a real alpha male [...], really athletic, capable and clever'.[44] Such comments often reveal a conflicted position on the Duke of the 1940s and 1950s, and by extension his later life too. For all his popularity with the public during his youth, he is positioned in interviews as a figure in need of restoration, simultaneously human and 'mythological': Claire Foy (who plays Elizabeth), for example, observed of the character: 'I think it's unfair to judge him by modern standards, in the sense that I think he is incredibly forward-thinking [...] and modern in his attitude.'[45]

One element of this 'recuperation' is the casting of Matt Smith, whose previous role as the 'eleventh Doctor' of the long-running *Doctor Who* (BBC, 1963–89; 1996; 2005–) was an inevitable point of comparison for reviewers and audiences. That programme's central conceit of a regenerating alien hero – so suggestive of the fluidity of masculinity itself – has spawned much scholarly deconstruction of its gender politics. Piers Britton, for example, compares the 'supremely authoritative narcissistic hero' of the previous two Doctors, with Smith's 'theatricalised and queer' take on the role.[46] But for Claire Jenkins, the actor/character's appropriation of 'geek chic' evokes 'metrosexuality': 'both Smith's persona and performance depict a shift towards a post-feminist masculinity that re-asserts the traits of hegemonic masculinity in the face of the "threat" posed by shifting gender boundaries.'[47] Such a reading, in line with Smith's status as 'unlikely' sex symbol,[48] extends fairly neatly to his performance as Philip, which conveys both the appeal and the danger of his displaced, challenged 'alpha' masculinity. Smith's repertoire of physical quirks (and quite possibly performance decisions rather than scripted demands) include an interrogative, domineering finger point and click and – at moments of strain – a neck/shoulder spasm, as if the character is trying to contain a restless physicality.

Naturally, as with all historical drama, *The Crown* represents its period and its attitudes through the prism of contemporary politics and culture. Some British commentators have critiqued the show for sharing a similar impulse to *Downton Abbey* (ITV, 2010–15), one of the most discussed series of the austerity-driven, Conservative-led era, in making the 'entitled

'No Need to Matronise Me!'

the heroes of narratives about our national collective past', and overlooking, in the view of Harry Leslie Smith, the key development of the depicted epoch, namely the creation of the welfare state.[49] Although conceived before the events leading to Britain's culturally and politically divisive referendum on leaving the European Union, *The Crown* portrays Philip as a concerned observer of anti-imperial sentiments, and a mouthpiece for 'declinist' anxieties about the nation's insignificance on the world stage. Its author, Peter Morgan, has noted parallels between its depiction of the build-up to the Suez Crisis (of 1956 and likely the subject of the second series), and the vote for Brexit: both involve a 'country mortgaging its international respect as a stable democracy'.[50] Yet Morgan also noted that, whilst he would by no means consider his project as pro-monarchy nostalgia, in light of 'our current betrayal by a whole political class', and the 'failure of the democratic process', the kind of benign, stable continuity symbolised by the Queen may take on an unexpected appeal.[51] Herein lies one of the paradoxes of *The Crown* in the context of the supposed forces of anti-elitism behind the Brexit (and Trump) victory: the series re-purposes the privileged Queen and consort as anti-establishment pathfinders.

The Crown's take on Philip as a manly but symbolically emasculated malcontent, sensitive to the nation's 'decline' but unreconstructed in his attitudes to gender roles, is similarly riven with contradictions. Unlike the disenfranchised victims of the world wars described by Claire O'Callaghan, Stella Hockenhull and Julie Anne Taddeo in their chapters in this book, Philip's characterisation would seem to refute any notion of 'masculinity in crisis'; indeed, there are parallels with Louise FitzGerald's analysis of David Walliams's character in the contemporaneously set *Partners in Crime* (BBC, 2015) as multifaceted yet ultimately conservative in its resolution of contradictory signifiers of masculinity.

The Crown also frustrates easy interpretation at the time of a resurgent wave of popular feminism. The series appeared on Netflix just a handful of days before Donald Trump's presidential victory, and his reputation for obscene comments about women – a videotape was uncovered in which he bragged of his ability to 'grab them by the pussy' – cast a dark cloud over the series' depiction of a King using comparably objectionable language, and (to some degree) the casual boorishness and racism of its prince consort hero. A number of commentators also jumped upon Matt Smith's claim that, upon asking Philip's grandson for advice on undertaking the role, Prince William merely used the epithet 'legend',[52] presumably in the sense of an archetypal figure far removed from the sensitivities of the present. To its credit, *The Crown* allows scope for viewers to make their own judgement on whether the kind of masculinity symbolised by someone, in Philip's words, 'ripped from the pages of some bizarre mythology', is worth recuperating or not.

Notes

1. Andrew O'Hagan, 'All hail, sage lady', *London Review of Books*, 38/24 (15 December 2016), p. 15. Available at https://www.lrb.co.uk/v38/n24/andrew-ohagan/all-hail-sage-lady\ (accessed 1 February 2017).
2. Esther Zuckerman, 'Claire Foy and Matt Smith on royal asses (literal and metaphoric) in *The Crown*', *The AV Club*, 3 November 2016. Available at http://www.avclub.com/article/claire-foy-and-matt-smith-royal-asses-literal-and-245075 (accessed 1 February 2017).
3. Laurie Penny, 'Shame of thrones: *The Crown* needs dragons, and a decent plot', *New Statesman*, 8 November 2016. Available at http://www.newstatesman.com/culture/tv-radio/2016/11/shame-thrones-crown-needs-dragons-and-decent-plot (accessed 1 February 2017).
4. Debra Birnbaum, '"The Crown" Star Matt Smith on How Prince Philip Compares to "Doctor Who"', *Variety*, 15 November 2016. Available at http://variety.com/2016/tv/news/the-crown-matt-smith-prince-philip-doctor-who-1201905271/ (accessed 1 February 2017).
5. James Hawes, 'Praise Philip, the Prince of Misrule', *Guardian*, 7 May 2017. Available at https://www.theguardian.com/commentisfree/2017/may/06/philip-prince-of-misrule-said-what-we-darent (accessed 21 June 2017).
6. Terence Blacker, 'We can't blame Prince Philip – we were the ones who indulged him', *Guardian*, 4 May 2017. Available at https://www.theguardian.com/commentisfree/2017/may/04/prince-philip-duke-deference (accessed 21 June 2017).
7. Ibid.
8. Lucy Mangan, 'The Crown review', *Guardian*, 4 November 2016. Available at https://www.theguardian.com/tv-and-radio/2016/nov/04/the-crown-review-netflix-100m-gamble-on-the-queen-pays-off-royally (accessed 1 February 2017).
9. Ibid., The argument that *The Crown* would have been inconceivable as a BBC production is slightly diminished by its broadcast in May 2017, around the time of Philip's retirement, of a film version of Mike Bartlett's play *King Charles III* – which concerned the death of the reigning monarch, and was deemed in some quarters of the conservative press to be in 'appalling bad taste'

and a 'republican fantasy'. Christopher Stevens, 'BBC's republican fantasy is more risible than revolutionary – and grindingly dull', *Daily Mail*, 10 May 2017. Available at http://www.dailymail.co.uk/tvshowbiz/article-4493614/BBC-s-republican-fantasy-risible-revolutionary.html (accessed 21 June 2017).
10. For an overview of the monarchy and cinema, see Jeffrey Richards, 'The Monarchy and Film 1900–2006', in A. Olechnowicz (ed.), *The Monarchy and the British Nation, 1780 to the Present* (Cambridge: 2007), pp. 280–314. The most detailed volume on the subject to date is M. Merck (ed.), *The British Monarchy on Screen* (Manchester, 2016).
11. Mandy Merck, 'Introduction', in M. Merck (ed.), *The British Monarchy on Screen*, p. 3.
12. Ibid., pp. 3–4.
13. Ibid., p. 3.
14. Ibid., p. 14. See also Basil Glyn, '*The Tudors* and the post-national, post-historical Henry VIII', in M. Merck (ed.), *The British Monarchy on Screen* (Manchester, 2016), pp. 309–38.
15. Márta Minier, 'Joining history to celebiography and heritage to documentary on the small screen: spotlight on the content of the form in the metamediatic royal bio-docudrama', in M. Minier and M. Pennacchia (eds), *Adaptation, Intermediality and the British Celebrity Biopic* (Oxon and New York, 2016), p. 97.
16. Mandy Merck, 'Melodrama, celebrity, *The Queen*', in M. Merck (ed.), *The British Monarchy on Screen*, pp. 363–83.
17. Nicola Rehling, 'When words fail: *The King's Speech* as melodrama', in M. Merck (ed.), *The British Monarchy on Screen* (Manchester, 2016), p. 384.
18. Ibid., p. 384.
19. David Cannadine, *History in Our Time* (New Haven and London, 1998), pp. 65–6.
20. Dennis Bingham, *Whose Lives are they Anyway? The Biopic as Contemporary Film Genre* (New Brunswick, 2010), p. 213.
21. Hannah Andrews, '*Women we loved*: Paradoxes of public and private in the biographical television drama', *Critical Studies in Television*, 12/1 (2016), p. 65.
22. Amanda D. Lotz, *Cable Guys: Television and Masculinities in the 21st Century* (New York, 2014), p. 6.
23. Michael Albrecht, *Masculinity in Contemporary Quality Television* (London and New York, 2016), p. 15.
24. Ibid., p. 7.
25. Charles Beem and Miles Taylor, 'Introduction: The Man behind the Queen', in C. Beem and M. Taylor (eds), *The Man Behind the Queen: Male Consorts in History* (New York, 2014), p. 3.
26. Ibid., pp. 3–4.
27. Ibid., p. 4.

28. Karina Urbach, 'Prince Albert: The Creative Consort', in C. Beem and M. Taylor (eds), *The Man Behind the Queen: Male Consorts in History* (New York, 2014), p. 146.
29. Ibid., p. 147.
30. Charles Beem and Miles Taylor, 'Introduction: The Man behind the Queen', p. 7.
31. Frank Prochaska, *Royal Bounty: The Making of a Welfare Monarchy* (New Haven and London, 1995), p. 258.
32. Tim Heald, *The Duke: A Portrait of Prince Philip* (Kent, 1991), p. 224 and p. 226.
33. Ina Zweiniger-Bargieolowska, 'Prince Philip: Sportsman and Youth Leader', in C. Beem and M. Taylor (eds), *The Man Behind the Queen: Male Consorts in History*, p. 223 and p. 225.
34. Sonya O. Rose, 'Temperate heroes: concepts of masculinity in Second World War Britain', in S. Dudink, K. Hagemann and J. Tosh (eds), *Masculinities in Politics and War: Gendering Modern History* (Manchester and New York, 2004), p. 192.
35. John Tosh, 'Hegemonic masculinity and the history of gender', in S. Dudink, K. Hagemann and J. Tosh (eds), *Masculinities in Politics and War: Gendering Modern History* (Manchester and New York, 2004), p. 178.
36. Sonya O. Rose, 'Temperate heroes', p. 178.
37. John Tosh, 'Hegemonic masculinity and the history of gender', p. 48.
38. Sonya O. Rose, 'Temperate heroes', p. 178.
39. Hugo Vickers, 'A royal affair: does The Crown bend the truth about the Windsors?', *The Times*, 24 November 2016. Available at http://www.thetimes.co.uk/article/a-royal-affair-does-the-crown-bend-the-truth-about-the-windsors-9r8dlbt6z (accessed 1 February 2017).
40. Andrew O'Hagan, 'All hail, sage lady', *London Review of Books*, p. 16.
41. Hannah Furness, 'Prince Philip as you've never seen him before: Matt Smith stars as the "touchy-feely" Duke in The Crown', *Telegraph*, 29 October 2016. Available at http://www.telegraph.co.uk/news/2016/10/29/prince-philip-as-youve-never-seen-him-before-matt-smith-stars-as/ (accessed 1 February 2017).
42. Debra Birnbaum, '"The Crown" Star Matt Smith on How Prince Philip Compares to "Doctor Who"', *Variety*, 15 November 2016. Available at http://variety.com/2016/tv/news/the-crown-matt-smith-prince-philip-doctor-who-1201905271/ (accessed 1 February 2017).
43. For a detailed account of Philip's early life, see Philip Eade, *Young Prince Philip: His Turbulent Early Life* (St Ives, 2011).
44. Hannah Furness, 'Prince Philip as you've never seen him before: Matt Smith stars as the "touchy-feely" Duke in The Crown'.
45. Esther Zuckerman, 'Claire Foy and Matt Smith on royal asses (literal and metaphoric) in *The Crown*', *The AV Club*, 3 November 2016. Available at http://www.avclub.com/article/claire-foy-and-matt-smith-royal-asses-literal-and-245075 (accessed 1 February 2017).

46. Piers Britton, *TARDISbound: Navigating the Universes of Doctor Who* (New York, 2011), p. 108.
47. Claire Jenkins, '"I'm saving the world, I need a decent shirt": Masculinity and Costume in the new Doctor Who', in S. Bruzzi and P. C. Gibson (eds), *Fashion Cultures Revisited* (London, 2013), p. 378.
48. Chris O'Dowd, 'My looks: the unlikely sex symbols', *Guardian*, 27 July 2012. Available at https://www.theguardian.com/culture/2012/jul/27/unlikely-male-sex-symbols (accessed 1 February 2017).
49. Harry Leslie Smith, 'The Crown's portrayal of history is an insult to my generation's struggles', *Guardian*, 8 November 2016. Available at https://www.theguardian.com/commentisfree/2016/nov/08/the-crown-portrayal-of-history-insult-to-my-generations-struggles (accessed 1 February 2017).
50. Trevor Johnston, 'Drama Queen', *Sight and Sound* (December 2016), p. 48.
51. Ibid., p. 48.
52. Morgan Jeffery, 'Matt Smith reveals he asked Prince William for advice on how to play Prince Philip in The Crown', *Digital Spy*, 31 October 2016. Available at http://www.digitalspy.com/tv/news/a812644/matt-smith-admits-he-asked-prince-william-for-advice-on-how-to-play-prince-philip-in-the-crown/ (accessed 1 February 2017).

Bibliography

Adams, J. E., *Dandies and Desert Saints: Styles of Victorian Masculinity* (Ithaca, NY, 1995).
Adams, Michael C., *The Great Adventure: Male Desire and the Coming of World War I* (Bloomington, IN, 1990).
Adkins, Roy and Lesley, *Jack Tar: Life in Nelson's Navy* (London, 2008).
Agamben, Giorgio, *Homo Sacer: Sovereign Power and Bare Life*, trans. Daniel Heller-Roazen (Stanford, CA, 1998).
Aiden, Hardeep and McCarthy, Andrea, *Current Attitudes Towards Disabled People* (London, 2014), p. 3. Available at http://www.scope.org.uk/Scope/media/Images/Publication%20Directory/Current-attitudes-towards-disabled-people.pdf (accessed 20 June 2016).
Akbar, Arifa, 'TV review: The Village gives viewers – finally – a proper, grown-up period drama', *Independent*, 1 April 2013. Available at http://www.independent.co.uk/arts-entertainment/tv/reviews/tv-review-the-village-gives-viewers-finally-a-proper-grown-up-period-drama-8555619.html (accessed 31 August 2016).
Akilli, Sinan and Öz, Seda, '"No More Let Life Divide . . .": Victorian Metropolitan Confluence in Penny Dreadful', *Critical Survey*, 28/1 (2016), pp. 15–29.
Albrecht, Michael, *Masculinity in Contemporary Quality Television* (London and New York, 2016).
Anderson, Eric, *Inclusive Masculinity: The Changing Nature of Masculinities* (Abingdon and New York, 2009).
Andrews, Hannah, '*Women we loved*: Paradoxes of public and private in the biographical television drama', *Critical Studies in Television*, 12/1 (2016), pp. 63–78.
Anon., *Man Points: The Definitive Guide to Measuring your Manliness* (London, 2015).
Asch, Adrienne and Fine, Michelle, 'Introduction: Beyond Pedestals', in M. Fine and A. Asch (eds), *Women with Disabilities: Essays in Psychology, Culture and Politics* (Philadelphia, 1988), pp. 1–37.
Atkinson, Will et al. (eds), *Class Inequality in Austerity Britain: Power, Difference and Suffering* (Basingstoke, 2013).
Bakare, Lanre, 'Benedict Cumberbatch apologises after calling black actors "coloured"', *Guardian*, 26 January 2015. Available at https://www.theguardian.

Bibliography

com/culture/2015/jan/26/benedict-cumberbatch-apologises-after-calling-black-actors-coloured (acessed 15 August 2016).
Baker, Brian, *Contemporary Masculinities in Fiction, Film and Television* (New York, London, Oxford, New Delhi, Sydney, 2016).
Banished BBC Press Pack (2015).
Barber, Nicholas, '*Pride and Prejudice* at 20: the scene that changed everything', *BBC Culture* (22 September 2015). Available at http://www.bbc.com/culture/us (accessed 2 September 2016).
Barrington, George, *The History of New South Wales* (London, 1802).
Bataille, Georges, 'Sacrifice, the Festival and the Principles of the Sacred World', in F. Bottin and S. Wilson (eds), *The Bataille Reader* (Oxford, 1997), pp. 210–19.
Beem, Charles and Taylor, Miles, 'Introduction: The Man behind the Queen', in C. Beem and M. Taylor (eds), *The Man Behind the Queen: Male Consorts in History* (New York, 2014), pp. 1–9.
Béhar, Henri, 'Interview with Benjamin Ross on "The Young Poisoner's Handbook"', *Filmscouts*. Available at http://www.filmscouts.com/scripts/interview.cfm?File=ben-ros (accessed 15 August 2016).
Bell, Ian, 'It was all shipshape in a voyage packed with every known emotion', *The Herald* (Glasgow), 21 July 2005, p. 23.
Berns, Nancy, *Framing the Victim: Domestic Violence, Media and Social Problems* (New Brunswick, NJ, 2009).
Bibbings, Lois S., 'Images of Manliness: The Portrayal of Soldiers and Conscientious Objectors in the Great War', *Social & Legal Studies*, 12/3 (2003), pp. 335–58.
——, *Telling Tales About Men: Conceptions of Conscientious Objectors to Military Service During the First World War* (Manchester, 2011).
Biernoff, Suzannah, 'Flesh Poems: Henry Tonks and the Art of Surgery', *Visual Culture in Britain*, 11/1 (March 2010), pp. 25–47.
Bingham, Dennis, *Whose Lives are they Anyway? The Biopic as Contemporary Film Genre* (New Brunswick, NJ, 2010).
Birnbaum, Debra, '"The Crown" Star Matt Smith on How Prince Philip Compares to "Doctor Who"', *Variety*, 15 November 2016. Available at http://variety.com/2016/tv/news/the-crown-matt-smith-prince-philip-doctor-who-1201905271/ (accessed 1 February 2017).
Blacker, Terence, 'We can't blame Prince Philip – we were the ones who indulged him', *Guardian*, 4 May 2017. Available at https://www.theguardian.com/commentisfree/2017/may/04/prince-philip-duke-deference (accessed 21 June 2017).
Bland, Lucy, *Modern Women on Trial: Sexual Transgression in the Age of the Flapper* (Manchester, 2013).
Blott, Unity et al., 'Sex scenes are a turn off for prudish Brits as Versailles' viewers switch channel during the raciest moments of the BBC drama', *Daily Mail*, 3 June 2016. Available at http://www.dailymail.co.uk/femail/article-3623370/Viewers-switch-sauciest-scenes-Versailles-drama.html (accessed 11 July 2016).
Botting, Fred, *Making Monstrous: Frankenstein, Criticism, Theory* (Manchester, 1991).
Bramall, Rebecca, *The Cultural Politics of Austerity: Past and Present in Austere Times* (Basingstoke, 2013).

Bristow, Joseph (ed.), *Oscar Wilde and Modern Culture* (Athens, OH, 2008).
Britton, Piers, *TARDISbound: Navigating the Universes of Doctor Who* (New York, 2011).
Brockes, Emma, '*Call the Midwife*: an Unexpected PBS hit with Another Brit Import', *Guardian*, 26 April 2013. Available at https://www.theguardian.com/commentisfree/emma-brockes-blog/2013/apr/26/call-the-midwife-pbs-hit-import (accessed 15 September 2016).
Bruzzi, Stella, 'Tempestuous petticoats: costume and desire in The Piano', *Screen*, 16/3 (1995), pp. 257–66.
Burns, Amy, 'The chick's "new hero": (Re)constructing masculinity in the postfeminist "chick flick"', in Joel Gwynne and Nadine Muller (eds), *Postfeminism and Contemporary Hollywood Cinema* (Basingstoke, 2013), pp. 131–48.
Burrell, Ian, 'BBC defends taking liberties with the life of Charles II death', *Independent*, 12 November 2003. Available at www.independent.co.uk/news/media/bbc-defends-taking-liberties-with-the-life-of-charles-ii-death-77957.html (accessed 12 July 2016).
Butler, Judith, *Gender Trouble: Feminism and the Subversion of Identity* (Abingdon/New York, 2014; originally published in 1990).
Byrne, Katherine, 'Adapting Heritage: Class and Conservatism in *Downton Abbey*', *Rethinking History: The Journal of Theory and Practice*, 18/3 (2013), pp. 311–27.
——, *Edwardians on Screen: From* Downton Abbey *to* Parade's End (Houndmills, Basingstoke, 2015).
——, 'New Developments in Heritage: The Recent Dark Side of *Downton* "*Downer*" *Abbey*', in J. Leggott and J. A. Taddeo (eds), *Upstairs and Downstairs: British Costume Drama Television from* The Forsyte Saga *to* Downton Abbey (Lanham, Boulder, New York, 2015), pp. 177–90.
Cannadine, David, *History in Our Time* (New Haven, CT and London, 1998).
Carvel, John, 'Heckled, Jeered Booed – Blair Bombs at the WI', *Guardian*, 8 June 2000. Available at https://www.theguardian.com/politics/2000/jun/08/uk.labour3 (accessed 18 October 2016).
Chapman, James, *The British at War* (London, New York, 2000).
——, '"This ship is England": history, politics and national identity in *Master and Commander: The Far Side of the World* (2003)', in J. Chapman, M. Glancy and S. Harper (eds), *The New Film History: Sources, Methods, Approaches* (New York, 2007), pp. 55–68.
Christie, Agatha, *The Secret Adversary* (New York, 1922).
Christy, Desmond, 'Fighting Blackadder', *Guardian*, 30 October 1999. Available at https://www.theguardian.com/books/1999/oct/30/historybooks1 (accessed 31 May 2016).
Cixous, Hélène, 'Sorties', in Douglas Tallack (ed.), *Critical Theory: A Reader* (Abingdon, 2013), pp. 200–11.
Clark, Alan, *The Donkeys: A History of the British Expeditionary Force in 1915* (London, 1961).
Clarke, David B. and Doel, Marcus, 'From flatland to vernacular relativity: the genesis of early English screenscapes', in Martin Lefebvre (ed.), *Landscape and Film* (London, 2006), pp. 213–45.

Bibliography

Clogston, John, *Disability Coverage in 16 Newspapers* (Louisville, KY, 1990).
Cochrane, Kira, 'The fourth wave of feminism: meet the rebel women', *Guardian*, 10 December 2013. Available at https://www.theguardian.com/world/2013/dec/10/fourth-wave-feminism-rebel-women (accessed 29 July 2016).
——, *All the Rebel Women: the Rise of the Fourth Wave of Feminism* (Guardian Book, Kindle Edition, 2013), Available at https://read.amazon.co.uk/?asin=B00H7G1DMY (accessed 30 July 2016).
Collie, Hazel, '"I've been having fantasies about Regan and Carter three times a week": Television, women and desire', in R. Moseley, H. Wheatley and H. Wood (eds), *Television for Women: New Directions* (London, 2017), pp. 223–40.
Conway, Jill, 'Gender in Australia', *Daedalus*, 114/1 (1985), pp. 343–68.
Cook, Pam, 'Masculinity in crisis? Tragedy and identification in *Raging Bull*', *Screen*, 13/3–4 (1982), pp. 39–46
Cornwall, Andrea, 'Introduction: Masculinities under Neoliberalism', in A. Cornwall, F. G. Karioris and N. Lindisfarne (eds), *Masculinities under Neoliberalism* (London, 2016), pp. 1–28.
Du Coudray, Chantal Bourgault, *The Curse of the Werewolf: Fantasy, Horror and the Beast Within* (London, 2006).
Crompton, Sarah, 'Dan Stevens: Why I left *Downton Abbey*', *Telegraph*, 7 March 2016. Available at http://www.telegraph.co.uk/culture/tvandradio/downton-abbey/9765334/Dan-Stevens-Why-I-left-Downton-Abbey.html (accessed 3 June 2016).
Cuklanz, Lisa M., *Rape on Prime Time: Television, Masculinity and Sexual Violence* (Philadelphia, 2000).
Darke, Paul, 'Understanding Cinematic Representations of Disability', in T. Shakespeare (ed.), *The Disability Reader: Social Science Perspectives* (London, 1998), pp. 181–97.
Davies, Helen, *Neo-Victorian Freakery: The Cultural Afterlife of the Victorian Freakshow* (Basingstoke, 2015).
Davison, Carol Margaret, 'The Victorian Gothic and Gender', in A. Smith and W. Hughes (eds), *The Victorian Gothic. An Edinburgh Companion* (Edinburgh, 2012), pp. 124–41.
Dawson, Graham, *Soldier Heroes: British Adventure, Empire and the Imagining of Masculinity* (London, 1994).
Deacon, Bernard, '"The hollow jarring of the distance steam engines": images of Cornwall between west barbary and delectable duchy', in E. Westland (ed.), *Cornwall: A Cultural Construction of Place* (Penzance, 1997), pp. 7–24.
De Groot, Jerome, '"Welcome to Babylon": Performing and Screening the English Revolution', in M. T. Burnett and A. Streete (eds), *Filming and Performing Renaissance History* (London, 2011), pp. 65–82.
——, *Consuming History: Historians and Heritage in Contemporary Popular Culture* (London, 2016).
Dixon, Wheeler Winston, *Straight: Constructions of Heterosexuality in the Cinema* (New York, 2003).
Dowell, Ben, 'Lark Rise to Candleford escapes BBC costume drama cull', *Guardian*, 6 March 2009. Available at https://www.theguardian.com/media/2009/mar/06/lark-rise-candleford-escapes-cull (accessed 15 September 2016).

'Drama: best of 2004', *BBC Drama*, 28 October 2004. Available at www.bbc.co.uk/drama/bestof2004/best_drama.shtml (accessed 1 July 2016).

Dyer, Richard, 'Don't look now: The instabilities of the male pin-up', *Screen*, 13/3–4 (1982), pp. 61–73.

——, 'The white man's muscles', in R. Adams and D. Savran (eds), *The Masculinity Studies Reader* (London, 2002), pp. 145–83.

Eade, Philip, *Young Prince Philip: His Turbulent Early Life* (St Ives, 2011).

Earnshaw, Jessica, '"It treads a very fine line": Versailles' Alexander Vlahos on THAT Henriette rape scene', *Daily Express*, 10 August 2016. Available at http://www.express.co.uk/showbiz/tv-radio/698718/Versailles-final-Alexander-Vlahos-rape-scene-Henriette (accessed 5 June 2017).

Easson, Angus, 'Introduction', *North and South* (Oxford, 2008).

Elgot, Jessica, 'Benedict Cumberbatch stuns theatregoers with anti-government speech', *Guardian*, 30 October 2015. Available at https://www.theguardian.com/uk-news/2015/oct/30/benedict-cumberbatch-stuns-theatregoers-anti-government-speech-refugees (accessed 15 August 2016).

Elliot, Annabelle Fenwick, 'It's 2015! People have sex!', *Daily Mail*, 1 September 2015. Available at http://www.dailymail.co.uk/femail/article-3217419/Lady-Chatterley-star-James-Norton-defends-raunchy-BBC-adaptation-relevant-claims-encourage-youngsters-read-classics.html (accessed 29 October 2016).

Ellsworth-Jones, Will, *We Will Not Fight: The Untold Story of World War One's Conscientious Objectors* (London, 2008).

Ensor, Josie, 'Much more than just jam', *Telegraph*, 13 January 2013. Available at http://www.telegraph.co.uk/women/9797917/Much-more-than-just-jam-waiting-list-for-new-look-Womens-Institute.html (accessed 16 September 2016).

Faludi, Susan, *Stiffed: The Betrayal of the American Man* (London, 2000).

——, *The Terror Dream: What 9/11 Revealed about America* (London, 2007).

Feasey, Rebecca, *Masculinity and Popular Television* (Edinburgh, 2008).

Fellowes, Julian, *Downton Abbey: Season One – The Complete Scripts* (London, 2012).

——, *Downton Abbey: Season Two – The Complete Scripts* (London, 2013).

Ferguson, Euan, 'The week in TV: *The Frankenstein Chronicles; London Spy; Peep Show; Unforgotten*', *Guardian*, 15 November 2015. Available at https://www.theguardian.com/tv-and-radio/2015/nov/15/week-in-tv-frankenstein-chronicles-london-spy-peep-show-unforgotten (accessed 2 November 2016).

Finding, Deborah, 'Figuring Gender and Sexuality in Little Britain', *Media@LSE*, EP13 (2008). Available at http://www.lse.ac.uk/media@lse/research/media-WorkingPapers/pdf/EWP13.pdf (accessed 10 September 2016), pp. 1–29.

Foyster, Elizabeth, *Manhood in Early Modern England: Honour, Sex, and Marriage* (London, 2014).

Frost, Caroline, 'Partners in Crime review', *Huffington Post*, 27 July 2015. Available at http://www.huffingtonpost.co.uk/2015/07/26/partners-in-crime-tv-review-david-walliams_n_7875534.html (accessed 3 July 2016).

Furness, Hannah, '"I'm definitely middle class", says actor Benedict Cumberbatch', *Telegraph*, 28 April 2013. Available at http://www.telegraph.co.uk/culture/tvandradio/10023710/Im-definitely-middle-class-says-actor-Benedict-Cumberbatch.html (accessed 15 August 2016).

Bibliography

———, 'Prince Philip as you've never seen him before: Matt Smith stars as the "touchy-feely" Duke in *The Crown*', *Telegraph*, 29 October 2016. Available at http://www.telegraph.co.uk/news/2016/10/29/prince-philip-as-youve-never-seen-him-before-matt-smith-stars-as/ (accessed 1 February 2017).
Fussell, Paul, *The Great War and Modern Memory* (Oxford, 1975).
Gabaldon, Diana, *Cross Stitch* (London, 1994).
———, *Dragonfly in Amber* (London, 1994).
Gamman, Lorraine and Marshment, Margaret, *The Female Gaze: Women as Viewers of Popular Culture* (London, 1989).
Gaskell, Elizabeth, *North and South* (Oxford, 2008).
Gates, Phillipa, 'Detectives', in M. S. Kimmel and A. Aronson (eds), *Men and Masculinities: A Social, Cultural and Historical Encyclopaedia: A-J* (Santa Barbara, CA, Denver, CO, Oxford, 2003), p. 215.
Genette, Gérard, *Narrative Discourse: An Essay in Method* (Ithaca, NY, 1983).
Genz, Stéphanie and Brabon, Benjamin A., *Postfeminism: Cultural Texts and Theories* (Edinburgh, 2009).
Gerber, David A. (ed.), *Disabled Veterans in History* (Michigan, 2000).
Giddings, Robert and Selby, Keith, *The Classic Serial on Television and Radio* (Basingstoke, 2001).
Gilbey, Ryan, 'George Blagden on dressing up for Versailles', *Guardian*, 30 May 2016. Available at https://www.theguardian.com/tv-and-radio/2016/may/30/versailles-george-blagden-playing-louis-xiv-bbc2-interview (accessed 27 July 2016).
Gill, Rosalind et al., 'Body projects and the regulation of normative masculinity', *Body and Society*, 11/1 (2005), pp. 37–63.
Girard, René, *Violence and the Sacred* (Baltimore, 1977).
Glick, Elisa, *Materializing Queer Desire: Oscar Wilde to Andy Warhol* (Albany, NY, 2009).
Glyn, Basil, '*The Tudors* and the post-national, post-historical Henry VIII', in M. Merck (ed.), *The British Monarchy on Screen* (Manchester, 2016), pp. 309–38.
Goodfellow, Maya, 'Britain's raging racism calls for more than symbolic safety pins', *Guardian*, 1 July 2016. Available at https://www.theguardian.com/commentisfree/2016/jul/01/britain-racism-safety-pins-brexit-migrants-xenophobic (accessed 16 September 2016).
Goodman, Gemma and Moseley, Rachel, 'Why academics are interested in the male body in *Poldark* and *Outlander*', *The Conversation*, 2 June 2015. Available at https://theconversation.com/why-academics-are-interested-in-the-male-body-in-poldark-and-outlander-42518 (accessed 18 September 2016).
Green, Martin, *Dreams of Adventure, Deeds of Empire* (New York, 1979).
Gregor, Ian, *William Golding: A Critical Study of the Novels* (London, 2012).
Gullace, Nicoletta F., 'White Feathers and Wounded Men: Female Patriotism and the Memory of the Great War', *The Journal of British Studies*, 36/2 (1997), pp. 178–206.
Haefele-Thomas, Ardel, *Queer Others in Victorian Gothic. Transgressing Monstrosity* (Cardiff, 2012).
Hagelin, Sarah, *Reel Vulnerability: Power, Pain and Gender in Contemporary American Film and Television* (New Brunswick, NJ, London, 2013).

Halberstam, Judith, *Skin Shows: Gothic Horror and the Technology of Monsters* (Durham, 1995).
Hall, Edward, 'Agatha Christie's *Partners in Crime*', Press Release. Available at http://downloads.bbc.co.uk/mediacentre/partners_in_crime.pdf (accessed 7 July 2016).
Hamad, Hannah, 'Hollywood Fatherhood: Paternal Postfeminism in Contemporary Popular Cinema', in J. Gwynne, N. Muller and H. Radner (Eds), *Postfeminism and Contemporary Hollywood Cinema* (New York, 2013), pp. 99–115.
Hanna, Emma, *The Great War on the Small Screen: Representing the First World War in Contemporary Britain* (Edinburgh, 2009).
Harper, Sue, *Women in British Cinema: Mad, Bad and Dangerous to Know* (London, 2000).
Harris, Margaret, 'Taking bearings: Elizabeth Gaskell's *North and South* televised', *Sydney Studies in English*, 32 (2006), pp. 64–82.
Harris, Scott Jordan, 'The BBC's plans to show more disabled people on TV are good – but they should be better', *New Statesman*, 13 August 2014. Available at http://www.newstatesman.com/media/2014/08/bbc-s-plans-show-more-disabled-people-tv-are-good-they-should-be-better (accessed 29 October 2016).
Harris, Sian, 'Sharper, better, faster, stronger: Performing Northern Masculinity and the legacy of Sean Bean's Sharpe', *Journal of Popular Television*, 4/2 (2016), pp. 239–51.
Hatherley, Owen, *The Ministry of Nostalgia* (London, 2016).
Hawes, James, 'Praise Philip, the Prince of Misrule', *Guardian*, 7 May 2017. Available at https://www.theguardian.com/commentisfree/2017/may/06/philip-prince-of-misrule-said-what-we-darent (accessed 21 June 2017).
Heald, Tim, *The Duke: A Portrait of Prince Philip* (Kent, 1991).
Healy, Chris, *Forgetting Aborigines* (Sydney, 2008).
Heathorn, Stephen, 'How stiff were their upper lips? Research on late-Victorian and Edwardian masculinity', *History Compass*, 2/1 (2004), pp. 1–7.
Hechter, Michael, *Internal colonialism: The Celtic fringe in British national development, 1536–1966* (California, 1977).
Heffernan, Virginia, 'Ah, Life at Sea: Sweaty, Sodden and Light on Nobility', *New York Times*, 20 October 2006. Available at http://www.nytimes.com/2006/10/20/arts/television/20mast.html?_r=0 (accessed 15 August 2016).
Heilmann, Ann and Llewellyn, Mark, *Neo-Victorianism: The Victorians in the twenty-first Century, 1999–2009* (Basingstoke, 2010).
Hendershot, Cyndy, *The Animal Within: Masculinity and the Gothic* (Ann Arbor, MI, 1998).
Higson, Andrew, 'Re-presenting the national past: nostalgia and pastiche in the heritage film', in Lester Friedman (Ed.), *Fires Were Started: British Cinema and Thatcherism* (London, 1993), pp. 109–29.
Hitchings, Henry, 'Award for comedy: David Walliams', *Evening Standard*, 19 November 2013. Available at, http://www.standard.co.uk/goingout/theatre/london-evening-standard-theatre-awards-2013-how-we-chose-the-winners-8948507.html (accessed 3 August 2016).

Bibliography

Hogan, Michael, '*Partners in Crime*: episode 2: "jolly good show"', *Telegraph*, 2 July 2015. Available at http://www.telegraph.co.uk/culture/tvandradio/tv-and-radio-reviews/11776285/Partners-in-Crime-episode-2-review.html.

———, '*The Frankenstein Chronicles*, Review', *Telegraph*, 11 November 2015. Available at http://www.telegraph.co.uk/culture/tvandradio/tv-and-radio-reviews/11989543/The-Frankenstein-Chronicles-review-eerily-effective.html (accessed 21 July 2017).

Hughes, Robert, *The Fatal Shore* (London, 2003).

Hunt, Leon, '"What are big boys made of?": Spartacus, El Cid and the male epic', in P. Kirkham and J. Thumim (eds), *You Tarzan: Masculinity, Movies and Men* (London, 1993), pp. 65–83.

Hurley, Kelly, 'Science and the Gothic', in A. Smith and W. Hughes (eds), *The Victorian Gothic. An Edinburgh Companion* (Edinburgh, 2012), pp. 170–84.

Hutton, Ronald, 'Why Don't the Stuarts Get Filmed?', in S. Doran and T. S. Freeman (eds), *Tudors and Stuarts on Film: Historical Perspectives* (London: 2009), pp. 246–58.

Hynes, Samuel, *A War Imagined: The First World War and English Culture* (New York, 1991).

Jeffery, Morgan, 'Tom Hardy interview – on making *Taboo* the electrifying antidote to *Downton*: "People might not like this"', *Digital Spy*, 31 December 2016. Available at http://www.digitalspy.com/tv/interviews/a817930/tom-hardy-interview-taboo-bbc-one-fx-tv-series-2016-plot/ (accessed 16 February 2017).

———, 'Matt Smith reveals he asked Prince William for advice on how to play Prince Philip in The Crown', *Digital Spy*, 31 October 2016. Available at http://www.digitalspy.com/tv/news/a812644/matt-smith-admits-he-asked-prince-william-for-advice-on-how-to-play-prince-philip-in-the-crown/ (accessed 1 February 2017).

Jenkins, Claire, '"I'm saving the world, I need a decent shirt": Masculinity and Costume in the new Doctor Who', in S. Bruzzi and P. C. Gibson (eds), *Fashion Cultures Revisited* (London, 2013), pp. 377–89.

Johnson, Niall, 'Agatha Christie drama Partners in Crime tops Sunday viewing', Mediatel Newsline, 27 July 2015. Available at http://mediatel.co.uk/newsline/2015/07/27/agatha-christie-drama-partners-in-crime-tops-sunday-viewing (accessed 7 July 2016).

Johnston, Trevor, 'Drama Queen', *Sight and Sound* (December 2016), pp. 46–8.

Jones, Ellen, 'Partners in Crime, BBC 1: TV review', *Independent*, 26 July 2015. Available at www.independent.co.uk/arts-entertainment/tv/reviews/partners-in-crime-bbc1-tv-review-excellent-leads-just-lack-that-spark-of-sexual-chemistry-10416626.html (accessed 7 July 2016).

Jones, Paul, 'Jimmy McGovern's *Banished* the victim of "limited" BBC2 drama budget as BBC confirms cancellation', *Radio Times*, 7 May 2015. Available at http://www.radiotimes.com/news/2015-05-07/jimmy-mcgoverns-banished-the-victim-of-limited-bbc2-drama-budget-as-bbc-confirms-cancellation (accessed 1 September 2016).

Kalestky, Anatole, 'Trump's rise and Brexit vote are more an outcome of culture than economics', *Guardian*, 28 October 2016. Available at https://www.

theguardian.com/business/2016/oct/28/trumps-rise-and-brexit-vote-are-more-an-outcome-of-culture-than-economics (accessed 21 July 2017).

Karskens, Grace, *The Colony: A History of Early Sydney* (Crows Nest, NSW, 2009).

Kelly, David, 'A view of *North & South*', *Sydney Studies in English*, 32 (2006), pp. 82–95.

Keneally, Tom, *The Commonwealth of Thieves* (London, 2007).

Kennedy, Ellie, 'But I'm a lady: undoing gender bending in contemporary British radio', in Gaby Pailer, Andres Bohn, Stefan Horbacher and Ulrich Sheck (eds), *Gender and Laughter: Comic Affirmation and Subversion in Traditional and Modern Media* (Amsterdam and New York, 2009), pp. 251–67.

Kerley, Paul and Bates, Claire, 'The Archers: What effect has the Rob and Helen story had?', *BBC News Magazine*, 5 April 2016. Available at http://www.bbc.co.uk/news/magazine-35961057 (accessed 22 June 2017).

Kersten, Joachim, 'Culture, masculinities and violence against women', *The British Journal of Criminology*, 36/3 (1996), pp. 381–95.

Kestner, Joseph, *Masculinities in British Adventure Fictions, 1800–1915* (Farnham and Burlington, 2010).

Killeen, Jarlath, *Gothic Literature 1825–1914* (Cardiff, 2009).

Kohle, Marie-Luise and Gutleben, Christian, 'Introducing neo-Victorian family matters: Cultural capital and reproduction', in M.-L. Kohle and C. Gutleben (eds), *Neo-Victorian Families: Gender, Sexual and Cultural Politics* (Rodopi, 2011), pp. 1–42.

Kramer, Ann, *Conscientious Objectors of the First World War: A Determined Resistance* (Barnsley, 2014).

Lamont, Tom, 'Russell Tovey: "I was a scared, skinny little rat. Then I hit the gym ..."', *Observer*, 1 March 2015. Available at https://www.theguardian.com/tv-and-radio/2015/mar/01/russell-tovey-looking-banished-interview (accessed 17 November 2016).

Landy, Marcia, *British Genres: Cinema and Society, 1930–60* (Princeton, NJ, 1991).

Langhamer, Claire, 'The meanings of home in post war Britain', *Journal of Contemporary History*, 4/2 (2005), pp. 341–62.

Latour, Bruno, *We Have Never Been Modern*, trans. C. Porter (Cambridge, MA, 1993).

Lawrence, Ben and Gee, Catherine, '*Doctor Who*'s best historical figures', *Telegraph*, 7 September 2012. Available at http://www.telegraph.co.uk/culture/tvandradio/doctor-who/9528099/Doctor-Whos-best-historical-figures.html (accessed 21 July 2017).

Lawrence, Jacquie, 'Hollywood still trails TV when it comes to strong roles for women', *Guardian*, 22 April 2015. Available at https://www.theguardian.com/media/2015/apr/22/hollywood-tv-roles-for-women-the-fall-house-of-cards (accessed 30 July 2016).

Lawson, Mark, 'Frankenstein TV: what happens when literary classics drop out of copyright', *Guardian*, 16 November 2015. Available at https://www.theguardian.com/tv-and-radio/tvandradioblog/2015/nov/16/frankenstein-tv-what-happens-when-literary-classics-drop-out-of-copyright (accessed 21 July 2017).

Lehman, Peter, *Running Scared* (Philadelphia, 1993).

Bibliography

Levine, Philippa, 'States of undress: Nakedness and the colonial imagination', *Victorian Studies*, 50/2 (2008), pp. 189–219.

Light, Alison, *Forever England: Femininity, Literature and Conservatism Between the Wars* (Abingdon, 1991).

Linton, Phoebe C., 'Modern Rape Culture and BBC's *Banished*', *The Public Medievalist*, 25 June 2015, Available at http://www.publicmedievalist.com/modern-rape-culture-and-bbcs-banished/ (accessed 5 August 2016).

London, Bette, 'Mary Shelley, Frankenstein, and the Spectacle of Masculinity', PMLA, 108/2 (1993), pp. 253–67.

Longmore, Paul K., *Why I Burned My Book and Other Essays on Disability* (Philadelphia, 2003).

Lorna Doone Reviews and Ratings, Internet Movie Database, n.d. Available at http://www.imdb.com/title/tt0259786/reviews?ref_=tt_urv (accessed 17 June 2016).

Lotz, Amanda D., *Cable Guys: Television and Masculinities in the 21st Century* (New York, 2014).

Loughran, Tracey, 'Masculinity, Shell Shock, and Emotional Survival in the First World War', *Reviews in History*, August 2010. Available at http://www.history.ac.uk/reviews/review/944#f2 (accessed 7 July 2016).

——, 'Masculinity, trauma and "shell shock"', *The Psychologist*, 28 (March 2015), pp. 250–1. Available at https://thepsychologist.bps.org.uk/volume-28/march-2015/masculinity-trauma-and-shell-shock (accessed 31 May 2016).

Louttit, Chris, 'Victorian London Redux: Adapting the Gothic Metropolis', *Critical Survey*, 28/1 (2016), pp. 2–14.

MacIntyre, Stuart and Clark, Anna, *The History Wars* (Melbourne, 2003).

Macmillan, David S., 'Ross, Robert (1740–1794)', *Australian Dictionary of Biography*, National Centre of Biography, Australian National University. Available at http://adb.anu.edu.au/biography/ross-robert-2608/text3591, published first in hardcopy 1967 (accessed 23 August 2016).

Manderson Lenore and Peake, Susan, 'Men in Motion: Disability and the Performance of Masculinity', in C. Sandahl and P. Auslander (eds), *Bodies in Motion: Disability and Performance* (Michigan, 2005), pp. 230–42.

Manea, Dragos, 'A Wolf's Eye View of London: *Dracula*, *Penny Dreadful*, and the Logic of Repetition', *Critical Survey*, xxviii/1 (2016), pp. 40–50.

Mangan, J. A., *'Manufactured Masculinity': Making Imperial Manliness, Morality and Militarism* (Abingdon, 2012).

Mangan, Lucy, '*The Crown* review', *Guardian*, 4 November 2016. Available at https://www.theguardian.com/tv-and-radio/2016/nov/04/the-crown-review-netflix-100m-gamble-on-the-queen-pays-off-royally (accessed 1 February 2017).

Marriott, Emma, *The World of Poldark: The Official Companion to the BBC Television Series* (London, 2015).

Martin, Maureen M., *The Mighty Scot: Nation, Gender, and the Nineteenth-Century Mystique of Scottish Masculinity* (Albany, NY, 2009).

Martin, Tim, 'The boy in a dress: review', *Telegraph*, 26 December 2014. Available at http://www.telegraph.co.uk/culture/tvandradio/tv-and-radio-reviews/11310500/The-Boy-in-the-Dress-review-witty-and-heart-warming.html (accessed 3 July 2016).

Mavis, Paul, 'Agatha Christie's Partners in Crime: The Tommy and Tuppence Mysteries', *DVD Talk*, 29 January 2013. Available at http://www.dvdtalk.com/reviews/58818/agatha-christies-partners-in-crime-the-tommy/ (accessed 15 July 2016).

McArthur, Colin, *Brigadoon, Braveheart and the Scots: Distortions of Scotland in Hollywood Cinema* (London, 2003).

McClintock, Anne, *Imperial Leather: Race, Gender and Sexuality in the Colonial Contest* (London, 1995).

McGarry, Lisa, 'Has the reaction to David Walliams and Lara Stone's split been homophobic?', *UnrealityTV*, 27 July 2015. Available at www.unrealitytv.co.uk/britains-got-talent/has-the-reaction-to-david-walliams-lara-stones-split-been-homophobic (accessed 15 July 2016).

McGovern, Jimmy, '*Banished*: A new drama for BBC set during the founding of the penal colony in Australia in 1788', *BBC Writers Room*, 4 March 2015. Available at http://www.bbc.co.uk/blogs/writersroom/entries/219f38a4-5c17-43ae-aee4-8fcdcf55d7a2 (accessed 19 August 2016).

McKenna, Mark, 'First Words: A Brief History of Public Debate on a New Preamble to the Australian Constitution 1991–99', *Parliament of Australia* (n.d.). Available at http://www.aph.gov.au/About_Parliament/Parliamentary_Departments/Parliamentary_Library/pubs/rp/rp9900/2000RP16#Pre (accessed 31 August 2016).

McRobbie, Angela, 'Post-feminism and popular culture', *Feminist Media Studies*, 4/3 (2004), pp. 255–64.

———, *The Aftermath of Feminism: Gender, Culture and Social Change* (Los Angeles, London, New Delhi, Singapore, Washington, DC, 2009).

McWilliam, David, 'London's dispossessed: Questioning the neo-Victorian politics of Neoliberal austerity in Richard Wardlow's *Ripper Street*', *Victoriographies*, 6/1 (2016), pp. 42–61.

Meldrum, Claire, 'Yesterday's women: The female presence in neo-Victorian television detective programs', *Journal of Popular Film and Television*, 42/4 (2015), pp. 201–11.

Merck, Mandy (ed.), *The British Monarchy on Screen* (Manchester, 2016).

———, 'Melodrama, celebrity, *The Queen*', in M. Merck (ed.), *The British Monarchy on Screen* (Manchester, 2016), pp. 363–83.

Mesure, Susie, 'Andrew Davies: the man who made Colin Firth a sex god', *Independent*, 19 February 2011. Available at http://www.independent.co.uk/news/people/profiles/andrew-davies-the-man-who-made-colin-firth-a-sex-god-2219985.html (accessed 1 November 2016).

Meyer, Jessica, *Men of War: Masculinity and the First World War in Britain* (Basingstoke, 2009).

Michasiw, Kim, 'Camp, masculinity, masquerade', *differences: A Journal of Feminist Studies*, 6/3 (1994), pp. 146–74.

Michaud, Marilyn, 'The double as failed masculinity in David Ely's *Seconds*', *eSharp: Identity and Marginality*, 6/1. Available at http://www.academia.edu/893747/The_Double_As_Failed_Masculinity_In_David_Elys_Seconds (accessed 2 July 2016).

Minier, Márta, 'Joining history to celebiography and heritage to documentary on the small screen: spotlight on the content of the form in the metamediatic royal

Bibliography

bio-docudrama', in M. Minier and M. Pennacchia (eds), *Adaptation, Intermediality and the British Celebrity Biopic* (Oxon and New York, 2016), pp. 79–100.

Monk, Claire, 'Men in the 90s', in R. Murphy (ed.), *British Cinema in the 90s* (London, 2000), pp. 156–66.

——, 'The British heritage-film debate revisited', in C. Monk and A. Sargeant (eds), *British Historical Cinema* (London, 2015), pp. 176–98.

Morris, Jenny, *Pride Against Prejudice: Transforming Attitudes to Disability – A Personal Politics of Disability* (London, 1991).

Moseley, Rachel, *Growing up with Audrey Hepburn: Text, Audience, Resonance* (Manchester, 2002).

——, '"It's a wild country. Wild ... passionate ... strange": *Poldark* and the place-image of Cornwall', *Visual Culture in Britain*, 14/2 (2013), pp. 218–37.

Moulton, Mo, 'Watching *Downton Abbey* with an Historian: Cowardice, Shellshock, and a Right Memory', *The Toast*, 20 January 2015. Available at http://the-toast.net/2015/01/20/watching-downton-abbey-historian-right-memory/ (accessed 30 May.

Mulvey, Laura, 'Visual pleasure and narrative cinema', *Screen*, 16/3 (1975), pp. 6–18.

Nail, Brian, 'Austerity and the Language of Sacrifice', *The Critical Religion Association*, 15 October 2013. Available at https://criticalreligion.org/2013/10/15/austerity-and-the-language-of-sacrifice/ (accessed 21 August 2016).

Nancy, Jean-Luc, *L'Imperatif Categorique* (Paris, 1983).

Neale, Steve, 'Masculinity as spectacle', *Screen*, 24/6 (1983), pp. 2–17.

Negra, Diane and Tasker, Yvonne, 'Neoliberal frames and genres of inequality: Recession-era chick flicks and male-centred corporate melodrama', *The Sociological Review*, 16/3 (2013), pp. 344–61.

——, (eds), *Gendering the Recession: Media and Culture in an Age of Austerity* (Durham, NC, 2014).

New Matilda, 'Boycott Banished, an All-White Drama about a Black Part of Our History', *New Matilda*, 10 March 2015. Available at https://newmatilda.com/2015/03/10/boycott-banished-all-white-drama-about-black-part-our-history/ (accessed 8 August 2016).

Nikolaidis, Aristotelis, '(En)Gendering Disability in Film', *Feminist Media Studies*, 13/4 (2013), pp. 759–64.

Nye, Robert, 'Western masculinities in war and peace', *American Historical Review*, 112/2 (2007), pp. 417–38.

Nystrom, Lisa, 'Blood, Lust and the Fe/Male Narrative in *Bram Stoker's Dracula* (1992) and the Novel (1897)', in J. E. Browning and C. J. Picart (eds), *Draculas, Vampires, and Other Undead Forms: Essays on Gender, Race, and Culture* (Lanham, 2009), pp. 63–76.

O'Callaghan, Claire, 'Rape at Downton Abbey', *Feminist and Women's Studies Association Blog*, 17 November 2013. Available at http://fwsablog.org.uk/2013/11/17/rape-at-downton-abbey/ (accessed 13 June 2016).

——, 'The Downturn at *Downton*: Money and Masculinity in *Downton Abbey*', in H. Davies and C. O'Callaghan (eds), *Gender and Austerity in Popular*

Culture: Femininity, Masculinity and Recession in Film and Television (London, 2016).

O'Dowd, Chris, 'My looks: the unlikely sex symbols', *Guardian*, 27 July 2012. Available at https://www.theguardian.com/culture/2012/jul/27/unlikely-male-sex-symbols (accessed 1 February 2017).

O'Hagan, Andrew, 'All hail, sage lady', *London Review of Books*, 38/24 (15 December 2016), pp. 15–16. Available at https://www.lrb.co.uk/v38/n24/andrew-ohagan/all-hail-sage-lady\ (accessed 1 February 2017).

O'Neill, Carly et al., 'Advertising real beer: Authenticity claims beyond truth and falsity', *European Journal of Cultural Studies*, 17/5 (2014), pp. 171–88.

Paterson, Peter, 'Sail of the century', *Daily Mail*, 21 July 2005, p. 59.

Payton, Philip, *Cornwall: A History* (Fowey, Cornwall Editions).

Peberdy, Donna, *Masculinity and Film Performance: Male Angst in Contemporary American Cinema* (New York, 2011).

Penny, Laurie, 'Shame of thrones: *The Crown* needs dragons, and a decent plot', *New Statesman*, 8 November 2016. Available at http://www.newstatesman.com/culture/tv-radio/2016/11/shame-thrones-crown-needs-dragons-and-decent-plot (accessed 1 February 2017).

Pheasant-Kelly, Fran, *Abject Spaces in American Cinema: Institutional Settings, Identity and Psychoanalysis in Film* (London and New York, 2013).

Phillips, Nickie D., *Beyond Blurred Lines: Rape Culture in Popular Media* (Lanham, MD, 2016).

Plain, Gill, *John Mills and British Cinema* (Edinburgh, 2006).

'"*Poldark* made me feel inadequate!" Period drama hunk James Norton opens up!', *Woman Magazine*, n.d. Available at http://www.womanmagazine.co.uk/publication/woman-magazine/poldark-made-me-feel-inadequate-period-drama-hunk-james-norton-opens-up (accessed 29 November 2016).

'*Poldark* "rape" scene sparks controversy', *BBC News*, 24 October 2016. Available at http://www.bbc.com/news/entertainment-arts-37749637 (accessed 8 February 2017).

'*Poldark*'s topless tin bath scene voted 2016's biggest TV moment', *Radio Times*, 30 December 2016. Available at http://www.radiotimes.com/news/2016-12-30/poldarks-topless-tin-bath-scene-voted-2016s-biggest-tv-moment (accessed 5 February 2017).

Poore, Benjamin, 'The Transformed Beast: *Penny Dreadful*, Adaptation, and the Gothic', *Victoriographies*, 6/1 (2016), pp. 63–6.

Prochaska, Frank, *Royal Bounty: The Making of a Welfare Monarchy* (New Haven, CT and London, 1995).

Procter, James and Smith, Angela, 'Gothic and empire', in C. Spooner and E. McEvoy (eds), *The Routledge Companion to Gothic* (London, 2007), pp. 95–104.

Pyyhtinen, Olli, *The Gift and its Paradoxes: Beyond Mauss* (Abingdon, 2016).

Redmond, Phil, 'Public service content: the conditions for creativity', in D. Tambini and J. Cowling (eds), *From Public Broadcasting to Public Service Communications* (London, 2004), pp. 74–7.

Reed, John. R, *The Army and Navy in Nineteenth-Century British Literature* (New York, 2011).

Bibliography

Rees, Jasper, 'Versailles: sex, intrigue, and great hair – review', *Telegraph*, 2 June 2016. Available at http://www.telegraph.co.uk/tv/2016/06/01/versailles-sex-intrigue-and-great-hair-review/ (accessed 4 June 2016).
Rehling, Nicola, 'When words fail: *The King's Speech* as melodrama', in M. Merck (ed.), *The British Monarchy on Screen* (Manchester, 2016), pp. 384–405.
Reiff, Rachel Haugrud, *William Golding: Lord of the Flies* (New York, 2010).
Richards, Jeffrey, 'The Monarchy and Film 1900–2006', in A. Olechnowicz (ed.), *The Monarchy and the British Nation, 1780 to the Present* (Cambridge: 2007), pp. 280–314.
Richardson, Ruth, *Death, Dissection and the Destitute: The Politics of the Corpse in Pre-Victorian Britain* (Chicago, 1987).
Richmond, Aaron, 'Disabled at Downton', in William Irwin (ed.) *Downton Abbey and Philosophy: Thinking in That Manor* (Chicago, IL, 2016), pp. 71–8.
Rickard, John, *Australia: A Cultural History* (London, 1988; 2nd edn 1996).
Rieger, James. *Frankenstein, Or the Modern Prometheus: The 1818 Text* (Chicago, 1982).
Rocha, Lauren, 'Angel in the House, Devil in the City: Explorations of Gender in Dracula and Penny Dreadful', *Critical Survey*, 28/1 (Oxford, 2016), pp. 30–9.
Roper, Michael, *The Secret Battle: Emotional Survival in the Great War* (Manchester, 2009).
Rose, Jacqueline, 'The twin curse of masculinity and male-dominated politics helped create Brexit', *Guardian*, 2 July 2016. Available at https://www.theguardian.com/commentisfree/2016/jul/02/twin-curse-masculinity-male-dominated-politics-brexit (accessed 7 February 2017).
——, 'Donald Trump's victory is a disaster for modern masculinity', *Guardian*, 15 November 2016. Available at https://www.theguardian.com/commentisfree/2016/nov/15/trump-disaster-modern-masculinity-sexual-nostalgian-oppressive-men-women (accessed 17 November 2016).
Rose, Sonya O., 'Temperate heroes: concepts of masculinity in Second World War Britain', in S. Dudink, K. Hagemann and J. Tosh (eds), *Masculinities in Politics and War: Gendering Modern History* (Manchester and New York, 2004), pp. 177–98.
Saraiya, Sonia, 'The year in TV: how shows of 2014 remade "masculinity" on television', *Salon*, 16 December 2014. Available at http://www.salon.com/2014/12/16/the_year_in_tv_how_the_shows_of_2014_remade_masculinity_on_television/ (accessed 3 July 2016).
Schlesinger, Arthur, *The Vital Centre: Politics of Freedom* (Boston, 1949).
Scourfield, Jonathan and Drakeford, Mark, 'New Labour and the "problem of men"', *Critical Social Policy*, 12/4 (2002), pp. 619–39.
Seltzer, Sarah, '10 years later, "North and South" remains the greatest period-drama miniseries of all time' (2014), *North and South 2004*. Available at northandsouth2004.com (accessed 24 June 2016).
Sewell, William, 'A Theory of Structure: Duality, Agency and Transformation', *American Journal of Transformation*, 98/1 (1992), pp. 1–29.
'Sexual Health for Men', *Christopher and Dana Reeve Foundation*, n.d. Available at https://www.christopherreeve.org/living-with-paralysis/health/sexual-health/sexual-health-for-men (accessed 15 August 2016).

Shakespeare, Tom, 'The Sexual Politics of Disabled Masculinity', *Sexuality and Disability*, 17/1 (1999), pp. 53–64.
Shepherd, Jack, 'Versailles: Conservative MP outraged by BBC drama with "most graphic sex scenes in British TV history"', *Independent*, 13 March 2016. Available at http://www.independent.co.uk/arts-entertainment/tv/news/versailles-conservative-mp-outraged-by-bbc-drama-with-most-graphic-sex-scenes-in-british-tv-history-a6928651.html (accessed 9 July 2016).
Sherrow, Rita, 'Lie back and think of England', *Tulsa World*, 2 July 2005. Available at http://www.tulsaworld.com/archives/lie-back-and-think-of-england/article_b1476763-205b-5285-9378-9a24255d7428.html (accessed 21 July 2017).
Showalter, Elaine, *The Female Malady: Women, Madness and English Culture, 1830–1980* (New York, 1985).
——, 'Rivers and Sassoon: the inscription of male gender anxieties', *Behind the Lines: Gender and the Two World Wars*, in M. Higgonet et al. (eds) (New Haven, CT, 1987), pp. 61–9.
Shuttleworth, Russell et al., 'The Dilemma of Disabled Masculinity', *Men and Masculinities*, 15/2 (2012), pp. 174–94.
Simon, Jane, 'We love telly', *The Mirror*, 6 July 2005, p. 39.
Sinfield, Alan, *The Wilde Century: Effeminacy, Oscar Wilde and the Queer Movement* (London, 1994).
Singh, Anita, 'Benedict Cumberbatch: "*Downton Abbey* is sentimental, clichéd and atrocious"', *Telegraph*, 16 August 2012. Available at http://www.telegraph.co.uk/culture/tvandradio/downton-abbey/9480067/Benedict-Cumberbatch-Downton-Abbey-is-sentimental-cliched-and-atrocious.html (accessed 15 August 2016).
Slotkin, Richard, *The Fatal Environment: The Myth of the Frontier in the Age of Industrialisation, 1800–1890* (New York, 1985).
Smith, Andrew and Hughes, William, 'Introduction: Queering the Gothic', in A. Smith and W. Hughes (eds), *Queering the Gothic* (Manchester, 2009), pp. 1–10.
Smith, Harry Leslie, 'The Crown's portrayal of history is an insult to my generation's struggles', *Guardian*, 8 November 2016. Available at https://www.theguardian.com/commentisfree/2016/nov/08/the-crown-portrayal-of-history-insult-to-my-generations-struggles (accessed 1 February 2017).
Sontag, Susan, 'Notes on "camp": camp, queer aesthetics and the performing subjects', in *Against Interpretation and Other Essays* (New York, 1961).
Spicer, Andrew, *Typical Men: The Representation of Masculinity in Popular British Cinema* (London, 2001).
Spooner, Catherine, *Fashioning Gothic Bodies* (Manchester, 2004).
Stacey, Jackie, *Star Gazing: Hollywood Cinema and Female Spectatorship* (London, 1994).
Staniforth, John Martin, 'Re-Imagining the Convicts: History, Myth and Nation in Contemporary Australian Fictions of Early Convictism', unpublished PhD thesis, University of Leeds, 2015.
Stetz, Margaret D., 'The late-Victorian "New Man" and the neo-Victorian "Neo-Man"', *Victoriographies*, 5/2 (2015), pp. 105–21.
Stevens, Christopher, 'Sorry Walliams but you can't wince as well as Arfur Daley', *Daily Mail*, 16 August 2015. Available at http://www.dailymail.co.uk/tvshowbiz/

Bibliography

article-3200229/Sorry-Walliams-t-wince-Arfur-Daley-CHRISTOPHER-STEVENS-reviews-weekend-s-TV.html (accessed 3 July 2016).

———, 'BBC's republican fantasy is more risible than revolutionary – and grindingly dull', *Daily Mail*, 10 May 2017. Available at http://www.dailymail.co.uk/tvshowbiz/article-4493614/BBC-s-republican-fantasy-risible-revolutionary.html (accessed 21 June 2017).

Stevenson, Catherine Barnes, 'Romance and the self-made man: Gaskell rewrites Brontë', *Victorian Newsletter*, 91 (1997), pp. 10–16.

Sturgess, Gary, 'Convicts and sex slaves: sorting the fact from the fiction in British TV series "Banished"', *Sydney Morning Herald*, 10 March 2015. Available at http://www.smh.com.au/comment/convicts-and-sex-slaves-sorting-the-fact-from-the-fiction-in-british-tv-series-banished-20150309-13yvc9.html (accessed 1 August 2016).

Summers, Julie, *Jambusters: The Story of the Women's Institute in the Second World War* (London, New York, Sydney, Toronto, New Delhi, 2013).

Tasker, Yvonne, *Spectacular Bodies: Gender, Genre and the Action Cinema* (London, 2012).

Taylor, J. D., '"Hysteric or Neuresthenic": The Role of Class in the Treatment of Shell Shock in World War I', *The Drowned and the Saved*, 29 April 2013. Available at https://drownedandsaved.org/2013/04/29/hysteric-or-neurasthenic-the-role-of-class-in-the-treatment-of-shell-shock-during-world-war-one/ (accessed 1 June 2016).

Thomas, Liz, '"I'm tempted to quit 'posh bashing' UK" says star of Sherlock Benedict Cumberbatch', *Daily Mail*, 14 August 2012. Available at http://www.dailymail.co.uk/tvshowbiz/article-2188010/Im-tempted-quit-posh-bashing-UK-says-star-Sherlock-Benedict-Cumberbatch.html (accessed 15 August 2016).

Thompson, Lauren, 'Mancaves and cushions: marking masculine and feminine domestic space in postfeminist romantic comedy', in J. Gwynne and N. Muller (eds), *Postfeminism and Contemporary Hollywood Cinema* (Basingstoke, 2013), pp. 149–65.

Thorpe, Vanessa, 'Raunchy French TV epic Versailles enlists British Actors to usurp Wolf Hall's Crown', *Guardian*, 30 April 2016. Available at https://www.theguardian.com/tv-and-radio/2016/may/01/french-tv-versailles-enlists-british-stars-bbc2 (accessed 27 July 2016).

Tosh, John, 'What should historians do with masculinity? Reflections on nineteenth-century Britain', *History Workshop*, 38 (1994), pp. 179–202.

———, 'Hegemonic masculinity and the history of gender', in S. Dudink, K. Hagemann and J. Tosh (eds), *Masculinities in Politics and War: Gendering Modern History* (Manchester and New York, 2004), pp. 41–60.

'The Unlikely Cult of Mr Bates', *Evening Standard*, 3 November 2010. Available at http://www.standard.co.uk/lifestyle/the-unlikely-cult-of-mr-bates-6531833.html (accessed 28 January 2016).

Urbach, Karina, 'Prince Albert: The Creative Consort', in C. Beem and M. Taylor (eds), *The Man Behind the Queen: Male Consorts in History* (New York, 2014), pp. 145–55.

Urry, John and Larsen, Jonasa, *The Tourist Gaze 3.0* (London, 2011).

Vanacker, Sabine, 'Sherlock's progress through history: feminist revisions of Holmes', in S. Vanacker and C. Wynne (eds), *Sherlock Holmes and Conan Doyle: Multi-Media Afterlives* (Basingstoke and New York, 2013), pp. 93–108.
Van Riper, Bowdoin, 'Good-Bye to All That: Piece of Cake, Danger UXB, and the Second World War', in J. Leggott and J. A. Taddeo (eds), *Upstairs and Downstairs: British Costume Drama Television from* The Forsyte Saga *to* Downton Abbey (Lanham, Boulder, New York, 2015), pp. 153–64.
Vickers, Hugo, 'A royal affair: does *The Crown* bend the truth about the Windsors?', *The Times*, 24 November 2016. Available at http://www.thetimes.co.uk/article/a-royal-affair-does-the-crown-bend-the-truth-about-the-windsors-9r8dlbt6z (accessed 1 February 2017).
Vincendeau, Ginette, *Stars and Stardom in French Cinema* (London 2000).
Walliams, David, *Camp David* (London, 2012).
Walsh, Fintan, *Male Trouble: Masculinity and the Performance of Crisis* (Basingstoke, 2010).
Walsh, John. 'Andrew Davies: The man who put sex into the Victorian novel', *Independent*, 16 April 2004. Available at http://www.independent.co.uk/news/people/profiles/andrew-davies-the-man-who-puts-sex-into-the-victorian-novel-56380.html (accessed 1 November 2016).
Weaver, Matthew, 'Russell Tovey says sorry for effeminate actor comments', *Guardian*, 3 March 2015. Available at https://www.theguardian.com/tv-and-radio/2015/mar/03/russell-tovey-sorry-effeminate-actor-drama-school (both accessed 17 November 2016).
Webster, Wendy, *Imagining Home: Gender, 'Race' and National Identity, 1945–1964* (New Jersey, 1998).
Weissmann, Elke, 'Troubled by violence: Transnational complexity and the critique of masculinity in *Ripper Street*', in J. Leggott and J. A. Taddeo (eds), *Upstairs and Downstairs: British Costume Drama Television from* The Forsyte Saga *to* Downton Abbey (Lanham, 2015), pp. 275–86.
Wendell, Susan, *The Rejected Body: Feminist Philosophical Reflections on Disability* (London, 1996).
Westland, Ella, 'The passionate periphery: Cornwall and Romantic fiction', in I. A. Bell (ed.), *Peripheral Visions: Images of Nationhood and Contemporary British Fiction* (Cardiff, 1995), pp. 153–72.
Wexelblatt, Robert, 'The Ambivalence of *Frankenstein*', *Arizona Quarterly*, 36 (1980), pp. 101–17.
Wheatley, Helen, *Spectacular Television: Exploring Televisual Pleasure* (London, 2016).
Wilson, Carl, '*The Frankenstein Chronicles* Series 1, Episode 1 – "A World Without God"', *Popmatters*. Available at http://www.popmatters.com/review/the-frankenstein-chronicles-series-1-episode-1-a-world-without-god/#ixzz4HPZ-QO37ehttp://www.popmatters.com/review/the-frankenstein-chronicles-series-1-episode-1-a-world-without-god/ (accessed 16 November 2015).
Wolffe, Richard, 'Britain allowed its populist right to rise: America should heed the warning', *Guardian*, 24 June 2016. Available at https://www.theguardian.com/commentisfree/2016/jun/24/britain-right-wing-brexit-america-trump (accessed 19 September 2016).

Bibliography

Wollaston, Sam, 'Versailles review – all hail Louis the Phwoarteenth', *Guardian*, 24 July 2016. Available at www.theguardian.com/tv-and-radio/tvandradioblog/2016/jun/02/versailles-review-louis-the-phwoarteenth-is-a-lot-of-fun (accessed 24 July 2016).

Woodward, Clair, 'Why Extinguish ITV's *Home Fires*?', *Express*, 22 May 2016. Available at http://www.express.co.uk/comment/expresscomment/672669/ITV-cancelled-series-Home-Fires (accessed 18 October 2016).

Wootton, Sarah, 'The changing faces of the Byronic hero in *Middlemarch* and *North and South*', *Romanticism*, 14/1 (2008), pp. 25–35.

——, *Byronic Heroes in Nineteenth-Century Women's Writing and Screen Adaptation* (Basingstoke, 2016).

Zuckerman, Esther, 'Claire Foy and Matt Smith on royal asses (literal and metaphoric) in *The Crown*', *The AV Club*, 3 November 2016. Available at http://www.avclub.com/article/claire-foy-and-matt-smith-royal-asses-literal-and-245075 (accessed 1 February 2017).

Zweiniger-Bargieolowska, Ina, 'Prince Philip: Sportsman and Youth Leader', in C. Beem and M. Taylor (eds), *The Man Behind the Queen: Male Consorts in History*, pp. 232–39.

Zwierlein, Anne Julia, 'Satan's Ocean Voyage and Eighteenth-Century Seafaring Trade', in B. Klein (ed.), *Fictions of the Sea: Critical Perspectives on the Ocean in British Literature and Culture* (Aldershot, 2002), pp. 49–76.

Index

addiction, 138, 147
Anatomy Act (1832), 147, 159
'Armitage Army', 97–8
Armitage, Richard, 9, 96–108
Australia, 18, 23–33, 37–41

Banished, 5, 6, 9, 15–32, 155
BBC, 24–5, 29, 38, 53, 71–88, 98, 259, 272
Bean, Sean, 9, 147–61
bee-keeping, 249–51
Birmingham, postwar, 45, 178–81
Bond, James, 9, 128, 241, 246
Brexit, 62, 271
British Empire, the, 36–50, 129, 137, 141

camp, 3, 129, 239–56
Charles II, 72–88
Children of the New Forest, 73–6, 85
conscientious objectors, 7, 167, 171, 206–19, 222, 234
convicts, 6, 15–31
Cornwall, 52–68
cricket, 252
crime, 113–23, 130, 146–60, 181, 241, 246, 248 *see also* detective, figure of,
crisis of masculinity, 4–10, 16–28, 31, 56, 94, 135, 146, 157, 160
Crown, The, 3, 7, 8, 9, 257–72
Cumberbatch, Benedict, 38, 44, 48

detective, figure of, 6, 7, 9, 111–23, 146–60, 235, 240–54
disability, 3, 150, 172, 176–7, 187, 202
Doctor Who, 149, 270
doctors, 48, 147–60, 172, 221, 222, 229–30 *see also Doctor Who*
domestic violence, 231–35

farmers (men working as), 6, 9, 211, 221
fatherhood, 7, 77–9, 106, 121–41
female gaze, the, 8–9, 29, 53–68, 92, 95, 102, 108
Firth, Colin, 8, 9, 91, 92, 156
flogging, 56, 62–5, 229
fourth-wave feminism, 222–24, 235
Frankenstein, 127, 129–41, 148–52, 158–9

Gabaldon, Diana, 52–3, 57 *see also Outlander*
Golding, William, 35–8, 41, 43 *see also To the Ends of the Earth*
'Gothic masculinity', 132–5, 142

heritage television, 2, 5–6, 8, 15, 41, 44, 45, 52–3, 72, 92, 154, 195, 261–2
Heughan, Sam, 53, 56, 229
Holmes, Sherlock, 9, 250–1
Home Fires, 7, 208, 216–18, 221–35
homophobia, 28, 137, 255

Index

homosocial, 26, 37, 104–5, 106, 113, 121–3, 128, 132–3, 134, 139–2
Hornblower, 36, 41, 47, 50

ITV, 235, 241, 242

Little Britain, 239, 242, 243, 256
London, city of, 48, 57, 84, 102, 116, 127, 129, 130, 132, 134, 152, 157, 168, 183, 188, 225, 246, 268

Mad Men, 254
Marryat, F., 37, 73, 76
medical profession, 141, 147–60
  see also doctors; science, C19th
Military Service Act, 207
Musketeers, The, 74–86

Nelson, 36, 37, 41, 45, 47
neo-liberalism, 4, 6, 10
'Neo-Man', 120–1
neo-Victorian, 3, 95, 100, 111–12, 117–24, 127
Netflix, 259, 262, 271
North and South, 2, 6, 9, 91–110

Obama, Barack, 262
Outlander, 5, 15, 52–68, 95, 149, 229

Partners in Crime, 2, 4, 6, 239–59, 271
Peaky Blinders, 2, 6, 7, 9, 45, 94, 155, 167, 174, 178–83
Penny Dreadful, 2, 6, 9, 127–45, 147, 148
post-feminism, 53, 55, 56, 62, 91–110, 254, 270
Pride and Prejudice, 8, 36, 91–8, 102, 112, 156 *see also* Firth, Colin

queen consort, 3, 7, 9, 257–72

rape, 1, 5, 30–1, 56, 63, 66, 67, 81, 82, 124, 201

Rhind-Tutt, Julian, 16, 28
Ripper Street, 6, 7, 9, 45, 95, 111–26, 146, 147, 149, 188
Royal Navy, 36–8

scars, 5, 56, 65–7, 158, 160, 229
science, C19th, 3, 49, 129, 137–8, 147–60, 263
Scotland, 5, 52–70, 131
servants, 47, 131, 135, 168–70, 172, 174, 177, 181, 196–200
Sharpe, 149, 154–6
shell shock, 165, 167, 171–4, 175, 177, 181, 209, 214
soap opera, 2, 38, 75–6, 79, 209, 261
Spanish Influenza, 211
Stevenson, R. L., 37, 127
Suez Crisis (1956), 271
syphilis, 146, 149–60

teachers (men working as), 208–12, 234
To the Ends of the Earth, 35–51
Tovey, Russell, 16, 25, 28, 29
Trafalgar, battle of, 37, 45
Trump, Donald, 10, 271
Turner, Aidan, 1, 8, 29, 53, 56, 169, 229

uniforms, 20, 62, 66, 167–78, 207, 233, 266

Versailles, 3, 6, 7, 9, 71–88
violence, male, 1, 5, 15–16, 18, 20, 22–31, 35, 45–6, 55, 58, 72–3, 81–2, 85, 86, 98, 99, 113, 121, 123, 180–3, 197, 200, 201, 228, 229, 231–2, 235, 242

Walliams, David, 4, 7, 239–58
war, 3, 7–8, 9, 139
  American War of Independence, 15
  Cold War, the, 240, 241, 244, 246–56
  English Civil War, 73

World War I,
  representation on television, 153, 165–86, 189, 192, 195, 206–20, 245–46, 264 *see also* conscientious objectors; shell shock
World War II, 38, 221–38, 264

Welch, Sandy, 91–110
Women's Institute (WI), 225–6, 231, 234–5
working-class characters, 6, 16, 39, 58, 99, 104, 111–13, 152–6, 167, 168, 174, 180, 182, 247, 249, 267

Lightning Source UK Ltd.
Milton Keynes UK
UKHW020357160421
382081UK00006B/130